COMMUNICATION
Writing and Speaking

COMMUNICATION
Writing and Speaking

Richard A. Katula
Celest A. Martin
Robert A. Schwegler
University of Rhode Island

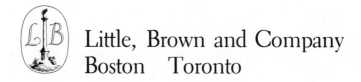
Little, Brown and Company
Boston   Toronto

Library of Congress Cataloging in Publication Data

Katula, Richard.
  Communication : writing and speaking.

  Includes bibliographical references.
  1. Communication. 2. Rhetoric. I. Martin,
Celest. II. Schwegler, Robert. III. Title.
P90.K345   1983   001.54   82-14017
ISBN 0-316-48314-1

Library of Congress Catalog Card No. 82-14017

ISBN 0-316-48314-1

9 8 7 6 5 4 3 2 1

BP

Published simultaneously in Canada
by Little, Brown & Company (Canada) Limited

Printed in the United States of America

Credits and Acknowledgments

The authors wish to thank the students whose work appears in this volume. All
student essays are used with the kind permission of the students. This material is
intended to demonstrate student writing techniques and is used solely as a teaching
device.

Photographs in Chapter 4 are by Gary D. Silvers.

Charles T. Brusaw, Gerald J. Alred, and Walter E. Oliu, from *Handbook of
Technical Writing*. Copyright © 1976 by St. Martin's Press and used by permission of
the publisher.

(Continued on page 383)

Preface

Communication: Writing and Speaking is a text that combines instruction in speech and written composition. For some time, many colleges and universities have taught speech and writing together, and speech and composition instructors who focus on one mode or the other often require at least one assignment that crosses over the traditional boundaries established by the disciplines. Furthermore, many who teach speech and/or writing courses would very much like to combine instruction as a way of making their classrooms livelier places where speaking and writing activities work together. Up to this time, however, this approach has been difficult for both instructors and students. Students have had to purchase two texts and have had to learn two separate vocabularies; instructors have needed to prepare the same material twice, once for speech instruction and once for instruction in writing.

This book integrates instruction in planned discourse, both spoken and written. Years of teaching and of learning from our students have developed the ideas presented here.

First, the book takes a conceptual-conventional approach to rhetoric. The conceptual patterns are based on a relationship between the way we think about our experiences and the way in which we organize them for discourse. These patterns—analysis, process, and cause-effect, to name a few—are presented to the students as ways of probing and organizing experiences into appropriate topics for discourse. The conventional patterns, on the other hand, are socially developed forms based upon audience expectations. These audience expectations provide standard questions that a composer must anticipate when shaping discourse designed to inform or motivate an audience. The book thus moves from composer-centered to audience-centered discourse.

Second, the book uses the terms *point*, *pattern*, and *detail* as the common elements of planned discourse, whether spoken or written. In this way, students learn a common vocabulary for thinking about both speeches and essays.

Third, the book uses a variety of models drawn from novelists, journalists, professional speakers, and students. These models apply to a wide range of writing and speaking situations.

Fourth, the book has realistic, practical assignments. We have tried to develop assignments so that they reinforce critical aspects of composing and lead students progressively through the most personal modes of communication to the most social. The organization of *Communication: Writing and Speaking* is geared toward aiding this progression.

The book begins with a chapter on human communication emphasizing the variable nature of communication events and the creative aspect of each. It distinguishes planned from unplanned discourse and elaborates on the similarities and differences between oral and written communication.

Chapters Two and Three discuss composing. We encourage students to view their experiences as potential topics for planned discourse. Rather than isolating steps in composing, the chapters focus on shaping experiences into planned discourse from two points of view: the mind of the composer and the viewpoint of the audience. We suggest that rewriting is a continuing process that allows composers to discover three things: their own thoughts and knowledge about the topic, the purpose of the communication, and the elements necessary for an audience to follow and be affected by the communication. We also encourage students to think about the entire communication situation: the communicator's role, the constraints on the occasion, and the audience's background and knowledge.

Chapters Four and Five are concerned with delivery and communication apprehension. Chapter Four provides a comprehensive treatment of delivery. Here, to accompany the text, we provide a number of photographs designed to show certain delivery techniques as well as to spark discussion about style of presentation. The goal of Chapter Four is to lead students to discover what works for them in particular situations.

Chapter Five presents the latest thinking on communication apprehension, both oral and written. The chapter discusses the psychological and physiological manifestations of communication apprehension and then discusses techniques for coping with it.

Chapters Six through Eight provide comprehensive coverage of patterns of discourse. Chapter Six discusses three conceptual patterns based on time: narration, process, and cause-effect. Chapters Seven and Eight are devoted to the static patterns: analysis, enumeration, description, definition, classification, and comparison. We discuss the patterns as natural mental activities and then relate them to discourse by showing how each pattern can be used to probe and organize a topic. We have added to the text numerous models with commentary, and have included assignments for both speeches and essays.

Chapters Nine, Ten, and Eleven are also pattern chapters; specifically, these chapters are concerned with conventional patterns of discourse, informative and argumentative. Chapter Nine presents a set of standard questions that one can use to probe and organize a topic for a comprehensive, balanced presentation of data in specific situations. Once again, we use models to show how the conventions are used in various informative situations, and we introduce three types of informative reports: curiosity, demonstration, and practical/technical reports.

Chapter Ten examines argument from the point of view of the composer. It discusses a set of standard questions that can be used to probe and organize a speech or essay for purposes of advocating a position one has taken. Chapter Ten also reviews the variables of audience motivation and speaker credibility.

Chapter Eleven looks at argument from the point of view of the consumer. It presents a new approach to an understanding of the structure of an argument—to an understanding of the reasons an argument works. Chapter Eleven shows how the two universal schemes of association and dissociation help make an argument effective, and uses a number of professional models to bring theory to life and to give a practical bent to our understanding of argument.

Chapters Twelve and Thirteen present a comprehensive treatment of paragraphs and sentences by discussing paragraph and sentence patterns in terms of readability and emphasis. The basic concepts of coherence and clarity are illustrated with both professional and student examples. Finally, the chapters examine stylistic distinctions between prose intended for the eye and prose intended for the ear.

Chapter Fourteen is concerned with critical appraisal of planned discourse. It teaches an audience how to ask and answer questions at the conclusion of a speech and how to share criticism of a composer's writing. This chapter should be particularly useful to those who would like to take a realistic approach to speaking in the classroom, as well as to those who find occasions for speaking and writing in real life.

Finally, the Instructor's Manual that accompanies this text is designed to help teachers cross boundaries easily. With this text, those who teach courses that deal primarily with writing will feel comfortable teaching, assigning, and evaluating speeches, and those who teach courses dealing primarily with speech will be given ample instruction in teaching, assigning, and evaluating essays. Perhaps most important of all, this book may be used either for a combined course or for a course that focuses entirely on writing or entirely on speaking. In fact, teachers of writing or speaking who use this text for their regular courses may decide that an assignment or two from the other mode will be an enriching experience.

We believe that using this text will provide many benefits. When oral and written communication are taught together the classroom becomes a livelier place, and teachers are better able to help those who write the way they talk and those who talk the way they write.

We believe, then, that students, teachers, and communication theory all benefit from the combined approach detailed in this text. We hope that after you have used the text, you will agree.

A project of this magnitude cannot be accomplished without the strength and support of many others. While we take full responsibility for the contents contained in this text, we would be remiss not to acknowledge those whose work or inspiration are part of this accomplishment.

First, we wish to thank our teachers and advisors without whose wisdom and patience we might never have pursued our course as teachers of speech and composition: W. Ross Winterowd, Marie H. Nichols, Joseph Comprone, William Ringler, Jr., Janel Mueller, and Randall Brune. A special thanks should be added here to Frank D'Angelo, whose theories underlie many of our beliefs about effective communication.

To those reviewers who prodded and pushed, but who also gave us the sound advice and encouragement to continue, we offer our heartfelt gratitude: Lois Einhorn, Sylvia Holladay, Gene Krupa, Mary McGann, Walter Minot, Donovan Ochs, Stephen North, Annette Rottenberg, Carl Schmider, Sara Stelzner, Donald Tighe, Rick Turner, and many others, unknown but to themselves.

No book would be complete without the phalanx of professionals who guide and shape the project from prospectus to page proofs. We acknowledge here those many patient souls: Paul O'Connell, Kevin Howat, Tom Gornick, Molly Faulkner, Carolyn Potts, Susan Schultz, Victoria Keirnan, Brian Walker, Carolyn Woznick, and Dorothy Seymour.

To those colleagues who wrote the grants, gave us time and counsel, or encouraged us, we salute you here: Richard Larson, M. Beverly Swan, Mary Sisney, Joseph Williams, Phyllis Roth, Jon Ramsey, Gerri Tyler, Dan Pearlman, George Dillavou, Winifred Brownell, and Joyce Allen.

Special thanks go to Ethel Thompson, our extraordinary, award-winning secretary, and to two others who helped in the manuscript process: Elaine Wichman and Betty Hanke. In addition, we want to thank our students, those whose models appear in this book and all those whose progress in the classroom continued to make this project worthwhile to us.

Finally, to our loved ones: Nancy Schwegler, Pat Katula, Riley Lamson, Christopher, Brian, and Michael, and our parents—we are back, and we love you.

Contents

1. Human Communication: Oral and Written   1

Formal and Informal Discourse   1

The Advantages of Studying Speaking and Writing
Together   2

Human Communication: Definition and Model   3

*Process 4 • Purpose 5 • Sending 5 • Receiving 5
Messages 6 • Shared Experience 6*

Conventions of Formal Speaking   7

Conventions of Formal Writing   10

Summary 12   Key Words 13   Exercises 13

References 15

2. The Composer as Self: Analyzing Experience   16

Responding to Experience: Exploring Thoughts and
Feelings   16

*Talking to Yourself on Tape 17 • Talking to Yourself on
Paper 17 • Talking to Others 19*

Discovering a Topic   20

Probing Experience 21 • Using Thought Patterns as Probes 23

Before Composing: Some Important Things to Consider   26

*Your Role as a Communicator 27 • Constraints and
Guidelines 28 • Your Audience 29*

Composing and Staying with It   32

*Advice from the Experts 32 • Getting Started 34 • False
Starts: Rereading and Rewriting 36 • Developing Form:
Looking for Key Phrases 37*

Summary 40   Key Words 41   Exercises 41

References 42

3. The Composer as Audience: Preparing a Final
Draft   43

Point   43

Subpoints 44

Pattern   45

Cue Words 45 • Conceptual and Conventional Patterns 47

Detail   47
   Personal Experience 48 • Examples 49 • Factual Support 50
   Quantitative Support 51 • Comparisons 54

Introductions   56
   Rhetorical Questions 57 • Humor 57 • Quotations 58
   Startling Statements 58

Conclusions   59
   The Quotable Quote 59 • Parallelism 60 • Reiteration 61
   Directing Attention to Beliefs or Action 62

Final Form   63
   Scripting the Essay 63 • Unscripting the Speech 65

Summary 67   Key Words 68   Exercises 68
References 69

4. Presentational Style   70

Types of Message Preparation   72
   The Memorized Speech 72 • The Manuscript Speech 73
   The Extemporaneous Speech 73

Physical Attributes of Presentational Style   78
   Gestures 78 • Posture 78 • Movement 79 • Facial
   Expression 79 • Dress and Appearance 80

Vocal Attributes of Presentational Style   80
   Pronunciation 80 • Fluency 83 • Rate, Pause, and
   Emphasis 83

Visual Aids: Preparation and Presentation   84
   Informative Aids: Preparation 85 • Informative Aids:
   Presentation 86 • Showing Aids: Preparation 86
   Showing Aids: Presentation 87 • Doing Aids: Preparation 88
   Doing Aids: Presentation 89

Visual Aids in Written Communication   90
Summary 91   Key Words 92   Exercises 92
References 93

5. Communication Apprehension   94

Speech Anxiety   95
   Understanding Speech Anxiety 95 • Coping with Speech
   Anxiety 97

Writing Anxiety   99
   Understanding Writing Anxiety 99 • Coping with Writing
   Anxiety 102

Summary 103   Key Words 104   Exercises 104
References 105

6. Time Patterns: Narration, Process, Cause-Effect   106

Narration   107
*Using Narration 107 • Getting Materials 110 • The Finished
Product 111*

Process   118
*Using Process 119 • Getting Materials 121 • The Finished
Product 124*

Cause and Effect   131
*Using Cause and Effect 131 • Getting Materials 135
The Finished Product 136*

Summary 141   Key Words 141   Exercises 141
References 147

7. Static Patterns: Analysis, Enumeration, Comparison   148

Static Patterns and Time Patterns   149

Analysis   150
*Using Analysis 150 • Getting Materials 157 • The Finished
Product 164*

Enumeration   171
Using Enumeration 171 • The Finished Product 175

Comparison   177
*Using Comparison 177 • Getting Materials 183 • The
Finished Product 184*

Summary 188   Key Words 189   Exercises 189
References 191

8. Static Patterns: Classification, Description, Definition, Exemplification   192

Classification   192
*Using Classification 192 • Getting Materials 197 • The
Finished Product 200*

Description   205
*Using Description 205 • Getting Materials 208 • The
Finished Product 210*

Definition   217
   Using Definition 217 • The Finished Product 219
Exemplification   222
Summary 222   Key Words 223   Exercises 223
References 226

9. Conventional Patterns: Sharing Information   227
Informative Discourse   228
Aims and Features of Informative Discourse   229
Planning Informative Reports   233
   Analyzing a Topic 233
Analyzing the Audience   236
Source Credibility   240
The Finished Product   241
   Point 241 • Pattern 242 • Detail 250
Summary 251   Key Words 251   Exercises 251
References 253

10. Conventional Patterns: Composing an Argument   254
Aims and Features of Argument   255
Planning the Argument   256
   Probing the Issue 257
Analyzing the Audience in an Argument   261
Source Credibility in Arguments   267
The Finished Product   269
   Point 269 • Pattern 271 • Detail 286
Summary 290   Key Words 290   Exercises 290
References 291

11. Beneath the Surface: What Makes an Argument Work   292
Associative Arguments   293
   Quasi-Logical Arguments 293 • Arguments Based on the
   Structure of Reality 298 • Arguments that Attempt to
   Organize Reality 303
Dissociative Arguments   308
Summary 312   Key Words 312   Exercises 312
References 313

12. The Paragraph: Details that Make a Point   314

Overall Structure: Fitting Paragraphs into Essays   314
*Paragraphs Within the Essay 314 • Sentences Within the
Paragraph 318*

Kinds of Coherence: Leading the Audience   320

Techniques of Exposition   324
*Using Patterns 324 • Topic-Restriction-Illustration 325
Broad Topic-Explanation-Restriction-Example 326
Example-Example-Example-Topic 327 • Problem-Solution 328*

Creating Emphasis   331

Composing Scene Setters   334

Summary 337   Key Words 338   Exercises 338
References 340

13. Sentence Varieties: Style as Choice   341

Agency: Who Did What to Whom   342
*Gerunds: -ing Subjects 343 • Dangling Modifiers 345
Misuse of Passive Voice 347*

The Relative Clause: Propositions   349
*Restrictive and Nonrestrictive Clauses 349 • Relatives in
Trouble: The Which-Trap 351*

Avoiding the Which-Trap: Using Shorter Structures to
Add Details   352
*Modifiers that Repeat 352 • Modifiers that Summarize
353 • Free Modifiers 354*

Creating Cohesion: Using Boundary Sentences to
Combine Old and New Information   355
Boundary Sentences 355 • Linking Discourse 357

Creating Special Effects: Emphasis and Parallelism   360
Emphasis: Beginnings and Endings 360 • Parallelism 362

Speaking with Style: Sentences to be Heard   364

Summary 366   Key Words 366   Exercises 367
References 367

14. Developing Critical Skills   368

Oral Communication   368
*Asking and Answering Questions 368 • Comments That Are
Not Questions 373*

Written Communication   375
*Reading and Responding to Essays 375 • Accepting
Criticism 379*

Summary 379   Key Words 379   Exercises 380
References 380

Appendix: Finding and Documenting Materials   381

Index   385

COMMUNICATION
Writing and Speaking

1. Human Communication: Oral and Written

And usually you just walk across . . . but it was high tide so I had to go over some cliffs and we were just kind of clinging to the edge of a sandstone cliff and I was stuck there . . . I mean I couldn't move — there's nothing for me to hold onto . . . and below me about twenty five feet was . . . uhm . . . this little cove with big sharp rocks sticking up . . . and I was looking down at them and I was clinging . . . and my only hope was this little patch of grass.

(Walcutt, 1977)

The woman quoted above is describing an experience to a group of friends in a style most of us use in our everyday communication, a style that is conversational and casual. We connect sentences with *and* or *so then*; we use such pronouns as *you* freely; we hesitate between phrases, and we shift tenses frequently. If we are not making ourselves clear we know that listeners will feel free to interrupt with questions or quizzical looks. On a one-to-one level, or with a group of friends, this informal communication style is quite appropriate, but there are times when it is not.

On many occasions communication needs to be more formal than casual conversational speech or writing. Formal situations are characterized by the role of the message sender, which might be that of *expert* or *guest speaker*, or *author*, and by the speaker's task, which might be to present a complete idea or experience without audience interruptions or the give and take of conversation. Public speaking, technical reporting, and essay writing are just three of many familiar situations that require us to use a more formal communication style.

FORMAL AND INFORMAL DISCOURSE

Communication in formal situations is called **planned discourse**. We feel the need in such situations to have a clear goal in mind — a point toward which we are moving. We also want to have our talking or writing carefully organized in advance so that we have anticipated questions from our listeners or readers. Words must be chosen precisely, and our language must be clear, lively, and vivid without seeming artificial or pretentious. Finally, if the message is to be spoken, we want to deliver it with appropriate tones and gestures or, if it is to be written, with the correct punctuation, headings, margins, and so on.

1

In order to see the difference between **informal** and **formal communication,** look at the following passage, which is a continuation of the informal narrative that opened this chapter:

> The worst part about it was I had a friend sitting up here and she's saying "ha ha" . . . and I was saying "Go get the police . . . go get someone" . . . I later learned that there are some people who do that in the face of disaster . . . I mean they just start cracking up as opposed to crying.

Later, this same woman was asked to tell her story in a composition class of about twenty students and to prepare in advance for a formal narrative. The passage just quoted above came out somewhat differently:

> My helpful friend, perhaps not realizing that I was serious, began laughing. Sue roared all the harder as my situation became more difficult. She claimed I looked funny, clinging there, screaming. I realized that she was laughing because she was incapable of acting: the situation must have been greatly disturbing to her, and so she treated it as if it were another situation. My abilities in psychoanalysis, even at age ten, were quite prodigious.

Notice that both passages were appropriate for the situation and that both were understood by listeners, but that they were different. Can you indicate the differences? Are the differences to be found in any of the distinctions already made between formal and informal discourse?

This book is concerned with formal speaking and writing. Achieving success in formal speaking and writing is a lifelong pursuit requiring continuous practice, but there is a body of knowledge about planned discourse which, when applied, can lead us consciously toward the development of successful skills. The development of your skills as a formal communicator is the central concern of this text.

THE ADVANTAGES OF STUDYING SPEAKING AND WRITING TOGETHER

One question you might immediately have is this: Why study speaking and writing in the same classroom? The integrated approach to the study of planned discourse has several advantages.

One advantage to studying speaking and writing together is that you can learn many terms and conventions that apply to both speeches and essays. The steps in composing, coping with communication apprehension, and critically appraising your ideas and the ideas of others are just a few topics common to both spoken and written discourse. In this text you will develop skills that you can use in any formal situation.

Secondly, skills most easily developed in one mode of communication can often be transferred to the other. Speaking situations, for instance, are most conducive to developing skills in audience analysis, since you must deal with a live group of people. Many writers have difficulty because they cannot clearly imagine an audience. The sense of audience you will develop in your speaking will help you "see" your audience and anticipate its needs more accurately in your writing.

Thirdly, many writing and speaking problems stem from improperly switching modes of communication. You may, at some time, have received a paper back from a teacher with this comment: "You shouldn't write the way you talk." Or perhaps you have heard someone comment like this about a speaker: "She sounds as though she's reading from *Time* magazine." Studying speaking and writing together will make you more aware of the appropriate style for each mode because your instructor will help you find the problems associated with switching these modes randomly in your own speeches and essays.

Finally, many who have studied speaking and writing together find that the classroom becomes a livelier, more interesting place because of this combination. Ideas are shared with a real audience, perhaps even debated. Essays are read aloud with a polished delivery style, since delivery is taught in the writing classroom. There ought to be something challenging but also enjoyable about a communications course. Studying speaking and writing together brings both challenge and enjoyment to your endeavors.

The next discussion concerns the basic components of the act of communication.

HUMAN COMMUNICATION: DEFINITION AND MODEL

Many times in our lives we will be asked to "say a few words to the audience" or "put it in writing." You might check this statement by listing on a sheet of paper five or six standard situations that call for planned discourse. Some examples appear in Figure 1-1.

Effective communication in such situations begins with an understanding of the communicative act and the principles governing both the spoken and the written mode.

> *Formal communication is a process with a clear purpose, involving the sending and receiving of messages as a way of sharing ideas and experiences.*

This definition of communication has the following key terms: **process, purpose, sending, receiving, messages,** and **shared experiences.** Look at what each of these terms means, and why each is essential to effective planned discourse.

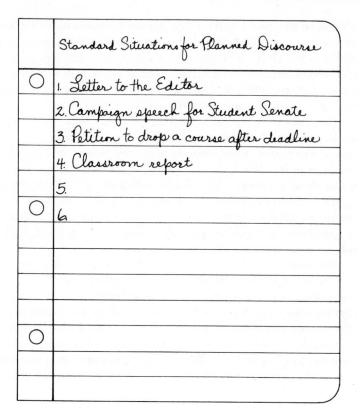

Figure 1-1 Standard Situations

Process

Planned discourse involves both preparation and production. Composers need to begin somewhere and end somewhere. What happens in between is called a process. We can think of the communication process as a series of stages, each of which reflects some growth in our speech or essay. Thus we might think of analyzing a topic, drafting a rough copy, revising, and proofreading as parts of a composition. We might also think of the communications process as a group of activities: finding a topic to fit the assignment, analyzing the audience, probing and organizing the message, setting goals, revising, proofreading, practicing, and so on. These activities occur not in a fixed order but together or in various orders at any time between planning the message and producing it.

Regardless of which method makes more sense for us, there is clearly a process involved. This process requires us to consider our role in the event, the topic, those who will receive the message, the environment or situation that has prompted the communication, and the interaction of all these variables. How we control this interaction will determine our success as communicators.

Purpose

Formal writing and speaking are directed toward a specific goal. The goal or goals may change as we move through the communication process. At some point in the process we might think to ourselves, "I'm going to find out exactly what the audience knows about this topic," or "Today I'm going to work on my conclusion." Eventually some final purpose will be reached: "I'd like to win this group over to my side," or "I'd like members of this audience to know how to care for their plants when I'm finished." These purposes may guide us through parts of the composing process, or they may shape the discourse as a whole. Goals and sub-goals become the directions we follow during communication.

Purposeful communication also suggests that there be a reason for communicating. We should try to communicate ideas that are worthwhile and relevant to those who will receive our messages. A good question to ask oneself is this: What can I say or write about this topic that is original, interesting, and valuable to my audience? Each one of us has something important to say; we need to search within ourselves to find it.

Sending

As speakers and writers we need to have a clear sense of our positions. We need to know what our credibility is with the audience, what our role is in the situation, and in the case of a speech what we look and sound like to our audience. The message sender has the responsbility to get the communication started — to get others involved and informed. Success in a speech or an essay depends a great deal on how much of us the audience sees in the message and how well it identifies with that vision.

Receiving

An **audience** receives a message, interprets it, and provides a response. The response to a message is called **feedback**. Speakers need to be aware of audience feedback and interpret it while they are speaking as well as when they have finished. Writers need to imagine audience feedback as they write. They must constantly ask themselves: How will the audience respond to this?

Messages

Messages in formal communication are conveyed through symbols. **Symbols** are words or nonverbal cues that represent, or stand for, actual objects, ideas, or experiences. Coffee is a beverage, but the word *coffee* only stands for that beverage; we cannot drink the word *coffee*. Similarly, sarcasm is a tone of voice, but it is a tone that stands for something else — an underlying attitude, perhaps.

The point of emphasizing that communication is symbolic is this: Because words and tones and gestures only stand for the real thing, they are easily misused and misinterpreted. One symbol can mean many things to different people, and what one person chooses to stand for something is quite often not what another person would choose. For instance, a listener might judge that a speaker's tone is sarcastic, but some speakers would deny that, saying that they were simply emphasizing a point in a humorous way. Who is right? The symbolic nature of messages makes this a difficult question to answer.

Words are very rarely arranged by two people in the same way. Speech is a constantly creative, original phenomenon, so much so that most longer sentences (fifteen words or more) are unique to the speaker or writer and are not easily repeated by hearers or readers unless they memorize the sentence. You can prove this to yourself very easily. Try, without looking back, to write out the definition of communication given on page 3. If everyone in the class tries this without peeking, you will find that no one has written the definition exactly as it appears earlier in the text, and further that no one in the room has written a definition with the same wording as anyone else.

This experiment shows that receivers do not always get the same message that we send. Receivers translate the words we use, and the order in which we use them, into words and orders that make sense for them. Symbol-using is complex. Our experiment serves to remind us that we need to put our messages into terms that our audience can follow, to provide careful definitions for terms that are unfamiliar to our receivers, and to provide time for feedback as a way of clarifying our message.

Shared Experience

The impulse to communicate arises from a desire to share with others our experiences, ideas, values, and attitudes. We do this with the understanding that we need to agree and disagree with others so that we may find meaning in our own lives. We also need to feel a sense of community with others and to recognize that it is only through sharing, compromising, and agreeing that action as a group is possible. Thus, speaking and

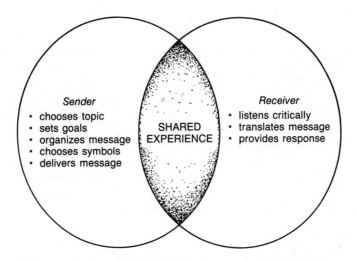

Figure 1-2 Communication as the Sharing of Experience

writing are social acts, ways of placing ourselves in the world, of establishing and maintaining relationships among people. Both forms of communication can perform a wide variety of social functions: they can persuade, amuse, express fear or pleasure, provide sympathy, create strong impressions, or even intimidate. And like most social acts, writing and speaking — particularly formal writing and speaking — involve conventions (rules and strategies) that need to be learned and that vary from situation to situation.

The model of communication shown above (Figure 1-2) will help us see more clearly the process we have just described. After looking carefully at those elements common to all formal communication, we can turn to a discussion of the special conventions of oral communication and written communication.

CONVENTIONS OF FORMAL SPEAKING

Conversations and other forms of casual speaking are governed by a sequence known as "dialogue." One person talks for a brief period, then someone else does, then another person, or the original talker, and so on. Informal speech requires this back-and-forth movement — it is natural. Long-winded talkers are often thought of as rude, boring, and self-centered. Because of our natural inclination to engage in dialogue, it takes practice and concentration to listen to one person speak for an extended period of time.

There are situations, however, in which the extended chain of speech is necessary, even expected. You may already have thought of many such occasions in response to the request on page 3, and you probably listed such events as classroom presentations, sermons, business conference reports, testimony at public hearings, and political speeches. These formal speaking situations require us to break from the natural back-and-forth sequence of conversational communication and to adopt procedures designed to help us succeed. What are some of these procedures?

Formal presentations are usually composed in advance so that we avoid rambling or losing our place during the presentation. Formal speaking also requires us to shift to a form of speech somewhere between our casual speech and the highly formal speech we use when writing. Most important, we need to draw on techniques of language usage and delivery that will counteract the audience's natural tendency to let its attention wander. In short, formal speaking requires us to speak for an extended period of time, but in such a way that we maintain the basic oral nature of the event.

Even on formal occasions the speaker must pay careful attention to the live audience being addressed. Effective communicators respond to the nonverbal, visual cues the audience provides as the speech proceeds; the speaker will interpret this reaction and respond to it immediately. If, for instance, someone's eyes have drifted to another part of the room, the speaker must respond to this nonverbal cue and draw the person back into the event, perhaps with direct eye contact or a change in tone that catches the person's attention. This is not an easy skill to develop, and it is one we will need to discuss at length later in the text.

We mentioned briefly that formal speech lies somewhere between the casual speech of conversation and the formal language of writing. What does this mean? Casual speech is usually somewhat relaxed and **colloquial**: it contains filler words, clichés, and references that have meaning only for the group present. Formal writing appropriate to research papers or essays requires language that will make sense to a larger audience; it requires careful attention to complete sentences and paragraphs and to mechanics. Formal speaking must maintain the closeness of the speaker-audience relationship but also have little filler speech, few colloquialisms, and few repetitions. Abraham Lincoln's famous Gettysburg Address illustrates formal speaking intended for both the ear and the eye.

> Fourscore and seven years ago our forefathers brought forth on this continent a new nation, conceived in liberty and dedicated to the proposition that all men are created equal.
> Now we are engaged in a great civil war, testing whether that nation or any nation so conceived and so dedicated can long endure.

We are met on a great battlefield of war. We have come to dedicate a portion of that field as a final resting place for those who here gave their lives that that nation might live. It is altogether fitting and proper that we should do this.

But, in a larger sense, we cannot dedicate — we cannot consecrate — we cannot hallow this ground. The brave men, living and dead, who struggled here, have consecrated it far above our poor power to add or detract. The world will little note, nor long remember, what we say here, but it can never forget what they did here. It is for us, the living, rather, to be dedicated here to the unfinished work which they who fought here have thus far so nobly advanced. It is rather for us to be here dedicated to the great task remaining before us — that from these honored dead we take increased devotion to that cause for which they gave the last full measure of devotion — that we here highly resolve that these dead shall not have died in vain — that this nation, under God, shall have a new birth of freedom — and that government of the people, by the people, for the people, shall not perish from the earth.

What is so remarkable about this piece of discourse? For one thing, Lincoln did indeed intend it for the ear. Say the phrases aloud, listening to their rhythm and balance, the pleasing quality of their sound: ". . . we cannot dedicate — we cannot consecrate — we cannot hallow this ground." Notice the crescendo effect as these synonyms, each a shade stronger in meaning than the previous one, build to the end of the sentence. Listen for the careful placement of emphasis in the sentence "The world will little note, nor long remember, what we say here, but it can never forget what they did here." The contrast is effortless but unforgettable. The final parallel phrase, ". . . government of the people, by the people, for the people," is one of the most quoted in American speech. Why? Because both the words Lincoln chose and their arrangement in the sentence increase the force of the sentiment behind the speech. Lincoln wrote these words to be heard, not to be read, but he had to plan his discourse and to strive consciously for a speech that would not only involve his immediate audience but also have broad, lasting appeal for future generations.

Although Lincoln's speech was so short that the photographer present did not get his camera adjusted in time, it was so appropriate in every way that Edward Everett, the man who spoke before Lincoln, and a famous orator of the day, paid him this compliment: "I should be glad if I could flatter myself that I came as near the central idea of the occasion in two hours as you did in two minutes."

Formal speaking, then, is planned in advance and follows certain conventions of language usage and delivery that distinguish it from conversational speech. As opposed to formal writing, a speech must be directed to the immediate audience and adjusted, when necessary, as the occasion progresses. An audience will react negatively to excessive filler speech — "you know," "uhm," "like" — and in-speech — jargon, technical terms — but will also think poorly of speech that is too formal and appears to be recited from a prepared text. Finding a middle ground is an essential part of composing a successful speech.

CONVENTIONS OF FORMAL WRITING

Most of us are aware of the important role that speech plays in our lives; writing is equally important. Think for a minute: have you recently gone through a day without writing something or reading something that was written? Whether writing a letter to the editor, reading a novel, or even browsing through the ads in a magazine, chances are that you need to write and read every day.

Even some familiar forms of oral communication follow the conventions of writing. Newscasters on the radio and television present the news from a written script, and as a member of the audience you are probably aware, either consciously or unconsciously, of the underlying form of their presentation. No television reporter would say, "uhm . . . there was a shift in the gold market today. Some trading has caused panic . . . Oh, wait a minute — first I should tell you, there was one country that . . . " We might accept this in casual conversation, but in the formal speech of newscasters, speech that is virtually identical to writing, such **repair sequences** are frowned upon.

A repair sequence occurs when we interrupt ourselves to change the order of our information — to add to it, to switch levels of vocabulary, or to alter in any way the expected flow of the text. Because writers generally have a chance to revise their work and to anticipate problems that would require repair sequences, readers expect that a piece of writing will not contain such shifts. Many beginning writers mistakenly let chatty interruptions carry over to their formal writing; successful writers realize that writing must maintain a regular progression and a consistent level that makes it easy for readers to follow.

While formal speaking is a social, public phenomenon, written communication is a private activity. Whe we write we generally need to be alone; as one successful writer, John Ciardi, puts it, "The major problem in writing is to go into a room, close the door, and put your butt firmly on the chair and leave it there." Writing requires an extended focus on the topic and a good deal of solitary thinking.

Written communication also requires an extended view of the audience. Writers must conceptualize the audience that will read their discourse and must fix upon that concept throughout composition in order to make choices in tone, wording, content, and strategy.

Professional speakers and writers know that effective communication requires a heightened sense of audience. Experiences in formal speaking enhance this sensitivity. Some students were once asked by their instructors to give a speech that would provide to fellow students some new information about their university. Each interviewed someone, compiled and organized the information, and presented it to the class. At first, the students were reluctant to actually go out and start asking questions, but the results were excellent. The students learned about such activities as a food cooperative, the student judicial board, the rape crisis center, and religious organizations. Even more important, they learned something about audience. In the course of this experience the students found that they had something to say, and they found an audience eager to listen. After the assignment students were able to find their own voices and also to discover the realities of an immediate audience. This new sense of audience was then transferred to the students' next essay: they began to write to a clearly defined group of people — in this case, their classmates and instructor.

Written communication requires precise use of form and mechanics: punctuation marks, pronoun usage, subject-verb agreement, and so on. Since written communication is observed primarily with our eyes, it lacks tone of voice and gestural cues. Writers must compensate for these missing components by following **semantic** (meaning) and **syntactic** (structural) conventions or rules. Punctuation is the writer's equivalent of the orator's facial gestures and tones of voice. A dash used effectively can mean "get this." The exclamation point (!) can emphasize irony, warn of disaster, or show excitement. In other words, punctuation suggests tone. Adjectives, adverbs, phrasing, and clause placement can also create emphasis like that of the gestures of oral communication.

Good writers use the semantic, syntactic, and mechanical devices of the language. When you think of a television show, a mental picture quickly flashes in your mind of the actor or actress who represents that show. The writers developed this image so that when you think of that person, you will think of the television show. As a writer, you must "show" your audience this same kind of visual detail in words. One of the most difficult tasks for a beginning writer is to create a scene for the reader, a scene that will take what is in the writer's mind and move it to the page and then into the mind of the reader.

Written communication, then, is a private activity, which requires an extended view of the topic and the audience, anticipation of audience response, and careful attention to word choice, structure, and mechanics. Formal written communication requires a special and consistent style that will make it acceptable in a number of contexts in which it might be read.

SUMMARY

Human communication in effect defines our humanity. Through the process of communication we learn to understand ourselves, others, and the world. Mastering the arts of formal oral and written communication is a life-long pursuit, but a worthwhile one if we are to participate intelligently in our society. Working with this text and with your instructor will stimulate your interest in speaking and writing and give you the essential skills you will need to become an effective communicator.

This chapter began by distinguishing formal communication from informal. It then analyzed communication by indicating those elements common to both formal speaking and writing. Following this, the discussion turned to the special conventions of formal speaking and the special conventions of formal writing.

Now that this core of principles has been introduced, your attention must turn to each individual aspect of the communication process. In the two chapters that follow, you will learn how to probe a topic by asking the right questions of it. You will also learn about making the communication satisfying to an audience — putting your ideas into some final form that will meet the audience's needs.

Chapters Four and Five will help you deliver your message effectively, and will help you understand and cope with that most common of problems: communication apprehension.

Chapters Six through Eleven will introduce a variety of patterns, or structures, that you can use to both probe a topic and organize the topic. You will learn, for instance, how to write a story, explain a process, describe a scene, analyze an issue, and argue for your point of view.

Chapters Twelve and Thirteen introduce the notion of style at the paragraph and sentence levels. Writing with greater emphasis and creating prose that will please the ear are two of the central concepts in these chapters. Finally, Chapter Fourteen presents methods of critically appraising your ideas and those of your classmates.

In all the chapters to follow the emphasis will be on *doing* communication. There is a unifying theory that underlies the entire text, and you will be asked to learn some new terms and apply various steps. But the key to becoming more effective at communicating is to practice communication, and this text will give you that practice in an orderly, sequential manner designed to accelerate, from one assignment to the next, your skill as a communicator.

Studying speaking and writing together is a challenging task, but it can also be enjoyable. We are sure that this will be the case for you.

Listed below are terms you should know before you move on to Chapter Two. If you are unsure about the meaning of any of these words, look back through the chapter and study the way in which they are used. Those you should know are in boldface.

KEY WORDS

planned discourse	shared experience
informal communication	audience
formal communication	feedback
process	symbols
purpose	colloquial
sending	repair sequences
receiving	semantic
messages	syntactic

EXERCISES

1. For which of the following speaking situations would you be likely to plan well ahead of time what you are going to say? What form would your planning be likely to take? Would you write out the whole speech, imagine what the audience would like to hear, prepare notes or an outline, rehearse important phrases and explanations, or do some other things to get ready to speak?

   a. a sales presentation at a convention
   b. a lecture for a college class
   c. an interview for a job you want
   d. door-to-door sales of cleaning products or cosmetics
   e. presentation of research results at a scholarly conference
   f. testimony before a legislative committee
   g. a sermon
   h. a debate about nuclear power
   i. a patriotic speech on a national holiday

2. Attend a speech or lecture on campus. Observe the level of formality the speaker uses. Is it appropriate for the audience? Look back at the questions asked regarding the quotation about hanging on the edge of a cliff. Following these questions, decide whether or not the speech you hear is an effective piece of communication.

3. When you shift your communication patterns for different situations, what changes do you notice in your own communicative behavior? How do you change it for a speech or essay, talking to friends about an experience, or talking in a more organized group, such as the classroom?

4. Interview the following people about the kinds of writing they do in their jobs: your parents, a brother, sister, friend, or celebrity, if you happen to know one. Then make a list and bring it to class. Bring all types of writing, even what may seem trivial to you: a grocery list, a note, letters, business reports or memos, invitations, job descriptions, and so forth. When gathering this information use the *who, what, when, where, why* questions of journalism. Who is doing the writing? What kind of writing is being done? For what purpose? When is it being done? Where? Remember to discuss whether the writing is appropriate for its intended audience.

5. Make it a point to watch both the local and national news for several days in a row. Then compare the styles of your local news commentator with those of the network newscasters. What differences do you notice? Are the levels of formality different? Is humor more acceptable in either of the situations? What about the vocabulary? Probe these differences as much as possible. You may also want to compare interviewing styles: Watch a news broadcast and listen to the reporters. How do they compare with other reporters? With other media interviewers? What factors account for the differences in interviewing styles?

6. The following paper was written by one of our students as her first essay in our course. Read it, and then discuss what features make it seem like unplanned or informal speech. Try applying this checklist:
   a. use of sentence connectors (*and, so then, but*)
   b. use of personal pronouns, especially first and second person
   c. shifting of tenses
   d. inclusion of humor

Lasting Friendships

Close, mature friendships can last a lifetime. But when friendship and responsibility conflict, many arguments may occur. The example that follows is a true one. It explains how and why many of my closest friends and myself overcame our disputes and remained friends—closer friends than before.

Almost everyone I hung around with in high school was a cheerleader, including myself. We were considered the so-called "popular group." Well, in the beginning of my senior year it was time to elect a new captain and two new co-captains. Everyone had a chance at being elected. It just so happened I was elected as captain and two of my closest friends as co-captains. I accepted the job as captain, knowing it would be just that—a job—a tough one, too. Tough because I would be in charge of my closest friends. This was a challenge I had accepted.

Well, practice went fairly well at first. Getting everyone's attention was the hardest part. No one wanted to listen to me. I let it go for awhile, but nothing was getting done. I knew I had to motivate and use discipline, and that's exactly what I did. A few hard feelings existed at first, but diminished as soon as practice was over. The real test would be when the season started. I was not looking forward to that.

Sure enough the season started and just as I had figured, there were many conflicts. For one thing, no one was listening to what I said. Everyone just wanted to have a good time. That was great, I wanted to have a good time, too, but we would have fun and cheer at the same time. Many of my friends could not understand this. I had been the same way they were the year before, but now all of a sudden I had changed. I had to make the change. I had the responsibility of the whole squad on my shoulders and I wanted us to look good. Not only for my sake, but for the sake of the group.

During the year, many problems and arguments arose. Some people weren't showing up at games. Others just weren't talking to me at all. This wasn't just going on during cheerleading but during school, too. I finally decided to have a talk with everyone. I laid it right on the line that I did not like the job I had, but I had it, and I was determined to do my best. I asked everyone to please leave cheerleading on the field, not bring it to school. I also asked that if anyone had any complaints, they should talk them over with me. Maybe they could be resolved. I finally broke down in tears and admitted that I hated the job and that my friends meant more to me than what I was doing. I loved all of them. From that one little talk I had everything resolved and the rest of the season was a lot more fun. Everyone understood how I felt which made me feel so much better. There were still a few conflicts here and there, but compromises were made and our friendships lasted.

So our friendships were, and still are, stronger than they ever had been. Looking back, it all seems pretty ridiculous. We all laugh about it now. All of us profited from the experience, especially me. I had learned how tough responsibility is and how special my friends really are.

— Brooke Thomas

7. What changes would you make if you were going to tell this student's story as a planned formal speech?

REFERENCES

Einhorn, Lois. "Oral and Written Style: An Examination of Differences," *The Southern Speech Communication Journal* 43 (Spring, 1978), p. 302.

Walcutt, Judith. "The Typology of Narrative Boundedness," in Elinor O. Keenan and Tina L. Bennet, eds., *Discourse Across Time and Space*, Southern California Occasional Papers in Linguistics, No. 5 (Los Angeles, University of Southern California, 1977), p. 56.

2. The Composer as Self: Analyzing Experience

> How can I know what I think till I see what I say?
>
> — E.M. Forster

As E. M. Forster implies, finding out what we think and why we think it frequently requires verbalizing our thoughts, either orally or on paper. How many times do we have to wait until we hear ourselves speak before we realize just how we feel about something? Sometimes having heard our words, we wish we could take them back or change them. That is the the advantage of planned discourse: we have the opportunity to analyze what we think and to deal with it before someone else does.

This chapter discusses how we analyze our personal experience and knowledge and then convert it into **discourse**: purposeful communication designed to affect an audience. The process has several stages or elements, which the chapter covers in this order: (1) responding to experience, (2) selecting and shaping the topic, (3) evaluating the communication situation, and (4) composing. Although these stages are discussed individually they do not always occur in a particular order, nor do they always occur separately in time. Considerations of topic, audience, and situation frequently overlap as we struggle to shape our experience into words.

This chapter examines the elements of communication from the perspective of the communicator. The next chapter looks at discourse from an audience's perspective, suggesting what a communicator must do to turn a rough version of a speech or essay into a finished product. Taken together, the two chapters provide an overview of composing from analyzing experience to preparing the final version of a speech or essay.

Careful preparation when beginning to compose is worth every minute of time it takes. Just as a successful carpenter spends time choosing the right tools and drafting plans, so a composer needs to bring to the preparation of a speech or essay a complete set of tools and plans appropriate to the task. Beginning to draft your work before you are ready can cause frustration and failure. On the other hand, setting about your work with adequate preparation can be a rewarding and confidence-building experience.

RESPONDING TO EXPERIENCE: EXPLORING THOUGHTS AND FEELINGS

Not all writing and speaking is intended for an audience. Sometimes we record experiences for our own ears and eyes alone. This helps in two important ways: it provides a necessary release of emotion and it gives one the luxury of ignoring an audience.

A spontaneous emotional release is one way of finding out what we care about enough to communicate to others. Releasing emotion privately is sometimes better than directing it toward others before we have had time to reflect on our feelings. Many of us have written an angry or sarcastic letter that we wisely destroyed after thinking more calmly about what we wanted to say and why we wanted to say it. Being able to ignore an audience has a purpose similar to releasing emotion: it allows us to be wordy and disorganized while finding out what we think in order that we may communicate more clearly at the appropriate time.

Of course, in addition to recording our experiences privately, we may respond to them by talking them over informally with others. This allows us to sort ideas in a way that prepares us for more formal communication.

Effective communication grows out of a desire to share experiences. Communication fails when it is artificial. The paragraphs below suggest three strategies for using personal experiences as a means of self-discovery: using a tape recorder, keeping a journal, and talking with others.

Talking to Yourself on Tape

> His novels are produced in an uncustomary way — talked first to friends, then told to a tape recorder, typed up and endlessly revised.
>
> (Clemons, 1981)

At first, many people feel a little silly sitting alone in a room and talking to a machine as Clemons claims William Wharton composes. However, they usually find that feeling a bit foolish is a small price to pay for storing a flow of thoughts and feelings to draw upon when they are running a dry spell. Business people, politicians, writers, and public speakers frequently keep tape recorders in their cars or offices to record those occasional flashes of insight that come to us as we drive, daydream, or consciously focus on a specific problem or situation.

Some people use tapes only to record their initial inspiration, preferring to give shape to their thoughts on paper; others actually talk out the whole speech, essay, business report, or even, as the quote above indicates, the whole novel. If you are more comfortable speaking than writing, using the tape recorder instead of the pen may make it easier for you to become involved in self–expression as a way of preserving your experiences.

Talking to Yourself on Paper

> I find myself on the very edge of creativity. My days in the world of words are numbered, and I find myself falling back into the world of numbers, data and facts. My imagination and creativity have grown in

size, but my interpretation and memory capabilities have become jealous and are now in the process of kicking them out of my brain. For one last time, I will delve into the world of words. In an attempt to paint an unbiased picture of myself, I will share my thoughts from my journal. From that picture, I will persuade people that keeping a journal is the best way to learn and know about yourself.

— Dede Demetroulakes

Like tape recorders, journals can capture the ideas that result from thinking deeply about the world and help us to reflect this thinking in our communication. An excerpt from Dede's journal illustrates this concept. Thinking about how to describe herself led Dede to an unusual metaphor:

> The thing that first comes to mind in presenting myself is the major driving force in my life, my desire to do research in the medical field. This goal makes all things subordinate to academics. I am an arrow directed at a target, coiled and about to be released. I expect to be released at any moment. I am in a more difficult dimension than most of my friends. I am potential energy while they are floating about in convection currents.
>
> The energy differential is evident in my personality. I am charged, nervous, and poised. I have learned to hide my energy behind a laid-back, more casual facade. But people who know me well and have seen the facade crumble know better. They know I am driving. I honestly don't know where it began, maybe parents, maybe friends, but as long as I can remember I pushed myself. I decided to make the move that changed my life. That is to go to college.

What should be emphasized here is that journal writing is rarely organized in any conscious way. In fact, another term for this kind of outpouring is simply **free writing**; however, any sustained piece of discourse usually shapes itself into one of the patterns discussed in this text. In this case, after the concept of analysis was explained and assigned, Dede realized she had the basis for the essay on self-examination excerpted above.

Students who use tape recorders, keep journals, or do both find that when it is time to choose a topic they have a recorded source of their own ideas. Of course, it still requires ingenuity to take the raw experience and organize it for an audience. Neither journals nor tapes will magically lead to complete assignments. They will, however, help you keep in touch with your thoughts, and the more often you express your thoughts verbally, the easier it becomes to shape them into formal discourse. If you were to browse through the journals of philosophers like Thoreau, writers like Hemingway, and statesmen like Adlai Stevenson, you would see how their public speech and writing grew from a continuing record of their experiences.

Talking to Others

> The general group discussions were most enjoyable. The atmosphere was always informal, friendly and relaxed. Since we had such a small class, I feel I got to know some very nice people. The topics we talked about covered a wide range but usually related to an assignment, and I found myself taking part where normally I might shy away. Hearing personal views and ideas was often fascinating. I think we all learned and profited from those discussions.
>
> — Marie Cobleigh

> The most significant experience I have had is the exposure to people whom I would not have chosen as friends. It was good for me to see how my "flaming liberal" views were received by other people. The kindness was unending, and indeed, even strange opinions were listened to with interest.
>
> — Maureen Wilcox

The students quoted above have discovered the value of sharing experiences and opinions informally with people other than their close friends. The discussions they refer to occurred during **brainstorming** sessions in class. Brainstorming helps in combating the fear that no one, outside of friends and family, could possibly be interested in our experiences or in what we have to say.

Brainstorming works like this: the instructor asks you to break up into groups of four or five and gives you a general topic, or simply asks you to exchange some recent experiences with each other. As you begin to talk and others respond you will develop a perspective on what aspects of your experience are interesting to others and why. Because you are not among your close friends, you are more likely to hear opinions you had not thought of, and you will begin to get a sense of the audience that successful communicators must keep in mind when preparing formal discourse.

One lively classroom discussion developed when a social worker realized her views on prostitution were not shared by others in the class, and in fact differed greatly from those of a young man who had just finished his military service. Far from being discouraged, the student welcomed the diversity of opinion. Sharing her views informally and receiving frank response to them allowed her to write a paper that successfully anticipated various reactions and arguments from a general audience. Had the topic not arisen in class discussion, the student said, she "would have written the paper only from my viewpoint, and ended up sounding self-righteous and narrow-minded."

It is important to stress that you need not have a topic when you begin discussion. The purpose of the discussion is much the same as that behind taping your thoughts or writing them in a journal: to put your experiences into words, to discover how you think and feel about them, and to learn to see them from other perspectives.

This split perspective — "How do I see it? How do others see it?" — is the most basic element of the analytical thinking that governs effective communication. As such, it must be considered at all stages of communicating, from the moment of the initial experience to the final presentation in formal speech or writing. For this reason we encourage you to begin viewing your everyday experiences as potential bases for planned communication.

Reflect on your experiences by asking yourself the following questions:

- What do I think about this experience?
- How does it make me feel?
- Would I share this experience with others?
- What would I tell them about it?

We suggest that you record the answers to these questions on tape or in a journal so that your immediate impressions are not lost. Then, when you talk about your experiences informally, ask yourself this set of questions:

- Are my listeners' reactions to the experience the same as mine?
- Do they see something in it that I missed?
- What aspect of the experience seems to interest them most?
- How do I view the experience differently now?

You probably already ask these questions unconsciously; most of us do. If you train yourself to become aware of the answers, the information you store as a result will become more readily available when you need to draw upon it. The pursuit of many professions and careers like art, music, medicine, psychology, and journalism, to name a few, requires heightened sensitivity to people and their reactions. This sensitivity develops in part from continual, conscious application of the questions listed above, as well as questions you develop in response to your own communication needs.

All of the methods described so far — using tapes, keeping journals, and talking informally with others — provided ways of examining immediate, organized responses to experience. The next section looks at ways to classify and organize raw experiences into possible topics for formal communication.

DISCOVERING A TOPIC

Have you ever gone through a whole day without talking to anyone at all? Without experiencing an opinion? Even if only to express our preference for a restaurant or movie, most of us communicate our thoughts to others daily and with little prompting. Communication in casual, interpersonal settings is as natural and normal as eating or sleeping. The things we talk about grow out of our experiences and how we think about them. The crowded parking lot that makes us late for class, the break-up with a friend, the decision to quit a part-time job — such events, relationships, and shifting viewpoints give us much to say, and the social side of our nature impels us to say it, thus sharing our experiences. We may not always be able to express exactly what we are thinking, and others may not always follow us completely, but having thoughts to express is rarely a problem.

Probing Experience

The idea of engaging in formal discourse nonetheless seems to paralyze the otherwise natural translation of experience into words. The composition student, the commencement speaker, the local column writer — all have asked themselves the painful question: "What am I going to talk (write) about?" After hearing "Pick a topic that you know something about," writers and speakers alike panic as they say to themselves, "I don't know anything interesting!" Our everyday experiences seem somehow trivial when we must come up with a topic to interest not our immediate circle of friends but rather that evasive body, the general audience. You should be able, however, to shape your planned discourse from the same experiences that inspire your natural, everyday urge to communicate.

We have two kinds of experiences: personal and vicarious. Personal experiences happen to us; we walk on the beach or we ski down a mountain. Vicarious experiences happen to others, but we participate indirectly in them by reading or hearing about them. Regardless of whether an experience is personal or vicarious, our perspective on it is unique; no one else will view it in quite the same way. Each time we process our experiences we are generating ideas for communication.

Why, then, does it seem that when we sit down to write a speech or an essay, we have nothing to say? Perhaps because we store experiences subconsciously. The conscious mind must have available the information it needs for day-to-day living: data for exams, shopping lists, birthdays of friends and relatives, bank balances, and so on. The conscious mind relies on the subconscious to preserve experiences and the sensory impressions that accompany them.

Although these experiences and impressions provide the basis for planned discourse, they are stored in raw form. To communicate effectively we must probe our experiences systematically; otherwise we offer our audience a jumble of impressions that have meaning only to us. The process of communicating in an organized fashion to a general audience goes beyond simply recounting an experience; it places upon the communicator the burden of giving meaning to the experience for others. To put it another way:

. . . writers [and speakers] don't *find* meanings, they *make* them. A writer in the act of discovery is hard at work searching memory, forming concepts, and forging a new structure of ideas, while at the same time trying to juggle all the constraints imposed by his or her purpose, audience, and language itself. Discovery, the event, and its product, new insights, are only the end result of a complicated intellectual process.

(Flower and Hayes, 1980)

Earlier, the importance of recording the initial emotional response to experience was suggested; now look at how we may process an event intellectually, in the manner described above: "searching memory, forming concepts, and forging a new structure of ideas." Imagine the following event:

The
Experience

The Thinking
Process

Scott's brother asks him to be his best man at his wedding. They talk for awhile and Scott accepts.

As the day draws near, Scott learns more and more about being a best man. Some of this knowledge he seeks out, some he learns vicariously, but all of it becomes part of his total experience. Questions naturally occur to Scott: What will the day be like? What is likely to happen? What are my duties and responsibilities? Why do we even have a best man? What kind of best man will I make?

Doubts may even arise as Scott thinks about the expensive tuxedo he will have to rent. He may wonder if all of this ritual is not actually a hoax perpetrated on young couples solely for the benefit of their parents and the wedding industry. He wonders why people go through all of this nonsense. "Why not just go down to the park with close friends, a guitar, and some good food, and simply pledge to share a life together?"

Later, recording the event in his journal or on tape, Scott may describe what the day meant to him. Impressions of friendship, celebration, and tradition as well as a sense of exploitation, falseness, and unnecessary expense may all run together in his recollections. Given an essay or speech assignment, Scott may naturally turn to his recent experience as the topic for his discourse. If, however, he views writing the essay or giving the speech as an end in itself, he is likely to see the event only as a topic, and thus try to cover all aspects of his experience, entitling his presentation something like "My Experience as a Best Man." Such an attempt will confuse and frustrate the members of his audience because they have not experienced the event. As spectators rather than participants, audiences look for focus, a point of view with which they can identify because it reflects not just individual but universal feelings or concerns.

On the other hand, if Scott views his tasks as engaging in a significant act of communication rather than as doing as assignment, he must consciously probe the experience. Certainly he should turn to his personal account of the whole event, but this time with an objective eye, looking for the social, other-directed implications of his personal feelings. Scott's anger at the expenses involved in a traditional wedding, for example, is a sentiment shared by others in society. He might explore this with a topic like "Buying the American Wedding: Time for a Change," an argument against the profit motive built into the wedding ritual, with some suggestions for change.

More sentimentally, he might decide to talk about the deepening of friendship and family ties that result from being involved with a couple's wedding; thus "Gaining a Sister" could be a description of the bride and the groom on their wedding day from the best man's point of view. There are numerous ways Scott could organize his experience. Here are two others; perhaps you can think of some you might want to add.

"How Not to Be a Best Man, Including the Obligatory Forgetting of the Ring" — a humorous guide to being a best man.

"The Best Man: A Time–Honored Tradition" — a historical tracing of the term "best man" and its place in the wedding ritual.

The point is this: recording experiences is an important first step in composing because it allows writers or speakers to capture in sharp detail the uniqueness of perceptions that could be forgotten or blurred over time. Extracting a topic from personal experience requires in some sense that we look for the universal as well as the unique, that we find a feeling, an idea, an issue that we have in common with others. Informal brainstorming can aid here because taking "what happened to me" and turning it into "how what happened to me affects you" is an essential step in composing.

Using Thought Patterns as Probes

Look at another experience and then at how you might sift it carefully and consciously for possible topics:

The Experience
You walk into a food store and pick up a few items. At the checkout counter you pick up a candy bar, pay for it, open it, and start to eat it on your way home.

The Thinking Process
As you munch on the candy bar, certain thoughts suddenly pop into your head. "I've been eating lots of candy lately. Here I am doing it again, and I hardly even realized that I bought it." Or "I wonder how they make candy anyway . . . . in a big candy factory?" Or "What's in this candy bar?"

As you eat you might decide that another candy bar would have tasted better. In your mind you begin to rate and rank five candy bars that you like. Thinking more seriously now, you might recall that in a nutrition class you took, a great deal was said about the effects of excessive sugar in the diets of children. You conclude that candy bar ads should warn children about the dangers of excessive consumption.

Out of these reflections, thoughts most of us have had about similar experiences, you have generated numerous topics for speeches or essays. You could talk about one of the following, as shown in Figure 2-1:

1. "How I Became a Junk Food Junkie" — a personal narrative
2. "The Candy Factory — How Sweet It Is" — a demonstration (process) speech on how candy is made
3. "What's in a Candy Bar?" — a descriptive essay on the ingredients in a candy bar
4. "The Five Best Candy Bars in America" — an analysis of popular candy bars and what makes them so
5. "The Case Against Candy for Kids" — an argument in favor of monitoring candy bar advertisements during children's television programming

Notice that this time the patterns of thinking are labeled as they apply to the topic: narration, process, description, analysis, and argument. When we process our experiences at a conscious level, approaching them as problems to be systematically explored in order that they may be effectively communicated and shared, we use logical thought patterns. To use the patterns this way is to use them as *probes*, as sets of questions to apply to an event or experience to see how many topics it contains. Each of the patterns suggests a different set of questions.

Time Probes (time oriented ways to think about experiences or ideas)
  Narration
    What happened?
    To whom did it happen?
    When?
    Where?
  Process
    How does it work?
    How can it be done?
  Cause and Effect
    Why did it happen?
    What is likely to happen in the future?

Static Probes (static ways to think about experiences or ideas)
  Analysis
    What are the parts?
    How are they related to each other and to the whole?

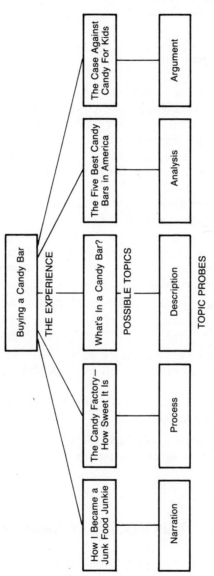

Figure 2-1 Probing an Experience Systematically

Enumeration
   How many parts does the topic have?
   Into what common serial or sequential arrangement do the parts fall?
   Can the parts be numbered?
Comparison
   Is it similar to other things?
   Is it different from other things?
Classification
   What categories does it fall into?
   What are the characteristics of each category?
Description
   What are the physical features?
   How is it organized in space?
   What are its mental or emotional qualities?
Definition
   To what class of things does it belong?
   What features characterize it and set it off from other things?
Exemplification
   What are reasonable illustrations of this idea or principle?
   What are some representative examples or instances in this group of
   things, persons, or events?

Conventional Probes (socially or culturally prescribed ways to think about
experiences or ideas)
Information
   What questions will an audience need to have answered in order to
   have all the information it wants or needs about a subject?
Argumentation
   What questions will an audience need to have answered in order to
   decide about an issue?

The following chapters will explore each pattern in detail and will
indicate how they may be used as organizing principles for discourse.

BEFORE COMPOSING: SOME IMPORTANT THINGS TO CONSIDER

Composing involves at least three variables: the communicator's **role**, the
constraints, and the **audience**. Each variable requires a different kind of
consideration. Before you can actually begin to draft, it is important to
analyze these preliminary considerations in some detail and perhaps make
some notes to yourself. This analysis may not help you with what to say
about your topic, but it will help considerably with how to say it.

Evaluation of each of the three variables — role, constraints, and audience — occurs throughout composition. The three work together, although one or another may dominate at some time during the actual preparation of a speech or essay. Remember that these factors need to be analyzed carefully before you draft a speech or essay. Then, as you draft, the knowledge you have gained from careful preliminary analysis may cause you to shift direction or focus, to reorganize your information, or to change the level of your language.   .

Your Role as a Communicator

Communicators must be sensitive to the way the audience perceives them so that they can adapt effectively to the situation. The student speaker at Commencement, for example, is aware that the audience will perceive that speaker differently from the way it will perceive the invited guest speaker, who is likely to be locally or nationally known. The guest speaker has already achieved a certain status in the audience's mind by virtue of reputation; the student speaker is an unknown, with ability that has yet to be proved.

If you are the student speaker, you know that the audience views you as a representative of the entire graduating class — what it has achieved, what it has to offer the community. Knowing this, you will probably spend time planning the appropriate tone and level of vocabulary for the speech, and even thinking about dress, appearance, and posture. Creating a profile for yourself ahead of time will help you with such considerations as the amount and kind of information needed, level of vocabulary, use of humor, appropriate dress, and so on. In making these decisions, consider the following factors:

- Has your credibility been previously established, or are you an unknown?
- Are you a member of the group you are speaking to or writing for, or are you an invited guest?
- Is your attitude toward the topic favorable or unfavorable?

Simply put, our direction to you is to know who you are in relation to your audience. Refrain from trying to be someone you are not. If you are not a member of the group, avoid trying to represent yourself as one. Your audience is well aware that you are an outsider and will probably expect you to act in that role. In the following interview for *Saturday Review*, journalist Tom Wolfe responds to the question, "Do you adapt to your subject?" His answer suggests the balance between sensitivity to others and awareness of self that communicators must maintain if they want to be effective.

When I first started at ESQUIRE, I made the mistake of trying to fit in. And given the kinds of things I was sent to cover — stock car racing, the Peppermint Lounge, topless restaurants in San Francisco — not only did I not fit in no matter how hard I tried, but I would deprive myself of the opportunities to ask very basic question that the outsider can ask. You just discover after awhile that people like to be asked questions they know the answers to.

(Haller, 1981a)

Constraints and Guidelines

Many beginning writers and speakers mistakenly assume that real writers and real speakers are so good that they are free to write and speak as they please, that regardless of the situation people will listen. This is not true. Even having a letter to the editor published requires that one conform to specific guidelines:

To the Contributor:

Thank you for your letter to the editor of the JOURNAL-BULLETIN.

The limited amount of space available means that many letters received cannot be printed. Those selected for publication are chosen on the basis of importance of the subject, the interest most readers would have in it, clarity and effectiveness of expression, and suitability of length (250-word limit). Unsigned letters are not used nor are duplicates of those originally sent to others.

Letters written as part of an organized campaign or in solicitation of funds are not acceptable.

Under normal circumstances, letter writers are restricted to one letter every 45 days so that as many readers as possible may have a chance to express their views.

The box checked below indicates the reason your letter will not be published.

   _____ 1. Your letter is too long.

   _____ 2. Your letter will be considered for publication if you will permit your name to be used.

   _____ 3. A previous letter of yours has been published or accepted for publication within the last 45 days.

   _____ 4. Your letter is apparently a duplicate of one sent to another party or publication. Only letters written specifically to the JOURNAL-BULLETIN are considered for publication.

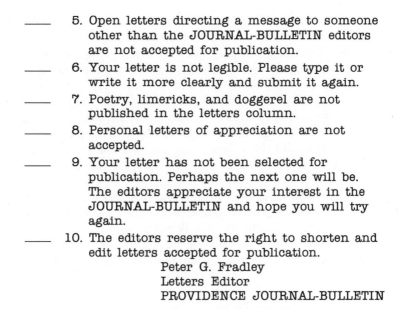

_____ 5. Open letters directing a message to someone other than the JOURNAL-BULLETIN editors are not accepted for publication.

_____ 6. Your letter is not legible. Please type it or write it more clearly and submit it again.

_____ 7. Poetry, limericks, and doggerel are not published in the letters column.

_____ 8. Personal letters of appreciation are not accepted.

_____ 9. Your letter has not been selected for publication. Perhaps the next one will be. The editors appreciate your interest in the JOURNAL-BULLETIN and hope you will try again.

_____ 10. The editors reserve the right to shorten and edit letters accepted for publication.

Peter G. Fradley
Letters Editor
PROVIDENCE JOURNAL-BULLETIN

Writers who want their letters published must adapt to the newspaper's guidelines. The same is true for most situations: if you want to be effective, you adapt. Public hearings will often limit speakers to five minutes. Research papers assigned in a classroom will quite often have page limits. Editors of magazines like _Time_ and _Newsweek_ assign their staff writers a topic and request a certain length. Conference speakers are frequently allowed only twenty minutes to present what may be the results of a year's worth of research.

The important thing to remember about the constraints on your writing or speech is that they are aimed at helping you, not hindering you. Carefully thought out constraints are often the results of what some unlucky soul had to learn by trial and error. They are actually clues about what works and what does not.

It is important to find out what constraints have been imposed on the situation in which you are communicating and even to ask "Why?" if that makes you more comfortable. If there seem to be no constraints, it is wise to ask about them; if none are suggested, provide your own.

Your Audience

Just as you must have a clear idea of your role in the occasion for communication, so it is important to know your audience. How does knowledge of an audience affect what we have to say? Think of this: When talking with your friends in a casual setting, and when talking about a topic familiar to all, you automatically adjust to the needs of your listeners. You can tell by their faces if you are giving too much detail about last weekend's ski trip, or whether they are more interested in the conditions of the slopes or the parties at the lodge. The entertainer in all of us tries to give our audience what we think it wants.

For this reason, effective communicators are adept at finding out ahead of time the background of their audience. This preliminary step helps them assess what the audience may already know about the intended topic and what it will need or want to know for the communication to be successful.

Those who make their living by writing also make it their business to know people, especially people who buy their books. Once *Saturday Review* analyzed "The World's Best-Selling Authors: Who They are and Why They Sell." The following passage reveals what these authors have come to know about their readers and how they try to satisfy the needs of their public:

> In the course of telling his or her tale, each writer imparts a great deal of "inside information." Whether the details are historical (as with Cartland and L'Amour) gossipy (as with Robbins and Wallace) or a combination of the two (Dailey), the data gives the manuscript legitimacy, and the readers a did-you-know dividend. Some of the information supplied here may be of no consequence — what good does it do most of us to know where to park when visiting the Kremlin? — but the facts represent an effort to enrich the reader and ennoble the book.
>
> (Haller, 1981b)

While you may never write or speak for financial gain, you will want to profit in other ways from your formal communication: getting a desired job, persuading your peers to support you for student body president, or convincing a graduate school that you deserve to be accepted into a program of study. In every case your communication should reflect an awareness of your audience and what it needs to know.

The following examples of topics, audiences, situations, and roles suggest considerations you might have when creating an image of yourself. By analyzing the considerations given in Table 2-1 you will begin to see how **information levels** and audience needs may differ.

Adjusting perspectives on a topic to fit diverse audiences and occasions as well as to meet the needs of your own shifting roles helps you in developing the flexibility of mind and spirit necessary to be an effective communicator. Here is how the information needs of the various audiences listed for the first topic might differ:

Topic	Audience	Needs to Know
An Ordinance to Stop Hazardous Waste Dumping: A Case for Passage	Residents of the town	1. Effects on drinking water 2. Presence of cancer-causing agents in ground and air 3. Increase in taxes for enforcement
	A biology professor	1. Chemicals in waste 2. Effects on flora and fauna
	Owners of the dump	1. Effect on profits 2. Increased responsibilities

There are three additional points to be made about audience analysis. First, audience considerations are meant to complement but not replace knowledge of the topic. We ought to be able to make a reasonable case for

Table 2-1 Analyzing the Communication Situation

Topic	Audience	Situation	You
An Ordinance to Stop Hazardous Waste Dumping: A Case for Passage	Residents of the town A biology professor Owner of the dump	Public hearing Research paper Letter	An angry citizen? A fellow scientist? An activist?
How to Study for a Test	Freshman orientation class Composition class School newspaper readers	Lecture 1,000-word essay Feature article	Counsellor? Colleague? Journalist?
Working On An Ambulance	Teenagers Townspeople	Career Day at local HS Open meeting on funds needed to operate ambulance Storytelling around the garage	Expert? Advocate? Co-worker?
Effectiveness Analysis for Insulating the Plant	Accounting officer, VP for business affairs, personnel director, plant manager, and worker representative	Conference report	Advocate? Information source? Salesperson?

what we have written or said regardless of the specific audience we are addressing. Second, it is quite helpful to write out, in a paragraph or two, a characterization of the audience. The act of constructing a verbal profile of the audience can be of great help in actual composition.

Third, what we learn from speaking to a live audience can aid us when we are trying to construct an audience during composition. The quotation below illustrates the value of this awareness of audience:

> It was all so personal. This was not some distant government official talking in governmentese; this was a voice connected to a warm human being; he knew them, he had visited them. He spoke of his wife and his children, even his dog. Some thirty-five years later an astonishing number of Americans who did not remember the names of the dogs of Harry Truman, Dwight Eisenhower, and John Kennedy, remembered the name of Franklin Roosevelt's dog because he had spoken with them about Fala, *my little dog Fala*, about Fala's Irish being up over Republican criticism. It was an awesome display of mastery. It was as if sitting in the studio he could visualize his audience sitting around their radios in their home, and he spoke not to the microphone but to those homes . . . . His touch was perfect.
>
> (Halberstam, 1979)

When we recall that Roosevelt was the only President in American history to be elected for a fourth term, we may attribute at least part of his popularity to the ability described above. Of course, Roosevelt had to imagine his audience not just at the moment of delivery in the radio studio but also while drafting his speech in the privacy of his room. Using this imagination is a skill that all communicators should work to acquire.

COMPOSING AND STAYING WITH IT

Advice from the Experts

> I'm a believer in doing it the hard way — getting into your small room, sitting at the table, excluding many of the pleasures of the world and very seriously writing and writing, doing the burden of work that has to be done . . . . You have to make your choice, which is to stay at your desk . . . and not to regret that the day is beautiful and other people are going to the beach.
>
> — Bernard Malamud (Pollit, 1981)

I try to set a quota of 10 pages — I triple space on the typewriter. For me it's about 1900 words. Any time I'm finished with that I can quit. I will quit even in the middle of a sentence at the end of the tenth page. The hardest thing is overcoming the inertia of beginning the next day. If I'm in the middle of a sentence or a paragraph, at least I know how the next day is supposed to begin. And I'll try to do a page or two before lunch. I always get up earlier than normal, but nothing gets done until just before lunch. I do a page or two. At that point I go outside, just walk around the block. I try to get five pages done in the afternoon, so that working after dinner is not going to be too much of a struggle. But I usually end up working late anyway. This is not a very good way to do it. Ideally, as I always used to gather Philip Roth does, one should get it all done before 2 PM. Then the rest of the day you can play tennis, go out in the evening, or whatever you like to do — just be a part of the world.

Tom Wolfe (Gilder, 1981)

I've always tried to work everyday when I'm in the course of a specific work. I try to write four hours each day but often it's three hours or two. I start in the midafternoon and try to work through six or seven. . . . When it's going well I can write a page in 15 minutes. When it's going hard I can take two hours.

William Styron (Mills, 1980)

No one has ever claimed that composing is easy. Quite a number of people falsely assume that if you've got the gift, you've got it, and words simply flow from the pen. Composing is much more work than gift. If you have enough discipline to remain in your chair for the time it takes to get started, chances are you have resolved the most difficult part of the whole composing process.

Composing involves its own set of rituals. You must find out at what time of day you work best and what you need to work with. Styron needs yellow legal pads and a supply of pencils; Tom Wolfe, a typewriter. The following excerpt from Jacques Barzun's "A Writer's Discipline" suggests the ways in which writers indulge their habits — and when to stop indulging.

In all such matters, I believe in humoring to the greatest extent the timid and stubborn censor which stops work on flimsy pretense. Grant, by all means, its falsely innocent preferences as to paper, ink, furnishings, and quash its grievances forever. We know that Mark Twain liked to write lying in or on a bed; we know that Schiller needed the smell of apples rotting in his desk. Some like cubicles, others vast halls. "Writers' requisites," if a Fifth Avenue shop kept them, would astound and demoralize the laity. Historically, they have included silk dressing gowns, cats, horses, pipes, mistresses, particular knicknacks, exotic headgear, currycombs, whips, beverages and drugs, porcelain stoves, and hair shirts. According to one of Bernard De Voto's novels, writing paper of a peculiar blue tint has remarkable properties, about which the author makes an excellent point . . . Quite simply, by yielding on such apparently irrational details, the writer is really outwitting his private foe — the excuse-maker in all of us who says: "I can't work today because I haven't any blue paper."

. . . suspect all out-of-the-way or elaborate preparations. You don't have to sharpen your pencils and sort out paper clips before you begin—unless it be your *regular* warming up. Give yourself no quarter when the temptation strikes but grab a pen and put down some words — your name even — and a title; something to see, to revise, to carve, to do over in the opposite way. And here comes the advantage of developing a fixation on blue tinted paper. When you have fought and won two or three bloody battles with the insane urge to clean the whole house before making a start, the sight of your favorite implements will speak irresistibly of victory, of accomplishment, of writing done.

(Barzun, 1980)

Getting Started

Let us say you are seated at your desk, curled on the sofa with a pad against your knees, or sipping coffee at the kitchen table — wherever it is you write. You have chosen a topic, considered your role, the constraints, and your audience, perhaps gathered information and jotted some rough notes on what you would like to include in your essay or speech. You sit, pen poised above paper. Nothing happens. You wiggle around in your chair, make some more coffee, pace a bit. Soon thirty minutes have gone by. Already it is one thirty and you are going out at five. This has to get done! You panic. You are stuck.

As Jacques Barzun suggests, the important thing is to get your pen moving across the paper. Remember that no one but you need ever see or hear what you say in a rough draft. What you write to get started is not final; it is simply getting started. Sometimes it helps to write out a **purpose statement**. This is not a statement to be included in your actual essay or speech, but a statement you write to yourself to lay out what you want to accomplish. The following are examples of purpose statements:

- I want to do a breezy, lighthearted piece on insurance salespersons. I want to classify them according to their selling techniques, from very hard to very soft. This is intended to entertain mostly, but it might also make readers a little more aware of the various gimmicks used to sell insurance. I'm thinking about 1,000 words or so for the entire essay.

- My goal in this speech is to get people to vote for me for Senate Treasurer. I've got five minutes, and during that time I want to present my ideas about the job and also give people a feeling for the kind of person I am. I may or may not get into my opponent's ideas, although I do plan to know them thoroughly: this I'll decide as things get going and I see what is right in the situation.

- My purpose is to say some things I have felt for a long time about welfare. I am sick and tired of the welfare issue being dragged into every political battle, and abused by both sides. I'm going to provide the facts about welfare: the system and the recipients, and then I'm going to make a plea for honesty and integrity on the part of politicians when they talk about the issue.

Your purpose statement may or may not turn out to be the basis for the **thesis statement** that will appear in your final draft. The difference between the two is that a purpose statement helps you, as the composer, to gain a clear understanding of why you are composing. It helps you to decide whether your goal is to tell a story, to present information, or to persuade your audience to adopt a particular viewpoint. A thesis statement, on the other hand, is generally a one-sentence signal to your audience of what your speech or essay can be expected to cover and of the pattern you will use to cover it. The thesis statement is an essential element of a finished product, but not of a rough draft.

Perhaps you have trouble starting to compose because you know that a good speech or essay should immediately involve the audience, or that the thesis should be stated soon after the introduction. These guidelines are generally true, but once again they apply to the finished product. The catchy introduction and the real purpose of our discourse frequently come to us only after we have begun to see our ideas take shape across the page. Struggling with the introduction and purpose and trying to shape them perfectly into a rough draft may interfere with your flow of ideas and cause you to give up before giving your thoughts a chance. Think back to the quotation that began this chapter: "How can I know what I think till I see what I say?"

Although this section suggests that a purpose statement can be helpful, keep up your courage even if you cannot put your purpose into words right away. Some people find it necessary to write down in random fashion everything they have learned about their subject before they can begin to organize it in an order appropriate for an audience. Spend some time thinking about how you write and about how ideas come to you. If writing out all you know about your topic is an important first step for you, recognize that this is part of your composing process. There is no right way to compose; all of us compose differently in the way that best fits how we think. But there are two suggestions that will help: discover the elements involved in your composing process and do whatever helps to get you started writing; then allow yourself enough time for your individual method. Once again, time varies. For some it is five consecutive hours; for others it is short periods of time spread out over several days. If you do these two things you will avoid the last-minute panic that may result in a finished product that fails to meet your standards.

False Starts: Rereading and Rewriting

There are many different styles of composing. Some people, like the writer quoted below, consider themselves single draft writers:

Q. Do you ever cross out or rewrite?

A. I try to interline. . . . Instead of crossing out I ususally erase, and
. . . I do a great deal of interlining. In general, my technique has almost never varied in that it is an accumulation of pages which I will never change in a major way. I don't write a first draft and then go back and dismantle it. I write very painstakingly from page one. It's like building a brick wall from the ground up . . . . I've written many pages and paragraphs that I've thrown away entirely.

William Styron (Mills, 1980)

Others write numerous drafts, each draft retaining the substance of the original ideas but shifting the point of view:

I'm one of the few people in the world who enjoy rewriting . . . . I change the stance, the teller, the characters, the time span.

William Wharton (Clemons, 1981)

Why do we rewrite? We rewrite because when our flow of ideas stops momentarily, we read over what we have already written to get us going again. As we look back on what we have said, our viewpoint may shift slightly, or it may change in a major way. We discover that we have left out things we meant to say, and we start to examine closely the connections among our ideas. What we are looking for is something — a word, an insight—that will move us along. Eudora Welty describes what happens in her rereading:

It's strange how in revision you find some little unconsidered thing which is so essential that you not only keep it in, but give it preeminence when you revise. Sometimes in the dead of night, it will come to me. Well, that's what I should do, that's what I'm working toward! It was there all the time . . . . I usually make a note right away: "Move something." Just a word. When I get back . . . in the morning, I just write.

(Haller, 1981a)

This backward motion of reading over and then rewriting a portion of the discourse helps provide the momentum to go forward again. Remember what Tom Wolfe said: "The hardest thing is overcoming the inertia . . ."

The rewriting process we go through as we struggle toward a complete draft is different from the revising we do to turn a draft into a finished product. In revising a completed draft, we attempt to respond to our discourse as an audience might; at this time, we concern ourselves with providing such necessary conventions as introductions, conclusions, clear transitions, and appropriate details, as well as with polishing our prose for the right sound. The next chapter looks at the process of final revision.

Developing Form: Looking for Key Phrases

The amount of rereading and rewriting we do varies according to our individual composing styles. Precisely how rereading triggers ideas for new material is a little-understood phenomenon, yet most writers would agree that it does. There are some definite cues we can look for as we read over what we have written.

The section on "Getting Started" suggested that you write out a purpose statement. When you feel yourself losing momentum, go back to your purpose statement. If you have omitted writing a purpose statement at this point in your composition, it may be the time to try putting one on paper. When you have finished doing so, read it over. One student's purpose statement appears below. Look at it and then at the clues it provides for giving direction to a speech or essay:

> What I really want to do is show the value of a varsity sports program at the school. I am not trying to convince anyone of anything — since I'm a varsity track member, no one would believe me. My goal is to provide information, to list what I see as the benefits of the program. I don't plan to argue about how much the benefits cost, or to compare the benefits to other extracurricular activities: I simply want the audience to be informed about the program, and to know that students are benefiting from it.
>
> — John Wallace

Having written out this statement to get started, John went on to begin writing about his own experience in the program. Writing about his personal experience led John to discover how many benefits he had personally derived from the program. At this point he became overwhelmed with the amount of material he was covering and simply stopped, wondering what to do next. What did he do?

He went back to his purpose statement and read over the last sentence: "I simply want the audience to be informed about the program and to know that students are benefiting from it." After reading this over, John said to himself, "OK, what's the best way to inform the audience? Maybe they don't need to hear all about my personal experiences; maybe I could just talk about the benefits to students in general."

Once John decided to talk about the benefits in general, he went back to the draft to cut. He read through his personal experience section, saving anything that illustrated benefits to the students in general but getting rid of material that described only what happened to him. As John started to rewrite, this time focusing only on the program's general benefits, a new problem surfaced.

John discovered that there are too many benefits to cover in a three-page essay or a five-minute speech. He realized that if he continued to keep writing, he could mention all the benefits involved but would be able to include only a sentence or two about each one, saying nothing in detail. He looked back once again at his purpose statement and found that the word "benefits" was causing his difficulty. He then asked himself, "Do I have to cover all the benefits? Which ones should I cover?"

Thinking about this, John was led to a purpose statement that provided more direction:

> Many benefits come from participation in the varsity sports program; I want to speak about three that I consider most important.

John was moving toward a specific pattern — in this case, enumeration. From this point on, his rereading focused on three major benefits of the varsity sports program. He reread to see if he had added enough details about the three benefits, but the focus of his discourse was clearer to him than it was when he first began.

It would be easier if we always knew exactly what we wanted to focus on when we began composing. Of course, some people do think out the whole piece before they put pen to paper. If you are lucky enough to be able to do that, there is no reason to change your composing style.

Most of us have to go through a process similar to the one that John used, writing randomly at first and then looking back for key words that will help us find direction.

The discussion of journal writing suggested that any sustained piece of discourse eventually shapes itself into an identifiable pattern or structure. The discussions of Scott's wedding experience and of buying a candy bar illustrated how this begins to happen. As this text suggests, patterns are the logical representations of the way we think when we begin to turn our experiences into forms that can be communicated.

Consider again how an experience actually happens or how an idea comes into your mind. Although you may immediately be conscious of some sequencing, for the most part the experience or the idea occurs holistically — that is, all at once. Suppose, for example, you are driving your car, minding your own business, and — CRASH — you are involved in an accident. The accident occurs all at once, and the events that preceded it and followed it are also only dim lights in your memory. Later that day when you return home you have an urge to tell someone about the accident, to share the experience. Think about how you do this. You cannot relate the experience holistically as it actually occurred; rather, the events must be somehow sequenced, put into phrases and sentences that your listener can understand. You make decisions, perhaps unconsciously,

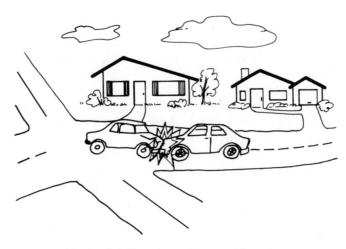

Figure 2-2 Experience Occurs All at Once

to highlight certain events, to drop events out, or to add the moods or feelings you may have recorded for yourself after the experience. What you are doing is quite natural; you are giving **form** to the event.

As we write about an event we are also giving it form. It is important that we keep reading over what we have written until we find that form for ourselves as composers. Words like *develop, cause, describe, list, trace, discuss* and so on help us decide upon the dominant thrust of our speech or essay, since each of these verbs implies a particular pattern of development that helps in thinking about a subject. The organization we begin to impose on our rough draft becomes much more defined in a final draft, where it serves to guide the audience through the speech or essay. As we are writing about an event we are also giving it form, pattern, structure, or organization.

Organization must be highlighted in a final draft because it is the method by which others can enter into our ideas and experiences and share them with us. The next chapter will help you develop audience-centered organizational skills.

This chapter has looked at the way discourse takes shape in the mind of the communicator, starting with the initial response to experience and moving it through various stages until it begins to assume a form apparent to the composer. Now "How do I see it?" begins to shift to "How do others see it?" — the other perspective a communicator should have. As one writer puts it, now it is time "to hear what it sounds like in other people's ears." (Pollit, 1981)

SUMMARY

Real communication grows out of a desire to share experiences. Before we engage in planned communication, however, it is useful to respond to experience informally in one or all of three ways: recording our thoughts on tape, writing them in a journal, or discussing them informally with people other than our close friends in brainstorming sessions. From an informal discussion we begin to develop the self-vs.-other perspective necessary to successful communication.

When we begin to think about our experiences as topics for planned discourse it is helpful to probe them systematically by using a set of questions. The answers to these questions suggest various directions for telling or writing about our experience. In this way we begin to impose a kind of informal order on our experiences, an order that will become more defined in composing and clearly marked in the final draft.

In addition to thinking about the experience itself there are three considerations to be analyzed before you begin a draft of your speech or essay. They are your role as communicator, the constraints imposed upon the communication situation, and the background of your audience, particularly what they need to know about your topic. Experience in speaking to a live audience will help you visualize whom you will be speaking or writing to as you are composing.

There is no easy way to start composing other than sticking with it as long as it takes to get started. To make the whole process easier for yourself you should pay careful attention to your own composing style and find out what you have to do and how long it will take you to do it. This will help you avoid the feelings of frustration and inadequacy that can be overpowering when we are trying to compose under the pressure of a deadline.

Finally, all writers get stuck at some point and have to read over what they have written to get started moving forward again. As you read try to look for clue words like *discuss, analyze, list, inform,* and *compare,* verbs that point to a specific pattern or direction for your work. In other words try to discover in your work an organization that seems natural to you. In a later draft you will have to make your organizational plan more specific so that an audience knows what to expect. When you are composing a first draft, however, discovering your real purpose and direction may take several false starts.

Everything suggested to you in this chapter is based upon the experience of professionals in writing and public speaking. Try the suggestions and keep adjusting your composing until you find what works for you. Communicating successfully is a rewarding experience, well worth the effort it takes. The first time someone approaches you after your speech with "I enjoyed what you had to say," the effort will seem minimal, and you will look forward to communicating again, despite the sometimes difficult process involved.

KEY WORDS

discourse	audience
free writing	information levels
brainstorming	purpose statement
probes	thesis statement
role	form
constraints	

EXERCISES

1. Look at the following list of familiar experiences. Choose one that you can relate to personally or vicariously, and think about the experience. Probe the experience by asking the questions on pages 24–27. Having probed the experience, list five possible topics for speeches and essays.

   - first day on the job
   - buying a car, a painting, a house, or a business
   - watching television
   - riding over or stepping on litter
   - student–teacher conferences
   - falling in love
   - meeting a handicapped person
   - raising a pet
   - studying
   - eating a piece of fudge
   - witnessing a crime, or being the victim of crime
   - hurting someone's feelings
   - designing or decorating a room, house, or office
   - having a run–in with the law
   - making friends
   - leaving home

2. "Brainstorming" means letting the mind run freely. With a group of about five persons, start talking about experiences. Make no attempt to organize your talk at first, but do attempt to pick up the conversation where the previous speaker has stopped. After fifteen minutes start writing down words and phrases, looking for similarities and differences among the experiences. Try to help the other members of the group find topics for speeches and essays by using the probing techniques introduced in this chapter. By the end of the period each person in the group should have a list of five topics.

3. Look back at the various audiences described in Table 2-1. Now write out, in a paragraph or two, a profile of the audience. In this paragraph include the points you think your audience will need to know.

4. Again using the material in Table 2-1, write out purpose statements for several of the topics, keeping in mind your role, the situation and its constraints, and your audience.

REFERENCES

Barzun, Jacques. "A Writer's Discipline," in Marcia Stubbs and Sylvan Barnet, eds., *The Little, Brown Reader*, 2nd ed. (Boston: Little, Brown, 1980), pp. 297–298.

Clemons, Walter. "Father & Sons," *Newsweek* (June 1, 1981), p. 82.

Flower, Linda, and John R. Hayes. "The Cognition of Discovery: Defining a Rhetorical Problem," in *College Composition & Communication* (February, 1980), p. 21.

Gilder, Joshua. "Creators on Creating: Tom Wolfe," *Saturday Review* (April, 1981), p. 43.

Halberstam, David. *The Powers That Be*. (New York: Alfred A. Knopf, 1979), p. 16.

Haller, Scot. "Creators on Creating: Eudora Welty," *Saturday Review* (June, 1981), p. 42. (1981a)

Haller, Scot. "The World's Five Best-Selling Authors," *Saturday Review* (March, 1981), p. 20. (1981b)

Mills, Hilary. "Creators on Creating: William Styron," *Saturday Review* (September, 1980), p. 40.

Pollit, Katha. "Creators on Creating: Bernard Malamud," *Saturday Review* (February, 1981), p. 34.

Providence Journal-Bulletin, "Letters to the Editor Response Form." (Providence, Rhode Island, 1981).

3. The Composer as Audience: Preparing a Final Draft

> It is a matter of looking at the kernel of what I have written, the content, and then thinking about it, responding to it, making decisions, and actually restructuring it.
>
> It means taking apart what I have written and putting it back together again. I ask major theoretical questions of my ideas, respond to those questions, and think of proportion and structure, and try to find a controlling metaphor. I find out which ideas can be developed and which should be dropped. I am constantly chiseling and changing as I revise.
>
> (Sommers, 1980)

The composers quoted above refer to the two selves of the successful communicator. The self as audience considers and questions the ideas put forth in the discourse, and the self as composer responds to these anticipated questions, putting the answers in a form or structure that will make them easily accessible to the audience.

The preceding chapter began with suggestions for a personal response to experience and ended by showing how to give form to that personal response as it turned into planned communication. This chapter asks you to respond to your experience in a different way, to provide it with the form that an audience expects and requires in order to participate in the meaning you are creating from your personal response.

The following are all features that audiences look for to guide them through discourse and to help them evaluate its merits: conventions of form, including a point, pattern, detail, introduction, and conclusion; credibility; and finally an effective style of presentation. The end of this chapter provides guidelines on how your finished essay should look and suggests alternative methods of preparing discourse to be spoken. Because a speech has that added element of delivery to a live audience, style of presentation will be covered fully in Chapter Four.

POINT

In the last chapter you saw a typical purpose statement about a varsity sports program. You saw how one composer, John, moved from a general statement to one that would give him more direction. The narrowed purpose statement looked like this:

> Many benefits come from participation in the varsity sports program;
> I want to speak about three that I consider most important.

In one sentence this composer developed a point of view that best cap-
tured his thoughts about the varsity sports program. In a final draft he will
want to move this statement toward the beginning of his speech or essay,
putting it soon after the introduction. In this position the narrowed statement will function as a thesis: it will alert the audience to the point of the
communication — that they are to hear about the three benefits of par-
ticipating in the varsity sports program. In most cases members of an audience expect the point of a discourse to be made clear soon after the
introduction so that they will know what they are to get out of the discourse — how they are to make sense of the rest of the information presented to them. Of course, situations occur that might lead the composer
to make an artistic decision to avoid actually stating the point (in a narrative, for example) or to place the point statement somewhere other than
after the introduction. Some reasons for such choices are discussed with
the concept of **point** in each of the pattern chapters, Chapters Six through
Eleven.

Subpoints

The audience in the sports example, having heard or read the main point,
would next expect to learn the three benefits of the varsity sports program.
In composing, John may not have listed the three benefits together but
written about each one separately as it occurred to him. In the final draft,
however, it is often useful to write an inclusive statement about the three
benefits and place it with the main point statement. Looking over his
rough draft John selected the three benefits this way:

> Subpoints: 1. Varsity sports provide a high level of competition.
> 2. Varsity sports contests provide an exciting and afforda-
> ble type of entertainment for spectators.
> 3. Varsity sports programs provide an excellent training
> ground for those aspiring to be coaches or physical
> education teachers.

Naturally, John shaped the subpoints more gracefully into one statement
for the final draft, in this way:

> Varsity sports provide a high level of competition, an exciting type of
> affordable entertainment for spectators, and an excellent training
> ground for those aspiring to be coaches or physical education teach-
> ers.

The main point statement, together with a listing of the subpoints, presents
the audience with a clear notion of the goals of the communication, giving
it definite cues to listen or read for.

PATTERN

Audiences expect the pattern of a discourse to flow from the point. In casual conversation most of us think very little about structure; it comes out as naturally as our words, and, just as we sometimes choose the wrong word, so do we make mistakes in organizing our communication. Most of us have, on occasion, gotten off the track of a story, or ended up talking about something completely different from our original thought. At the very least we have heard others drift aimlessly through a communication. In conversational speech our listeners may not mind poorly organized communication, but in planned discourse we need to provide our readers or listeners with an organized flow of words.

The thesis statement directs the audience to the point of the discourse, and it should usually contain a cue word or words that indicate how the point will be developed; that is, the **pattern** of the discourse. Look back for a moment at the quotes that opened this chapter and you will notice how much attention the authors give to structure as they revise their work into final form. One says she "tries to find a controlling metaphor." Setting up a pattern by appropriate use of words is one way of controlling the ideas in a discourse so that an audience can follow them.

Cue Words

The individual pattern chapters discuss the words appropriate to the development of various types of speeches and essays. The list given below shows how the pattern becomes cued in the thesis statement and illustrates some of the words that signal organizational pattern to an audience. Of course, only the pattern part of the statement is illustrated — you will need to imagine your own lead-in: "I'll attempt to," or "I intend to," or however you feel comfortable beginning, and then supply your own topic at the end of the statement. As you will notice, many times the cue words in italics appear in the thesis statement as verbs. The name of the pattern each statement illustrates appears in parentheses.

Tell what happened/*talk about my* experience with (Narration)
Illustrate the *process* of (Process)
Trace the *causes* of/examine the *effects* of (Cause–effect)
Analyze the issue/the components of/the problem of (Analysis)
Compare the qualities of/the methods of/the results of (Comparison/Contrast)
Describe the environment of/the day of/the life of (Description)
Define the properties of/usage of (Definition)
Categorize the events/classify the types of people who (Classification)

Present a *case history* of/give *examples* to illustrate (Information)
Argue the superiority of/against the decision to/for legislation to (Argument)

Now look at some specific examples of how cue words work in thesis statements. Here are three thesis statements:

1. There are three main causes of pollution in Chesapeake Bay.
2. Let me describe for you a day in the life of Chesapeake Bay.
3. The following is a report analyzing the major pollutants in Chesapeake Bay.

Each statement, by the way it is worded, suggests a pattern of development to the audience. The first statement, for example, indicates that the controlling idea is *causes*. The speech or essay will not be a narrative; it will not be an analysis; it will have no goal other than to trace the causes for pollution. Of course, some narrative may be necessary, definitions may be needed, description may play a part; but the dominant, underlying movement of the essay will be from cause one to cause two to cause three, and that is the movement the audience will look for.

Recognize, then, that the pattern flows out of the point, but that once a pattern is chosen, the entire discourse should move in one particular direction. Organization becomes, in a sense, a constraint on the finished product. If, for example, narrative is chosen as the dominant pattern of development, the discourse must move in narrative form; it should avoid moving into analysis, argument, or classification (although these elements may be present); the speech or essay must flow within the constraints of narrative form. Because of the audience's expectations it is quite important that the writer or speaker decide what the consequences are of a particular pattern. Look at the following example:

Point: One legacy of the Three Mile Island nuclear power plant accident is the stress and anxiety felt by the people in the area.

Pattern: Exemplification

Detail: Case studies of three families who have suffered and continue to suffer stress and anxiety related to the Three Mile Island nuclear power plant accident.

In this case, after the introduction the composer will probably begin with the point statement above and then add to it: "This essay will present case studies of three families who have suffered and who continue to suffer such stress and anxiety." Now the composer has alerted the audience to the fact that the essay is a classic thesis-support essay, and the audience will be able to follow it as such. The composer avoids saying that anything will be proved; rather, a point has simply been stated and the writer or speaker has indicated that the audience can expect to receive three examples to support it. The composer will not trace the causes of the accident at TMI, or analyze all the events surrounding it, or show how a nuclear power plant operates or fails to operate, or even argue that nuclear power is a safe or a dangerous form of energy production: the course is clear — the author will show by example one lasting effect of the accident at TMI. The composer may be criticized later for not taking another course, or the audience may feel the need for more examples to support the generalization, but after a rough draft that may have done some of the above, the composer has chosen a particular focus for the final product, and the audience is able to follow the communication.

Conceptual and Conventional Patterns

In the chapters that follow, Chapters Six through Eleven, several patterns of development will be treated in detail. The discussion of pattern centers around two types, conceptual and conventional. Conceptual patterns are derived from psychological studies into the way the mind normally operates as we attempt to make sense of events that occur. Conceptual patterns indicate how we actually think about the world around us. In contrast, conventional patterns are derived from social situations in which efficient forms have evolved to carry out communication purposes. Conventional patterns tell us how to anticipate the questions the audience will expect to have answered. Your knowledge of the conceptual and conventional patterns will be valuable to you as you shape your communication to various situations. In the chapters that cover communication patterns, the terms *conceptual* and *conventional* will be explained in greater detail.

DETAIL

Every idea, everything that we write or say, needs filling in. We can fill in by qualifying, by giving examples, by providing factual support — in short, by clarifying and supporting our ideas. When we communicate we want to give fullness to our ideas, and when we listen or read we naturally expect **detail**. If we think of the idea we are trying to communicate as a space shuttle, the point of our communication as the landing place, and the pattern as the plan we have devised for getting us to the point, then we can think of detail as the fuel and the software that support the idea throughout the journey.

Details range from the most personal to the most objective, just as the patterns move from narration to argument. The kind of detail we supply is a matter of artistic choice; however, certain points and patterns suggest one kind of detail over another. Each of the pattern chapters will give a good deal of advice concerning the kind of detail most appropriate for what you are planning to accomplish. This section of the chapter will indicate what the general kinds of detail are, with examples of each kind. The movement will be from the most personal forms of detail to the most objective.

Personal Experience

Personal experiences are a valuable form of supporting material. Giving first-hand details about the topic shows that you are involved in it and have a clear sense of what you are talking or writing about. Personal experiences add to your credibility as a communicator since they reveal to your audience that you have a basis for your comments and evaluations.

Personal experiences are subjective. As such, they may not be typical of everyone's experience, and an audience cannot always judge the validity of your experience or form generalizations based on them. Used alone, personal experiences fail to constitute sufficient proof except, of course, in personal forms of discourse, such as narrative. In the following student essay, which reviewed and analyzed research on communication apprehension in the elementary school classroom, notice how the student has applied to her own experience what she has read.

> Research into communication apprehension shows that teachers have misinterpreted reticent behavior as obstinacy. As an oral reader and reciter in the first grade, I was shaky and placed in slow groups where I quickly surpassed the requirements for written work and silent reading. One teacher told my mother that I thought I knew all the answers and I felt I did not need to participate in class. From the research I did for this paper, I now realize that this was simply a misinterpreted observation of reticent behavior. I was scared, not stubborn.
>
> — Linda Washington

This personal experience works well because it puts the literature review into concrete terms for the readers and also shows that Linda has applied the research to her own life, thus enhancing her **credibility** as a writer on the topic.

Personal experiences can be dramatic or funny, serious or lighthearted. They can be about events one has actually been a part of, or they can be vicarious experiences one has had through a book, a movie, or even another person. Regardless of where the experience comes from, if it serves the purpose of clarifying or establishing credibility it is a valuable form of supporting detail. Use personal experiences to break up long chains of information in oral reports and masses of data in arguments and to reestablish audience contact in a speech.

Personal experiences make useful asides in a speech because they help speakers to be spontaneous and allow them to keep audience focus and interest. Professional speakers often keep a stockpile of good stories in reserve and insert one into a speech, when it fits, as a way of keeping audiences involved. Nothing arouses audience curiosity like a revealing personal experience.

Examples

Examples are particular instances of larger generalizations. They are not as subjective as personal experiences but are chosen by the composer to support a point, so they are a form of subjective detail. Examples may be hypothetical or real.

Hypothetical Examples. Examples are often made up to support a point. Look at the following hypothetical case developed by a student to argue against the Equal Rights Ammendment:

> If ERA becomes law, it will mean that public bathrooms could not be marked for one sex or the other. Can you imagine, for example, what the student union would be like at noontime? Every pervert on campus would be camped out in the "Personroom."
>
> — Pete Levine

Hypothetical examples can also be serious characterizations of general occurrences, such as the following:

> Eleanor Rigby,
> Died in the church and was buried along with her name.
> Nobody came.
> Father MacKenzie,
> Wipes off the dirt from his hands as he walks from the grave.
> Nobody saved.
> All the lonely people,
> Where do they all come from.
>
> — The Beatles, "Eleanor Rigby"*

In this case the woman and the priest stand for, and are particular examples of, all the lonely people written about by the Beatles.

Factual Examples. Examples are often drawn from real events to support a generalization. In this case the purpose of the example is to typify the point. Too often, extreme examples are used to support an assertion. This is not the purpose of an example. In the following example the

---

* "Eleanor Rigby," by John Lennon and Paul McCartney. This song first appeared in 1966 on the Beatles' album *Revolver* (Capital ST 2576).
Copyright © 1966 Northern Songs Ltd. All rights for the U.S.A., Mexico, and the Philippines controlled by Maclen Music, Inc. % ATV Music Corp. All rights reserved. Used by permission.

writer, a student, supports her assertion that television violence is disturb-ing because the absence of blood and gore provides to the young viewer an unrealistic picture of the outcome of a violent act, such as murder:

> An example of this theory is the case of the six year old boy who shot and killed his mother with a gun that was poorly hidden in the closet. The child went into the kitchen with the gun where his mother was doing the dishes and said to her, "Hold it right there or I'll shoot . . . you have the right to remain silent. . . ." Whereupon the mother turned around and the child shot her twice. When asked by the police what he was doing, the child said he was pretending to be "Adam–12," the hero of a popular police series. The child did not know the gun was real and could not imagine the results, having seen only sterilized forms of killing on television.
>
> — Elizabeth McCabe

Use examples to give concreteness to a composition. Be certain that the examples actually support the point you are attempting to make, that they are typical rather than extreme (unless you clarify the nature of the example), and that they are developed fully.

Factual Support

We are a nation of facts and experts. It sometimes seems that information is everywhere and close by is an expert prepared to give it to us. While it is extremely important to scrutinize facts and the experts who so willingly offer them, factual support is a standard form of supporting material. When used as proof for an assertion factual data adds significance and credibility to a point.

Firsthand Facts vs. Secondhand Facts. Too often the only source of factual material is secondhand. How often have we heard a speaker quote from *Time* or *Newsweek* some fact that the reporter has interpreted from a study, a government publication, or an expert? How much more valid the statement would be were the speaker to quote from the document itself. A phone call to a legislator's local office can usually yield most government documents within two weeks; a personal visit or phone call to an expert can often give insights not available in secondhand accounts. Firsthand information is harder to come by but it is usually worth the effort.

Reporters and special-interest groups can often give facts, but out of context. Before using material from such sources be sure you know the context in which the fact was used, the date of the fact, and the position of the secondhand source who is using it. An example of how facts are taken out of context can be seen in the debate over container deposit legislation, or the so-called bottle bill. An opponent of the bill testified at a public hearing that "According to federal studies beer sales in Maine declined 4.4 percent between 1977–78, the first year of Maine's bottle law." He was using this fact to argue against the bill because decreased sales mean decreased sales taxes, something dear to every politician's heart. If we look at the study itself, a study easily attainable through the General Accounting Office, we discover the context of that fact:

> Beer sales declined 4.4 percent between 1977 and 1978, but grew again in 1979. One distributor stated that only part of the decline was attributable to the deposit law, adding that sales recovered and grew steadily. Maine changed its legal drinking age from 18 to 20 in 1977, which may have reduced beer consumption.
>
> (Comptroller General, 1980)

This kind of distortion occurs frequently and can lead an audience to erroneous conclusions. Be on your guard when using factual support.

Quoting from Authorities. This is a standard way of providing detail. When used as proof for an assertion, authorities add credibility and objectivity. When quoting directly from an authority give the person's credentials along with the quotation, as in the following example from an essay by a student on the ability of vegetarian diets to meet nutritional needs:

> Dr. Aaron M. Altshul, head of the nutritional program at Georgetown University School of Medicine, is enthusiastic about the ability to produce meat texture out of soy flour. He says, "It will probably rank with the invention of bread as one of the truly great inventions of food. It is possible to allow people the enjoyment they expect from meat-like components and yet avoid the excess in calories, fat, and high proportion of saturated fats that ordinarily come from such consumption.
>
> — Bonnie Bailey

Notice how the author gains credibility both through the quote and the credentials of the source. She has saved us the time needed to look at her footnotes to check the validity of her quote, or, if this had been a speech, the time required to answer our question about her source.

Use factual material whenever an assertion you are making might otherwise seem unreasonable to an audience. Be sure your facts are accurate, up-to-date, and authoritative.

Quantitative Support

Quantitative data is a special form of factual support. We are a nation not only of experts but also of numbers. Numbers define us and describe the world around us. We are Social Security numbers, credit card numbers, and license plate numbers. The American family equates to 2.5 children,

1.3 television sets, and .5 handguns. Numbers guide personal and public life, dictating what is known and what is to be done. As a form of supporting detail numbers provide a sense of objectivity and concreteness to our communication. Although our common sense tells us that numbers are created by human beings, quite often for self-serving purposes, and although our common sense tells us that "Garbage in means garbage out," statistical detail is a valuable, unavoidable form of detail.

A complete account of how to use quantitative data accurately and ethically is beyond the scope of this text, but there are proper ways to communicate statistical data that are appropriate and important for composers.

1. Use numbers sparingly, especially in oral presentations. Too much numerical detail overwhelms the receiver and can lead to frustration.

2. Translate numerical detail into understandable terms. If you say, for example, that "Energy reduction brought about by container deposit legislation would be about 160 trillion BTU's per year," you should relate that figure to something that can be visualized. Look at the statement above as it was rewritten for purposes of a speech given at a public hearing on the bottle bill.

> Energy reduction brought about by container deposit legislation would be about 160 trillion BTU's, or the equivalent of 81,000 barrels of oil per day. To put that into perspective, the State of Oregon has estimated that, with its switch to deposit containers in 1972, it has saved enough energy to heat the homes of 55,000 Oregonians per year.

3. Put numerical detail into visual aids. Charts, graphs, pictures, and maps allow you to keep your data displayed so that the audience can easily follow. In an essay, visuals can be placed in the text or at the end of the text in a section labeled Appendix. In a speech, visuals should be displayed prominently for easy audience viewing. The chapter on presentational style, Chapter Four, will tell you how to use visuals effectively.

4. Cite sources and dates. Audiences need to know where you obtained the data and when the data were gathered. Since numerical detail can change in importance very rapidly, it is important to use data that are recent.

5. Qualify numerical detail. It is helpful to an audience to see your data in relationship to other data. Comparisons are quite useful here. Note, for example, how pollster Daniel Yankelovich characterizes normative patterns in American life by comparing new survey data with previous data (Figure 3-1). By doing this Yankelovich is able to show not only what norms guide American life today but also how today's norms differ from past norms. Such qualifications aid our understanding.

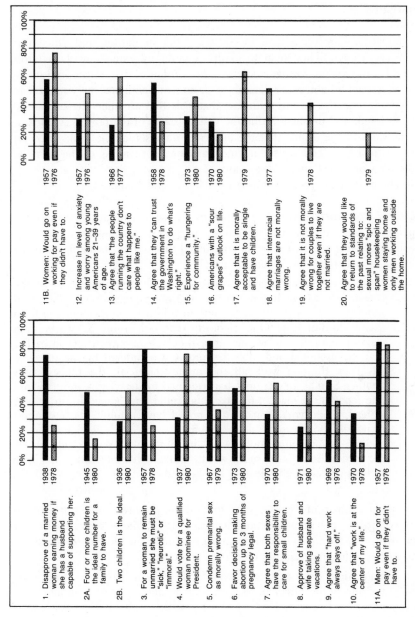

Figure 3-1 Twenty Major Changes in the Norms Guiding American Life
Source: From Yankelovich, 1981. Used by permission.

Comparisons

Comparisons are often used to point out the similarities and differences between things. They help to clarify a point by explaining it in terms readily understood by the audience. For instance, the stages in human development might be explained by asking the audience to visualize an assembly line that begins with raw materials that are then shaped, added to, colored, and finished during the various stages of the process. Comparisons work to the degree that the audience understands the terms used for the comparison, believes them, and transfers the meaning of the terms to the idea or object under discussion.

There are two types of comparison: literal and figurative.

Literal Comparisons. Literal comparisons use real instances to support a point. A program that has worked in one place, for instance, might be compared with one that is being considered for another location, as in the following excerpt from a student speech:

> Victim restitution programs work effectively in many parts of the country. In Massachusetts, victim restitution programs in 1980 saved more than 225 persons from going to prison for crimes ranging from assault to burglary. One eighteen year old, John X, works as a cleanup man and dishwasher in a Brockton restaurant owned by the man he assaulted and robbed. John X was ordered by the judge to pay back through work all the money taken in the robbery plus another $1,000 for personal harm caused to the victim. John X told one reporter, "I made a mistake, and could have gone to prison, but, instead, I am working it off and now I have a job." The restaurant owner is also pleased.
>
> Such a program could work in our state. We could reduce crowded prisons, save many youths from a life of crime, and give victims a feeling that justice has been done.
>
> — Steve Katzmann

Literal comparisons can be used to show why something is not working by comparing it with something that is. Further, literal comparisons can be used to make the unknown clearer or to make an idea more attractive, as in the following example used by a student:

> You might think that paying $435,000 for a half minute of advertising during the Super Bowl is an unbelievable amount of money. But look at it this way. If you had a job which paid $100 per week, you would probably not think that spending $10 on yourself was extravagant. Well, the companies that are paying the Super Bowl advertising rates are also only spending about 10% of their income. $435,000 to a company like AT&T means the same or maybe even less than that 10 bucks means to you.
>
> — Rich Cate

When using literal comparisons it is important to use instances that are closely related. The more that can be compared the more likely it is that the comparison will work.

Figurative Comparisons. Figurative comparisons involve the use of two topics which may be very different on the surface, but which share underlying similarities. Quite often the terminology of one aspect of life can be used to illustrate or explain the workings of something in another aspect. Even though baseball and politics, for instance, are much different from one another we often hear explanations like the following:

> Ward's campaign started out with two strikes against it: a lousy manager and little public support. It was inevitable that he'd strike out. I'll give him credit, though, at least he got up and took his swings.

Although baseball and politics differ, the language of one helps to describe the other. Figurative comparisons add color to descriptions, thus bringing clarity and maintaining audience interest. Scientists often use figurative comparisons to make an abstract idea more comprehensible, as in the following model:

> Discovering the smallest particle of matter in the universe, the elusive quark, is very much a hit or miss proposition. Electrons are sent racing around a long tube and then are bombarded by other electrons until they smash apart. This collision is photographed and then the scientist attempts to identify the individual parts. It is sort of like banging two watches together: you smash them against one another and look to see what falls out.

One further use of figurative comparisons is to change the mental picture that readers or listeners have for a phenomenon. In the following excerpt from a speech, Jesse Jackson attempted to change the audience's mental picture of America as a melting pot.

> . . . A better example is that we're more like a bowl of vegetable soup than a melting pot. First of all, vegetable soup is more digestible than steel . . . . The second point is that in vegetable soup, you may have a tomato base and that is the homogenous dimension of American culture. There are many things that we have in common. We have common geography, soil, common air, common water, common tax system, common military system, common government. There is an American base, that's more American than it is European, African or anything else. . . .
> But beyond . . . that American base, . . . corn and beans, peas and chunks of meat are floating up on the top of that soup. And those things appeal to us. Our Irishness, our Italianess, our Catholicism, our Protestantism, our Jewishness, our Blackness, our Arabness, appeals to us, and it's up on the top of the soup. And when it

gets hot, those elements do not lose their identity, but each one of them has extracted from it some of its vital juices. And that's what makes the soup tasty. Because there are some blacks and some whites, some males, some females, some young and some old, but no one loses his essential identity, just gives up some of his essence for the common wealth.

(Jackson, 1974)

As you read Jackson's comparison, see whether it gives you a clear picture of the American experience. Is it more accurate than the melting pot view of America? Has it advantages or disadvantages that the melting pot view lacks?

When using figurative comparisons consider the members of the audience. What terms do they already understand? Consider also the parts of the comparison. Are the things being compared similar enough to carry the comparison? Finally, ask yourself what other comparisons might be used to make the point, to make another point, or to argue against the point.

There are numerous other forms of supporting detail: definitions, descriptions, myths, fables, maxims, and documents, to name a few. Some of these will appear in models throughout this text and will be explained as they appear. What is most important at this point is that you understand how to use the major forms of supporting detail.

INTRODUCTIONS

Many composers find that they write their **introduction** last, after they have become thoroughly familiar with their material. By then they are excited about what they have to communicate, and they want the audience to become as involved in the topic as they are. Frequently, as you work through your drafts, some idea, some phrase will stand out, and you will say to yourself, "That's it — that's how I want to begin." Jot down a key word or phrase to remind yourself of this idea for an introduction. Avoid making the mistake of failing to get others involved in your discourse after all the work you have put into it. "My speech today is about the Susan B. Anthony dollar" is a common way to begin, but it is also the first step to failure. How much better it would be to excite the reader or audience with something like this: "Who heads the list of most unpopular female in America? What woman is almost completely unwelcome in grocery stores, banks, and restaurants? The answer: Susan B. Anthony. The reason: She appears on the Susan B. Anthony dollar."

In the latter example the audience is drawn into the presentation through the use of questions. Audience interest is aroused because of the natural curiosity to know the answer to the questions. Effective communicators plan their introductions carefully around certain purposes and methods chosen to meet the aim.

The functions of an introduction are to create interest in the topic, establish a foundation for understanding, establish good will with the audience, and prepare the audience for the point statement. Take a closer look at some of the methods available to composers for an effective introduction.

Rhetorical Questions

Rhetorical questions are questions to which an immediate response is obvious. Rhetorical questions stimulate curiosity about the topic and also lead to the point statement. The following introduction from a student speech shows how a rhetorical question can be used effectively:

> What would you do if you were in a restaurant and someone at your table started to choke? Would you hit him on the back? Would you scream for help? Would you panic? I hope you would do none of the above, since there is another alternative that is much better: the Heimlich maneuver.

> — Martha Hartt

There is another form of question sometimes used in speeches: the direct question to the audience. It often sounds something like, "How many of you would know how to save a choking person?" Asking for a show of hands or some other audience response is indeed one way to get the audience involved, but it may also backfire. If you use a direct question be sure you have anticipated all possible audience responses and have a plan for responding to whatever you hear. Such planning will save you anxious moments should the response be other than what you have anticipated.

Humor

Humor can be an effective device at any point in a composition, but it is especially valuable in the introduction. An amusing anecdote establishes good will, relieves some of the tension felt at the beginning of a speech, and gets readers or listeners involved. In the following example Adlai Stevenson, twice candidate for the presidency of the United States and then ambassador to the United Nations, begins his speech to a 1965 Honors Day Convocation at the University of Illinois with a humorous introduction that ingratiates him with the audience and sets the tone for his address:

It was just five years ago that I last spoke on this campus, and that's too long between visits for a former Governor of Illinois, former Trustee of the University, and a former resident of Bloomington and Libertyville.

I couldn't help but think that all of those "formers" brought to mind a story a young woman told me in Washington not long ago who said that her husband was being transferred to New York, and that her little daughter was crestfallen and upset when she heard the news. And that night she overheard her saying her prayers. She asked God to bless Mommy, asked God to bless Daddy, and her little brother, and then she said, "And now God, this is goodbye, we are moving to New York." [Laughter.] Well, I have news for you, New York is not so bad.

Of course, humor always works best when it is built into the context of the occasion and oftentimes does not work so well when taken out of that context. Writers and speakers need to consider using humor that will be tied closely to the message they are sending so that others will understand it in that context.

Quotations

Direct quotations from prose or poetry are often quite effective for beginning a speech or essay. Quotable statements are catchy and have a way of capturing interest for the topic at hand. A number of books, such as Hurd's *Treasury of Great American Quotations* or Bartlett's *Familiar Quotations*, are storehouses of catchy expressions that can get others involved in your speech or essay. For example, if you look at the chapters in this text you will notice that many begin with a quotation.

Startling Statements

Although startling statements can be used improperly as gimmicks, they can also function effectively to get others involved in your topic. Reporters and professional writers often use startling statements as lead-ins to the story. Look at the following introduction from *Time* magazine for an article on gun control:

A handgun is sold in the U.S. every 13 seconds, adding 2 million a year to the nation's estimated arsenal of 55 million automatics and revolvers. That is one pistol for every four Americans.

(Isaacson, 1981)

One final note about introductions. Experience shows that the introduction requires as much planning and development as any other part of the composition. First impressions are important and a carefully developed introduction will help your message receive the attention it deserves.

Reprinted by permission. © 1980 NEA, Inc.

CONCLUSIONS

The **conclusion** is as important as the introduction of a speech or essay. How often have we heard a speaker say at the end of an otherwise interesting speech, "Well, that's about it." When we hear this we sense that something is missing, and it is. What is missing is the conclusion. Effective communicators plan their conclusions. Take a close look at both the functions of a conclusion and the methods appropriate for carrying out the function.

The functions of a conclusion are to provide a sense of completeness, repeat and summarize key points and ideas to be remembered, and direct the receiver's attention to an appropriate belief or type of behavior. A variety of methods can help us achieve these goals.

The Quotable Quote

Audiences will often remember only parts of the discourse. Especially in lengthy or technical compositions it is often useful to heighten comprehension with a memorable quotation. Quotable statements, because they are easy to remember and because they contain the essence of an idea in a few words, make an effective device in a conclusion. In the following example a speech on the role of the individual in protecting the environment, the student speaker concluded in this way:

> So if each one of us would play a part in saving our environment; if each one of us would pay closer attention to those little habits of ours that waste water, litter the landscape, and pollute the air; if each one of us would become our own little environmental movement, we would make a lasting contribution to the future. As Mahatma Gandhi once said, "There is plenty for everyone's need, but none for anyone's greed."

> — Dawn Myers

Parallelism

Look once more at Dawn's conclusion and notice another rhetorical technique that is present: parallel structure. The repetition of the phrase "If each one of us . . ." gives the conclusion a memorable repetition of the key idea of the speech (that each one of us is responsible for the environment) as well as a literary touch that makes the conclusion pleasing to the ear.

Grouping ideas in parallel structure is an effective technique in a conclusion because it reinforces an idea and provides balance, contrast, and rhythm to a conclusion, thus making it memorable. Professional speakers and writers often use parallel structure, as in the following conclusion by Martin Luther King in his historic Civil Rights address of August, 1963, "I Have a Dream":

> This is our hope. This is the faith that I go back to the South with.
>
> With this faith we will be able to work together, to pray together, to struggle together, to go to jail together, to stand up for freedom together, knowing that we will be free one day. This will be the day when all of God's children will be able to sing with new meaning — "my country 'tis of thee; sweet land of liberty; of thee I sing; land where my fathers died, land of the pilgrim's pride; from every mountain side, let freedom ring" — and if America is to be a great nation, this must become true.
>
> So let freedom ring from the prodigious hilltops of New Hampshire.
>
> Let freedom ring from the mighty mountains of New York.
>
> Let freedom ring from the heightening Alleghenies of Pennsylvania.
>
> Let freedom ring from the snow-capped Rockies of Colorado.
>
> Let freedom ring from the curvaceous slopes of California.
>
> But not only that.
>
> Let freedom ring from Stone Mountain of Georgia.
>
> Let freedom ring from Lookout Mountain of Tennessee.
>
> Let freedom ring from every hill and molehill of Mississippi, from every mountainside, let freedom ring.
>
> And when we allow freedom to ring, when we let it ring from every village and hamlet, from every state and city, we will be able to speed up that day when all of God's children — black men and white men, Jews and Gentiles, Catholics and Protestants — will be able to join hands and to sing in the words of the old Negro Spiritual, "Free at last, free at last; thank God Almighty, we are free at last."

The chapters in this text on sentences and paragraphs will help you to create prose that is rhythmic and emphatic.

Reiteration

Reiteration means straightforward summary of key ideas or main points you want to be remembered. Reiteration is often used in cause-effect, analytical, and informative compositions as a way of pulling the topic together for the audience. In the following conclusion to an essay, "The Face of Modern Anti-Semitism," notice how the conclusion captures the key ideas of the composition and also shows that the topic is one for concern by all Americans.

> Jewish concern for the re-emergence of anti-Semitism should not be treated as a case of Jewish hypersensitivity. The phenomenon of anti-Semitism requires the most serious reflection and action, because it involves not only the Jews, but a much larger community, and, indeed, the whole fabric of democratic life. As the history of anti-Semitism has shown, hatred of Jews invariably reflects larger crises in society which directly affect the lives of all. The resurgence of anti-Semitism points to a resurgence of other forms of intolerance and hatred. And that poses a profound threat to all democratic life and institutions.
>
> (Hecht, 1981)

Hecht's conclusion is effective because each sentence summarizes a part of the essay. If we were to list each sentence rather than connecting them in paragraph form, we would be able to see the outline of the essay and have a clear sense of the movement of the paper to the warning sentence on which it ends.

Of course, Richard Hecht is a professional writer and recognizes that reiteration is a convention he is expected to follow whenever the topic is lengthy and complex. Composers must be sensitive to the need for a conclusion that summarizes so that their audience understands the ideas presented as completely as possible.

In the following example we see a conclusion to a student's report on robotics that uses reiteration as a way of projecting the audience into the future:

> Outside the factory and the lab, the work that needs to be done in this world is virtually limitless, and so is the robot's potential ability to do it. In the field of farming and food processing, for example, Unimation has been asked to design a robot that can pluck chickens. Australian technicians are already testing robots to shear sheep. Robots now on the drawing boards will soon be spraying crops with pesticides, digging up minerals deep under the oceans, and repairing satellites in outer space. That's not all, either. Designers are even working on a robot that will gently lift a bedridden patient while a nurse changes his sheets, and tucks him back into bed. The potential

list goes on and on, and although the robot revolution may be just beginning, it is moving fast and it is here to stay.

— Kim Sloat

Kim's conclusion is a slightly different type of summary. Her goal is to point us toward the future, since her key idea is that the robotics revolution has just begun. She succeeds with a compact listing of potential uses for robotics not previously mentioned in her essay — a list that shows in condensed form the depth and breadth of robotics. The conclusion ends with a restatement of her original point from the first page of her essay: "Robotics is promising to bring about a new revolution in American industry, and it could very well be the answer to the problem of stagnation in production which faces the United States today."

Directing Attention to Beliefs or Action

If you look closely at most magazine advertisements you will see that they usually tell you not only about the product and what it will do for you but also how to get it. Coupons are popular simply because they encourage you to do something — at the very least, cut out the coupon. Situations will often occur in your writing and speaking that require using the same technique. Look at the following conclusion to a student's speech on donating blood:

> Your blood is needed, then, to save lives and ease the pain of countless others. Next Tuesday, a blood drive will be held here on campus, at the Union, from 9:00 a.m. until 4:30 p.m. I think it would be great if we could meet as a group and go together. Please see me immediately after class if you agree. If you would rather go individually: fine. But please go. You might be saving a life.
>
> — Lauren Addessi

Similar conclusions might be more subtle and might be addressed to audience beliefs rather than specific actions. The point is that the conclusion tells the receivers specifically what it is you want them to do.

There is a temptation when writing action conclusions to use fear appeals. The tendency to write or say "If you fail to do such and such, then this or that will happen" is natural; we have all felt the urge to scold or goad our receivers. There is, of course, the right time and place for every strategy, but fear appeals give the conclusion a negative tone and quite often generate defensiveness rather than action. Use them sparingly. The following conclusion to a student's essay on student apathy is typical of the fear appeal:

> So I guess what I'm trying to say is that unless we get off our butts and become more active, we will get what we deserve. Not enough of us are pulling our load. We come to classes, and that's it.

> Remember, if tuition goes up again next year or if the food in the dorm gets worse, blame yourself.
>
> — Joe Meyers

Notice how the conclusion strikes you. Instead of telling you what to do, it is accusatory, and it causes you to think something like, "Well, who does he think he is, anyway?" When the urge strikes to use fear or scolding, fight it. Look for a positive way to conclude. How would you, for example, rewrite the conclusion to the essay on apathy?

There are as many conclusions as there are compositions, of course. Use the techniques discussed here, but be creative. Devote time to your conclusion. On a speaking occasion watch the time so that the conclusion need not be rushed. An effective conclusion can make your composition more successful. If it is memorable, lively, and balanced it will leave your readers or audience with a positive feeling about you and your ideas.

FINAL FORM

A wise person has said, "Writers turn blood into ink; speakers turn ink into blood." All that has been said so far applies equally to a speech or an essay. In their final form, however, the differences between oral and written communication detailed in Chapter One create special circumstances with regard to the presentation of a speech or essay.

Scripting the Essay

An essay is, we might say, completely **scripted**. It is given to its intended readers in finished form. All of the emotions and the dynamics of the event being written about must be conveyed in one medium: the written word. A writer relies on knowledge of punctuation, grammar, and other formal devices to give added precision to the words, but ultimately, the success of an essay depends upon the words on the page. A reader's judgment of the author and a reader's ability to share the author's ideas hinges on the script the reader has.

Understanding the written medium should lead us to some careful thinking about how to present an essay in final form. Here are some ideas for your consideration, starting with a quote from a professional writer:

> My cardinal rule in revising is never to fall in love with what I have written in a first or second draft. An idea, sentence, or even a phrase that looks catchy, I don't trust. Part of this idea is to wait a while. I am much more in love with something after I have written it than I am a day or two later. It is much easier to change anything with time.
>
> (Sommers, 1980)

Perhaps this professional writer gives the most practical advice on how to become your own best critic: don't fall in love with your prose. One of the first steps in revision involves getting past the notion of permanence, the notion that anything you write has to be perfect the first time and cannot be changed.

As you revise your essay for the last time, however, you will want to be sure that your word choice is effective, that your sentences are smooth and flowing, and that your paragraphs contain appropriate transitions. Of course, the more chapters of this text that you read and put into practice, the better you will become at final revision because you will begin to store chunks of knowledge that will provide you with a checklist for revision. The chapters on the sentence and the paragraph, Chapters Twelve and Thirteen, for instance, will show you how to develop stylistic alternatives. As you work with these alternatives you will notice that, depending on your message, some will heighten its effectiveness while others may detract from what you are trying to say.

At this point it would be unrealistic to provide a comprehensive discussion of all the stylistic considerations involved in a final revision. After all, although learning and working with these elements is a semester-long course and a lifelong project, there are some ways to make your final draft appear representative of all the work you have put into it. This process of cleaning up is called **editing**. Here are some general rules to guide you:

1. Be sure your verb tense and your pronoun usage are consistent. Avoid switching from past tense to present or randomly from *I* to *you* in your essay.
2. Use whatever handbook your instructor recommends to check punctuation; pay special attention to the rules for the colon and the semicolon.
3. Circle in your rough draft any word you are not sure how to spell. Check the spelling before using it.
4. Type your essay doublespaced on medium weight bond, unless your instructor specifies otherwise. Be sure to use a fresh ribbon and leave wide margins for comments.
5. Carefully proofread your typed copy. Correct typos neatly with a black pen or pencil. Perhaps ask a friend or someone in class to proofread your work.
6. Fasten the pages of your essay in the manner your instructor suggests; most prefer either paper clips or staples rather than fancy covers that take up extra room in the briefcase.

Editing your paper carefully and presenting clean copy are marks of a professional. Developing precise editing habits now will aid you throughout college and later in your chosen career.

When you have finished putting these final touches on your essay, it is completely scripted. It must stand on its own. Judgments about you will be made indirectly from judgments about your composition. Authors turn blood into ink.

Unscripting the Speech

A speech is also a composition. It too is scripted in the sense that many speakers, especially professionals, write the speech out completely or at least draft out whole segments of the speech or use a thoroughly filled-in outline. But a speech is presented to a live audience, and requires one to appear spontaneous, as though the speaker were just talking to us. Thoughts and ideas must seem to arise on the spur of the moment. Speakers who seem too rehearsed or who sound canned fail to capture their audience's attention. Speakers who are so rehearsed or so tied to a script that they cannot adjust to situations as they develop are breaking one of the cardinal conventions of the oral mode: spontaneity. Thus a speech needs to be scripted during the composing process and **unscripted** at the time of delivery.

An excellent example of how situations create restraints that call for on-the-spot unscripting is the public hearing. Presenting one's views before a legislative body, whether it be the student senate, the town council, or the state assembly, is a standard situation in our democratic society. Most public hearings are organized just before they begin. As moderators assess the size of the crowd and as speakers sign up or show hands to testify, moderators decide about how long each speaker will be given. It is not uncommon to hear a moderator say, "Each speaker will have ten minutes, but if we have too many questions I may have to shorten that toward the end of the hearing to five minutes." It is also not uncommon for moderators to announce about midway through the hearing something like the following: "I am going to ask all future speakers to restrict their remarks to facts and ideas that have not already been addressed. Please avoid repeating things that have been said up to now." In such a situation, the speaker must adjust or lose effectiveness.

When addressing a live audience, there are other techniques that can help you turn that ink back into blood. Professor William S. Howell of the University of Minnesota, an advocate of the need to unscript a speech at the time of delivery, conducted a survey with people who do a great deal of public speaking. He put his analysis of the survey this way:

> I once asked several top-notch professional public speakers three questions. The first, "When you give a speech do you find yourself saying things you did not plan to say?" All answered, "Yes." Next,

"As the years go by, are you doing more or less of this?" All replied, "More." And finally, "How do you feel about these unplanned interludes?" All responded, "Fine! These are the most successful parts of my talk."

(Howell, 1982)

What we learn through Howell's survey is that successful speakers go into a speaking situation with a great deal of preparation but not a complete script they have memorized and are thus tied to. Professional speakers trust in their competence on the topic, prepare note cards or an outline, and then rely on their impulses during the actual presentation to adjust and adapt to the response they get as they scan the audience.

Competence in public speaking requires continual adjustment to the present event. Many speakers have a stock of stories, experiences, quotable statements, and interesting examples they can plug into their speech as it progresses. This is sometimes called ad libbing, as in our accompanying cartoon. In the discipline of rhetoric we might call this inventory of information *commonplaces*, stock expression that fit into numerous situations and can be used as appropriate during a speech.

While writers must capture all of their feelings in words, public speakers can use body language and tonal cues to add to the meaning of their words. These attributes of effective presentational style are the subject of the next chapter; for now, it is important to realize that reacting naturally to your message with your body and voice tones is another way to unscript a speech.

Developing the level of confidence you need for standing in front of an audience without a complete manuscript requires practice and experience. The classroom is a good place to start, and if you will give yourself a chance you will discover that like Howell's top-notch speakers you will say things that come into your mind as you are actually presenting the speech.

Confidence comes from knowing your topic and from practice. There are also other ways to prepare for a speech that can help in the unscripting process. Some speakers, for instance, begin by writing out a speech completely so that they can see it all in one place. At that point they begin to highlight — that is, use colored ink to mark key points, phrases, dates, and anything else they want to use in the speech. Having highlighted the manuscript these speakers reduce it to outline form and often put this outline on note cards in the manner to be described in Chapter Four. The manuscript is then put aside and the speakers practice the speech from the highlights, attempting to simply talk their way through it. This method may work for you.

Another strategy for unscripting a public speech involves segmenting the speech. In this approach the speech is not written out completely or memorized. Rather the speaker prepares segments — point statements plus segments of information that support the point in a variety of ways. The segments are then brought into or left out of the speech as the situation dictates. The speaker simply knows enough about the topic to be able to concentrate on what is or is not working with the particular audience. With this method adjustments can be made on the spot.

One final method for unscripting a speech is called the talking manu-script method. In some real situations a speech contains a large amount of essential data, yet the speaker needs to be certain that everything gets said. For such occasions the speaker needs to rehearse the manuscript to the point of knowing it well enough to talk it out. Visual aids will help with this approach, as will a dynamic presentational style. If the audience is carefully attended to, and if the speaker knows the material well enough to adjust as the situation demands, this method can work.

In summary, an essay is completely scripted, while a speech requires unscripting. This is an area for inventiveness and consciousness of what works for you. Your instructor will help you with this, and practice in the classroom will also help. As we move on to a discussion of presentational style you will find additional differences between written and oral commu-nication.

SUMMARY

This chapter has attempted to help you view your speech or essay from an audience's perspective by reviewing those elements of discourse an audi-ence expects to find. Without these elements the speech or essay will not be accepted as a finished product.

Effective planned communication has a point toward which it is mov-ing, a pattern of organization that provides direction, and sufficient sup-porting material to give the speech or essay credibility. Additionally, the finished product contains an attention-getting introduction and a memor-able conclusion.

An essay is completely scripted; it is received by readers in its finished form. An essay, therefore, needs to be revised and polished prior to being turned in. A speech, on the other hand, needs to be composed prior to being presented, but then unscripted at time of delivery so that it appears fresh and spontaneous to the audience.

The fine arts of writing and speaking require us to see our work as others do. This critical step of turning away from ourselves and seeing our discourse from the perspective of the audience will ensure that we have not only expressed ourselves but also communicated something meaningful to others.

KEY WORDS

point   conclusion
pattern   scripting
detail   editing
credibility   unscripting
introduction

EXERCISES

1. It was mentioned earlier that advertisements often use an action concept, such as a coupon, to stir the audience. It is also true that many ads have all the components of a finished product, albeit in condensed form or partly visual form. Check this out for yourself by looking at or listening to (and taping) five advertisements. See whether you can label the five parts of the finished product for each ad: point, pattern, detail, introduction, and conclusion. If you can, go one step further and label the rhetorical technique used in the introduction and conclusion and the kind of detail that is used.

2. Write a 500-word essay on a topic of your choice, or on a topic assigned by the instructor. Prepare this topic in an oral presentation of three to five minutes. If at all possible, tape record the oral presentation. If you have followed the advice given for scripting and unscripting you should be able to make two observations: both the essay and the speech contain the five components of the finished product; and the speech sounds different from the way the essay reads. What are the differences? Why did you make the changes that you did?

3. List five topics about which you might speak or write credibly. Why did you choose these particular topics? Would some readers or audiences cause you to change your mind about your credibility for these topics? If your credibility shifted for a topic with a particular audience, what adjustments would you need to make?

REFERENCES

Beatles, "Eleanor Rigby," by John Lennon and Paul McCartney. This song first appeared in 1966 on the Beatles' album *Revolver* (Capital ST 2576).

Comptroller General of the United States, "The Effects on the States of Mandatory Deposits on Beverage Containers," General Accounting Office, 1980, p. 16.

Comptroller General of the United States, "Potential Effects of a National Mandatory Deposit on Beverage Containers," General Accounting Office, Washington, D.C., 1977, p. 28.

Hecht, Richard, "The Face of Modern Anti-Semitism," *Center Magazine* 16 (March/April, 1981), p. 27.

Howell, William S. *The Empathic Communicator* (Belmont, California: Wadsworth Publishing Co., 1982).

Isaacson, Walter, "The Duel Over Gun Control," *Time*, March 23, 1981, p. 33.

Jackson, Jesse. Speech given at the Speech Communication Association Convention (Chicago, Illinois, 1974).

Sommers, Nancy, "The Revision Strategies of Student Writers and Experienced Adult Writers," in *College Composition and Communication* 31 (December, 1980) pp. 383–384.

Yankelovich, Daniel, *New Rules: Searching for Self Fulfillment in a World Turned Upside Down* (New York: Random House, 1981).

4. Presentational Style

Most of us can recall hearing a moving public speech. What makes a speaker successful? The topic? The ideas? Cleverness of expression? Are speakers successful because of their style of presentation? The point of this chapter is that the way an idea is presented is as important as the idea itself.

One of the first judgments an audience makes about a speaker has to do with how real the speaker appears to be. Because it is an extended chain of speech a formal presentation must be planned well in advance. Successful speakers plan a speech carefully, but when actually presenting it they should appear unscripted, as discussed in Chapter Three, and should create the impression of **spontaneity**. Remember, good art is concealed art.

Public speaking is similar to writing an essay in the sense that it requires a certain formality. Because the situation is formal, the public speaker's language, tone, and presentational **style** must be formal. On the other hand public speaking is related to conversational communication because it is oral. Speakers must appear natural and allow their own distinctive styles to emerge. Effective speakers articulate clearly, use few filler words, and gesture meaningfully, but still appear to be themselves. If you are to be a successful public speaker you will need to develop this dynamic presentational style, which is somewhere between conversational communication and formal writing.

Since each of us has a unique way of communicating, there are few fixed rules for effective presentation. There are bad habits, however, and there are techniques that work well. One of the reasons rehearsal is so important is that it helps speakers get to know their own presentational style and leads to some conscious decisions about what mannerisms the speakers would like to eliminate or emphasize.

The presentational style that works for you will be the result of how well you adapt to the situation, the message, and the audience. In a narrative, for instance, you might decide that a speaker's stand or the furniture arrangement is creating a barrier between you and the audience, so you might ask the group to arrange itself in a circle while you sit comfortably on a table at the front of the room. You have created an environment that makes sense for you and for the message you want to communicate.

In a formal argument you might decide that the speaker's stand will work for you — that it will give you that authoritative edge you want in this situation — so you get behind the lectern and use it in an authoritative way. This is not unlike many real situations we have all observed. When a president gives a fireside chat he sits, restfully composed, in a large easy chair, using open, expansive gestures. When he delivers the State of the Union Address he stands behind a lectern, and his gestures become more emphatic. In the first situation the president's posture exudes a sense of informality, cordiality, and intimacy. In the second situation, the president's stance says, "I am the President, and I am here to tell you how things are." What is most important is that the presentational style be an integral part of the event. Look carefully at Figure 4-1 and ask yourself what messages are hidden in the two arrangements.

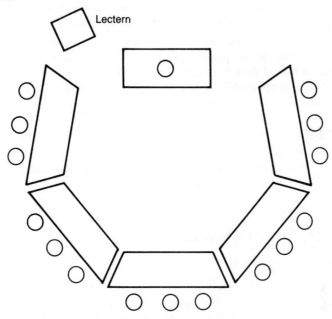

Comfortable Setting for a Narrative

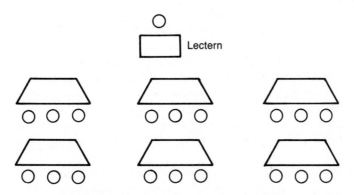

Possible Setting for an Argumentative Speech

Figure 4-1 Possible Arrangements for a Presentation

Each speaking situation requires adjustment on your part. Control the situation; prevent it from controlling you. If a group is larger than you anticipated, or if you should happen to overhear a comment hostile to your topic, you must have enough self-presence to remain calm. If you become flustered you lose your advantage. When the score is tied in the ninth inning of a World Series game and twenty million fans are watching, the great player goes to bat thinking, "Here is what I am going to do" rather than "What is the pitcher going to do to me?" Adjust the situation so that you are in control.

The rest of this chapter will focus on effective oral presentation. Accompanying the text to follow are photographs and exercises. Read the text, study the photographs, and do the exercises. Make judgments about the people you see in the photographs: reflect on how similar they are to you. There is no need to be an imitator; but in the same way that reading a variety of authors increases your stylistic options in writing, observing people who use different postures and gestures when speaking will expose you to a range of alternatives in choosing what works for you. As your instructor and classmates respond to you as a speaker, you will learn what techniques are most natural and appropriate for you. If you practice accordingly, your delivery style will improve.

TYPES OF MESSAGE PREPARATION

The Memorized Speech

Sometimes we are tempted to **memorize** a speech because we are afraid of forgetting the material, but memorizing the speech has its own pitfalls. While you may get the whole message out (or may not), your nonverbal behavior will all too often betray the fact that you are reciting lines, like a train conductor announcing stations, rather than communicating with an audience. When speakers are too intent on remembering every word of a speech, they often forget about interaction between themselves and us. The face and body fail to interact naturally with the message. Speakers who recite from memory may sound like neophyte actors in an eighth-grade play. Further, memorized speeches can provoke unintentionally humorous mispronunciations such as *ape-athy* and *nu-cu-lur*. Worst of all, if such speakers lose their place they may panic and bumble their way through the rest of the speech. At any rate, members of the audience have little sense that they are being communicated with.

It may be that, for you, memorizing some part of the speech, the introduction perhaps, is helpful. Sometimes a little rote memory provides a sense of security. Generally speaking, however, there are better ways to feel secure. Let your instructor and the material in this chapter be your guide.

The Manuscript Speech

Manuscript speaking means delivering an entire speech that has been written out. The speakers shown in the photographs are delivering their speeches from manuscripts. At times you may want to do this. When you do, avoid the common problems associated with manuscript speaking: face buried in the text, a reading rhythm, lack of eye contact, and few, if any, gestures.

If you must use a manuscript, use it not as a crutch or a barrier but as an aid to communication. Keep the audience as your central focus. Practice gesturing with one hand while following your manuscript with the other. Rehearsal is all-important in manuscript speaking, playing a role similar to the revision of a rough draft in the process of writing.

It is possible to read a speech, and read it well. Begin by preparing a triple-spaced manuscript with markings for your own use. This type of manuscript is shown in Figure 4–2. Practice reading a line or two ahead of delivery so that you can still make eye contact with the audience. Keep one hand free for gestures and use the other to keep your place. Finally, strive to keep your voice natural as though you were talking, not reporting the news.

Your instructor may or may not want you to speak with a manuscript in class. If you are permitted to do so and you want to try a manuscript speech, follow the advice given above and ask your instructor for help. A manuscript can be useful if used wisely. Remember that the first requirement is to be animated, audience-centered, and natural. Here is some advice in the form of a checklist for your manuscript.

1. Write the manuscript to be spoken, not read. Put into the script personal pronouns, fragments, and other language markers you would use orally.
2. Triple space the manuscript, and use markings and marginal notes as cues to yourself.
3. Use good, hard stock paper or five-by-seven inch cards for the script.
4. Practice reading aloud until the speech sounds natural. Remember, you must convey the idea that this is you, but you at your best.
5. Be prepared to change your prepared remarks should something unusual occur during your presentation. Responding spontaneously to audience reaction will make your speech more lively and realistic.

The Extemporaneous Speech

Extemporaneous delivery involves the use of notes (in some cases, a mental note system) as an aid to presentation. The advantage of this method is that it promotes natural response to the audience and the situation. Speakers who use an effective note card system are able to move from one idea to the next as they speak and are able to speak spontaneously about each idea as it arises.

I went through *gesture* six years of school, including kindergarten, marvelling and

envying my friends and fellow classmates who could get away with chewing *chewing gesture*

bubblegum in class. How I wish I had their *drawn out* boldness and their shrewd

look at class defiance. My day finally came! It was during the fifth grade when one of

my close friends had bought a brand new flavor of "Bub's Daddy," one of the

emphasize juiciest, most flavorful candy gums on the market. She offered me a piece

just before we rose to take the "Pledge of Allegiance," and say our morning

prayers. I could no longer stand being razzed and hearing those nasty,

familiar name callings: "*emphasize* worry wart," "scaredy cat" and "chicken." *hit hard* So I

took it. ! It must have been four inches *gesture* long, smelling so strawberry sweet;

with a tantalizing, tangy, light as a cloud coating, dusted softly in a buff

of powder. What a temptation! *faster* I grabbed it and sank *hand gesture* my teeth into it.

Oh! Sheer ecstasy at 8:15 a.m. I thought . . . if my mother, or dentist,

could see me now! *pause* But the only one who actually did see me was Miss Ruffin, *lower voice*

my teacher.

— Carolyn Senerchio

Figure 4-2 A Manuscript Speech Format

Successful extemporaneous speakers put direct quotes and other precise details on content note cards to insure accuracy, while the outline of the entire speech is put on the process note cards. Figure 4–3 shows how to construct both the content and the process note cards.

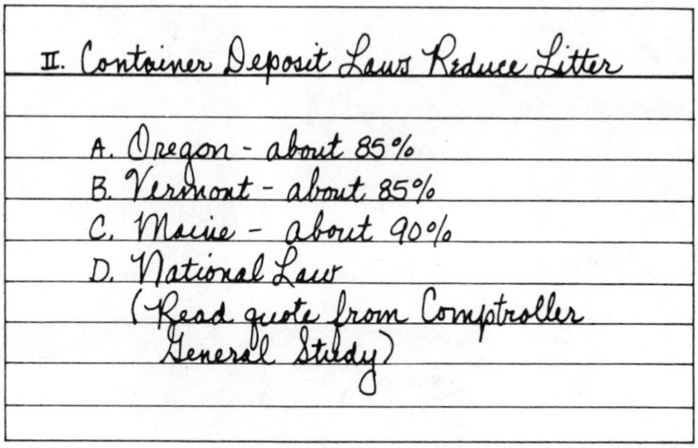

II. Container Deposit Laws Reduce Litter

    A. Oregon – about 85%
    B. Vermont – about 85%
    C. Maine – about 90%
    D. National Law
        (Read quote from Comptroller
        General Study)

Process Card

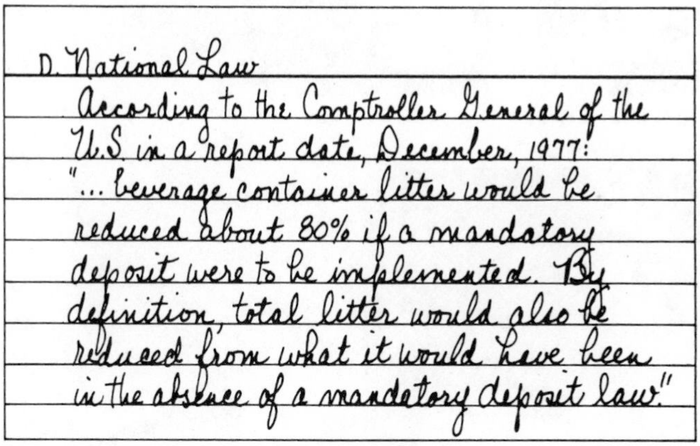

D. National Law
    According to the Comptroller General of the
    U.S. in a report date, December, 1977:
    "... beverage container litter would be
    reduced about 80% if a mandatory
    deposit were to be implemented. By
    definition, total litter would also be
    reduced from what it would have been
    in the absence of a mandatory deposit law."

Content Card

Figure 4-3 Note Card System

76

*Effective Use
of Gestures*

Memorized Speech

*Good Posture;
Side of Podium*

Effective Presentational Style

Using the Manuscript Effectively

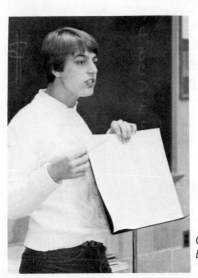

*Good Posture;
Effective Use of Lectern*

Reading the Speech

Ineffective Presentational Style

Hiding Behind Lectern

Slouching Posture

Extemporaneous Speech Style

When speaking extemporaneously the speaker is able to concentrate on the audience, which becomes the focus of the event. Speakers can **gesture** naturally as they reflect on the ideas listed on their note cards. The voice is close to a conversational voice, projected to the needs of the situation, and the speakers are usually much closer to actually talking with the audience than in either the memorized or the manuscript style.

One of the speakers shown in the photographs is delivering quite well. As you look at the photos, note which speakers appear to be using notes well, focusing on the audience, and generally appearing to be natural and spontaneous. How do you look to others when you speak? Which photo best captures your presentational style?

PHYSICAL ATTRIBUTES OF PRESENTATIONAL STYLE

Gestures

All of us gesture naturally when communicating informally; however, when we find ourselves in a formal situation, gesturing naturally becomes more difficult. In the formal presentation each gesture must be purposeful; the random, often unconscious gesturing that accompanies conversational speech must now become conscious and meaningful. You will find that the first step toward effective gesturing is to be totally prepared for your speech, so much so that you are able to let your hands and arms move with the flow of your words. Gestures should reinforce ideas and feelings: they should be used to give a visual dimension to words. Gestures in a formal presentation need to be exaggerated just a bit (but not much) from casual speech. Slow them down and make them smoothly, but always in your own particular style.

Posture

In casual speech, **posture** reflects our style and personality. It also reveals how attracted we are to the person with whom we are talking and how we feel about the topic of conversation. An important step toward improving speaking style is to become aware of various postures so that you are able to use them as aids to communication, and so that you display the right attitude toward your topic and the audience.

Look at the photo of a young man with hunched posture and hands prominently displayed on a chair. What is his posture communicating to us? Look too at the photo of the young woman standing too casually and appearing to hide behind the lectern. To the audience she communicates a lack of concern, so that the audience will most likely feel unconcerned as well. Good use of the lectern is shown in the photo of the young woman gesturing with her left hand. She has taken a comfortable stance — not slouched, yet not rigid; her stance has made the audience feel comfortable. There are numerous ways to use posture to make an audience feel comfortable, and you should be searching for the posture that works best for you.

Movement

Moving while speaking may involve the whole body or just the head. Generally speaking, **movement** toward the audience connotes a sense of intimacy or sharing with them. If you are forced behind the lectern because of the occasion you can still lean toward the audience to achieve this sense of closeness.

Movement is most effective when it coincides with the message and when it is subtle. For instance, a speaker may move unobtrusively to the side of the lectern, rest one arm on it, take an erect but comfortable posture, and lean slightly toward the audience. Few audience members have consciously noticed, but the speaker has created a positive effect. The speaker appears to be out there with the audience, relaxed but aware, comfortable but confident. The movement has been purposeful, and the audience has been made to feel more involved in the total event.

Facial Expression

Every speaker has felt the freezing of the face that occurs in formal presentations: muscles tense, jaws lock, lips go numb. Practice and experience will help loosen you up; as you gain confidence in yourself, your face will reveal that confidence. Work toward animated and lively **facial expressions** that fit smoothly into the character of the speech. Do not be afraid to smile at yourself or display emotions. You will find, if you look carefully, that audiences often mimic the facial expressions of the speaker: smile and they will smile back at you, frown and they will frown also, stare blankly and you will get stared at in return.

Eye contact is important to effective delivery. Look audience members in the eyes; scan the entire audience, but avoid excessive staring or focusing on one person. Use your eyes to draw back people who may have drifted away. Use your eyes to express feelings about your message. The eyes are most significant in developing the quality of the relationship between you and the audience. They are also the main interpreter of audience response. Continuous, conscious, but natural eye contact is a key element in successful presentational style.

Dress and Appearance

We all have our own standards for dress and appearance. In class, or in the real speech setting, **appearance** standards may be rigidly enforced or only suggested. Research indicates that the way a speaker is dressed is related to the speaker's credibility. Audiences tend to favor those whose clothing suggests high status, and these speakers are viewed as more persuasive. You might talk to your instructor if you are interested in learning how your appearance affects your speaking. Make some judgments about the speakers who appear in the photographs on page 81. What do you think about their attire?

Gestures, posture, movement, and facial expressions occur all at once in a planned speech. They make up a large part of the total energy that you want to exchange with an audience. In the photos that follow, look for behavior that you like and dislike, behavior you would feel comfortable with yourself, and mannerisms you find distracting. Which pictures represent most closely your speaking style? What qualities or characteristics could be represented here that are not?

VOCAL ATTRIBUTES OF PRESENTATIONAL STYLE

Research studies indicate that vocal cues are another important factor in shaping the audience's perception of a speaker. Vocal cues combine with what we say, how we look, and how we move and gesture to create an image upon which the audience bases its judgment of a presentation. The opening of this chapter stressed the fact that effective oral presentation involves creating a feeling of naturalness and spontaneity in a less than natural setting, the public speech. This point reinforces the importance of vocal attributes in presentational style.

Pronunciation

Clear pronunciation and a standard speech style are important characteristics of effective presentations. In natural, spontaneous speech, many of us clip off the sounds at the end of many words. In particular, we say *goin* for *going* and *stayin* for *staying* and we make similar clips of *ed* and *s* endings. Similarly, in our casual speech we may not say some words correctly, using "fer" instead of "for" and *nucular* rather than *nuclear*. While these are certainly inaccurate, in conversational speech they are seldom corrected by others, and our meanings are not much distorted. When we are put, however, in that middling situation — an oral presentation in a formal setting — we need to maintain our naturalness while subtly shifting to a more formal articulation pattern.

In a planned presentation one should say, "We are reaching the age of individualism," rather than "we're reachin' the age of indavidyalism." Avoid excessive contractions and make all of the sounds in the words, but unobtrusively. Clear, standard pronunciation should in fact be practiced in all of your speaking rather than only in planned presentations. Those who succeed during their student years in developing a natural but clear standard speech style have achieved a valuable end product of education. It is a mark of distinction to be in control of one's language, and having such mastery will speak well for you.

Because pronunciation is so critical to effective presentational style, it seems worthwhile to stop here and try a drill. Do not read on, then, until you have practiced saying these words. Remember, make all of the sounds in the words, neither adding nor subtracting any, but avoid exaggerating. Try using each word in a sentence so that you can practice it within the natural flow of speaking. These words are representative of common omissions, additions, and transpositions in pronunciation. If you are not sure of the preferred pronunciation of a word, check an up-to-date dictionary.

little	business	environment	compulsory
problem	vegetables	athlete	for
police	euthanasia	drowned	because
strength	government	escape	picture
literature	laboratory	electoral	tobacco
genuine	library	February	walked
often	unusual	statistics	just
hundred	relevant	strategy	nuclear
larynx	remuneration	prodigy	vehemently

Finally, the following advice should prove helpful.

1. Clear and correct pronunciation is a mark of maturity and professionalism. You will be expected to display this quality when you have graduated from college and are looking for employment.
2. Improvement in control of standard pronunciation results from constant attention.
3. Be especially careful about pronunciation in formal presentations, but avoid exaggeration. If you are practicing clear standard speech all the time, your speech in formal situations will soon appear to be an extension of your normal presentational style. Be careful not to hypercorrect — for instance, to start pronouncing the sound for *t* in *often* or the one for *b* in *dumb*, or put other sounds in words where the letters do not stand for any sounds.

Fluency

The term **fluency** refers to the stream of speech. Most spontaneous speech is laced with hesitations, pauses, and other fluency errors. Unfortunately, audiences generally view in a negative way such nonfluencies as *um* and *you know*; in-sentence switches ("I need time to, uh, well, the book is longer than, you know. . ."); repetitions; stutters; tongue slips; and incoherencies. Although it is unclear whether nonfluencies lower audience comprehension or the persuasiveness of your message, they certainly fail to add to your success. For this reason, try to eliminate as much nonfluency as you can.

In formal speaking, of course, eliminating nonfluencies as much as possible is even more important. Because the stereotypical public speaker is someone with a forceful, steady, uninterrupted flow of speech, this has become the standard by which others are judged. Most of us need to concentrate extremely hard at first to rid our speech of the filled pauses — the *like, you know, right*, and *um*, pauses — that have crept into our conversational speech. There are at least three ways to begin the task of ridding our speech of these nonfluencies.

1. Practice fluency all the time — make it a conscious effort on your part.
2. Minimize nonfluencies by picking a person, a role model, whose speech is quite fluent, and keep this person in mind when you speak. This idea has worked for many students.
3. Ask a friend or classmate, or your instructor, to count your filler words. If the count is, for instance, twenty filler words in a five-minute presentation, reduce that by half before midsemester. By the time the course is completed, see whether you can eliminate seventy-five percent of your filler speech. Whatever time you spend on this problem is worth it.

Rate, Pause, and Emphasis

A significant amount of nonfluency results from speaking too quickly, a problem that is sometimes related to speech anxiety and sometimes to habit. A normal rate of speech is somewhere around 150 words per minute, but individuals may successfully vary widely from this norm. The key to success is audience comprehension: you should speak at a rate that is natural and comfortable for you but one adapted to the needs of the particular audience you are addressing. Generally speaking, if you are pronouncing words clearly and correctly, and if you are adjusting to the acoustical demands of the setting, your speaking rate should cause no problems for the audience.

Rate is directly related to **pause** and **emphasis.** When you are in control of your rate of speech and talking in a natural manner, you will notice that some words and places in your presentation are more important than others. An effective speaker hits key words and places slightly harder than usual in a speech and gets added meaning out of them.

Use pauses and emphasis the way a good writer uses punctuation. A pause that is just slightly longer than usual can catch an audience's attention (as well as give you time to look at your notes and get composed). Consider each three-dot segment in the following examples to be a normal pause, and then read the statements, adding a pause of equal duration for each three dots:

- If unemployment among teenage Blacks hits twenty percent . . . the streets will light up again.
- If unemployment among teenage Blacks hits twenty percent . . . . . . the streets will light up . . . again.

Now add emphasis to this sentence, stressing what you think are the key words. Notice how the meaning changes as you move the stress marks around. Here are three ways, among many, that you might add emphasis to the statement depending upon the preceding text:

- If unemployment among teenage Blacks hits *twenty percent* . . . . . . the streets will light up again.
- If unemployment among *teenage* Blacks hits twenty percent . . . . . . the streets will light up . . . again.
- If *unemployment* among teenage Blacks hits twenty percent . . . the streets . . . . . . will light up again.

Rate, pause, and emphasis, when used as an aid to communication, will add vocal variety to your presentational style. At first you may feel inhibited using rate, pause, and emphasis in your speaking, but as you become more comfortable with yourself in this role you will become more aware of the fact that manipulating rate, pause, and emphasis is normal and natural for the vast majority of us, and that you are simply projecting your rate, pause, and emphasis to meet the demands of the situation. Think of it as oral punctuation.

VISUAL AIDS: PREPARATION AND PRESENTATION

A **visual aid** is a device the speaker or writer uses to reinforce a point. Visual aids add clarity and color to a message. They can also help to relieve communication apprehension in a speech by redirecting the audience's eyes and giving the speaker a handy source of information. In an essay visuals can highlight a point made in the text, provide perspective for the readers, and even give readers a breather as they work through the material. Many professional communicators make a practice of using visual aids for the reasons just mentioned.

There are three ways to provide visual aids. Informative aids can be used in both speeches and essays. They are usually in the form of such displays as charts, maps, and graphs. In the case of a speech, informative aids might involve a handout or some chalkboard work.

The second way to provide visual aids is through a showing aid. Show aids are used in speeches and may be in the form of pictures, illustrations, photographs, exhibits, transparencies, audio- or videotapes, or demonstrations by the speaker.

The last type of visual aid is the doing aid. In a speech, Do aids involve dramatizations, role playing, and such audience participation activities as filling out a questionnaire.

Visual aids must be carefully prepared and effectively presented. The guidelines below are offered as a way of checking the quality of a visual aid. Follow the guidelines and look carefully at the model visuals given in the text as ways to make your visuals an integral part of the presentation.

Informative Aids: Preparation

Visual aids must be large enough to be seen by all members of the audience. Check the size of the room and pace off the distance from the person who will be farthest away; then check your visual aid to be certain that the person farthest away can see or read your information. Adjust the shape of the visual and the size of the detail accordingly.

Use only information actually related to your point. A visual aid is more than a decoration; it must do something. It is not enough to have a large picture of a handgun for a speech on handgun control; it is better to have a chart with statistics on handgun ownership. It is important that the visual aid add a dimension to the presentation.

Visual aids must simplify the material. If the source from which you draw your information has more than you need, make your own chart using only the relevant data. Label your visuals at the top or bottom so that they make sense by themselves.

Think about what you will need for exhibiting your visuals. Bring thumbtacks, tape, or whatever you need to display your visuals properly. Avoid counting on the chalkboard ledge or on a friend in class to hold the visuals for you.

Practice working with your visuals. Know the data as well as you can. Use a pencil to write notes to yourself lightly on the visual if that will help you cover the material.

Informative Aids: Presentation

When presenting informative aids it is important to station yourself in a spot where you can see both the audience and the visuals. Be sure that the speaker's stand does not obstruct the audience's view.

Unless you have had experience with the chalkboard, consider using poster board for your visuals. If you want to try using the chalkboard anyway, be certain to practice in advance and ask if what you have written can be read. While writing on the board try to maintain as much audience contact as you can. You can do this by limiting your visual material to one word or phrase or by taking a position to the side of your writing and looking occasionally at your audience as you write. Avoid turning your back to the audience for extended periods of time, and work from left to right or in some organized manner. Most important, bring your own chalk.

Handouts can be effective informative aids, but using them before or during the presentation can be risky. You take the chance that the handout will distract the audience or that chaos will result as the handouts make their way around the room. Better to use handouts at the end of the speech, perhaps as part of your conclusion. Be sure the handout reinforces the topic and has your name on it.

Showing Aids: Preparation

Showing aids need to be made understandable. A picture or a photograph usually needs to be captioned; transparencies need headings, and audio or video material must be of good quality. Demonstrations should be done in clearly labeled steps or stages.

Showing aids must be carefully timed. A five-minute tape played in an eight-minute speech creates a lack of balance. Only a certain number of photographs can be shown in an allotted time. Make sure that your visual does not become your speech. Demonstrations should show only the step itself, not the time between intervening steps. The time between can be mentioned; then move along by having the step completed in advance.

Rehearsal is important when using showing aids. Know how to thread the tape deck or the projector. Know whom to call if the equipment fails, or if you need an outlet or an extension cord. Plan to use your voice to keep audience interest if the visuals lack a sound track. If you are using someone else as a demonstrator be sure that person is reliable and has rehearsed with you. If lights need to be dimmed, plan to use your voice to keep audience interest in the presentation.

Avoid dangerous or gimmicky aids. Check with your instructor ahead of time to be sure that your aid is acceptable in the classroom.

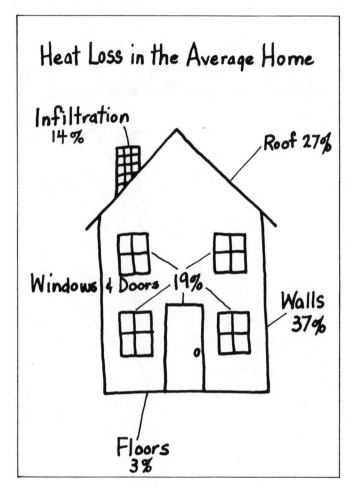

Figure 4-4 Home Insulation Visual Aid

Showing Aids: Presentation

If you are going to be using showing aids, arrive early to set up and check the equipment. Arrange the room to suit your purposes.

Keep the presentation lively. Time your slides or photos so that you avoid gaps of silence. Ask someone to help you run the projector, if necessary, so that you can attend to the speech. Have enough material to go around the room if the speech involves a demonstration. If you are demonstrating how to press flowers, for instance, it is a good idea to have enough to give to each member of the audience so that they can try doing it themselves.

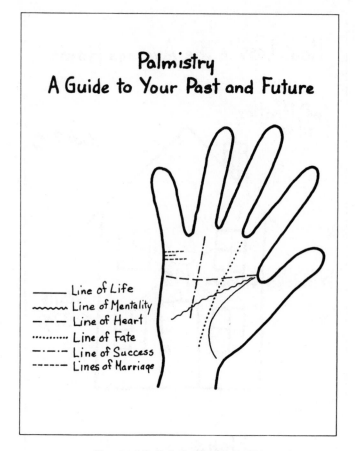

Figure 4-5 Palmistry Visual Aid

Doing Aids: Preparation

Doing aids can work, but you must know your audience well to insure success. Role playing, in particular, can be dangerous. Know the members of your audience and what they are capable of. If you suspect that role playing will cause problems, be ready to handle them, or look for a better way to visualize your point. Check with your instructor in advance if you plan to use the audience.

Doing aids must carefully timed. Exercises take time; dramatizations can be long and drawn out beyond their value in the presentation. Be certain that the speech avoids becoming one long exercise.

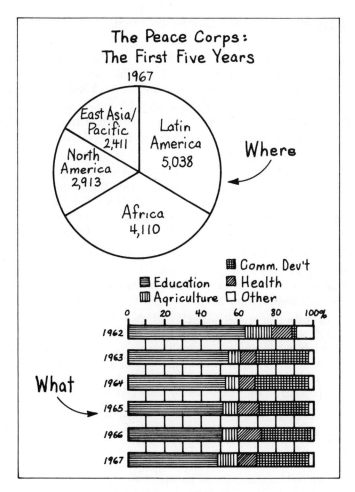

Figure 4-6 Peace Corps Visual Aid

Doing Aids: Presentation

Doing aids require that you cue the audience ahead of time. Members of the audience need to know what they are getting into. If they are going to arrange flowers, do macramé, sing a song, play a game, work out a puzzle, or make something, they will appreciate knowing about this in advance.

Answer questions as you go along, and show patience. An audience appreciates a running commentary that reassures and guides them. Some speaking while the activity is going on also prevents awkward gaps of silence.

VISUAL AIDS IN WRITTEN COMMUNICATION

Visual aids in written communication are of the informing variety, so some of the guidelines already given for oral communication should be followed for the written mode. There are some additional practices, however, that help to make visuals in written communication effective.

Most important, refer to the visual in the actual text. Sometimes it is enough to simply indicate in parentheses that a visual accompanies the text, in the following way:

> A new baby boom began in 1978, as many women in their 30s decided that it was "now or never." This latest birth boom is not as large as the one following World War Two (See Figure I), but it is substantial and it does mean that teacher training will become an active part of the college curriculum in the 1980s once again.

In other cases, it will be necessary to describe in the text the terms or numbers or pictures used in the visual. Do this whenever the visual must be long or technical (which should be rarely), or when you want to provide your own interpretations of the data, as in the following example:

> The baby boom following World War Two continued until about 1964. As Figure I shows, births before and after the period 1946–64 are lower, creating what some have called *the pig in the snake* effect. That is, as this mass of humanity moves through the snake of time it creates a huge bulge that affects every aspect of our lives from politics to popular music, from sexual values to religion.

In the example just given, two visuals might be used: one with the chart of birth rates on it and the other with a picture of the pig in the belly of the snake (see Figures 4-7 and 4-8).

The writer must decide whether to place the visuals in the text or at the end of the text in the form of an appendix. Decide which placement is best by judging how essential the visual is to the text, how long it is, and how complex it is. If you want to be certain that readers look at the visual, it is probably best placed as close as possible to the information it illustrates. Then direct your readers to it. If the material is supplementary or if the text will be much broken up by the visual, consider placing it at the end in the form of an appendix.

Visual aids in written communication must be carefully constructed. Such visuals should be as neat as the text itself. Photographs and pictures or snapshots are often lacking in quality and will detract rather than add to your material. Similarly, photocopies of charts or maps taken from newspapers or magazines are not as presentable as those you make yourself. Take the extra time to prepare the visuals yourself. and do them neatly.

It is essential that credit be given for all visual material. Unless you are

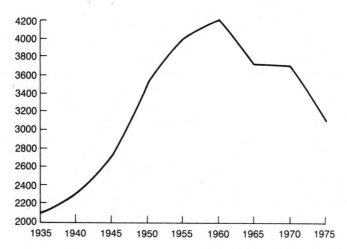

Figure 4-7 Birth Rates in the United States, 1935–1965

Figure 4-8 Pig in the Belly of the Snake

the author or the artist or both, put a standard footnote reference at the bottom of the visual giving credit to the originators.

Visual aids can lend clarity and color to your presentation. If used incorrectly, however, they can actually detract from the message. Many instructors have special ideas about how to construct and use visual aids, and you should follow your instructor's guidelines as well as those in this text. Look at the visuals presented in this text and discuss what you like and dislike about them.

SUMMARY

Effective presentational style is critical to success in oral communication. Each of us has a unique style; the goal is to become conscious of one's style, emphasize what works well, and become conscious of and eliminate distracting behavior. Through practice and criticism your presentational style will emerge; audiences will see you as natural and spontaneous, despite the fact that you have planned for the communication event.

There are three types of presentation: memorized, manuscript, and extemporaneous. One type will be more appropriate for a particular occasion than another, although the extemporaneous style offers the most advantages in naturalness and spontaneity. Most important, know what the advantages and disadvantages are of each presentational style as we have discussed them here, and plan in advance for solutions to problems.

Effective oral communication requires liveliness and animation. The speaker's sense of enthusiasm and attraction to both the audience and the topic will be picked up by the audience and often imitated. A dynamic presentational style is achieved through the use of body and voice. Gestures, movement, facial expressions, and posture are the predominant avenues of expression through the body. Care in pronunciation, fluency, and timing are the key vocal variables for effective presentation. Finally, dress and appearance communicate a great deal about attitude toward the topic, audience, and situation.

Visual aids can add to the effectiveness of spoken or written communication. They need to be prepared and presented properly so that their relationship to the speech or text is clear to the audience or the readers.

KEY WORDS

spontaneity	facial expression
style	appearance
memorized	pronunciation
manuscript	fluency
extemporaneous	rate
gestures	pause
posture	emphasis
movement	visual aids

EXERCISES

1. In a descriptive essay of three to five pages, characterize your personal presentational style. Use the section on description as a guide. If possible, evaluate your style and make a list of virtues and flaws.

2. Using your descriptive essay from Exercise #1, or a list of terms you have prepared that characterize your presentational style, pair off with a member of the class and ask the other person to react to your essay or list of terms. Do the same for the other person. Pay close attention to how others see you as compared with how you see yourself. Make some judgments and commitments about your style to share with the other person.

3. When convenient, record yourself on an audiotape in a conversation with someone. The following day, play the tape back and make some observations about your style, using the material from this chapter on vocal aspects of speaking. Later on in the semester record yourself again and take note of any changes in your presentational style.

REFERENCES

Bassett, Ronald E., Ann Q. Staton–Spicer, and Jack L. Whitehead, "Effects of Source Attire on Judgments of Credibility," *Central States Speech Journal*, 30 (Fall, 1979), pp. 282–285.

Knapp, Mark. *Nonverbal Communication in Human Interaction* (New York: Holt, Rinehart and Winston, 1972), p. 174.

5.   Communication Apprehension

It ranks right up there on the fear scale with cancer, tall buildings, and cramped spaces. Many normally sophisticated, reasonable, and intelligent adults have been known to wither in its grip. Students tell us it is their single most recurring problem. It has ruined more dinners than stringy roast beef and rubbery chicken combined. We are talking, of course, about communication apprehension.

Communication apprehension is a broad term that covers all levels of fear or anxiety associated with real or anticipated communication with another person or persons. Apprehension may be present in all communication situations from the most casual conversation to the most formal public speech. Communication apprehension is as prevalent in writing as it is in speaking. Many a person has forsaken an opportunity to advance in a career, to speak out on an issue, to write a letter to a friend, or to ask a special person out for an evening because of communication apprehension. Students report that it is their most recurring fear when faced with a course in communication. Communication apprehension, however, like any other fear, is controllable if we can first come to understand it and learn a few techniques for dealing with it when it occurs. The objective of this chapter is just that: to help you understand communication apprehension, and to help you cope with it.

Notice that our objective is to understand and cope with communication apprehension. We have said nothing about getting rid of it. In fact, the fear we feel in a communication situation is a natural component of the event. It is the same anxiety we feel the first day on a new job, before a big test or important date, or at the start of a crucial athletic contest. We might even say that the anxiety we feel on such occasions is the result of an energy flow in our bodies that we need in order to do our best. When we say, for instance, that we are *psyched up* for an event, aren't we actually saying that there is a flow of energy in us that we are using to get into the situation? We need to begin the discussion of communication apprehension with this important point in mind: we cannot rid ourselves of it; rather, we need it to help us prepare emotionally for the event.

If we remember that most human beings feel anxiety in threatening situations, we can more easily accept it as a natural component of communication events. After all, communication, especially formal communication as discussed in this book, is a threatening event. Formal communication is a revelation of ourselves; it puts us in the spotlight, so to speak, and that is often intimidating. Thus when we feel apprehension we are experiencing a common reaction that each and every one of our peers is feeling. It is helpful to remember from the start that everyone around you is to some degree feeling communication apprehension.

Communication apprehension can come from two sources, although they are not distinct and involve a great deal of overlap and interaction. The first source is a general anxiety **trait**: that is, each of us feels anxiety to a greater or lesser degree depending upon our personalities, our backgrounds, and our expressive levels. Some of us simply like to talk more than others do, some of us are generally more outgoing than others, and some of us are more easily intimidated than others. So communication apprehension is a trait we exhibit in one situation or another, one we need to be conscious of as we attempt to cope with it.

The second source of communication apprehension is the specific situation in which we find ourselves. This is **state** anxiety. For some of us, if we do not consider ourselves glib or witty or high talkers, casual conversation can be intimidating, while for others of us the public speaking situation generates the most anxiety. There are those of us who feel comfortable writing a complex technical report but who block completely when faced with writing a letter home. Traits and states, then, are the sources of apprehension; they exist on a continuum and are present in varying degrees with each communication event.

Communication Apprehension

Trait Apprehension ———————————— State Apprehension
(US)   (SITUATIONS)

For the purpose of studying formal communication, we are most concerned with the reaction to a planned speech or essay. What follows are some specific ways to deal with the anxiety you feel in these two situations. If you will make a conscious effort to think about and apply this advice in your assignments, we believe you can come to grips with much of your communication apprehension.

SPEECH ANXIETY

Speech anxiety may occur at any stage in the process from choosing a topic to answering questions after the speech. Those anxieties that occur while you are composing will be discussed in the next section of the chapter. For now, let us consider those anxieties specifically related to presenting a speech.

Understanding Speech Anxiety

Self-Anxieties. Many of us defeat ourselves before we begin. Look at the following statement by a student about her feelings just prior to her first speech:

While I was speaking, I felt self–conscious and very much aware of the physical symptoms caused by my anxiety. I kept thinking that everyone could see my heart pounding. And when my speech was over, I refused to believe that I spoke well. Others in the class said I did a good job, but I felt terrible and felt that they were just saying that to be nice.

— Sandra Starr

Sandra learned, as many of us have, that we can be our own worst enemies. As the semester progressed she came to realize that she had ideas worth sharing, and that unless she believed in herself she could not ask others to do so.

The last sentence of Sandra's statement is worth thinking about. Notice that her audience thought she did a good job. The reason for the apparent contradiction between Sandra's and her audience's analysis has a reasonable explanation: Sandra was concentrating on herself, and her audience was listening to her message.

We have come to call self-defeating tendencies the **speech anxiety syndrome**. It works something like this: I am nervous, and I am aware that I am nervous. As I prepare to speak I think that the audience knows that I am nervous. Not wanting to be embarrassed by appearing nervous, I get more nervous now that I know the audience knows. Now that I am more nervous I think that the audience knows I am more nervous, and on and on and on.

Notice that all of this anxiety takes place in the speaker's head. Nowhere does it say that the audience actually reflects consciously on the speaker's anxiety, and, in fact, the audience most likely lacks a great concern for the speaker's anxiety. How many times have you said, or heard anyone else actually say, "Let's go watch So-and-So get nervous during a speech"? Audiences come to a speech for a variety of reasons, one of the least of which is to check out speaker anxiety. You must realize this, tell yourself this, and avoid talking yourself into unnecessary anxieties. If you have something to say, that will become the most significant audience concern.

Message Anxieties. There is no substitute for thorough knowledge of the topic. Many of us have had the experience recorded by a student in the following simple comment: "I have found that it is easier to speak on topics in which I had some personal interest, and had researched thoroughly." Such a commonsense realization reminds us that knowing our material and having a point, pattern, and detail will relieve many of our anxieties. If, however, you have picked your topic the night before, scrambled about for information you are not personally interested in, and have not practiced the material, you will indeed feel much anxiety. Your body is giving you the same message it might give if you were to do a solo flight your first time in the cockpit of an airplane. If you know your message you will find that you feel much more comfortable presenting it to an audience.

Audience Anxieties. Many of us make the mistake of having false expectations about our audience. Too often we feel that the audience is more critical than it actually is. There are critical audiences, but generally speaking the members of an audience know less than the speaker about the topic, since it is the speaker who has done the preparation. Further, audiences, especially classroom audiences, are generally willing to give the speaker and the message a fair hearing if only for self protection in their own speeches. As one student put it in his self-evaluation:

> After my first speech in class, I learned to control my anxiety by realizing that the audience is almost never as frightening as it sometimes seems to be.
>
> — Dave Geary

Situational Anxieties. Many of us who speak frequently have come to understand what we call the speech anxiety peak experience. That is, if we have a ten–minute speech, for instance, most of our anxiety occurs just prior to and during the first moments of the presentation. If we know this, and consciously tell ourselves this, we come to the realization that we are indeed going to feel anxieties, but they will peak at the beginning, and if we can get past this part and are prepared, we will feel increasingly comfortable as the speech progresses.

One student who applied this idea of talking to herself about the **speech anxiety peak** reported the following in her speech journal:

> One aspect of public speaking that I feel I can handle better is pre-speech stress. Particularly helpful was the idea of allowing yourself to be nervous, while telling yourself that it will dissipate as soon as the speaking begins. Every time I got up in front of the class I felt more comfortable than the time before. My pre-speech anxiety level decreased a great deal.
>
> — Karin Powell

Three mental operations, then, can help you understand speech anxiety more clearly. First, avoid the speech anxiety syndrome. Second, develop realistic audience expectations. Third, recognize the speech anxiety peak experience. If you will add to this advice careful and thorough preparation, you will feel much more secure about your speaking. Now add to this new understanding some methods for coping with those anxieties that we feel.

Coping with Speech Anxiety

Preparation and practice are essentials for coping with speech anxiety. There are, however, some do's and don'ts that work in the speaking situation.

1. Use visual aids. Visual aids help to relieve speech anxiety in two ways. First, they become a body of data or an organizational scheme you can refer to; thus you need not worry as much about losing your place or stumbling on your note cards. Second, visuals redirect some of the audience's focus away from you and to the visual aid. As you look out at members of the audience you will see that the visual has caught their attention, and you will feel more comfortable. Well prepared, informative visuals are a useful coping mechanism.

2. Know your introduction. Remember the speech anxiety peak experience. Many speakers have a humorous or dramatic introduction that generates some audience response. These speakers realize that if they can redirect energy toward the audience at the beginning of the speech, they get that extra moment or two to calm down and get involved in the event. Many speakers memorize their introductions or use familiar stories or expressions, realizing that if they can get off on the right foot they will be able to get past the anxiety peak and into a more relaxed attitude in general.

3. Breath deeply before starting to speak. Too often speakers rush to the lectern and start in immediately. It is usually better to move to the lectern, or to the front of the room, settle oneself by breathing deeply (but not obviously) two or three times, look out at the audience for a brief moment, and then begin.

4. Look for a friendly face. Usually you will find someone in the audience who is willing to give you an A right from the start. As you scan the audience look for a person or persons who are reacting favorably. You will find that these positive cues make you feel more comfortable.

5. Avoid memorizing your speech. The following comment by a student sums up the problem with memorizing a speech:

> At the beginning of this course I was very shy and extremely nervous. For my first speech I decided to memorize the whole thing, but when I stood in front of the class, and all eyes were on me, I forgot most of it. From that point on, I decided I needed a few note cards. Just to have a few note cards in front of me made me more confident and less nervous.
> — Mary Ann DiMaio

Memorizing the speech takes away from your ability to cope with yourself and the situation, since it puts all the focus on the message. It takes practice and effort to deliver from notes, but the time spent is well worth it.

6. Don't give up. Controlling speech anxiety is a tough assignment. You will feel more and more confident as you apply what we have said here and as you gain experience in public speaking. Most of us can cope, and you will be able to if you make the effort. Le us turn now to a consideration of communication apprehension in writing.

WRITING ANXIETY

Some students are gripped by writing anxiety from the time they receive an assignment to the moment when, sighing with relief, they hand in the paper. Others claim to experience their most anxious moments when choosing a topic. Once this decision is made they enjoy the rest of the composing process. Still others are perfectly at ease choosing a topic and researching it but panic when the time arrives to put pen to paper.

Just as with public speaking, it is natural for even the most professional writers to pass through stages of apprehension during composing. Novice writers sometimes feel that their fears stem from inexperience; this is not necessarily so. Let us look at how a professional explains writing apprehension, the various ways in which students experience apprehension, and what all of us can do to cope with what is commonly called **writer's block**.

Understanding Writing Anxiety

Self-Anxieties. It has often been said that writing is a lonely business. Writers sit in a room, the pen and the blank page their only company; yet unlike public speakers, writers are free to change their words if they decide that what they have written is not really what they mean. There is no need to worry about stumbling over words in front of a live audience.

On the other hand, neither are there smiling faces in front of the writer to provide encouragement. Writers can only imagine their audience, and what we imagine can be more frightening than reality when our egos are on the line. In the quote below, Tom Wolfe explains how we can let fear of our own inadequacies overcome us:

> What is called writer's block is always here. It's me-fear, fear that you can't do what you announced. Maybe you only announced it to a few people, or only to yourself. The awful thing about the first sentence of any book is that as soon as you've written it, you realize this piece of work is not going to be the great thing that you envisioned. It can't be. That's one kind of fear. Another would be not coming up to the expectations of editors, authors, and all the rest.
>
> (Gilder, 1981)

Although as a student you may not have experienced the pressure of editors, your teachers and classmates' expectations can be equally frightening. Notice that Wolfe refers to the first sentence as one of the key problems for writers. Getting over the notion that the first sentence has to be perfect can relieve much of the anxiety connected with writing. Me-fear is partially a fear of seeing your own words across the page, fear of sounding silly, if only to yourself. We naturally desire to present ourselves as best we can at all times, and many of us cannot bring ourselves to write that first sentence, knowing that it will not be our best. Realize, then, that some of your anxiety is a reflection of your self-esteem rather than of your inadequacies. Then make this self-esteem work for you — be critical of yourself during your final draft, but not when you are getting started. The student quote below illustrates the danger of first-sentence block:

> One of my major writing problems is beginning. I often find that once I start and get over that first hurdle, I don't encounter many problems after that. But the starting problem can last for hours and I find that I lose a lot of valuable time in the beginning.
>
> — Gail Gariepy

Try to convert preliminary worrying time into time spent rewriting and polishing after the first draft takes shape.

Many students experience a more deep-rooted kind of anxiety, stemming from lack of preparation in the basic subjects of grammar and spelling. They become so discouraged with mechanical problems that they lose sight of the fact that they have something worth communicating.

> I have a fear of writing and always have. I believe it stems from my background in grammar school as well as in high school. I do not remember having a good basic course in writing and I didn't have to write that much in high school. I always felt that the less I had to write the better.
>
> I can recognize some of my trouble areas but I find it difficult to correct them. Some of my concerns are spelling and grammar. I really feel that the worst thing anyone can do to me is to have me write something in front of someone — even if it's a simple telephone message. I cannot stress the amount of anxiety it causes me to write a message and to have to give it to someone right away.
>
> — Paula LaMontagne

As with any task we are not good at, the longer we put off learning how to do it properly the more convinced we become that we are unequal to it. Many students, like Paula, believe that they will never master grammar and spelling. These, then, become the two aspects they associate most with writing. Consequently, they view the whole writing process as unpleasant.

Certainly, mechanical problems cannot simply be overlooked. Muddled grammar and poor spelling interfere with your message. If, like Paula, you are embarrassed to write a note in front of someone, then you need help. Paula found that working with a programmed spelling text and reviewing a grammar handbook weekly with her instructor alleviated some of her anxiety. In fact, once she had brought herself to ask for help — both from her instructor and from the Writing Lab — she began to enjoy the other aspects of writing, even discovering that she had a flair for humor in her work. For years her flow of ideas had been trapped by what she knew to be her weaknesses. Making a decision to confront your problems and to begin to master them is like going on a diet — you feel better just knowing you are doing something about them.

Message Anxieties. If you have probed your topic thoroughly before you begin to write and spent time at the library when necessary, you should have little problem with what to say. Occasionally you may be assigned a topic in which you have little interest. Instead of writing an essay that reflects your boredom and thus bores your readers, try to find an unusual aspect of the topic and learn something you might otherwise not have known. For instance, suppose you are assigned the general topic of health. You are tired of hearing about running, and you cannot face another essay about the pleasures of a sprouts sandwich or a dish of yogurt and fruit. Forget the fads, then. Avoid allowing the immediate connotations a topic has for you to dominate your attitude toward the topic. Remember that there are mental, social, and financial aspects of health as well as physical ones, and allow yourself to get past your initial dislike of a topic to an exploration of its less common aspects.

Audience Anxieties. Look at the following comments:

I'd be embarrassed for a classmate to read my writing.

— Joan Harrington

You mean you want me to read what I wrote *out loud*?

— Bob Weisberger

At first, everyone was afraid to read their journals. But then we started to realize how much we enjoyed hearing somebody else's, so it became a little like group therapy.

— Mary Zeff

One of the things I liked the best was getting to read the other students' papers.

— Lisa Reed

Sooner or later, you will be asked to share your writing with someone other than the teacher. The first two reactions quoted above are typical of the initial shock this can cause to students who are accustomed to handing in essays to the teacher as one of twenty-five or thirty students and having their work returned in the same anonymous way. But after all, when your communication is worthwhile, you will want to reach the broadest possible audience. As the last two quotes indicate, your classmates are eager to hear and read your ideas. If you have the opportunity to exchange research papers in class, you will be pleased to discover that more than likely, your reader has learned something new from your paper. We have found that fellow students are appreciative of one another's efforts and will express that appreciation openly. On the other hand, when criticism is required, remember that your peers are trying to help you become a better communicator. They want to aid you in your attempt to convey your exact meaning, so they may question the arrangement of your ideas or your choice of words. As one student put it:

> For the first time in my school writing, I didn't feel I was just writing for the teacher. In the group sessions, I learned to give and receive constructive criticism. I was excited when others told me they had learned from my paper. Also, I got to read about parapsychology, nursing, plant science, and other things I had never known much about.
>
> — Jean Thompson

Situational Anxieties

> Write something, Oh, no, what? Can I spell? Once I get going, it's OK.
>
> — Maureen Wilcox

Some students like Maureen momentarily panic when faced with an in-class essay. In fact, this experience is similar to the speech anxiety peak syndrome. Initially, the writer panics and blocks, much as speakers may feel they are choking over the first few words before gaining control of themselves as the panic subsides. Prepare yourself for the anxiety of on-the-spot writing by realizing that after a minute or two, your mind will begin to clear and words will start to flow. If you have practiced brainstorming with your other assignments you will unblock and allow this technique to take over.

It is best to avoid clockwatching; if you keep telling yourself you are unable to write anything worthwhile in fifty minutes, you will only reinforce the block and prevent your mind from working freely. Write and make corrections as neatly as you can, and resist worrying about allowing yourself time to write the essay over. Instead, spend your time on the essential elements of point, pattern, and detail. As long as you remember to shape your essay around those elements, even one class period will be enough time for you to convey your ideas meaningfully.

Coping with Writing Anxiety

Writing anxiety is a normal response to the stress of communicating clearly. However, there are a few hints, **coping mechanisms**, that will lessen this anxiety for you, and make composing the pleasurable experience it can be.

1. *Get help if you need it.* Avoid allowing yourself to be tyrannized by old habits and weaknesses. If you know you are weak in the basics of grammar and spelling, let your instructor know immediately that you are serious about getting help with them. Mastering old problems will give you the confidence to explore the other aspects of writing.

2. *Spend time with your topic.* Once you have chosen a topic, try talking about it with your friends. Listen to the vocabulary they use in discussing it; listen to yourself. Make a mental note of any phrases or quotable statements that might provide a good introduction or conclusion to your essay. Rehearse a few openings mentally as you drive or walk to school. Live with your topic. Then when you sit down to write, the blank page will not look so formidable. You will have achieved enough familiarity with what you want to say to at least have a beginning.

3. *Keep a list of possible topics.* It is a good idea to keep a pocket-sized notebook with ideas for think pieces, essays you could write without any outside research. Jot down thoughts about things that make you angry, unusual scenery you would like to describe, mannerisms of someone you know, anything at all. Then when you are asked to do a free theme essay in class, you will have a store of ideas to look over to help you get through those first few moments of panic.

4. *Concentrate on a feeling of accomplishment.* Once you have written something successfully (you may judge your success by the reaction of your readers), try to keep the good feelings from this experience in your mind when struggling with composing. Imagine the favorable comments of your classmates as you work at making a description real, or an argument convincing. Keep the rewards of writing well before you always, and remember that a little anxiety is a natural reflection of the fact that you care about your audience.

SUMMARY

Communication apprehension is a common, recurring phenomenon. Each of us experiences some communication apprehension on some occasions. Rather than trying to rid ourselves of our apprehension we should attempt to understand it and cope with it.

Communication apprehension is the result of both personal traits and communication situations. For the purposes of this book we have focused on speech anxiety and writer's block. We have indicated the common psychological symptoms associated with speech anxiety and writer's block and then attempted to provide some coping mechanisms that have proved useful to others. If you will follow the advice given in this chapter and your instructor's advice, you should begin to notice that your anxiety has lessened.

There is, of course, no substitute for practice in speaking and writing. The more opportunities you accept, the more you will come to understand your own personal brand of communication apprehension. If you think about this discussion we believe you will agree that cancer, death, and cramped spaces are indeed much worse.

KEY WORDS

trait apprehension	speech anxiety peak
state apprehension	writer's block
speech anxiety syndrome	coping mechanisms

EXERCISES

1. Fill out the Speech Anxiety Graph given here. In groups of five, discuss your results. Is there a pattern of response in your group? Does there appear to be a speech anxiety peak? If so, go back to the chapter, page 97, and see if the coping mechanisms listed for the speech anxiety peak are helpful. Can you think of others?

Speech Anxiety Graph

Instructions: Think about the last speech you presented for this class. Think particularly about the speech anxiety you experienced. Describe this anxiety with the help of the graph given below. On the vertical axis at left below are terms describing speech anxiety from No Anxiety or 1 to Very High or 7. On the horizontal axis below right are terms prior, to, during and after a speech presentation. Graph the amount of anxiety you felt by making an X at each of the points A to E. Then connect the Xs with a line.

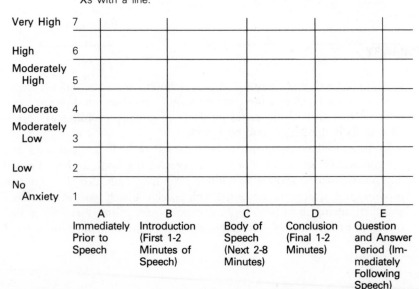

Very High	7
High	6
Moderately High	5
Moderate	4
Moderately Low	3
Low	2
No Anxiety	1

A	B	C	D	E
Immediately Prior to Speech	Introduction (First 1-2 Minutes of Speech)	Body of Speech (Next 2-8 Minutes)	Conclusion (Final 1-2 Minutes)	Question and Answer Period (Immediately Following Speech)

2. Analyze your own communication apprehension. Write down those traits you have that might cause apprehension and those situations that generate anxiety in you. Next write down ways that you have discovered to cope with your anxieties, as the students cited in this chapter have.

3. Interview someone who speaks or writes professionally. Find out about the person's apprehensions, and also about coping mechanisms the writer or speaker has found useful. Are the anxieties of this communicator similar to yours? Could you use any of this person's strategies for handling anxiety?

REFERENCES

McCroskey, James, and Virginia Richmond. *The Quiet Ones: Communication Apprehension and Shyness.* (Dubuque, Iowa: Gorsuch and Scarisbrick, 1980).

Gilder, Joshua. "Creators on Creating: Tom Wolfe," *Saturday Review* (April, 1981), p. 43.

6. Time Patterns: Narration, Process, Cause-Effect

What if you lost your ability to remember?

You would not be able to bake a cake because you would forget the ingredients and would fail to recall when you put the cake in the oven. You would not be able to make a decision about buying a house or a car, about getting married, or about choosing a college major or a career, because such decisions depend on an ability to anticipate future events on the basis of past experience. A person who has lost the ability to remember through illness or physical injury is

> . . . like someone who is forever arriving in the middle of a ball game and is compelled to check the scoreboard to see what is going on; or who is always entering a movie house in the midst of a showing, and is forced to attempt to reconstruct the plot. Every time his attention wanders for an instant, there is a new ball game, or a new film; he does not know how he got there, what has happened, and what is likely to occur next.
>
> (Gardner, 1965)

Memory rests on the ability to evaluate and catalogue events as they occur, to ask and answer such questions as "What happened?" "How did it happen?" and "Why did it happen?" Because some unfortunate individuals are unable to ask these questions, they cannot perceive time and change.

For most people, however, *What? How?* and *Why?* are tools of understanding. They represent basic mental patterns we use to understand and control experience. These conceptual patterns appear in our speaking and writing as well, reflecting the way we think about a topic and making it easier for an audience to understand what we have to say. When they appear in speaking or writing, the patterns can be called conceptual patterns of discourse. The conceptual patterns include time patterns (narration, process, cause and effect) and static patterns (analysis, enumeration, comparison, classification, description, definition, exemplification). This chapter discusses time patterns; the chapters that follow it discuss static patterns.

Narration, the first pattern to be reviewed, presents an event or a series of events, including the setting and characters, in effect creating or recreating the event. Narration answers the question "What happened?" Process, the second pattern, isolates the steps or states that make up a series of events, making clear their functions and answering the questions "How does it work?" and "How can it be done?" The third pattern, cause and effect, looks backwards and forwards from an event, asking what is responsible for making it happen ("Why did it happen?") and what further events it is likely to cause in turn ("What is likely to happen in the future?").

These patterns appear more or less directly in many kinds of speaking and writing:

Narrative — oral and written stories, novels, biographies, television dramas, testimony before a committee, travel books, oral and written reports

Process — explanations and demonstrations, instruction manuals, recipes, textbooks

Cause and effect — accident reports, scientific papers, memoirs, political speeches, editorials, business reports

By being aware of the patterns, by developing a kind of form consciousness, you can improve your own writing and speaking considerably.

NARRATION

Using Narration

Narration is a basic mental pattern. We use it to store and process much that we experience in the course of a day. There are, of course, other ways to remember and deal with experience. We can create lists (enumeration); we can break something down into its parts (analysis); or we can set up categories as pigeonholes for facts and ideas. For the most part we use mental patterns like these in special circumstances, such as when we have to remember lecture notes for a test or when we are learning an important procedure. When it comes to everyday sorts of remembering, most of us use a narrative pattern — we remember what happened to us.

Test yourself for a moment: What did you have for breakfast two days ago?

If you are like most people, the answer didn't come to mind immediately because most of us do not store eating experiences in a special mental pattern like this:

Meals: (1) breakfast, (2) lunch, (3) dinner, (4) snacks (morning) (afternoon) (evening)

When you tried to figure out what you ate, you probably went to a narrative slot in your mind, one labeled "What happened to me two days ago." There you found something like this:

> I got up early because Physics, my first class of the day, is tough, and I needed the extra time to study for the scheduled quiz.
> I was tired, so I put on some old jeans and a wrinkled shirt, washed quickly, brushed my hair, then . . .
> I went over to the cafeteria; I could smell bacon and eggs cooking . . .

> That's it: scrambled eggs — I had scrambled eggs, and they were terrible.

Narration not only helps us store information, it also allows us to experience an event again. When something especially pleasant or unpleasant happens we often store it in our memories in order to be able to call it up again hours, days, or weeks later to enjoy the pleasant moment, relive an embarrassment, or bring back anger. Often an event keeps running through our minds in this manner:

> I can't believe how nasty she was to me today; I mean, I hadn't seen her in a couple of days and I was feeling so good because it was a beautiful day outside, so I stuck my head into her room and said "Hi! How's everything going?" And she looked up with a really mean look on her face and said, "Everytime I really get involved in something, you figure out a way to interrupt me. Leave me alone!" I can't believe it; I can't believe how nasty she was. I mean, all I did was . . .

In speaking and in writing, narrative patterns make it possible to share experience, to examine it, to relive it, and even to imagine it. As a result, narrative patterns can be used for a variety of purposes.

Narratives can inform. Newscasts, newspapers, and magazines are perhaps the most obvious places where narratives provide information, but histories, biographies, scientific reports, and business reports also present information through narratives. Accident reports, insurance claims, speeches at banquets, and testimony before legislative committees all contain narratives that inform.

Narratives designed to inform usually try to present events as accurately as possible, but not all narratives of this sort need to be completely objective. A narrative that reports personal experience will inevitably be shaped by the attitudes and limitations of the person on whose experience it is based. Some situations call for objective narratives: scientific reports and accident reports, for example. Others may encourage a personal viewpoint: an invitation to speak on travel experiences to a social, church, or community group, for instance.

Narratives can also argue. Such narratives generally avoid trying to present all the details of an event; they are selective, and they emphasize certain aspects of an event in order to persuade an audience or move it to action. Editorials and political speeches are two occasions that call for narratives that argue. Narratives used to argue seldom take up a whole speech or essay; they are usually used to make a point powerfully, often in an opening, and to support the argument.

Narratives can also express feelings about an event and try to get the audience to understand and share the feelings. Narratives of this kind, however, occur primarily on informal occasions: in conversations in which we want to share our feelings with friends, in letters, or in diaries and journals. In formal writing and speaking, however, expressive narratives are often simply elements of stories whose main purpose is to bring pleasure to the audience, to entertain.

Most written and spoken narratives come into being simply because creating them brings pleasure to the author or speaker and pleasure to the audience as well. Storytelling is an ancient art, practiced around campfires, over dessert at the dinner table, and in short stories and novels. Many people claim that the purpose of stories is to combine pleasure and instruction, to entertain while shedding light on human behavior. While this is true, it is also true that many good stories aim at nothing more than providing the pleasure of a well-told story, one that allows the audience to experience the world created by the storyteller, its **setting**, its events, its characters. The following student speech combines some of these different elements. Although it is clearly designed to make the audience laugh, it also invites the audience to share the emotions the speaker felt at the time of the events.

> When I was a boy I attended St. Joseph's school. As was tradition, most of the male students were also altar boys at the adjoining church. One particular Sunday in November stands out in my mind as a truly embarrassing experience. I was in the Sanctuary, which is the back part of the church, dressing up in my vestments, which consisted of a long, black hooded frock secured at the waist with a white rope belt. It was at this time that I first noticed that my frock was a bit too long and might cause me to trip. But I carelessly disregarded this notion.
>
> Upon leaving the Sanctuary, I noticed that the church was extremely full for a regular Sunday. But I wasn't afraid, for I was an altar boy of several years' experience. The Mass proceeded well under the direction of Father Reilly, the eighty-four-year-old pastor of the church — until the time came for me to bring the container of wine and the empty chalice to Father Reilly, who was standing behind the altar. The altar was constructed of white marble and was accessible only by a series of steps followed by a landing and another series of steps on either side.
>
> I grasped the container of wine and assaulted the steps with ease. I then returned for the empty chalice. The antique silver chalice had been with the church since the church had opened. I grasped the heavy silver chalice at the base and again at the stem and started to ascend the steps. I reached the second to last step, and that is where fate had sealed my destiny. It seemed that my frock had gotten caught under my left foot, preventing me from putting my right foot on the next step. Feeling myself falling forward in slow motion, I threw my arms out to break my fall. This resulted in my hurling the heavy silver chalice at Father Reilly. It narrowly missed his shoulder, landed, bounced, and began its way down the first flight of stairs.
>
> I was now lying face down on the cold marble floor and I noticed that the organist had stopped and the church was silent except for the incessant clanging of the chalice as it bounced down the stairs. Then, as a final insult, it rolled on the landing approaching the second flight of

stairs, paused momentarily on the edge, and continued down the second flight of stairs, allowing the parishioners another chance to view the spectacle if they had missed the first. Finally it came to rest against the first pew.

Then I gathered up as much self-confidence as I could, lifted myself up, and slowly limped over to the now dented chalice. I replaced it with another and continued on with the Mass amidst a field of stifled laughter. It was after this incident that I always made sure that the frock I was wearing was at least six inches too short.

— Jerry Thibeault

Getting Materials

Materials for narratives can come from three places: experience, imagination, and research. Which you use will depend in part on the writing or speaking occasion and in part on your purpose.

If the occasion requires you to communicate about some event you have not experienced directly, your research skills will come into play. In a history class, for example, you might be asked to prepare a review of the events leading up to the Civil War. In this case you would turn to books and scholarly articles. On the job you might be asked to prepare a report on an accident in a factory. In this case your research would consist of interviews with participants and an examination of the scene.

If the occasion calls for you to speak or write from your personal experience, then most of the techniques described in Chapter Two of this text will help you probe your experience and turn it into a speech or essay. In business and in social settings, your audience will often be very interested in hearing what special experiences you have had, so as you probe your experience you should try to remember as many events and details as you can. While you are likely to uncover much more material than a good narrative can employ without losing focus and overwhelming the audience with irrelevant detail, you can always prune your material as you revise or rehearse what you have to say. Starting with a wealth of detail will aid you in recreating the events of your narrative so that the audience can experience what happened as fully as possible; cutting can come later.

One thing to remember as you probe your experience is that your memory is probably lazy. At first it will probably not yield up all the events and detail necessary to recreate an experience. You may need to probe it again and again, forcing it to recover all the sensory information, all the words, gestures, and actions that made up the experience and need to be conveyed to the audience.

If your imagination is the source of your narrative, you can probe it using the same techniques you use to probe your memory. Your imagination can also be a bit lazy, and you may need to push it some to get the detail you need for a successful narrative.

The Finished Product

Point. A narrative should have a purpose, or point. The purpose may be to get readers or listeners to agree with your opinion about something (the silliness of most high school regulations; the need to preserve our natural environment); it may be to get the audience to share the feelings you had as the result of an experience; or it may be simply to get the audience to laugh or feel sad. In most cases the purpose needs to be clear at the beginning of the narrative; otherwise the audience may fail to understand why the story is being told or how the events support the point the author is trying to make. At worst, the audience may react improperly, laughing at events the author wants to present as part of a chain of tragic misunderstandings.

Titles are an important device for conveying purpose. A title like "Ginger, Pup, and the Dead-end Kids," for example, suggests a light-hearted look at childhood, while "The Day Grandfather Died" suggests a sad, perhaps sentimental reminiscence. Some narratives make use of an explicit thesis statement to indicate purpose. A narrative argument, for instance, might begin, "I had an experience this past summer that reflected the unfairness of a town ordinance prohibiting glass containers in the park." The story of the dropped chalice announces its purpose less explicitly, but no less clearly: "One particular Sunday in November stands out in my mind as a truly embarrassing experience."

Choosing whether or not to begin with a thesis is an important decision because it is, in effect, a decision about the purpose of a narrative. If you believe that your narrative is most interesting for the characters or events it presents, or if your primary aim is to get your audience to react in a certain way — to laugh, to wonder, or to cry — then you probably do not need an explicit thesis statement. If you believe that your narrative is interesting for some statement it makes or for the support it lends to an idea, then you probably want to open with a thesis or end with a general statement or moral. Since a good narrative ought to be interesting both on its own and for what it has to say, the choice of a strategy is often difficult. Curiously enough, though storytelling for pleasure is one of the oldest human pastimes, when it comes to writing or speaking in public most of us find it hard to let a narrative stand on its own. If in writing a draft or rehearsing a speech you find that you have included a thesis statement, take a close look at your work and decide whether the thesis belongs in the final version.

As you read the following student essay try to decide what its point is, and once you have decided consider whether or not it should have been indicated in an explicit thesis statement:

Popcorn or Not?

My stomach growled as the woman in front of me walked away with her puffy, buttery, and mouthwatering bucket of popcorn. I stepped up to the counter and said, "Can I have two small boxes of popcorn?" The tall man behind the counter looked right by me.

"May I help you?" he said to the couple in back of me.

At first I was confused. Then I figured that he probably did not hear me, so I patiently waited for the couple in back of me to get their order. When they were through, I said in a louder tone than the first time, "Could I please have two boxes of popcorn?" I was sure that he heard me; however, he turned to the young girl beside me and said, "What would you like?"

She, with a look of surprise on her face, hesitated for a second and then ordered. My first reaction to the actions of the man behind the counter was vexation. I knew for sure that he had heard me, and I knew that he was not blind. I stood there as the popcorn in the machine began to pop, and I thought to myself, "Those other people were probably here before you. Go ahead and order. He'll take your order this time for sure." As an elderly man walked up to me and stood beside me, I said, once again, "Could I please have two boxes of popcorn?"

The man behind the counter looked right into my eyes. His eyes looked like two lifeless and cold planets, and his facial expression conveyed indifference. "May I help you, sir?"

"Oh, my God! That man just came and the guy asked him before he asked me!" At that point I knew the guy behind the counter was purposely ignoring me because I was black and he was white. "You ignorant jerk!" I thought — I dared not say it. I did not want to start any trouble.

The man continued to wait on the white customers. I knew that I was not going to get any popcorn, so I slowly turned around and began to walk back to my seat. As I approached the seat, my girlfriend turned around.

"Where's the popcorn?" she asked. My eyes suddenly began to fill up with tears.

"I can't cry in front of her — in front of all these people; I've got to hold it in," I thought. "Oh, the popcorn! My girlfriend who was at the counter told me that it was stale, so I didn't bother to get any."

The lights dimmed, and Act Two was about to begin. I sat there in the dark. I was empty-handed, hurt, and alone in my sorrow.

— Roxann Jeffreys

Pattern. The action of a narrative consists of characters operating within a specific setting. Most narratives begin, therefore, by providing necessary background through answers to the questions *Who? What? When? Where? Why?*

Who — main character or characters
What — beginning of the action
When — time
Where — setting or place
Why — thesis or indication of purpose; cause of the events

Often, however, an author will leave out one of these elements in order to create a sense of mystery and to keep the audience reading or listening to find out what is going on. The opening of "Popcorn or Not?" for example, leaves out the *why* so that people will keep on reading to get an explanation of the events.

After the introduction, the events in most successful narratives come in clear order, following a pattern common in one form or another to all narratives:

Introduction (who, what, when, where, why)
   Event 1 (or Episode 1)
   Event 2 (or Episode 2)
   Event 3 (or Episode 3)
   Event 4, 5, 6, (or Episodes 4, 5, 6) . . .
Conclusion (falling action)

In the early stages of drafting a narrative speech or essay we usually follow the simplest narrative pattern, beginning with the first event and moving chronologically to the final event. Good narratives, however, may begin with a long description of the setting or with some dramatic material from the middle of the chain of events. Note how the student narrative below begins in the middle of things and then fills in the prior events by means of a flashback — that is, memories or dreams of earlier **episodes**:

My Turn

"Bob Hamann."

I was never more displeased at hearing my own name. At once, my heart began pounding at about twice its normal rate. She had actually called on me; it was my turn to give my oral presentation to the class.

I realized at that moment how much I disliked Miss Hall. She had more than twenty students to choose from, and she had to select me. I was partially hidden behind the bouffant hairdo of the girl who sat in front of me; I had hoped desperately that Miss Hall wouldn't notice me that morning. I had looked everywhere except towards the front of the room, not wanting to meet her glance. But all of my ploys were unsuccessful; I would not be given another reprieve. I had been called upon; today was my day.

"Robert."

"Don't get nervous; I'm coming," I thought, further annoyed by her use of my proper name.

With sweating hands, I gathered my notes, which I had tucked away in my notebook. She watched me with that familiar half-smile of hers. It was an annoying look that seemed to say she knew I wasn't well prepared. She seemed to take pleasure in knowing I was about to make a fool of myself. My legs trembled slightly as I stood up.

It wasn't as though I hadn't had enough time to prepare for the presentation. It was no surprise assignment. For weeks we had gone over the fundamentals of writing a research paper. On the first day of class, we had been warned that we would be required to hand in a twenty-page paper and orally present our subject to the class.

Unfortunately, I had typically waited until the last few days. I had thumbed desperately through an encyclopedia for a suitable topic. I had settled on a particular poet whom I knew nothing about. William Blake became my subject because the school library had a phonograph record of some of his works; I figured that would take up part of the required time that I had to fill. The paper was due in less than a week, so I began immediately. When three days and three long nights were over, my paper was finished. Never had I written a paper so quickly, or one with so little content.

These thoughts raced through my mind as I walked to the podium. Once I was in place before the class, my main thought was getting the thing over with. With very little feeling, I told the rest of the class what I knew about William Blake, poet. My mouth was so dry I wasn't sure, at times, whether or not it would open again for my sentence. My hands shook uncontrollably as I turned the pages in front of me. Finally, referring to my notes more often than was expected of me, I finished the oral part of my presentation.

All that was left was to play the record; the worst was now over. There was no more need to be nervous.

With what I considered to be complete control, I lifted the arm of the record player. Before I even realized that my hands were still shaking, I scratched the needle over the entire record. The piercing sound screeched through the room for what seemed like minutes until finally the needle fell into the proper groove.

— Bob Hamann

In order to avoid confusion and to demonstrate the relationship between individual episodes and the purpose of the whole discourse, narratives need to make clear the pattern they are following. One important way to alert an audience to the pattern is to use transitions, cue words and phrases like *a little bit later, yet, so* (meaning *therefore*), and *when*, to indicate where episodes begin and end and to indicate how events are related to each other. Here is a list of some useful words and phrases for narratives:

then	while	at that time
when	yet	simultaneously
next	first	before long
later	second	presently
afterwards	third	following that
shortly	once upon a time	finally

The events in most narratives are arranged in order of increasing intensity (**rising action**). The conflict or mystery builds until it is resolved (crisis → resolution) and then ends quickly (**falling action**). When a narrative is designed to support a thesis, it also usually follows an ascending order ending with the events that most clearly support the thesis.

Detail. The detail necessary for a successful narrative varies from case to case. There is not much concrete detail in the story of the dropped chalice, but what there is has been carefully chosen. Because of it the audience can see the layout of the church and hear the sound of the chalice as it bounces down the stone steps. If there were many more visual or auditory details, however, the drama of these events would be diluted and attention would be drawn away from the sense of embarrassment the altar boy feels as he and the congregation watch and hear the chalice rolling and falling.

Written narratives usually contain more detail than oral narratives because a lot of detail can make an oral narrative hard to follow. Readers, on the other hand, can always reread a passage if they have lost track of the story. A narrative whose aim is to display the richness of an experience and to explore the characters' reactions would also usually contain a lot of detail. The following student essay, for example, draws heavily on senses like sight, sound, and touch to describe the character's mood and the events themselves. Take note of how specific the detail is; by describing objects specifically, even down to their color, the author helps readers visualize the scene and thereby share the emotions that the character feels.

A Cold Night for Camping

I am freezing. Every inch of my skin is covered with goose bumps. That is, every inch excluding those few that make up my left knee. The knee is hot and swollen from being twisted on a hike earlier in the day. My sprained knee really makes me feel confined. I will be forced to stay at this New Hampshire campground for a good long while.

In an effort to avoid freezing, I am wearing every bit of clothing that I brought on this mountain camping trip. This includes a red-and-white striped tube top; a white, short-sleeved T shirt; my favorite navy blue sweat shirt; two pairs of cutoffs; and three pairs of white sweat socks. I should explain that these were appropriate clothes before a freak storm turned a warm June day into a twenty-five-degree June night. As I lie here shivering, I am furious with myself for not planning better. I did not even bring a pair of long pants! I was carried away by the romantic aspects of summer camping and neglected to be practical. If I do get frost-bitten while stranded on this mountain, I probably deserve it.

The fluffy, down-filled sleeping bag that I am curled up in is guaranteed to keep the camper warm until twenty below zero. I would guess from the way my teeth are chattering that the warranty is up.

My flashlight, which I refuse to turn off, focuses a sharp ring of light on the right-hand side of the yellow and blue vinyl tent. I stare at the sides of the tent being violently sucked in and billowed out as the wind howls through. It was that same wind that kept putting out the campfire earlier in the evening. Because of that there was no way to cook any food. The noisy growling of my stomach is competing with the howl of the wind, and I am beginning to wonder just how long I can put up with this.

The hail is falling in erratic patterns. At one moment only four or five hailstones will bang intermittently against the vinyl. Then, a second later, the tent will be bombarded with a flurry of hailstones. The noise becomes deafening, and I start to worry. I am worried about freezing, or starving, or the tent collapsing from the wind, or a thousand other things that could happen during a mountain storm in the middle of the night.

Closing my eyes, I try to calm myself down. I remember the daytime when I enjoyed the outdoors. I think about the grassy plateau that the tent is on and the deep, scented pine grove around this small clearing. In my mind I can see the sparkling brook that gurgles as it runs past the campsite and on down the mountain. Best of all though are the giant mountain peaks that completely surround this beautiful scene.

I wish it were daytime so I could see all of this around me.

I wish it were daytime so that sun could warm things up and I could get some food. But instead it's dark, without even the moon or stars, and it's freezing, with the wind and hail making the cold more bitter. I do not know the exact time, but I do know that it has to be day before long. So I will just wrap myself a little tighter in my sleeping bag and wait for morning. Sometimes when you find your-

self helpless in a bad situation that is all you can do, just hang on
. . . and wait for morning.

— Monica DeCubellis

Style. The success of a narrative depends to a great extent on the verbs it contains. Since the narrative pattern focuses on what happens, the verbs need to be interesting in themselves so that they capture the relationship between characters and events:

> grasped, towed, watered, smashed, emerged, thinned, gathered, burst, chased, saw, chattered, thought, drove, passed, played, jumped, flew, sighed, fell, hit, dozed, gnawed, shattered.

Verb tense — past, present, and future — is important, too, because it helps clarify the relationship among events. Choosing verb tense carefully is particularly important in a narrative like "A Cold Night for Camping," where the action takes place in the present but includes memories of things that happened in the past — that is, earlier in the day. If all the events in a narrative or in one of the sections in a narrative belong in the same time frame, however, then it is important to present them in the same tense to avoid confusing the audience. In informal discourse, nonetheless, we sometimes shift from the past tense to the present in order to make events seem more intense and dramatic:

> After all these thing had happened, I decided that nothing else could possibly go wrong, so I stretched out on my bed and put my head under the pillow to try to shut everything out and get a little sleep when all of a sudden [tense shift] in comes Joey and she shouts that the stove is on fire and the kitchen is filling up with black smoke. . . .

This device fails in formal speaking situations, though, because the audience finds it distracting; it makes a formal speech sound like a chatty, loosely-structured story being told to a small group of friends. In addition, speakers are often misled by the tense shift. They begin to lose sight of the plan they are following and start filling up the speech with irrelevant detail. The consequences of such a tense shift can be even more serious in writing because a reader lacks the visual and aural cues signaling that a tense shift is for emphasis rather than an indication that the events occurred at a different time. Many readers will either lose track of the events or become irritated over the writer's seeming lack of control over the time frame of the narrative.

Pronouns also play an important role in narratives. In some stories the speaker (**narrator**, in written works) appears directly as *I* or, as part of a group, *we* or *us*. Since *I*, *we*, and *us* are first-person pronouns, stories that use this strategy are said to be **first-person narratives**. In other stories there is no *I* and the characters are referred to by third-person pronouns, *he, she, it, one, they*. Stories of this kind are **third-person narratives**. Few stories turn away from the action to address the audience directly as you, though this tactic can sometimes be useful. It is most effective in an opening thesis statement or a closing generalization designed to involve the audience directly in the action of the narrative and in its implications. This passage from the narrative essay shown on page 74 begins with *you* and shifts to *I* for the body of the story:

Learning the Hard Way

Did you ever dare to do something that you knew was wrong, yet did it because everyone else did? Well, I did.

I went through six years of school, including kindergarten, envying my friends and fellow classmates who could get away with chewing bubblegum in class. How I wished I had their boldness and their shrewd defiance. During fifth grade, however, one of my close friends brought to class a brand new flavor of "Bub's Daddy," one of the juiciest, most flavorful bubblegums on the market . . .

— Carolyn Senerchio

Finally, the words spoken by characters can be an important part of a good narrative. In many cases, of course, it is enough to report indirectly what characters have to say: "As soon as he felt the water through his sneakers, John started yelling for a bucket or a coffee can or anything else that he could use to bail and keep us from sinking into the black, smelly water of the pond." Every time you come across a phrase like *he said that* in a draft of a paper or in a speech you are rehearsing, you should consider whether a bit of dialogue or a monologue would be more effective. Look at "My Turn" and "Popcorn or Not?" to see how effective direct quotations can be.

PROCESS

. . . underlying all Nixon's political qualities, good and bad, is curiosity — a fascination with How Things Work. In any private conversation with Nixon, this characteristic surfaces almost immediately: how do things get done? Those who have perceived this quality only at its most vile in the famous transcripts should be reminded that these were conversations held in the worst season and the worst crisis of the man's life. The same qualities of curiosity, probing, suspicion, reflection as I have heard them over the years, in and out of the Oval Office, can make him also one of the most absorbing and impressive of conversationalists . . . . The conversations have run from the brilliant to the humdrum — but always as a theme, the same theme: How Things Work. If you knew how to get the proper buttons, you could press them.

(White, 1975)

The curiosity about how things work that is the distinguishing characteristic of Nixon's personality is really not unique. In fact, the desire to understand processes — the workings of things — is basic to the way our minds operate.

Magazines are filled with articles that answer the questions, "How does it work?" and "How do I do it?":

"How to Stay in Shape Naturally"
"Do-It-Yourself Solar Heat Pool and Hot Tub"
"Medical Emergency Guide"
"How to Water Your Plants"
"Home Repairs Made Easy"
"The ABCs of Appraisals — Why, How, and Where to Find the Best Appraiser for Your Important Objects"

Billboards are filled with announcements of lectures on:

"How to Plan Your Estate"
"How to Assert Yourself"
"Home Gardening in Three Easy Stages"

Despite wide differences in subject matter, these presentations have a common approach. They take a complex procedure, mechanism, or event and divide it into the steps or stages that lead from the first event to the final one, or from raw material to finished product. This act of division makes it easier to understand the complex and often subtle changes that occur around us every day: how a flower grows, how decisions get made, how a poem gets written, and how a house gets built. To view anything as a series of steps leading to a particular end result or product is to view it as a process.

Using Process

Process is concerned with how things happen, with changes and with the patterns or operations that make change possible. Viewing any event as a process is a basic and essential operation of the human mind.

Events occur rapidly, sometimes seemingly all at once, and it is often difficult to understand at first how they happen. A tennis player throws the ball in the air and serves it perfectly into the opponent's courts; a good knitter's fingers move so quickly it is difficult to see them, let alone figure out what they are doing. It is even harder to follow such internal events as the process by which someone creates a good essay, prepares a good speech, or makes a correct decision about a complicated problem. Our minds normally respond by splitting events into parts, thereby slowing down the process of change so that we can better understand it and perhaps come to control and manipulate it.

When we first observe a complicated machine or an assembly line, for example, we tend to notice only a blur of wheels and gears and a rush of people going in all directions with tools in their hands. But soon our minds begin to impose order on the activity, turning it into clusters of parts and of actions linked together for a specific purpose.

In our complex technological society, speakers and writers are often called on to explain a complicated procedure or a new product. On these occasions, process as a pattern of thought provides a way of understanding a subject, and as a pattern of expression it provides a way to convey the understanding to an audience. Thus people who write operating manuals for home computers or who demonstrate and sell word processors make use of process patterns. So do people preparing business reports describing an efficient new manufacturing procedure, or people outlining for a community group a speech on inexpensive ways to insulate homes.

Most occasions calling for a process pattern are ones in which your purpose will be to inform or persuade. As a nurse, physician, or medical technician, for example, you may decide to use a process pattern to help explain to your colleagues a delicate new medical procedure or a piece of complicated equipment, or you may use the pattern to help demonstrate to administrators the effectiveness of a product or procedure in such a way that they will be willing to put money behind it. As a student you may need to write up the procedures for bringing a band to campus so that the other members of the campus entertainment committee will know how to do it. Or as a member of a food cooperative, you may find that you are responsible for explaining the organization's operating procedures to prospective members, just as in this excerpt from a student speech:

> You are also provided with an opportunity to learn how a co-op operates. All members are required to work a minimum of two hours per month or pay a twenty percent markup. The work is divided into various committees with diversified duties, such as running the cash register, ordering and maintaining food stocks, or publishing a monthly newsletter.
>
> Now how does this work for you? Let me try to show you. Each member is required to make a refundable deposit that is used as operating capital. It is approximately equal to the amount they spend each week with a five-dollar minimum. The work obligation for working members is related to the amount they have on deposit. For

instance, if you put down five to fourteen dollars, you are required to work three hours a month, and so on.

— Lori Walker

Process can have other uses, too. You can use it to appeal to your audience's curiosity, or you can use it to convey feelings or recreate a scene, as in an account of how your grandmother prepared Thanksgiving dinner, or how you played a complicated game with your friends when you were a child.

Getting Materials

Sometimes the writing or speaking situation will dictate the topic and require you to follow a process pattern. Your supervisor at work, for example, might say, "Write me a report outlining the steps we should take to introduce our new product to the Los Angeles area." At other times the occasion may dictate the topic but leave you free to choose process as the best and most interesting approach: "I've been asked by a local consumer group to talk about auto repairs (or deceptive advertising, or income tax preparation), and I already know a good deal about the topic. Perhaps the best way to approach the speech is to tell how most auto repairs are done and what members of the audience can do on their own, because that way they will come away from the speech not only knowing more about the topic but also with some practical knowledge for everyday situations." Sometimes you will be free to choose both the topic and the approach:

> What do I know about? Lacrosse — I've played it for three years. It's an unusual game and perhaps people would like to hear about it. I could entitle my speech, "Playing Lacrosse for Fun and Pain."

> What would I like to find out about? FDA approval of new drugs — I've always wondered why it takes so long and I'll bet my potential readers have too. I could call my essay, "From Laboratory to Drug-store: How a New Drug Gets FDA Approval."

Once you have chosen a topic and have decided to view it as a process, you need to begin gathering materials for your discourse. For many topics, of course, your knowledge and experience will provide enough material. Yet even if you already know a good deal about a topic you may discover, as you begin jotting down your ideas, that you need to know more about it before you can explain it clearly to an audience. If the topic has been dictated to you or if you have chosen it because you want to learn more about it, then you will clearly have to do some searching for materials.

Magazines and books are good sources of information, but interviewing people is a particularly effective way to find out how things happen. In order to get the necessary information from an interview you need to ask appropriate questions. This is also true for written sources. "How does it happen?" is the basic process question, but each topic requires its own set of more specific questions: "How many people are involved?" "How quickly can it be done?" "Can any steps be skipped?" "What are the most difficult procedures?" You may not know enough about your topic at the beginning to be able to formulate such probing questions; the people you interview, however, will be able to suggest pertinent questions, as will any background reading you do.

Most people you interview will be quite helpful and will provide you with more information than you can use. The most helpful people of all will be those who have a service to offer (director of a rape crisis center —. "What can I do if I am raped?"), or those who want to defend the job they are doing (the director of campus food service — "How is dormitory food prepared?").

If you choose a topic you already know something about, then you probably will not have to do extensive interviewing or reading; yet you will still need to ask questions about your topic, particularly questions that take into account the reader's point of view: "Have I left out any essential steps?" "Have I indicated what materials are necessary for the process?" "Have I made the dangers clear?" The more familiar you are with a process the more likely you are to leave something out or to fail to understand what your audience needs to know about it. Many students enjoy writing essays or giving speeches on how a particular sport or game is scored or refereed — rugby, basketball, tennis, backgammon. Quite often they become so caught up in creating the situation for a potential score that they use technical terms for maneuvers, forgetting that the audience is probably not familiar with either the terms or the maneuvers. A student explaining rugby forgets to define *scrum*; a tennis player forgets to say what *let* and *rally* mean. Definitions and explanations are an essential part of a process presentation.

The questions you choose to ask will depend both on your topic and on what you are using the process pattern for: to give directions, to explain an unusual and interesting phenomenon, to provide the facts for an analysis of a situation or a problem, or to provide supporting evidence in an argument. Whatever the aim of the discourse, asking the appropriate questions is an important step in applying the process pattern to speaking and writing. The following selection is from the opening of a book on the federal budget — admittedly, a complicated topic and, one would think, a dull one. In the opening paragraph the author shows how process questions can be used to uncover the most important and interesting aspects of the topic. In the second paragraph he tells how questions helped guide the research that provided materials for the book. In the third paragraph he indicates the two major ways the process pattern is used in the book: to describe the budgetary process and to provide data for an analysis of the procedure.

Confronted with the vast array of figures in the Budget of the United States, one is likely to think of budgeting as an arid subject, the province of stodgy clerks and dull statisticians. Nothing could be more mistaken. Human nature is never more evident than when men are struggling to gain a larger share of funds or to apportion what they have among myriad claimants. Budgeting deals with the purposes of men. How can they be moved to cooperate? How can they find ways of dealing effectively with recalcitrant problems? Serving diverse purposes, a budget can be many things: a political act, a plan of work, a prediction, a source of enlightenment, a means of obfuscation, a mechanism of control, an escape from restrictions, a means to action, a brake on progress, even a prayer that the powers that be will deal gently with the best aspirations of fallible men.

How does the budget (the funds appropriated by Congress and actually spent) get made in American national government? In an effort to begin to answer this question, interviews were held with approximately 160 of the participants in the budgetary process — agency heads, budget officers, Budget Bureau staff, appropriations committee staff, and Congressmen. Although this research was approached from the perspective of the administrative agency, corresponding information at crucial points was sought from the standpoint of appropriation subcommittees and Budget Bureau divisions. Two basic questions were posed: How does your agency determine how much it will try to get in a particular year? How do you go about trying to achieve this goal? (A Congressman or Budget Bureau official would be asked how his unit decided what to allocate to a particular agency or program and how it sought to make its decision stick when there was a disagreement.) In the course of the interviews it was discovered that answers to these questions could not be gotten without asking still more questions. How much do you have to fight for? Where do you get clues about what is likely to be acceptable to other participants? What is the pattern of your consultations with your counterparts throughout the government? What do you have to do to be successful? How do you spend your time? The answers serve both to extend our knowledge of the budget as a political process and to challenge existing concepts of the ways in which budgetary problems are formulated and resolved. . . .

This book has a dual purpose: to describe the budgetary process and to appraise it. In the second and third chapters we seek to increase our understanding by describing the kinds of calculations made in budgeting and the types of strategies that the participants use to accomplish their purposes. In the fourth chapter proposals for reform are analyzed and it is shown that these proceed in the dark because of the lack of knowledge of how the budgetary process actually works. In the final chapter is presented an appraisal of the budgetary process and the major suggested alternatives based on the descriptive material advanced in the previous pages. An appendix on the formal powers of the participants and the timing of the budgetary cycle is included for those who are not familiar with these facts.

(Wildavsky, 1965)

The Finished Product

Point. Because the process pattern focuses on how things happen, papers and speeches that employ it are generally filled with detailed explanations and descriptions. Something that takes only a moment to do may take a long time to explain, as anyone who has tried to teach a child to tie a shoe or tell time can testify. Nurses who give vaccinations and diabetics who require insulin can fill a hypodermic needle with a few quick motions. A clear explanation, however, requires many details, as witness this student's exposition:

> Before you can make an injection you need to fill the needle in the proper manner. First, shake up the bottle (vial) of insulin to make sure the solution is mixed properly. Then open an alcohol swab package and wipe off the top of the bottle. Put the bottle down and pick up the needle. On either end of the needle are protective caps covering the needle on one end and the plunger on the other. These must be removed. Pull the plunger back to the desired dose (five units, for example). Now pick up the vial again and, holding the vial in one hand upside down and the syringe in the other hand, inject the needle into the vial through the protective covering on the top of the vial. Push the plunger all the way in. Then pull it back a little past the amount wanted (five units past the desired dosage). Inch the plunger back up to the desired amount. This will eliminate all air bubbles. Now that you have five units of insulin within the needle shaft, withdraw the needle from the vial. You are ready to make the injection.

— Cini Miller

Audiences will not tolerate such a complicated presentation for long unless they know that it has a purpose, that it leads up to something important. Thus the aim of a process speech or essay needs to be made clear from the start, either through a thesis statement or an introductory paragraph that leads the audience to expect a particular use of the process pattern.

After the opening paragraph of the following student essay, the reader knows the essay will present a set of directions:

So you have a plant two and a half feet tall growing out of a six-inch pot. Don't you think it is about time you repotted it?

To repot your plant you will need a bigger pot, plant soil, newspaper, a knife or spoon, and if your pot has no drainage holes you will also need rocks, clay pieces, or charcoal. Before you begin to dig in, place the newspaper over a large working surface. Now take the plant in the pot and using the knife or spoon go around the edge of the pot and pry the plant, roots, and soil out of it. Next, take the bigger pot, and if it has no drainage holes, place either rocks, charcoal, or broken clay pieces one to two layers deep on the bottom. Then place some of the new soil in the center of the pot so that the base of the upper part of the plant is approximately a half-inch below the lip of the pot. After you have done that, put some more soil around the plant so that it is held firmly by the soil. Now you can water and feed your plant (feeding is optional.)

Congratulations, you have just successfully repotted your plant. Another tip for repotting; if you consider your plant to be your friend, talk to it during the process. Some plant owners find that it is helpful to tell the plant what is happening and let it know how much better it will feel once it is in the new pot.

— Lisa Dickey

As the preceding paper clearly indicates, a thesis statement alone is not enough. The opening of a paper or speech needs to motivate its audience; readers and listeners must feel a need for the directions or explanation that follows. If they feel no need, they may stop reading or simply close their eyes and think while the speaker drones on.

While a set of directions usually appeals to a narrow audience — to those who want to accomplish what the directions aim at — explanations of an interesting process often aim at a wider audience. Explanations try to show that a process is interesting in itself. This point usually has to be made not only at the beginning of a discourse but throughout, either directly by comments on the importance or uniqueness of the process or indirectly by examples and details that help make the process vivid and lively.

Pattern. The structural pattern for process discourse is quite straightforward:

Process Pattern

Introduction (thesis, background, materials)
    Step 1 (stage 1) . . .   Step 4 (stage 4) . . .
    Step 2 (stage 2) . . .   Step 5, 6, 7 (stage 5, 6, 7)
    Step 3 (stage 3) . . .
Conclusion

Few process speeches or essays implement the pattern in such a simple form. Even a simple process has many small steps, and if we organize a discourse so that each step in the process corresponds to one section of the discourse, the audience may soon get bogged down in detail. The steps in a process, therefore, have to be clustered so that the discourse is divided into a few major sections, each of which in turn contains smaller steps.

Modified Process Pattern

Introduction (thesis, background, materials)
Section 1
   Step a (stage a)
   Step b (stage b)
   Step c (stage c)
Section 2
   Step x (stage x)
   Step y (stage y)
   Step z (stage z)
Sections 3, 4, 5
Conclusion

Depending on the topic and the audience, some of the smaller steps may need to be spelled out in detail while others may need to be mentioned only briefly, if at all.

To call the audience's attention to the different steps in a process and to the way the steps are related, process discourse makes frequent use of cue words. Here are some examples:

Words that identify the different steps in a process — stage, event, step, procedure, phase, condition, state, development, operation, task, occurrence

Words that link the steps by emphasizing their relationship in time — when, next, after, first, second, third, now, before, soon, while, during, the next day, much later

Words that indicate what kind of change takes place at each step — combines, changes, transforms, varies, mixes, alters, displaces, inverts, reverses, concludes, destroys, completes, disassembles, fixes, builds, refines

In the following student essay the process is divided into four major sections, each containing a number of smaller steps. The cue words at the beginning of some of the paragraphs (indicated in the reprinted essay by italics) are signals to the reader of the beginning of each major section in the process.

Strike Three

Books and pamphlets of all kinds have been written for young players just learning the game of baseball. The pages of these manuals are filled with illustrations and detailed instructions covering virtually every aspect of the game: hitting, fielding, pitching, bunting, and sliding. However, each one of these books is missing an element which is a crucial part of baseball — the strikeout!

Introduction

It takes a great deal of hard work and mental preparation to be able to strike out consistently. Most well-known major league ballplayers have been unsuccessful. However, it becomes much easier if a player knows the proper techniques.

Section 1

The *first step* in *preparing* to strike out occurs in the on-deck circle. You should have a minimum of three bats. As the pitcher throws to the batter at the plate, you swing the three bats lightly to get the feeling of hitting nothing but air. You must swing only three times; you then kneel on your left knee, place the bats under your right arm for support, and glare at the pitcher until your turn at bat.

Section 2

The *next step* is *making your way* to the plate. It is important not to appear too eager. You walk slowly, dropping one bat and then another, finally reaching the batter's box with a single weapon. You then grab a handful of dirt and rub it gently over both hands and the bat. Next, you situate yourself at the plate by furrowing large holes in the dirt with your cleats, scattering as much dirt as possible onto the plate. After a couple of half-swings, you are ready for the first pitch. You always let this pitch go by without swinging, in order to find out what kind of "stuff" the pitcher has on that particular day. "Strrrrike One!"

Section 3

Preparing for the *second pitch* is more complicated. There are several adjustments that must be made. You push your batting helmet down over your ears more securely, casually rearrange your jock strap, and spit on your hands for added grip. Before stepping back down into the footholes, you hesitate and squint down at the third base coach, who appears to be searching frantically for a misplaced tobacco pouch. You then pull your batting gloves on a little more tightly as you step to the plate. As the pitcher releases the ball, you focus your eyes on the rotation of the pitch; you want to know exactly where the ball will be when it sails across the plate. You swing the bat with moderate power, coming as close to the ball as possible without risking a hit.
"Strrrrike Two!"

Section 4

The most exciting *strike* is always the *third*. Coaches, teammates, and fans are all screaming at you now, and your adrenaline begins to soar. You yell at the skinny little batboy to get you the pine tar rag, and throw it just beyond his reach when you're done with it. You step to the plate looking fierce and determined as though the pitcher is your worst enemy. As he starts his windup, you call time out, step out of the batter's box, and wipe an imaginary speck of dirt from your eye. Now that you have broken his concentration, the pitcher is less effective. This is your chance. As the ball reaches the plate you swing with every available ounce of energy. As a cloud of smoke rises from the catcher's mitt, you listen for the sweet sound of success. "Strrrrike Three!"

— Bob Hamann

Readers of a process essay can go back and review passages they failed to understand the first time, or they can choose to re-read the whole essay. People listening to a speech, however, seldom can ask the speaker to repeat the entire speech or large portions of it; the most they can do is ask the speaker to clarify a few points in a question-and-answer period at the end of the speech. As a result, good speakers generally try to make sure that listeners understand as much as possible of the speech on first hearing. To do this they use not only frequent cue words, but also previews, internal summaries, and final summaries that repeat important information and keep listeners aware of the pattern of the speech. (Writing can use these devices too, of course.) Here are some excerpts from a student speech that makes use of all three devices:

Preview   Getting ready to go scuba diving means doing a lot more than just putting on your equipment and going into the water. Today I would like to tell you about the proper way of getting ready for a safe and enjoyable dive, a process that has three stages: 1) preparing and checking the equipment, 2) putting on the wet suit, and 3) putting on the mask and breathing equipment. . . .

Internal Summary   At this point in the process you should have checked over carefully each of the pieces of equipment on which your life will depend during the dive: the tanks, the regulator, the gauges, and you are now ready to begin putting on the wet suit. . . .

Final Summary   Your equipment is on and you just can't wait to get into the water — but don't go yet. Take a minute to run over this checklist to make sure that you have prepared yourself properly . . . .

Detail. In preparing a process paper or speech we generally end up including too much detail in the early versions because we want to make sure that every step is clear and easy to visualize. During revision or rehearsal, therefore, we have to make sure that the remaining details are those most helpful in accomplishing the purpose of the discourse. If we eliminate too much detail, however, we run the risk of boring our audience with explanations that are vague and uninteresting. The answer is to include only a few details in each section but to choose them wisely. One or two well-chosen and representative details (examples) are often enough.

Here is how one student went about explaining "How to Tell when It's the Flu (and Not Just a Little Cold)":

. . .The onset of the third symptom tells you for sure that you are experiencing the flu. Your body becomes hot with fever and your throat stings with pain. Each swallow feels like a two-inch golf ball with spikes going down your throat slowly, so very slowly.

— Mary Chabot

To explain the symptoms of flu, this student had to find details that would convey physical sensations exactly and would also agree with the experience of those readers who have had the flu. She chose well, particularly in the case of the golf ball with spikes.

In a set of directions it is usually important to present somewhere near the beginning of the piece all the materials necessary for the process. This procedure resembles a recipe, but should not be as obvious or as detailed. A list like a half-cup of flour, a quarter-teaspoonful of imported paprika, a quarter-cup of shortening, two eggs, a half-cup sugar, a square of baker's chocolate, and a dash of salt is hard to remember on a single reading or hearing, and everyone in the audience will have forgotten it after a few minutes anyway.

Sometimes the necessary detail can be supplied through graphics or visual aids. Graphics can also supplement a complicated written explanation without seeming repetitive. Figure 6-1 and Figure 6-2 are examples of visual aids that accompany written communications.

The form of illustration most appropriate for process is the **flowchart**.

A flowchart is a diagram of a process that involves stages, with the sequence of stages shown from beginning to end. The process being illustrated can range from the steps involved in assembling a bicycle to the stages by which electromagnetic waves are intercepted and modified in a radio receiver.

When creating a flowchart, consider the following points.

1. Title the flowchart clearly.
2. Assign a figure number if your report contains several illustrations.
3. Use arrows to show the direction of flow.
4. Label each step in the process . . . . Steps may also be represented pictorially or in captioned blocks.
5. Include a key if the flowchart contains any symbols your reader might not understand.
6. Have adequate white space on the page. Do not huddle your steps and directional arrows too close together.
7. As with all illustrations, place the flowchart as close as possible to that portion of the text which refers to it.

(Brusaw, Alred, and Oliu, 1976)

In a process speech, the speaker often needs to make effective use of **visual aids** — charts, pictures, and graphs. Illustrating a process, giving it a visual dimension, enhances audience comprehension and adds liveliness to

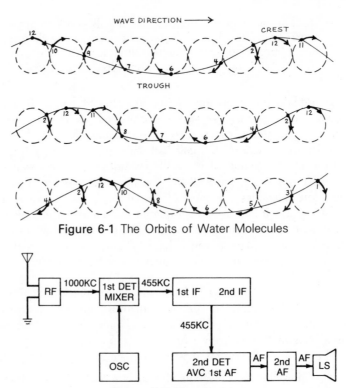

Figure 6-1 The Orbits of Water Molecules

Figure 6-2 Flowchart

the presentation. In addition, the visual aids may suggest new ways of viewing the topic and thereby help the speaker probe it more thoroughly.

In both speaking and writing, visuals should be an aid to clarification or an ornament to make the discourse more interesting. They should not be a substitute for the written or spoken text. If the text has a clear pattern and abundant detail, a visual aid may be unnecessary.

Indeed, unless you are giving a demonstration speech (see Chapter 3, "Conceptual and Conventional Patterns") you will probably want to use visual aids primarily to summarize your main points, to help explain difficult procedures, or to aid the audience in memorizing essential steps. In order to be an effective part of the text the aid needs to be detailed, listing the specific activities or characteristics of your subject.

Style. A process discourse in which the writer or speaker appears as I or we is said to be in the first person, and one in which the characters or subjects (a firefly, an exploding star, a person) are referred to as *he, she, it, one,* or *they* is said to be in the third person. This is the same as in narration. Process, however, has a third alternative. The audience can be addressed directly in the **second person,** *you.* This tactic is rarely used in narratives, but it is widely used in giving directions or in explanations. It is useful because it gives the impression of involving the audience directly in the process being described. Highly technical or scientific processes are often presented in the third person because this tactic makes the explanation sound objective and authoritative.

A first-person presentation is often chosen as a way of integrating narrative techniques with the process pattern; this strategy is particularly effective with humorous or touching material drawn from the author's experience, as in this student essay:

> "Slow down," I say to my niece. "Make little circles, not big ones."
>
> Ann Marie, my niece, is standing on a chair in front of the bathroom sink brushing her teeth. Her blue, child's soft-bristled toothbrush is gripped tightly in her hand. Toothpaste mixed with saliva is running down her chin dripping in the sink.
>
> "Spit out so you don't drip all over." I try to keep my patience as this five-year-old imp keeps wiggling around getting toothpaste all over the bathroom counter, mirror, and floor.
>
> We started out putting some Crest on her toothbrush and moistening it with water. Then guiding her hand with my own, I placed the toothbrush on the outer surfaces of her teeth and brushed them in small circular movements. Of course, she tried to bite the brush and close her mouth, but finally the outer surfaces were cleaned. Now to begin the inside surfaces.
>
> This is no easy task, for my fingers have been bitten twice, but if I can guide her hand without acquiring any more tooth marks, and have her brush the chewing surfaces with short horizontal strokes, our task will be accomplished.
>
> "No more fooling around," I say to Ann Marie. "We have only a little bit more to do." So we brush the insides, using a circular motion again, then the chewing surfaces; now her teeth are finally cleaned. I look at Ann Marie; she has toothpaste all around her mouth and water all down the front of her. I wonder what her mother will say when she sees her, but that doesn't matter for I am proud of my niece. She has accomplished a task which is not easy, and with a little more help and patience, she will soon be able to brush her teeth properly on her own.
>
> — Joan Goulart

CAUSE AND EFFECT

Using Cause and Effect

Have you had an argument lately? Have you tried to persuade a friend to do something because you think the results will be worthwhile? Have you tried to place the blame for your present situation on a friend, a relative, a teacher, or a politician? If so, you have been using the cause-and-effect pattern.

When we ask why an event has occurred or what force is responsible for creating a particular situation, we are searching for a **cause**. A cause is anything that brings about, creates, is responsible for, or produces a result. The result of a cause is an **effect**, which can be an event, situation, or object. When we talk about what is likely to happen as a result of some present action or what happened as a result of an event in the past, we are talking about effects.

Because you neglected to have the brakes on your car checked (cause), they failed and you hit a tree (effect).

Because the city made very few repairs on its sewage disposal plant during the past two decades (cause), the plant failed and began spilling raw sewage into the bay (effects).

Since the university is more interested in tuition money than in student welfare (cause), it accepted more people than the dormitories can properly accommodate, and students now have to sleep in the lounges (effects).

Some scientists claim that if we continue burning coal at the present rate (cause), the carbon dioxide released by the process (cause) will create a dangerous greenhouse effect in the atmosphere (effect).

The coach recruited a seven-foot, one-inch center last year (cause), and as a result our team finished first in the league this year (effect) and did very well in the post-season tournament (effect).

Any discussion of public policy needs to pay attention to effects: Will the bottle bill help reduce litter? Will it put people out of jobs? Will solar power be a practical source of energy? Will it help reduce our dependence on foreign oil?

Attempts to solve problems or to look to the past as a guide to the future require the isolation of causes: What changes in operating procedures will help prevent welfare fraud? What can past accidents at nuclear power plants tell us about avoiding future problems?

Public policy is not the only subject in which identification of causes and effects is a frequent pattern in thought and expression. Scientific discussions, medical texts and lectures, histories, technical reports and explanations, and even arguments about sports make regular use of the cause-and-effect pattern. More personal kinds of expression often follow cause-and-effect patterns too, just as this student essay does:

Fear of Lobster

Almost everyone has a phobia: heights, flying, a dark room. My fear is lobsters. My lobster-alarm began ten years ago and the fear is just as overwhelming today.

For as long as I can remember, my mother has loved lobster, and I have adored strawberries. This led to the horrid experience which began my phobia. After a busy morning at the market, my mother entered my playroom and enthusiastically announced, "There is a paper bag in the crisper bin of the refrigerator for you, dear."

"Must be strawberries," I said to myself as I dashed to the avocado-green refrigerator.

My small hands hurriedly opened the creaky door and proceeded to slide out the crisper compartment. The wrinkled brown bag lay in the bin waiting to be opened as I thought happily that my mother *had* brought me a surprise.

I quickly tore open the bag, then began screaming hysterically. Instead of succulent strawberries, much to my horror I found two beady-eyed lobsters clinking their threatening claws at me. The cool reddish-blue living bodies squirmed in the bag as I peered at them advancing toward me. I feared that at any moment they would escape their chilly prison and attack me with their huge pinching claws.

Hearing my screams, my mother flew into the kitchen and found me lying on the floor, quivering and sobbing uncontrollably. I cried continuously for two hours and couldn't seem to forget the shock of finding the frightful lobsters instead of juicy red strawberries.

From this time on I was very cautious of any lobster that my mother brought home for her treat. I would warily watch and listen as the monster from the deep was submerged into a large dented tin cauldron. At a safe distance, I would hesitantly watch her drop the lobster into the boiling water and I would cringe at the scraping sound it made struggling to be freed from its bubbling death.

Several years later, my new boyfriend Carl, a lobsterman, of course, brought my mother two fresh lobsters as a surprise present. I met him enthusiastically at the front door. I glanced immediately at what he had in his hands and yelled, "Stay away from me with those things, I'm afraid of lobsters!"

Being a professional lobsterman, he laughed at my outburst and retorted, "There is nothing to be afraid of; they can't hurt you at all, SEE!" He plunged toward me as I backed into the white aluminum door, shaking. The lobsters' claws grabbed onto the skin on my midsection through my aqua-blue Speedo bathing suit as Carl tried to teach me their harmlessness.

The grotesque lobster hung flapping from my stomach as I screamed and shook helplessly and my boyfriend tried to unhinge the locked claws from my flesh. I yelled frantically, "I told you I was afraid of lobsters; I told you . . .!"

Three years later, my boyfriend, the same Carl, brought me to his fishing vessel to teach me about the many wonderful aspects of lobstering. I hesitantly climbed onto the large deck hoping no lobsters would be aboard. Carl assured me once again that there was nothing to be afraid of and that the lobsters would not come into the boat and attack me. But he didn't realize that the deckhands would come onto the boat and attack me with two lobsters in each hand. This time I didn't have to explain my fear of lobsters; Carl declared it for me. "Don't go near her with those lobsters; she is really afraid of them," he warned his workmates.

Of course they laughed and skeptically replied, "Let's see just how scared she is of lobster!" The two workers slowly approached me as I backed up towards the stern of the boat. Just as I was about to fall overboard with the four lobsters, Carl caught me and pushed the pranksters away. Once again my phobia was resurrected.

This summer at a family clambake another incident occurred to reinforce my lobster phobia. The clams, clamcakes, and delicious clambake extras had been devoured and the last (and supposedly) best element was yet to be served — the lobster.

As usual, I was on kitchen duty with the other family cooking crew. Across the chaotic kitchen, I could hear Carl's father asking me to turn down the boiling pot of lobsters. I slowly trudged across the kitchen toward the stove, looking at the gigantic pot, fearing the contents passionately. I assured myself that they must be cooked, or almost, so how could they harm me. This brilliant deduction gave me a sense of security that soon proved false.

The tin cover bobbed up and down as the pot boiled. The closer I got, the louder the incessant bubbling and clanging rang in my ears. As I looked directly down at the pot and reached toward the selector knob to turn down the heat, the banging suddenly became an ear-shattering crash as the cover flew off the pot and onto the floor.

The sickly clink-clank of the dying shellfish replaced the bubbling sound. My head throbbed as I watched the massive claws threaten me from above the outer rim of the pot. I stood frozen with fear as I watched the entwined bodies roll over and over in the boiling water. I stared hypnotized at the black eyes of the sea creatures.

I finally snapped out of my lobster trance and into reality when I heard someone yelling at me to replace the cover of the pot. Once again my fear overcame me and I ran from the room crying hysterically.

I am so affected by my fear of the red-bodied shellfish that I have refused to eat, touch, or even look at lobster since the first traumatic incident. Nowadays whenever someone is cooking, consuming or catching the beast in my presence, I quiver uncontrollably. When questioned about my odd behavior, I reply, "I am afraid of lobsters!"
— Diane Elliot

When it is used to address scientific subjects, questions of public policy, and topics about which there has been much debate, cause-and-effect discourse usually pays considerable attention to logic in order to establish a logical relationship between causes and effects. Even when it is applied to more personal topics, as in "Fear of Lobster," cause-and-effect discourse pays attention to the relationship of causes and effects. Thus, although cause and effect is closely related to both narrative and process and often deals with the same kind of topics they do, it has a different emphasis: it focuses on the why of events rather than the what or how; it investigates the linking of events. "Fear of Lobster," for example, contains narrative material, but instead of telling a single story from start to finish, it begins by stating an effect — fear of lobsters — and then presents the causes in the form of four separate episodes arranged chronologically.

Getting Materials

Isolating causes and effects and describing their relationships can sometimes be a tricky business. Suppose your town contains several ponds with high levels of chemical X, the output of industries that have since left town. Suppose, too, that people living in the vicinity of the ponds have an abnormally high cancer rate. You might leap to the conclusion that chemical X is the **primary cause** of the cancer, while the manufacturing process that put it in the pond, the building of houses near the ponds, and the decision of people to live in the houses are **secondary** or **contributing causes.** This kind of argument would satisfy most of us because it seems to fulfill our standards for a logical explanation. It takes into account the factors most of us would believe are necessary to consider and it appears to have no major flaws in logic. We would consider it plausible because it fulfills the rules we have set up for judging whether or not an explanation is valid. It specifies both the cause and the necessary conditions that had to exist before the primary cause could bring about the effect.

Public health officials would not be satisfied by this train of thought, however. They would want to know if there are any other toxins or any viral substances in the water that might have caused the cancer, and they would ask if there is any evidence that the people living around the ponds actually came in contact with the chemical X in the water. In short, they would ask for a lot more evidence before they would consider chemical X the cause of the disease.

Different audiences clearly will have different standards of proof. What one listener accepts as a probable cause may seem to another to be related only loosely to the effect in question. The natural sciences like biology, chemistry, and medicine demand, for example, that all the possible contributing causes be investigated before any one is declared the probable cause. For most other audiences, however, a high correlation between cause and effect is enough. Most of us will accept something as a probable cause if, in our experience, it is usually associated with a particular result. This is the standard you can follow in your writing and speaking unless you are addressing a specialized audience.

The Finished Product

Point. When we use the cause-and-effect pattern to explore our own experience or to guide informal discussion with other people, we do not necessarily expect answers to our questions: "Why can't I get a raise?" "Will course X give me the kind of training I need to get a job?" "Why do people tolerate corrupt businessmen and politicians?" When we use the pattern in public speaking or writing, however, our audiences generally expect us to reach conclusions, to isolate specific causes and effects. To employ the pattern in a speech or essay is, in effect, to promise that you will attempt to answer the questions it poses; if you fail to do this, your audience may reasonably complain that you have contributed little to its understanding of events.

You need not always identify the primary reason for an event or predict future effects with great accuracy. Many situations are so complex that the most we can hope to do is to explore the causal links in an accurate, detailed manner. Even specialists find it difficult to accurately assess the causes of social unrest in Third World countries or to predict the outcomes of the turmoil; but after a little research most of us could point to several contributing factors (poverty, primitive farming practices, insensitive governments) and some likely results (left-wing revolutions, rise of dictators, land redistribution).

Our audiences have a right to expect that we will try to draw specific conclusions, no matter how limited, and that we will make the conclusions plain to readers and listeners. Because most causal relationships are complex and difficult to follow, a successful cause-and-effect speech or essay usually relies on multiple signals to make sure the audience understands the point being made and can follow the discussion easily. The signals fall into two categories: direct statements and cue words. A concise statement either indicating what relationships the author plans to examine or proposing a specific explanation for events is particularly useful if it comes near the opening of a discourse, as does the thesis statement in this student essay:

> Why did it happen? This is the question many people asked about the Boston Celtics basketball team. They made a 180-degree turnaround, from the second-worst record in the league one season to the best the next season, 56–18. All the players did a better job, of course. But Larry Bird, a rookie who was already a superstar and who led his Indiana State team to the NCAA basketball finals, was the main reason for the Celtics' success.
>
> — John Grossamanides

Terms that identify causes and effects can be used throughout an essay or speech as cues or reminders for the audience of the point you are trying to make and of the relationship between the causes and effects. Here are a few such terms; there are, of course, many more (those that help highlight the structure of a particular piece of discourse are listed on page 140):

result	consequence	product	origin
outcome	effect	reason	motive
cause	antecedent	accomplishment	agent
means	instrument	source	development

In discussions of history, cause and effect is often combined with narrative; in scientific discussion it is often combined with process. In these and similar situations it is important for a speaker or writer to use direct statements and cue words to guide the audience's attention to the causes and effects being discussed. In the following student essay, words and phrases that act as signals for the audience have been italicized; note how the writer uses them to keep the focus of the essay on the why of the phenomenon as well as the how:

The *Effect* of Light on Plant Growth

Introduction: Effects of light on plants — Phototropism, Circadian, Rhythms, and Photoperiodism

Anyone who grows houseplants knows that *light affects plants in many ways.* The phenomenon called phototropism (the bending of plants toward light) has been known to man for centuries. This *response* is exaggerated in houseplants since their major source of light usually comes from one direction. You may have also observed that some plants open their flowers or leaves in the morning and fold them closed at dusk. But did you know that all plants undergo twenty-four-hour cycles called circadian rhythms? If you grow Christmas cacti or other flowering houseplants you may have noticed that the amount of light they are given partially *determines* when (or if) the plants flower, a phenomenon called photoperiodism. Although scientists do not fully understand why these *responses* occur, they can now describe how they occur.

Phototropism Explanation

Phototropism is not as simple as it seems to be. In actuality plants do not bend toward light; they bend away from darkness. A plant hormone called auxin, present in the growing tips of a plant, *causes* cells on the shaded side of a plant to elongate more than the cells on the lighted side. *Why* does auxin *affect* the cells on the dark side

Possible Causes

more than the lighted side? Scientists suggested three *hypotheses* to *answer* this question. The first *explanation* was that light decreases a cell's sensitivity to light. Another possible *answer* was that light chemically deactivates or destroys auxin. The third *hypothesis* was that light *causes* auxin to migrate to the shaded side of a plant shoot.

Actual Causes

Winslow Briggs shows that the third hypothesis is true. In his experiment, he split open the growing tip and placed a thin piece of glass between the two halves. He then placed the plants before a light source, so that the glass was perpendicular to the light. The glass barred the movement of auxin to the shady side of the tip, and the shoot did not bend. Shoots with no glass plate in them bent toward the light, and when tested for auxin had much higher levels in the shaded side of the tip (unlike the plants with the glass barrier).

Circadian Rhythms Explanation

Circadian rhythms (approximately twenty-four-hour cycles which occur regularly in plants) can be seen in the wood sorrel which folds both its leaves and its flowers toward its stem at dusk. In 1729, Jean-Jaques de Mairan noticed that these movements continued in plants when they are placed in a constant, dim light. More recent studies have shown photosynthesis auxin production and the rate of cell division also have daily cycles which continue at constant environ-

Possible Causes

mental conditions. For years biologists debated whether circadian rhythms are *caused* by some environmental force other than light (such as rotation of the earth, or magnetic waves) or if they are internal factors *controlled* entirely by the plant.

Actual Causes

Biologists eventually determined that circadian rhythms are part of an internal mechanism often referred to as a biological clock. Although they will continue during constant environmental conditions, they will eventually get out of step with the earth's 24-hour day and night cycle. Light and temperature cycles *help* the plants synchronize their own internal cycles with the earth's daily cycles. Since photosynthesis can occur only in light, and bees will not pollinate flowers open only at night, it is necessary for a plant's daily rhythms to correspond to the earth's light and dark cycles.

Photoperiodism Explanation

Over fifty years ago, two scientists working for the Department of Agriculture, W. W. Garner and H. A. Allard, were experimenting with the Biloxi soybean. Even when the soybean was sown in successive two week intervals, all the plants came into flower in September. After testing the plants in a variety of controlled environments, Gardner and Allen discovered that the plants would not flower until the days became short enough. They called this biological *response* to changes in the length of days and nights photoperiodism.

Contributing Causes

There are three basic ways a plant may *respond* to the length of light in a day. Short-day plants must have a light period less than a certain critical length (which varies depending on the particular plant) to flower. Long-day plants have a specific minimum length of light each day to flower. The third category, day-neutral plants, flower regardless of the length of light in a day. More recent studies have found that if the length of darkness is interrupted briefly (one to two minutes) by light, a short-day plant will not flower. However, interrupting the daylight with darkness has no *effect* on a long-day

Primary Causes

plant. *Therefore*, it can be said that the length of light it receives significantly *affects* the time in which a plant flowers.

Conclusion:
Possible
Consequences
of the
Knowledge

Now that biologists are understanding how plants *respond* to light, this knowledge can be used to benefit man. By restricting or increasing the amount of light plants receive we can *cause* them to blossom earlier or later than usual. With today's technology we are able to get crocuses and daffodils all year long instead of only in the early spring. When we fully understand how light and other environmental factors *affect* plants, we may be able to grow fruit and other foods right here in New England that we must import now.

— Therese Mersereau

Although this essay does explain how light affects plant growth, its primary aim is to identify the correct explanations (causes) for the effect of light on plants, to show why light affects plants. The second paragraph, for example, examines three different explanations of phototropism and indicates why the third one is correct.

Pattern. Cause-and-effect discourse can follow several patterns, with the choice depending on whether we want to emphasize causes or effects.

Cause-to-Effect Patterns
Introduction (including thesis)
    Cause 1
    Cause 2
    Cause 3
    Cause 4, 5, 6 . . .
    Effect
Conclusion (summary)

Introduction (including thesis)
    Cause
    Effect 1
    Effect 2
    Effect 3
    Effect 4, 5, 6 . . .
Conclusion (summary)

Effect-to-Cause Patterns
Introduction (including thesis)
    Effect 1
    Effect 2
    Effect 3
    Effect 4, 5, 6 . . .
    Cause
Conclusion (summary)

Introduction (including thesis)
    Effect
    Cause 1
    Cause 2
    Cause 3
    Cause 4, 5, 6 . . .
Conclusion (summary)

In actual speaking and writing, however, cause-and-effect relationships are often more complicated than these paradigms suggest because in life causes and effects are closely entwined, and any event may have multiple causes, all of which seem equally important.

Treating each cause or effect in a separate section of a speech or separate paragraph in an essay is one way to help make clear the pattern behind a discourse. Another way is to make use of cue words that highlight the pattern, such as verbs like these that make clear the links between events:

leads to	happens	results in
causes	affects	brings about
contributes to	changes	produces
becomes	determines	makes possible

Use transitions and prepositions like these that specify relationships among causes and effects:

therefore	because	in effect	in
as a result	since	then	so
consequently	due to	owing to	of
thus	on account of	by	if . . . then

Detail. Details in cause-and-effect discourse have to be lively and vivid, of course, but they also have to help convince the audience that causes and effects have been correctly identified. The detail has to be **sufficient**; that is, there has to be enough detail to convince an audience that the causal links you have made are actually there. If the relationships you are describing are unusual, you will of course need more support to help persuade the audience than if they are relatively common. The detail has to be **comprehensive** to the extent that it covers all the important factors you have isolated; otherwise your audience may feel that you have left unsupported an important part of your argument or explanation. Finally, the detail has to be **logical**; that is, it has to show that there is a close and logical relationship between events. When the detail meets these three criteria, then the audience will be likely to find the discourse as a whole both believable and easy to follow.

SUMMARY

This chapter has reviewed each of the conceptual time patterns — narration, process, cause and effect. It has also examined the questions they ask of events: What happened? How did it happen? Why did it happen, or What is likely to happen? These patterns help shape spoken and written discourse and can be called on to meet the needs of a variety of speaking and writing occasions.

In the case of discourse organized around any of these patterns, a communicator has to remember that the finished discourse must have a point, a clear pattern, and appropriate detail. The point, pattern, and detail of a particular discourse will depend on the subject matter, the occasion, the audience's needs, and the communicator's purpose. At the same time most successful speeches and essays will employ some variation of the speaking and writing technique discussed in this chapter.

KEY WORDS

narration	visual aids
setting	second-person discourse
flashback	cause and effect
episode	cause
rising action	effect
falling action	primary cause
narrator	secondary or contributing causes
first-person narrative	sufficient detail
third-person narrative	comprehensive detail
process	logical detail
flowchart	

EXERCISES

Narration

1. List a number of speaking occasions for which a narrative would be appropriate, either as part of a speech or for the whole speech. Describe each occasion briefly and indicate the possible purpose for the narrative.

2. List a number of possible audiences for a written narrative and indicate what purpose a narrative written for each audience might have.

3. Here are three openings for narratives. Which is the most effective, and why? How could each one be improved?

a. The impact of the gray car hitting the fire hydrant was abrupt and hard. My glasses flew off my nose and through the steering wheel as my head hit the wheel. The screeching sound of metal being mangled traveled through the air. My milkshake spilled from the falling cup and into my lap. The car suddenly sat as motionless as my heartbeat. My legs started to feel cold and damp as the shake penetrated my clothes. I did not know what hit me.

b. When I was eight years old, my father did something that changed the way I viewed the people around me and has continued to affect me to the present day. No event I have ever witnessed has had such a great impact on me, and I can remember every detail of it clearly.

c. Comfortably sipping a glass of orange juice, I look out the window of the northbound Eastern Airlines DC–9 at the Atlantic seaboard 33,000 feet below. A melancholy mood overtakes me, born in the knowledge that I must shift my mental gears once again to prepare myself for school after a week's vacation in Costa Rica. The studying I brought to do in my spare time has been left untouched until now, and as I glance over the books in my carry-on, my thoughts wander back to Central America.

4. Indirect discourse reports what is said or thought but not in the actual words of the speaker or character. Direct discourse reports what is said or thought in the exact words used, relying on quotation marks and tags like *he said* or *she thought* to indicate that the words are being reported directly. Here is a passage making use of indirect discourse. Turn it into direct discourse:

As I looked out at the pitcher, I began to think that there were already two strikes on me and that if I missed the next pitch I would never be able to live it down. There were two outs in the ninth inning, and as I had begun to make my way out to the plate my coach had shouted out that all I had to do was get a little bit of a hit to bring the runner home from third base. Now as I stood at the plate I could hear my teammates yelling for me to get a hit and the opposing players telling me to miss the next pitch. Worst of all, I could hear my older brother telling me that in a similar situation he had got a hit. I could hear him telling me this because I was already sure I was going to swing at the next pitch and miss it completely.

5. a. Write an action-focused narrative about some personal experience that you remember clearly. Choose an event that happened in less than one day. Try to recreate the specific details of the experience, making sure that all the events, things, and people in the narrative are presented clearly to the reader. Your goal is to make the reader see, feel, and understand what happened.

Write as quickly as you can, trying to fill the equivalent of two typewritten pages (300–400 words). As you write try to recall the impact the experience had on you. Was it particularly funny, beautiful, or puzzling? Make sure the reader feels the impact too, but let the experience speak for itself, and avoid talking at great length about the meaning of the event.

b. Look over your narrative. Try to find the central, most dramatic point of it. The few moments, even seconds, when everything seemed to come together: when the crash occurred, when you realized all along that you had been misjudging your friend, when you opened your mouth before the crowd and tried to speak your lines, but nothing came out. Rewrite your narrative so that it focuses on these few minutes or even seconds. You may also wish to include an earlier incident that sets the scene (perhaps as a flashback) and one later incident to show the consequences; for example, you might wish to show yourself daydreaming as you drive along on a beautiful autumn evening, then go to the moment of the crash and finally to your reactions after it.

c. After you have revised the narrative so that it concentrates on the central incidents, look for phrases like *he said, she said,* and *I thought.* When you find them, try to insert dialogue or monologue as a substitute for indirect reporting of speech and thought.

When you finish this step, you should have a polished, dramatic, focused narrative ready to hand in.

6. Jot down ideas for a speech on a topic similar to the assignment in #5 above. Set it aside for a while, then outline it or write it out, working as quickly as you can. Then find a friend as a trial audience and deliver the speech.

After you have given the speech, ask these questions of your performance:

a. Did it have a clear purpose or point?

b. Did it have a clear pattern? What were the incidents? Why were they included? Should some be dropped? Are others needed?

c. What kind of detail was included? Setting? Dialogue? Did it help accomplish the purpose of the speech?

Now you are ready to revise the speech for formal presentation.

Process

1. Think of a topic for a process essay that would be appropriate for each one of the following periodicals:

a. *Popular Mechanics*

    b. *Glamour*
    c. *Motor Trend*
    d. *Woman's Day*
    e. *Bon Appètit*
    f. *Sports Illustrated*
    g. *Consumer Report*
    h. *Strength and Health*
    i. Your favorite magazine

2. Think of a topic for a process speech that would be appropriate for each one of the following audiences:
    a. a group of senior citizens
    b. the graduating class at a local high school
    c. the local chamber of commerce
    d. a local environmental group
    e. a group of auto dealers or other merchants
    f. a boys' or girls' camping organization
    g. a church or community social group
    h. citizens protesting the tax rate or a similar problem
    i. your classmates

3. Here is the opening of a process essay. How would you change it to make it more effective, either as the opening for an essay or a speech?

> Changing spark plugs may seem to be an easy task to some people, yet until the task is experienced firsthand, the frustration, anger, and feeling of total helplessness cannot be imagined. The following may not always be true, but it may persuade the uninformed members of society to think twice before they conclude that the replacement of spark plugs is a simple task.
>
> First off, you must go to the nearest automotive parts store and purchase a new set of plugs. The number of spark plugs you'll need is determined by the number of cylinders your car has. If you have a four-cylinder engine, you'll need four spark plugs; a six cylinder engine needs six spark plugs, and so on. Your car needs a specific size and kind of plug, so be sure you get the right one. Now that you have the plugs, the main tools needed are a socket wrench with a rubber-lined three-quarter-inch socket and a torque wrench. The rubber lining of the socket wrench is to protect the ceramic head of the spark plug from damage during replacement. It is also wise to keep a pile of rags handy because you will probably become grease-covered from head to toe. Wear old clothes. Now you are ready to begin.

4. Here is a list of topics for a possible process speech or essay. In order to determine which ones would make good topics, answer these three

questions: Who would want to know about this? How could the topic be introduced so that a relatively broad audience would have a reason for wanting to learn about it? What major divisions of the process would the speech or essay emphasize?

   a. packing grocery bags at a supermarket
   b. tying a shoe
   c. filling out an income tax form
   d. serving customers at a fast-food shop
   e. writing a poem
   f. playing field hockey
   g. wine tasting
   h. polishing shoes
   i. piercing ears

5. Write a description of one of the following simple processes, making use of appropriate technical terms. Define the terms in such a way that a complete novice will be able to follow the description but someone who is familiar with the process will not feel insulted or bored. The terms you would use to describe the process of changing a tire, for example, might include winged nut, spare tire, jack base, big wrench, bumper jack, bumper, hubcap, nut.

   a. changing a tire
   b. sewing on a button
   c. baking a cake
   d. using a tape recorder
   e. using a thirty-five millimeter camera
   f. making a serve in tennis
   g. water skiing

6. Choose two people from the class, one to be blindfolded and one to give directions. Ask the person to be blindfolded to stand on one side of the room, and then put the blindfold on. Now rearrange the furniture in the room to create obstacles of moderate difficulty. The person charged with giving the directions should try to guide the blindfolded subject across the room by using verbal directions only — no guiding by touch. The blindfolded person may not ask questions or say anything at all. If the blindfolded person touches any of the obstacles before reaching the other side of the room, stop and begin again with a new pair of participants. Keep trying until someone makes it across the room successfully.

7. Choose a topic similar to the ones in exercises four and five above and prepare a speech or essay on it. Try to write or present it so that it serves the needs of a particular audience, perhaps your classmates.

Cause and Effect

1. Take a current political or social crisis and list all the possible causes you can think of. Circle all those you think it would be necessary to mention in a speech or essay designed to isolate the important causes as a way of understanding events. Follow a similar procedure with the possible effects of some current social or political upheaval. Now write a speech or essay focusing on the causes or effects.

2. Do the same as in the first exercise, but this time focus on a campus or local situation or problem that deserves attention. If you wish, you may address your speech or essay to a local or campus audience.

3. In preparing a cause-and-effect essay or speech it is wise to explore as many possible causes and effects as possible so that nothing important is missed. One way to do this is to prepare a list of possible causes or effects, a list that is much more comprehensive than you will be able to use in an actual speech or essay. To train yourself in discovering causes and effects, take an everyday event and make a list of all the possible causes or effects. Here, for an example, is a list of the possible causes of an auto accident:

location of accident	vehicles involved
condition of vehicles	road surface
road defects	traffic control
light	weather
condition of operators	operators' driving skills
pedestrian involvement	features of the environment
passengers in the vehicles	animals or inanimate objects on the road

4. Describe three occasions for which a cause-and-effect speech might be appropriate. What standard of proof might be appropriate for the identification of causes and effects in each situation?

5. Describe three possible audiences for a cause-and-effect essay. What standard of proof might each audience demand for the identification of causes and effects?

6. Rewrite the following passage so that the causes and effects are clearly identified. Add material if necessary.

   More than sixty percent of the students in Math 141 classes failed last semester. It's obvious, students agree, that the course wasn't doing its job. Since such a large percentage of students failed, the Math Department, rather than failing all of them, gave them a no-grade report. The students were told to take the course over. This led to an over-scheduling of students for this calculus class during this semester. Now the classes are extra-large, a problem that makes it even harder for a professor to cater to the problems of each individual student.

REFERENCES

Brusaw, Charles T., Gerald J. Alred, and Walter Oliu. *Handbook of Technical Writing* (New York: St. Martin's, 1976).

Gardner, Howard. *The Shattered Mind* (New York: Alfred A. Knopf, 1965).

White, Theodore J. *Breach of Faith: The Fall of Richard Nixon* (New York: Athenaeum, 1975).

Wildavsky, Aaron. *The Politics of the Budgetary Process* (Boston: Little, Brown, 1965).

7. Static Patterns: Analysis, Enumeration, Comparison

Our minds have the ability to freeze events in time and space. We can store an important event in our memories, where it will be available for years any time we wish to call it up, with all the colors, gestures, and sounds more or less intact. We can approach a difficult problem by breaking it into parts, then sorting and rearranging the parts until we arrive at a solution. We can set our everyday lives in order by making lists of all the different kinds of things we have to do:

Shopping	*Errands*	*Bills*
1. grocery store	1. post office — mail letters	1. rent
2. drug store	2. library — return books	2. electric
3. discount store		3. water

In order for our minds to operate in these ways, we have to make use of patterns of thought (conceptual patterns) known as static patterns. To store an event in our memories we make use of the description pattern; solving a problem requires analysis; and list-making draws on the skills of classification and enumeration. These and the other static patterns — definition, exemplification, comparison — enable us to view events as if they were frozen in time and space, that is, as if they were static or unmoving. By making use of these patterns we can examine our experiences in considerable detail. Thus the static patterns provide a very different perspective than that of the time patterns (narration, process, cause and effect) discussed in Chapter Six.

The static patterns and the questions they enable us to ask of experience are as follows:

Chapter 7

Analysis — What are the parts? How are they related to each other and to the whole?

Enumeration — How many parts does it have and into what common serial arrangments do the parts fall? Can the parts be numbered?

Comparison — Is it similar to other things? Is it different from them?

Chapter 8

Classification — What categories does it fall into? What are the characteristics of each category?

Description — What are its physical features? How is it organized in space? What kind of thing is it?

Definition — To what class of things does it belong? What features characterize it and set it off from other things?

Exemplification — What are reasonable illustrations of this idea or principle? What are some representative examples or instances of this group of things, persons, or events?

STATIC PATTERNS AND TIME PATTERNS

It may be easier — at first — to prepare a speech or essay that follows a time pattern than to prepare one that follows a static pattern. The order of events in a simple narrative, process, or cause-and-effect discourse is from beginning to middle to end; that is, the same order in which the parts of a paper or speech need to be arranged for the benefit of an audience: introduction, body, conclusion. Thus if you decide to tell a story (describe a process, present causes and effects) by following the natural, chronological order of the events, this order will provide a satisfactory arrangement for your speech or paper and you need not spend much time worrying about organization.

In contrast, if your speech or essay follows one of the static patterns, you will probably need to spend considerable time working on its organization. The parts into which you split a subject through analysis, the groups you form through classification, or the points you cover in a comparison fail to fall by themselves into any particular order. This is because the mental processes of analysis, classification, and comparison do not impose a particular order on these points. If you are a member of a committee formed to investigate complaints about your local public library, your analysis of the problems might produce a list like this: small size of book collection, lack of adequate staff, poor physical facilities, confusing layout of books and materials, and old-fashioned circulation arrangements. The order in which these problems occur to you during the process of analysis is probably not important; it could be the result of chance, of personal experiences, or of prejudice. It probably does not matter to you, either, if your fellow committee members put the problems in a different order on their lists, just as long as you all agree, more or less, on what the problems are.

When you have to present the results of your investigation to the public in a written or oral report, however, the arrangement of the parts becomes very important. If your purpose is to convince the town or city council to make improvements in the library, then the order in which you cover the problems (and the amount of attention you give to each) should put emphasis on those improvements which are most likely to receive funding. In such a situation, the most important problem is often discussed first. If, on the other hand, you wish to convince the public of the seriousness of the situation at the library, then you might arrange the problems in an ascending order of importance, ending with a discussion of the most serious, so that your audience will be left with the strong impression that the local library is in grave trouble. The arrangement of parts within a piece of discourse based on a static pattern should depend, then, on who the audience is, what the situation is, and what the communicator's purpose is. When you are working with static patterns, therefore, you should be aware of this extra step.

Of course, there are many times when you will have to pay just as much attention to the organization of a speech or essay that follows one of the time patterns. For example, if you begin a story in the middle of things and use flashback, if you describe two processes that occur simultaneously, or if you present an involved cause-and-effect sequence, you will have to make sure that the material you present is arranged in the order best designed to convey your purpose and meet the needs of your audience. In these cases the time patterns pose the same kind of difficulties as the static patterns.

ANALYSIS

Using Analysis

When we face a difficult problem or a new and confusing situation we generally turn to the mental process of **analysis** for help; that is, we analyze the problem or situation by breaking it into parts that are relatively easy to understand, and then we try to discover how the parts fit back together to make up the whole. The same process of understanding works with other subjects — with issues that have provoked considerable disagreement, or with objects that excite our intellectual or scientific curiosity.

Since analysis can help us deal with such a wide variety of subjects, it should come as no surprise that people call on their powers of analysis for help on a wide variety of occasions. Here are some common situations that call for analysis:

In business activities from selling soap to building steel mills to flying people around the world, solving problems and analyzing new situations are everyday activities.

In academic and professional activities, from the study of art history to the observation of cancerous tumors in mice, analyzing objects and events is a central part of research.

In politics and public service the analysis of issues and disagreements provides a basis for decision-making and action.

In our personal lives, whether we are trying to figure out why the car failed to start, trying to understand a disagreement among friends, or trying to deal with the new information and puzzling situations presented by activities like stamp collecting, reading mystery stories, building model airplanes, or cooking special dishes, we rely on our powers of analysis.

On many of the occasions when we use analysis as a pattern of thought we also have to be ready to use it as a pattern of expression. That is, we have to be ready to present our analysis to readers or listeners so that they can understand how we went about analyzing the subject and so that they are likely to agree with our conclusions. This can be a difficult task because analysis is a very widely used pattern of thought and expression, and it takes a variety of relatively distinct forms. As a communicator you need to decide early in the process of preparing a speech or essay which form of analysis best meets the needs of the situation in which you find yourself. All the decisions you have to make about the point pattern, detail, and the performance style of your discourse will be determined, to a considerable extent, by the form of analysis you have chosen.

To begin with, then, you need to be able to recognize different forms of analysis. In addition, you need to decide what form of analysis is appropriate for a particular occasion.

Analysis, both as a pattern of thought and as a pattern of expression, can be divided into four forms depending on the subject being analyzed: a problem, a situation, an issue, or an object (that is, an isolated aspect of reality).

Problem Analysis. Problems come in all shapes and sizes — someone fails a test; a marriage collapses; the radio just assembled from a kit blows up as soon as it is plugged in; a new bridge has to be closed because it is unsafe; negotiations between two countries break down and a war erupts. What all these incidents have in common is a malfunction of some sort: an element in a complicated system fails to work the way it should. **Problem analysis** sorts through all the different elements to isolate the central problem or conflict along with any contributing factors; problem analysis then tries to understand the relationship between these and the other elements that make up the incident or circumstance under examination. Problem analysis does not set out to provide solutions, but in the process of exploring a problem, the general outlines of a solution may become apparent.

Situation Analysis. All of us spend a lot of time trying to learn about the circumstances that surround us (and other people as well), both because we may need the information as a basis for future actions and also because we want to satisfy our curiosity. At work you may spend time exploring the social and economic characteristics of an area your company is considering as a potential market for its products. At home you may spend the evening watching an informative television program on China, learning about its political structure, economic situation, and social behavior, all aspects of a country most Americans find puzzling but intriguing. **Situation analysis** focuses on any state of affairs, large or small, breaking it into parts in order to isolate all the personalities, forces, institutions, or objects that make it up, exploring the functions of each element and the relationships among them.

Issue Analysis. Analysis can be applied to ideas and issues as well as problems and situations. **Issue analysis** focuses on a dispute or disagreement and examines opposing points of view, isolating the major and minor features of each side as well as the facts and examples that provide support. Any issue, from a dispute over the hunting of baby seals for their fur to an argument among family members, can be the subject of this form of analysis.

Object Analysis. Academic and professional fields have their own methods of analysis, **object analysis.** Biologists examine the molecular structure of cells, psychologists study the different elements of the process of thought, medical doctors observe the effect of viral infection on healthy organs, and literary critics ask how the parts of a poem work together to create an effect. Though the methods of analysis differ from field to field, the aim of this form of analysis generally remains the same: to examine carefully a small section of reality — an object — identifying its parts and determining how the parts are related to each other.

The form of analysis you choose for a speech or essay should depend in part on your subject, but it will also depend on the occasion and on the needs of your potential audience.

If your audience believes that things are not going well, or if the audience can be convinced that a problem exists, problem analysis is an appropriate form. Testimony before legislative committees on dangers to the environment, on the regulation of industry, or on difficulties in the welfare system generally takes this form, as do presentations before boards of inquiry looking into marine disasters, fires, floods, and the like. Speakers before professional societies, before business organizations, and before special interest groups like student coalitions often choose to analyze problems the group is facing: government regulation, declining profits, rising tuition.

The written report analyzing a problem is a standard feature of our society. Executives in business and government write memoranda on problems of all sorts, and consulting companies produce numerous reports each year on leaking dams, highway safety, and the rising cost of essential services.

The following memorandum from a student-faculty committee looks at a problem common to many college campuses:

> To: Donna Mullen, President, Student Senate
> William Gomes, President, Faculty Senate
> James Sarducci, University President
>
> From: Joint Faculty-Student Committee to Investigate the Library
>
> Re: Report on the Library
>
> On January 15 the Committee began collecting and investigating student complaints about the condition and operation of the library. The committee received seventy-five written comments and, in addition, fifteen verbal comments on "Speak to the Committees Day." Even

though the committee asked for complaints, it received much praise for the library, particularly for the energy and dedication of its staff, which one student described as "a really helpful group of people working in a tough situation."

Student complaints focused on the physical plant, the arrangement and condition of the book collection, and the training of student help. Other features of the library received negative comment, but not to the same extent. After reviewing the complaints, the committee has come to agree with the students that these aspects of the library pose serious problems. In each case, moreover, the committee noted that the problems were caused by a lack of adequate funding, not by any negligence on the part of the staff. What follows is a discussion of some of the more significant problems facing the library:

1) *Physical Condition* Students at this university spend a lot of time studying in the library, and they were quick to point out that conditions have deteriorated beyond what might be expected through normal use. The upholstery on chairs is torn; wooden chairs are broken; the facilities in the restrooms function poorly, if at all; and broken windows are repaired with cardboard, seldom replaced. Because of the reduction last year in maintenance staff, the tables, chairs, and shelves are covered with gritty dust, and pieces of paper often litter the floors.

2) *Arrangement and Condition of the Book Collection* The problems in this area are less obvious than those affecting the physical condition of the library, but they are still irritating and may have serious consequences in the future. Two years ago the library had to stop in the middle of changing from the Dewey Decimal System to the Library of Congress System.

Students find the use of two cataloguing systems confusing, and they waste a lot of time searching for books. For the past five years, moreover, the library has not been able to replace damaged or stolen books. Damage up to this point has been limited somewhat, because of the vigilance of the staff, but if the present situation continues, the collection will develop serious gaps.

3) *Training of Student Help* Most students, particularly those who work part-time for the library, feel that the training given to student help is inadequate because the library cannot spare enough staff for training or supervision. As a result, books end up misshelved; circulation mistakes are frequent; and unless there is a regular staff member available, students who need help locating a book have no one to turn to for advice.

Since each of these problems can be directly traced to a lack of adequate funding, the committee recommends that the appropriate faculty and student organizations make every possible effort to have funding levels for the library increased.

This memo opens with a description of the background of the problem, its purpose stated clearly in a thesis, "What follows is a discussion of some of the more significant problems facing the Library." The memo then goes on to isolate and explore each aspect of the problem and its impact on library services. According to the memo, the link between each one is a lack of funding, and the final paragraph indicates the direction a solution might take. A memorandum like this covers each aspect briefly; a report or speech might cover only one or two aspects, but in greater detail.

When the people making up a potential audience are facing a new or confusing situation, they want information about it so they can respond in an appropriate manner. Situation analysis is the proper form for such occasions. For example, orientation sessions for new students or new employees often consist of speeches covering such topics as important campus services and the new students' responsibilities, or the highlights of a company's organization and operation. Booklets distributed to the same groups (A *Student's Guide to State U; Working for Widget Manufacturing*) have a similar function.

On other occasions, situation analysis may serve an audience's desire for general information — that is, its curiosity. Newspaper articles and investigative reports on television analyzing scandals, successes, and disasters serve this need.

The following student speech is directed both at immediate needs and at curiosity about a popular subject. For some members of its audience the information in the speech will be of use as the basis for an important and expensive decision; for others the information will be interesting because the topic is a popular one.

Stereo Receivers

Today's college society is more influenced by music than any other in the past. Everywhere you look people are studying, sleeping, eating, and partying to music. A survey conducted by *Stereo Review* at Harvard University showed that sixty-one percent of the students' rooms had stereos in them. And the heart of any stereo system is the stereo receiver. A receiver is a component that combines a tuner, AM and FM, a preamplifier, which takes the weak signal from the tuner or turntable and makes it clear, and an amplifier, which makes the signal loud and clear and passes it on to the speakers. If you want to have a stereo in your dorm room, you will need to spend a good deal of time shopping for a receiver.

There are many stereo stores around ranging from national name stores to local shops. Stereo specialists usually offer better buys, better service, and lower prices than local department stores.

In choosing a receiver, you should always keep in mind what you want it to be able to do. Will you want to hook it up to a turntable or to a tape player? Or will you just want to listen to FM or AM stations? You should also keep in mind the size of the room you live in because that will determine the power or wattage you need. For most dorm rooms twenty-five or forty-five watts of power per channel are plenty.

Prices of receivers vary greatly, too. A good receiver can cost as little as a hundred and seventy five dollars and a very good one can cost as much as nineteen hundred dollars. Most college budgets dictate a receiver costing between a hundred and seventy five dollars and two hundred and fifty dollars.

There are many brands to choose from, too; names like Fisher, JVC, Harmon-Kardon, Kenwood, Pioneer, Realistic, Phillips, Sherwood, Technics, Sony, and Panasonic come to mind among many others. All the models offer the same features with only slight differences among them. I'd like to give you some idea of the choices facing you using information accumulated from *Stereo HiFi Equipment Annual Review*:

Fisher: well-engineered receiver; good price and can be repaired almost anywhere; about twenty watts per channel

JVC: higher quality than Fisher and a slightly higher price; a bit overdone with its many knobs and gadgetries such as mixers and equalizers, but it is an excellent receiver with very good durability and a good buy. Averages around twenty-five watts; you can get them all the way up to fifty or seventy-five watts.

Kenwood: equal to Fisher, less than JVC. It has only fourteen watts and is not known for durability; not a very good buy.

Harmon-Kardon: good quality but low wattage (about 20) for what most students expect from a receiver. A good buy for the money. A bit hard to find and to get repaired, but it should last longer. . . .

All the foreign receivers are good or excellent, but most are harder to get repaired or serviced. Quality outsiders include Marantz, Toshiba, Yamaha, and Hitachi. . . .

For the rest of your equipment you will find that there are many magazines to read to find the best bargains. Check newspapers, too, since weekly sales are always happening. I would like to be able to give you some advice about buying the rest of your system, too, especially speakers, but I don't have the time; the magazines will give you plenty of help.

Those of you with big bucks might be interested in the ultimate system: a Technics SA1000 receiver for $1900, a Technics RS9900 cassette deck for $2000, a Sony BSB180 turntable for $1800, Pass model 1A speakers for $1770 each, for a total of $9,240 dollars excluding taxes, of course. Personally, I'll stick to my AM-FM clock radio for $11.99.

— Donald Duncan

When the members of your potential audience are facing a disagreement over important matters or a choice between two or more courses of action, issue analysis can help make the alternatives clear. Essays and speeches on topics like "The President's Economic Program: Pros and Cons," "Alternatives for the Oil Industry in the Next Decade," and "The Debate Over Nuclear Energy" can help clarify points of disagreement over important social, economic, and political policies by representing fully and clearly the views of each side on an issue.

The audience for object analysis usually consists of specialists in a particular academic or professional field, and the occasions when this form of analysis is appropriate usually call for writing: papers in advanced courses, articles in technical journals, and scholarly books. Most object analysis is complex, and it can be difficult to follow. As a result, it appears primarily in print so that the audience has a chance to review the analysis thoroughly and evalute the evidence. When object analysis is presented in a speech, the speaker usually reads directly from a written text to make sure that the wording is unambiguous and all the facts are correct.

One form of object analysis useful to you as a communicator is the analysis of a speech or essay. This can consist of an analysis of your own work or an analysis of a fellow student's work, as in this brief essay:

Peer Analysis of "Crazy Jim Flanagan"

In the opening of David Jones's narrative about his boyhood friend Jim Flanagan, the reader is told the *when, who, where,* and *why* of the story, but left to discover the *what* through further reading. The phrase, "we were youngsters" indicates when the story takes place, and the introduction of Jim Flanagan, "a good friend," indicates whom the story is about. The events take place in a small town, Templeford, New Hampshire, but the opening of the narrative says little about them, enticing the reader to go on to find out what happened by referring to Jim as "Mental Man" and his actions as "crazy" and "sadistic."

There are three main events, arranged in chronological order, in the body of the paper. The first event occurs during the author's childhood. This incident is the "hog-spogging" of Paul Landreux, introduced by the words "One day." Jim's behavior in this event illustrates his nasty sense of humor. David leads the reader to the second event with transition words suggesting the passage of time, "as Jim grew older." "Confirmation class" also indicates a later period since members of a confirmation class are generally teenagers in junior or senior high school. Extortion of money from the other students is the topic of this event, actually a cluster of events, which ends when "Jim entered his high school years." The last major event, preceded by background information, is the bombing of the

Volkswagen. The story ends with an ironic twist, a physical description of "mental man" as "short, thin, and quiet looking."

— Angela Fedorcuk

Getting Materials

To analyze a subject, you ask such questions as "What are the parts?" "How are they related to each other and to the whole?" An analysis essay or speech presents the results of an act of analysis, arranged for the benefit of an audience. Most of the investigation of the subject and the gathering of material needs to be done, therefore, before you sit down to write your essay or prepare your speech, but the process of analysis should continue while you are preparing your discourse.

Whether you are just starting to analyze a subject or are in the middle of preparing a speech or essay, this three-step procedure can help you do a thorough job of examining your subject and finding the material you need for your discourse:

1. decide what you want to analyze,
2. divide it into parts, and
3. relate the parts to each other and to the whole.

Each time you follow these steps you are likely to do things a bit differently depending on the subject you are examining and the form of analysis you are using. No matter what the occasion, however, a clear but flexible plan like this one will help you do a better job.

Decide. Try to state to yourself, briefly and in concrete terms, exactly what it is you want to analyze and why. This step may sound easy, but it often takes a good deal of time. We frequently start out analyzing one subject only to discover that we are really interested in a different one, or we begin by defining a subject in such broad terms that effective analysis is impossible.

Suppose, for example, you find it difficult to understand why people slaughter large numbers of wild animals like whales, seals, and coyotes. You assume, however, that people who do such things have arguments to justify their actions. You state the issue to yourself in this way: "What arguments do people make for — and against — slaughtering wild animals?" and you decide to prepare a speech or essay analyzing the different points of view. As you begin to think about the different arguments, perhaps doing a bit of research along the way, you realize that the issue is quite complicated because the killing of wild animals takes place in very different situations for a variety of reasons:

- Farmers in the western part of the United States poison large numbers of coyotes each year to protect their herds of sheep and cattle; opponents claim that coyotes actually kill relatively few farm animals.
- Several countries allow whale hunting for meat and for other products; opponents claim that whales are endangered by this practice, that whale meat is a luxury food and not an essential source of protein, and that there are easily-obtainable substitutes for the other products.
- Large numbers of baby harp seals are killed each year for their fur; hunters claim that the herd can easily support this annual harvest, whereas opponents argue that the hunting methods are needlessly cruel and that the hunt endangers the species.

Each one of these topics is a complicated matter in itself, and if you tried to touch on them all you would probably end up doing a superficial job of analysis on each one and would fail to contribute much to your reader's understanding of the larger issue. Besides, covering all these topics in detail would require a good deal of research — probably a lot more than you have time to do.

When you discover that your topic is too broad you should realize that your potential audience will learn a lot more from a detailed discussion of one of the smaller issues than from a general, and perhaps vague, discussion of the larger question. You will therefore have to choose one of the smaller issues. One way to do this is to state each of the smaller issues to yourself in terms of specific situations and specific events. This will allow you to visualize what your final paper might look like and how much time and research it will take. Because it will force you to carefully examine each issue on its own, this procedure will also help you decide which subject you like best and are most willing to work on. For example:

Broad, vague subject: The slaughtering of wild animals
Specific subjects: The killing of coyotes by farmers in the western United States to protect their herds of livestock
The killing of whales by Japanese whalers for meat and for by-products
The killing of baby harp seals to meet the demand for their exquisite fur

As you go through the process of deciding what your subject is to be and stating it in concrete terms, you will start noticing almost unconciously what the most important elements of the problem, situation, or issue are, and this will form the basis for the next step in the process of analysis.

Divide. Split the subject into parts so that you can understand it more fully. Dividing a subject into parts is the heart of analysis. It is in the acts of dividing and examining that we come to understand in detail what it is we are analyzing and begin to understand how the parts are related to each other and how they make up the whole.

The parts into which a subject should be divided are not, however, always obvious. Frequently you will need to try splitting up a subject several ways until you encounter the way that helps you understand it best. There are, nonetheless, some standard places to begin. Look for obvious divisions. A play that the author divided into three acts can be analyzed along the same lines. A government department like the Bureau of Alcohol, Tobacco, and Firearms has three main divisions, just as the name suggests. Most issues have two sides, a pro and a con: Should there be a tax cut this year or not? Should the drinking age be raised or not? In addition, positions on each side of an issue can usually be divided into three parts — major arguments, minor arguments, and supporting evidence.

It is a good idea to have a pen and paper handy at this stage to jot down all the different ideas you have for dividing your subject. As you jot them down you may begin to see some system emerging, and this will help you decide which way of dividing the subject is best. It may also suggest how the different parts of your subject are related. Figure 7-1 is a sample jotting sheet for a paper on the topic, "The Killing of Baby Harp Seals."

Relate. Bring the analysis to a conclusion by stating how the parts are related to each other and to the whole. Once you have identified the parts, you can come to an understanding of how they fit together by asking questions appropriate to the form of analysis you are using.

Problem Analysis — What is the central problem or conflict? How is it linked to any smaller problem? How do these problems work together to prevent the system from operating correctly or to make conditions less than ideal?

Situation Analysis — How do the different elements of the situation fit or work together? How do they limit the operation of each other? What are the responsibilities and powers of each element? What does each contribute to the working of the whole?

Issue Analysis — How do the major arguments, minor arguments, and supporting evidence fit together to form a point of view on an issue? How are the points of view related to each other?

Objective Analysis — How do the different parts of the object, organism, or event work together to help it accomplish its aim (remain alive, operate correctly, remain stable)? Can any general laws of nature, scientific principles, or standards of art and culture explain the relationship of the parts?

Your statement of the relationship may be in the form of a tentative thesis statement for your speech or essay, or it may be in the form of a list

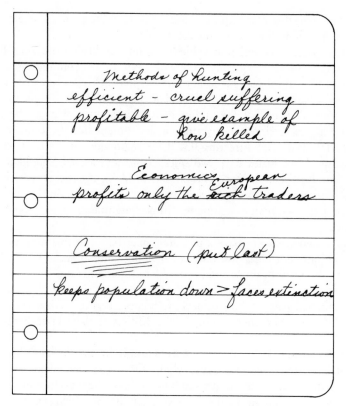

Methods of hunting
efficient – cruel suffering
profitable – give example of
how killed

Economics, European
profits only the such traders

Conservation (put last)

keeps population down > faces extinction

Figure 7-1 A Jotting Sheet for Collecting Ideas

that suggests a pattern of arrangement for the discourse. Here is a list for the paper on "The Killing of Baby Harp Seals."

Pro
(hunters and Canadian government)

Con
(humane societies)

1. Methods — hunting techniques (including clubbing) are efficient and cause the seals no excessive suffering
   (supporting examples and arguments)

1. Methods — hunting techniques (including clubbing) are cruel and painful to the seals
   (supporting examples and arguments)

2. Economics — the seal hunt is a major source of income for one of the poorer Canadian provinces
   (supporting examples and arguments)

2. Economics — the hunters make very little money; only European fur traders benefit significantly from the hunt
   (supporting examples and arguments)

Pro *(hunters and Canadian government)*	Con *(humane societies)*
3. Conservation — the hunt does not threaten the existence of the harp seal; it keeps the population within manageable limits (supporting examples and arguments)	3. Conservation — many forces are threatening to make the harp seal extinct; hunting only makes its existence more precarious (supporting examples and arguments)

When your thoughts are in this form, you may be ready to give your attention to the point, pattern, and detail of your discourse.

Here is the way one student chose to develop the material in the list of arguments over the killing of baby harp seals:

The Pros and Cons of Seal Hunting

The bitter controversy over the killing of seals has been going on for over twenty years. During this time the public outcry has been so tremendous that many animal humane societies have begun fighting for the seals and pressuring governments to pass legislation to prohibit slaughtering of the seals. The humane societies have tried many different ways of stopping the hunt, but so far they have been mostly ineffective.

Every year hundreds of thousands of seals are killed for their furs. It is the small baby harp seal furs that are the most sought after because the fur is snowy white and very soft. The major seal hunts take place in the Pribilof Islands of the United States, in the Canadian Gulf of St. Lawrence and Newfoundland, and in South Africa.

It is the way in which the seals are killed that concerns the humane societies most. The sealer attempts to kill the seals by smashing the skull of a seal with a blow from a long wooden club called a hakapik. He then punctures the throat of the seal with a knife, causing it to bleed to death in case the blow from the hakapik did not kill the animal. After that, he peels off the pelt and blubber, usually leaving the carcass on the ice.

Sealers argue that clubbing and exsanguination is the most humane method of killing seals under field conditions. They have experimented with trying to shoot the seals and with poisoning them, but they found that both of these methods took too long and were too expensive. Canadian officials claim the seals are dead or unconscious from the moment they are clubbed. As a result, they claim the killing of the seals is humane and that the seals feel no pain and do not go through any suffering.

The humane societies contend that this is not true. They claim that it takes a great deal of skill to fracture a seal's skull on the first blow, thus causing the seal to die or become unconscious. If a seal is not killed or knocked unconscious on the first blow, then it has to go through a tremendous amount of pain before it dies; some seals are skinned while they are still conscious. Humane societies argue that seals go through a great deal of pain and suffering before they die, and sealers should therefore either develop a new way of killing the seals or stop killing them altogether.

A second argument is over the economics of the hunt. The Canadian government contends that the annual seal slaughter is a major source of income for Newfoundland. During the past fifteen years, fur seal pelts have sold at an auction for average prices of sixty-eight to one hundred and twenty-seven dollars each. The government claims that the loss of the seal hunt would cause much unemployment and hardship for the men who count on the seal hunt for their income.

The humane societies say this is not true. They say that half the clubbers make one hundred dollars a year or less from the hunt and the most any hunter makes is approximately $1,700. These figures come from official Canadian government publications. The humane societies claim that the only people making any significant money are the European fur dealers who sell coats made from the furs.

A third major argument is that the hunt is causing a serious threat to the existence of the harp seal. The Canadian government insists that the annual seal hunt is "good resource management." It denies that the number of seals is diminishing and claims that this year's "pup" population will be between 345,000 and 358,000. It plans to allow 180,000 baby whitecoats to be killed this year and claims that an annual reduction in the size of the seal herds is necessary to maintain the seal population within numbers compatible with the available supply of food and habitat.

The humane societies have a different point of view. They feel the harp seal is in danger of eventual extinction due to a high mortality rate from weather conditions, habitat contamination, predators, and hunters. In the 1940s there may have been as many as ten million harp seals in Canadian areas. Today, the herds number about one and a half million by all estimates. Humane societies believe the number of births this year will be around 250,000 nearly 100,000 below the Canadian estimate. Dr. D. M. Lavinge of the University of Guelph, Canada, found that the status of the harp seal in the Western Atlantic may be severely threatened in the future if the seals continue to be managed on the basis of the more optimistic population assessments. The humane societies point out that arguments about keeping herd size down so there is enough food and habitat are ridiculous. They point out that in the Pribilof Island hunt only bachelor males are killed, and these animals do no breeding at all. The societies feel that neither the Pribilof nor the Newfoundland hunt is necessary to keep seal population within limits and that the seals are facing a very serious threat of extinction if the hunts are not called off or toned down.

There are more pros and cons to the seal hunt, but these are the three major arguments. Each side has strong arguments, and it is obvious that the battle over killing seals will be going on for a long time. Neither side is willing to make any concessions, so in the meantime the seal killing will go on.

— Kay Hoban

Unless you already know a good deal about the subject, an analysis of a topic like seal hunting will generally require some research in newspapers and periodicals. For topics of local interest, however, interviews or surveys may provide the best information. An informal survey can often provide you with the information or the range of viewpoints you need for your analysis: just ask your friends and instructors how they feel about the topic. If you want to make the survey more formal, here are some helpful steps:

1. Make up a basic question and also follow-up questions that will allow you to probe the issue to uncover further arguments and evidence:

   Do you approve or disapprove of smoking in restaurants? What do you think about when you see someone light up a cigarette, cigar, or pipe in a restaurant? Does smoke bother you while you are eating? Would you go up to a smoker and ask the person to stop smoking, or would you stop smoking if someone asked you to?

2. Prepare a questionnaire to be administered orally or filled out in writing:

   Survey: Smoking in Restaurants
   Subject's name:_____
   Subject's age, background, or other relevant information:_____
   _____

   Basic question: Do you approve or disapprove of smoking in restaurants?_____
   _____
   _____

   Follow-up Questions:
   Do you smoke?_____
   What do you think about when you see someone light up a cigarette, cigar, or pipe in a restaurant?_____

   Does smoking bother you while you are eating? Do you feel compelled to smoke while you are eating?_____

   Would you go up to a smoker in a restaurant and ask the person to stop smoking, or would you stop smoking if someone asked you?_____
   _____

   Additional comments:_____
   _____

3. Before you administer the questionnaire, try it out on your classmates or friends.
4. Administer the questionnaire to a group of people large enough and diverse enough to represent the major points of view on the subject.
5. Let people ramble a bit in their answers; this will allow them to bring up minor arguments and supporting evidence that can help make your analysis complete.

A questionnaire like the one above can be easily adapted to a variety of situations. You may, however, prefer a less formal approach. If, for example, students on your campus are constantly complaining about parking facilities, you can look into the matter by interviewing. Interview the head of the campus security force and ask for a statement on the parking problem. Ask what the administration policies are and how they are implemented. Ask for a response to common complaints like the lack of parking space and erratic ticketing. Then talk to individual police officers. They will probably welcome the chance to give you their view of the situation, and they may even pass on some hints on how to avoid tickets. Finish the job by interviewing students and staff — secretaries, custodians, administrators. When you are done you may have a different view of the problem and good material for a speech or essay.

This interviewing procedure need not be restricted to campus topics (living conditions, dormitory food, tuition raises); it works equally well with such civic topics as land pollution and plant closings and such social problems as the role of farmers in an increasingly urban society.

The Finished Product

Point. Analysis is a basic and important mental process but, as the focus of an essay or speech, analysis is not very interesting in itself. It is interesting instead for what it reveals about the subject of analysis. Thus effective analytical writing and speaking needs to make clear from the start why the subject needs to be analyzed and what the audience can hope to gain from the analysis. A clear thesis statement can help do this, but it is usually not enough. The introduction has to indicate why a particular issue deserves a close look or why a problem or situation needs detailed examination. If the analysis leads to a particular conclusion, this, too, needs to be made clear, not only at the beginning but throughout the discourse.

The student author of the following analysis essay has a point to make and tries to convince the members of her audience that they need to pay attention to the problem she is exploring.

Old Suites/New Suites

During the past decade dormitory fires in American colleges and universities have killed a surprising number of students. The causes range from careless smoking, to faulty wiring, to, worst of all, arson, but the result is always the same — a tragic loss of life. Last year the state legislature passed new regulations governing dormitory design, and these regulations meant that remodeling was required in all six buildings of the George Butterfield complex at this university. Students have always had to pay extra for the privilege of living in the suites that all the buildings in the complex contain, but the remodeling done to comply with the new fire laws, though clearly necessary, has created a new problem: the suites no longer provide the luxuries students pay for.

In previous years each suite had one private entrance opening into a livingroom shared by all residents of the suite. Suites also contained four private bedrooms and two private bathrooms. No one except the students living in a suite had access to the livingroom, the bathroom, or the bedrooms.

The redesigned suites have one main entrance that is not private and can be entered by anyone. The main door opens on a hall containing doors to the four bedrooms on one side and to the two bathrooms on the other side. The lounge is at the end of the hall. At the far side of the lounge is another entrance connecting the suite to a different section of the building.

The lounges were once places where residents of a suite could gather and relax in privacy. This is no longer the case. Since traffic flows right through them, the lounges are no longer like livingrooms and resemble instead the lounges in regular dorms. The new lounges cannot be locked up to protect private property, and because of the fear of theft they no longer contain pictures, posters, television, refrigerators, or stereos. They now lack any personality and resemble the barren study rooms in other dorms.

The bathrooms have become a major inconvenience. In previous years they were within the enclosed area of the suites. They are now out in the hallway. The rooms can be locked only from the inside, so when no one is using them, they are unlocked. Personal items can no longer be kept in the bathrooms without fear of theft; towels, toothbrushes, soap, and all personal items now frequently disappear from the bathrooms. The result is rooms that lack any personal touch. There aren't even shower mats or throw rugs for the cold, damp floors. Just as in a regular dormitory, the bathrooms are accessible to anyone walking through the hall.

The students are not getting what they have paid for, and the conditions that accompany the change make matters even worse. Since the first day of school workmen have been in and out of the suites. Loud construction takes place at all times during the day.

Many suites have no lounge furniture. There are rooms without phone availability or TV antenna outlets. There are rooms with holes in the ceiling, broken windows, broken desks, and much more.

— Amy Keene

This essay reviews three characteristics of the old and new suites: entrances, lounges, and bathrooms. In each case it shows that the changes have created considerable inconvenience and, when taken together, make for a deplorable situation. The analysis clearly supports the author's conclusion that something is wrong with living arrangments in the new suites and that they are no longer worth the extra money. The closing details about the mess created by the construction provide added urgency to the author's demand that immediate steps be taken to correct the problem.

Pattern. The pattern that informs an analytical essay or speech depends to a great extent on the purpose of the discourse. Situation and objective analysis usually employ a variation on this pattern:

Analysis Pattern #1
Introduction (need, thesis)
    Characteristic 1 (or cluster of features 1)
    Characteristic 2 (or cluster of features 2)
    Characteristic 3 (or cluster of features 3)
    Characteristic 4 (or cluster of features 4)
    Characteristic 5, 6, 7 (or cluster of features 5, 6, 7)
Conclusion (summary, comment)

A problem analysis may follow a slightly different pattern:

Analysis Pattern #2
Introduction (problem, thesis — may identify central problem or conflict)
    Central Problem (central conflict)
    Sub-problem 1
    Sub-problem 2
    Sub-problem 3, 4, 5
Conclusion (summary, solution)

In contrast, because an issue analysis examines two or more positions, its patterns are a combination of the basic **analysis pattern** (#1) and the comparison patterns to be mentioned later (pages 185–186):

Issue Analysis Pattern 1   *Issue Analysis Pattern 2*
Introduction (issue, thesis)   Introduction (issue, thesis)

Argument 1 (pro)
  Minor arguments
    Details and Examples
Argument 1 (con)
  Minor arguments
    Details and Examples
Argument 2 (pro)
  Minor arguments
    Details and Examples
Argument 2 (con)
  Minor arguments
    Details and Examples
Arguments 3, 4, 5 (pro and con)
  (including minor arguments,
  details, and examples)
Conclusion (summary, comment)

Argument 1 (pro)
  Minor arguments
    Details and Examples
Argument 2 (pro)
  Minor arguments
    Details and Examples
Arguments 3, 4, 5 (pro)
  (including minor arguments, de-
  tails, and examples)
Argument 1 (con)
  Minor arguments
    Details and Examples
Argument 2 (con)
  Minor arguments
    Details and examples
Arguments 3, 4, 5 (con)
  (including minor arguments, de-
  tails, and examples)
Conclusion
  (summary, comment)

Moreover, analytical discourse generally makes use of terms like the following which help identify for the audience the different elements of the subject being analyzed:

part	argument	section	sum
characteristic	position	unit	mass
element	stance	piece	totality
aspect	issue	factor	however
segment	point of view	detail	on the other hand
trait	opinion	division	in contrast
component	belief	whole	meanwhile

The following issue analysis is a good example of how a well-executed pattern and the skillful use of cue words can guide an audience through a complex discussion. Cue words are italicized.

Introduction Every year millions of college-bound high school juniors and seniors gather in auditoriums, lecture halls, and gymnasiums across the country to test their abilities against the SAT and the Achievement Tests. These exams, along with many other standardized tests, are created by the Educational Testing Service (ETS) for the College Board and are used by most of the colleges and universities in this country as a criterion for admission. Recently, however, these tests and the ETS have become an issue of fervent debate with groups such as DETEST (Demystify the Established Standardized Tests) claiming that ETS judges not aptitude or achievement but exposure to upper-middle-class American culture. These groups are pushing to radically alter or even abolish the tests, which they feel are racially and socially biased against individually creative modes of thought, and abused by the institutions they are designed to assist.

Argument 1 (pro)   ETS has always held with pride the *belief* that their tests open opportunities to the less fortunate by presenting a means by which students from all economic and social backgrounds can be judged equally. They look back on a long and prosperous evolution starting with the first version of the SAT, 90 years ago. These days each test question is thoroughly inspected by as many as thirty reviewers before being student tested. The testers boast production costs of $100,000 per test, reflecting the care with which the items are designed and chosen to effectively measure individual likelihood to succeed. Nothing, they maintain, could more fairly reveal personal talent.

Argument 1 (con)   DETEST, *on the other hand*, claims that, whatever the methods, the intentions of the ETS are not being satisfied. It charges that the test questions are socially and racially biased. Statistics show that test scores vary with family income, specifically that the states with the greatest per capita income produce the highest mean test score. This, anti-test lobbyists contend, is due to the ability of wealthier families to provide their children with education better geared toward the type of skills required for success on College Board exams. Thus the tests are seen as a measure, not of individual likelihood to succeed, but of exposure to a type of education not readily available to economically disadvantaged people.

Argument 2 (pro)   Anyone who has ever taken an ETS exam is familiar with its concept of the "best" answer. Most of the multiple choice questions do not contain one completely right answer and a number of all wrong answers but one response that is "more right," perhaps only slightly so, than any or all of the other choices. The ETS maintains that this "best answer" technique makes possible fine distinctions between exceptional and average individuals. Fine students are, according to the testers, those who can consistently distinguish a choice which is sixty-five percent correct from another that may be sixty percent right. Thus the tests are, theoretically, making maximal use of a minimum number of questions.

Argument 2 (con)   DETEST supporters, *however*, take a *different stand* on the "best" answer issue. They suggest that the ETS's concept of the "best" response is not universal, saying that any answer that can be deduced logically is equally acceptable (as shown in the example below).

EXAMPLE:

The first three figures below are alike in a certain way. Which one of the four choices is most related to the first three?

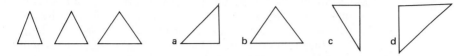

The correct answer is obviously (b), which follows the first series in being a triangle with a progressively wider base. Another conceivable answer is, however, (d), if we see the three models as being equilateral. This example is simple but illustrates DETEST's point.

Detest also points out that any veteran of ETS tests is at an advantage over the novice since a little experience will lead almost anyone to familiarity with the ETS's specialized view of the best answer. Thus these standardized tests penalize individuals with unusually creative modes of thought and students who are not used to the type of questions asked.

Argument 3 (pro)

Yet, one of the most forceful arguments for keeping the present testing system remains that colleges and universities need some standards by which to judge students. The hard line stand taken by many ETS supporters is that today's students have few standards imposed on them and that, though the existing exams may not be infallible, they are the best we have yet devised. The scores, they say, are used only in conjunction with other information to determine admissability of a student. In fact, since at least ninety percent of all applicants are accepted to the college of their choice, the test results are usually significant only at the most selective schools (Harvard and Yale for example). Still, the scores tell a great deal about a student in relation to his peers and are therefore helpful in the decision making process. The tests' advocates are saying that they play a vital role in today's university system and must continue to fulfill this need, at least until something better can be designed.

Argument 3 (con)

In response, anti-test groups acknowledge our need for standards but contend that the ETS tests are being badly abused. They complain that the results are being used for selection rather than as cutoffs for qualification. Currently many schools are receiving applications from so many highly qualified students that they have resorted to choosing between these individuals purely by virtue of a small difference in these scores. Some DETEST officials claim to have witnessed the choice of students by a difference of as little as 30 points, a fluctuation well within the range of chance. Such abuse of these scores is viewed as a terrible tragedy since it implies that applications are not being thoroughly screened and some of the finest applicants are not being accepted simply because their scores do not match up to the rest of their achievements.

So the debate rages on. The Educational Testing Service and its supporters maintain that the tests are fair and necessary. DETEST and other groups attack this view saying that the exams are socially biased and abused by many colleges and universities. Individual conflicts have been settled in court, but no major advance has been gained by either faction. It appears unlikely that a clear victory will soon be obtained in either direction. A compromise is imperative, however, as millions of students are affected annually by our present testing system.

— Peter Bakwin

Detail. Analysis can be very complicated and as a result can make for dull reading or listening. Writers and speakers therefore need to pay special attention to detail; they need to use vivid detail and a variety of examples to make sure their audiences can visualize each aspect of the subject and become emotionally involved when appropriate. At the same time, authors and speakers need to provide enough technical explanations and details so that their audiences can fully understand a problem, situation, or issue.

Object analysis is an exception to these rules. It is neutral in tone, and the author seldom addresses the readers directly. It uses the third person (*he, she, it, they*) almost exclusively and avoids trying to appeal to the reader's emotions. The burden of proof, as a result, lies almost entirely in the facts the author presents to support the conclusions reached in the analysis. The audience for this kind of discourse is for the most part already interested in the general topic and needs no vivid detail in order to be attracted to it.

Issue analysis is also a somewhat special case because although the analysis needs to be objective, the discourse may make use of highly emotional language and examples. By definition an issue is an area of disagreement, and when people disagree about something important they get angry and try to use interesting and vivid examples to support what they have to say. Issue analysis forces you to become involved in the argument, to get inside each position in the debate so that you can present it effectively. The more important the issue — abortion, drug use, nuclear power — the more emotional each side is likely to be. In addition, even though your treatment of an issue has to be even-handed, you can at times permit your emotions to show. If the arguments you are presenting appeal to the emotions, so should your treatment of them. If in the course of your analysis you decide that one side is clearly stronger, let your audience know by presenting your judgment in a concluding statement or by commenting on the quality of individual arguments. The author of the student essay, "The Pros and Cons of Seal Hunting," on pages 161–162, has a clear point of view but still manages to cover both sides of the issue. She uses emotional detail effectively in the beginning of the essay to establish the importance of the issue. In addition, she uses a wide variety of detail in the body of the paper and contrasts effectively the emotional, moral language of the opponents of seal hunting with the technical, relatively unemotional language of the proponents.

ENUMERATION

Using Enumeration

Enumeration as a pattern of thought means:

I. Arranging things in numerical order (first, second, third, and so on)
II. Putting things in order using some other standard sequence
   A. Alphabetical order (a, b, c, and so on)
   B. Large to small, short to tall, narrow to wide, and so on
III. Putting things in order using a spatial scheme
   A. Left-to-right, clockwise and counterclockwise, and so on
   B. Outline form
      I.
        A.
        B.
           1.
           2.
      II.

Enumeration is primarily the power of arrangement, the ability to put matters in manageable order. It is not a way of coming to any special understanding of a subject. To arrange the books in your personal library according to size may make your bookshelf neater, but it will not reveal anything about the content of the books or their importance to you. To put the addresses and phone numbers of your friends and family in alphabetical order may make it easier to locate the information when you need it, but it will not reveal anything about your relationship with the people or their importance to you.

In short, enumeration as a pattern of thought can help us organize our experience so that we can deal with it effectively and maybe come to understand it, but in most cases enumeration cannot contribute directly to an understanding of experience. Yet though it is more concerned with arrangement than with comprehension, enumeration is particularly useful in a complex society like ours because it makes information easier to use and to remember. Teachers put student names in their grade books in alphabetical order to make it easy to find a particular name when recording a grade or noting an absence. Airplane pilots assign numbers to the steps in an emergency procedure to make them easier to remember and to insure that they are carried out in the proper order even in a crisis. Library catalogues are arranged in alphabetical order by author, title, and subject so patrons can find one book among 40,000 or more.

The pattern can be helpful on a variety of occasions. When your subject is quite complicated, or when you think your audience may have trouble following what you want to say, enumeration can add clarity and emphasis to the primary pattern of your speech or essay. In both versions of the essay quoted below, for example, the directions are arranged in a process pattern. Yet notice how much easier it is to understand and remember the steps in the second version:

> When the materials are assembled, you are ready to begin. Set a log on its flattest, most stable end. Make sure any knobs are pointing perpendicular to the plane of the intended split since the grain is discontinuous in these areas and a clean cut is difficult. It is best to work in loose dirt or sand because the wood will be more stable on this kind of ground.
>
> Step back and grip the end of the sledge handle so that the head rests on the center of the log when your arms are fully extended. Swinging the sledge without bending at the elbows assures your accuracy and reduces muscular strain in your arms. Secure your stance with your feet shoulder-width apart and dig those steel-toed boots into the dirt. Think lumberjack!
>
> Bring the sledge behind your back, holding it so as to strike the wood with the sledge-shaped side of the head. By straightening your arms at the elbow, lift the sledge above your head so that your arms and the sledge handle are in one vertical line. . . .

> When the materials are assembled, you are ready to begin. First, set a log on its flattest, most stable end. Make sure any knobs are pointing perpendicular to the plane of the intended split since the grain is discontinuous in these areas and a clean cut is difficult. It is best to work in loose dirt or sand because the wood will be more stable on this kind of ground.
>
> Second, step back and grip the end of the sledge handle so that the head rests on the center of the log when your arms are fully extended. Swinging the sledge without bending at the elbows assures your accuracy and reduces muscular strain in your arms.
>
> Third, secure your stance with your feet shoulder width apart and dig those steel boots into the dirt. Think lumberjack!
>
> Fourth, bring the sledge behind your back, holding it so as to strike the wood with the sledge-shaped side of the head. By straight-

ening your arms at the elbow, lift the sledge above your head so that your arms and the sledge handle are in one vertical line . . . .

— Peter Bakwin

When you need to summarize the points you have made so the audience can remember them and act on them, enumeration can provide a compact format. When you go in for that job interview,

1. Keep saying to yourself, "I'm good enough for this job."
2. Pay attention to what the interviewer has to say and answer all questions concisely and honestly.
3. Ask any important questions you have about the company and the job.
4. Try not to panic if things don't seem to be going well — things may not be going as poorly as you think, and besides, there's always another chance.

When the time you have for a speech is limited or you believe your potential readers will not tolerate a long discussion, you can choose to cover only a few aspects of a topic, arranging them in an enumeration pattern:

> Debate over the future of nuclear power has been going on since the early 1950s and shows no signs of stopping. Neither you nor I have enough time tonight to review all the points that have been made by each side in the controversy. I will, therefore, limit what I have to say to three important aspects that have been regular features of the debate for the last three decades.

> The rapid rise to national prominence in 1977 of the National Music, Ballet, and Opera Company – West was followed three years later by its equally spectacular collapse. Now, a few years later, the causes of what was, at the time of the breakup, an astonishing event are becoming clear, and there are enough to fill a book — or two. I would like to concentrate on three that have received little attention, though they may well be among the most important factors. They are: (1) the breakdown of labor negotiations with stagehands in spring, 1979; (2) the failure of the advertising campaign for the expensive new production of *Turandot* in fall, 1979; and (3) the deterioration of the once-close relationship between the company's executive director and its chief patron.

The same strategy will work with topics that are too broad for a comprehensive treatment or that fail to fit within the kind of tight, logical organization provided by patterns like analysis, classification, comparison, or cause and effect. If, for example, you want to analyze an issue like gun control, and if your knowledge of this complicated issue is not extensive or you are unable to find a satisfactory way to organize all the points and subpoints on each side, you may want to limit yourself to a thorough discussion of two or three points, making no attempt to deal with the topic comprehensively:

> . . . As the examples I have just given indicate, gun control is both a very important and a very complex issue. In the time I have this afternoon, therefore, I would like to cover two of the major areas of disagreement over gun control. . . .

Here is how one author sees this use of enumeration:

> There are times when you have some "things to say" about a subject, but the best you can do is to put them into some reasonable order. You could probably say more about the subject, but you limit yourself to a representative number, and this order at least serves your purpose.
>
> (D'Angelo, 1980)

On an occasion when you are speaking and need to organize your thoughts quickly, enumeration can provide a convenient framework. If you are answering a question before an audience (or asking one), your answer will probably have several parts that may or may not be closely related. Setting up a pattern based on a quick estimate of the number of parts in your answer will give you better control over your discourse, allowing you to distinguish clearly between your ideas and to develop each one fully:

> My answer has two parts.
> First, . . .
> Second, . . .

Even when you have planned a speech ahead of time, you may at the last minute have to make adjustments based on changes in the situation or a new understanding of the audience's needs. Political candidates have to do this frequently. Despite having prepared a thorough and consistent set of statements on tax policy, a candidate may end up adapting them to a variety of audiences, changing the organization of the statements without greatly altering their content. To a group of business people, a candidate might say,

> I have three proposals for using tax policy to increase investment in business and decrease the tax bite on legitimate profits . . . .

To a group of suburban parents, the candidate might say,

> I have two proposals for decreasing your tax burden: first, an increase in the tax deduction for the interest on your home mortgages; second, credit for your children's college and private school tuition. Let me explain these in detail . . . .

The Finished Product

Point, Pattern, and Detail. Enumeration is seldom the only pattern controlling a piece of discourse, and the point and detail you choose for your speech or essay will need to reflect the overall purpose (to analyze, to classify, to inform, to persuade, and so on).

The organization of your discourse should, however, be based on the **enumeration pattern**:

Enumeration Pattern
Introduction (including thesis)
  First (one, A)
  Second (two, B)
  Third (three, C)
  Fourth, (four, D)
  Fifth, sixth, seventh (five, six, seven; E, F, G,; last)
Conclusion (including summary)

Whatever pattern of enumeration you choose (numerical, alphabetical, spatial, and so on), you should stick to it throughout the essay or speech. Your audience will probably lose track of the pattern unless you use cue words consistently:

Inconsistent	*Consistent*
First	First
Second	Second
Next	Third
And then	Fourth
In addition	Fifth
Moreover	Sixth

The following paper, an objective analysis, makes good use of the pattern and the cue words:

Critique of Magazine Article

The article I have chosen to critique appears in the April, 1981, issue of *Quill*, a magazine published for journalists and journalism students by the Society of Professional Journalists, Sigma Delta Chi. The article discusses the availability of jobs for journalism graduates and gives advice about locating a job.

The article is well done, as one would expect in a magazine that is published by such a highly qualified group. But what makes it so good? Why does it appeal to readers of the magazine? In the following paragraphs, I will cover six features that make the article successful.

First of all, the article appeals to its readers' interests. The audience for the magazine is made up primarily of people who have a position in journalism or who desire one. The split is about fifty-fifty. Half the audience, therefore, is directly interested in what the article says, and the other half is also interested, though less directly. The college seniors among the readers especially want to know about the job prospects they will face when they get into the working world in just a few short months.

Second, the timing of the article is excellent, and next to content, timing is the most important factor for attracting a reader to an article. This point may seem obvious, but what interest would most readers have in an article that deals with an election scheduled for two years from now? Probably not much at all. This article appears in the April issue of *Quill*, right before graduation time, when most seniors are thinking very seriously about jobs.

A *third* feature of the article is its uncomplicated layout. The article is divided into six basic parts; each one is clearly related to the whole. For example, one of the sections is headed "Hints for Hunters." This section contains tips that are useful for finding a good job. The tips are presented in an inspirational manner, which contributes to the overall impact by helping motivate readers to go out and get a job.

A *fourth* good aspect of the article is the use of graphics. In the middle of the article there is a half-page chart that lists (by percentage) the fields that recent journalism graduates have entered. The fields include newspaper work, wire services, advertising, and a number of others. The chart is particularly clear and indicates the wide range of opportunities in journalism.

A *fifth* quality of the piece is its use of first-hand sources. The article contains four first-hand accounts of actual job hunts, including descriptions of problems the people encountered. The material is presented in a straightforward manner, and the readers are left to judge what the market conditions are.

A *sixth* and *final* good point of the article is its attempt to predict the future job situation for journalism students. In this way it serves the needs of students who are not yet looking for jobs, but will be soon, and it also serves the needs of those readers who at some time in the future will be looking for a second or third job. The article presents a visual aid at the end that forecasts what jobs will be available during the 1980s. This, I think, is the single most important part of the entire article. What it does, in essence, is to summarize the entire outlook for journalism students.

This article is not perfect, however, and the major shortcoming is too serious to overlook. The problem is this: the author paints too rosy a picture of the job market for journalism. Despite her attempts to be realistic in describing the job situation, the author often gives the impression that it is relatively easy to find a job if you have a journalism degree. Well, this is not true. Only the highly skilled and motivated get the few available jobs out there in the working world. You have to really want to do this kind of work in order to get a job in journalism or a related field. This phrase used by journalists all over the nation sums up the job situation:

You gotta pay your dues
if you wanna write the news.

— Scott Schmitt

COMPARISON

Using Comparison

Comparison answers the question, "Is it similar to other things?" **Contrast** answers the question, "Is it different from other things?" When people use the term comparison they usually also mean to refer to the companion pattern, contrast, and that is how the word will be used here unless otherwise indicated.

Comparison is one of the most basic mental patterns our minds use to deal with experience. One of the first things a baby learns to do is to distinguish between a blanket and mother, between thumb and bottle. It is not surprising, then, that many of the other conceptual patterns make use of comparison.

Analysis notes differences in order to break a subject into parts. Definition often provides information about a word or concept by indicating what other words it is like (synonyms) and what ones it is not like (antonyms). In singling out a scene, character, or emotion, description points to its uniqueness, its specialness, in effect contrasting it with other less noteworthy experiences.

Nor is it surprising that while comparison can stand on its own as a pattern of expression, when it supports a particular point it is frequently used in combination with other patterns. Issue analysis is perhaps the most obvious example of a mixture because it openly compares differing points of view and its structural pattern is a blend of the analysis and comparison patterns. Comparison appears in other patterns as well — in classifications that isolate groups with widely differing qualities in order to explore their similarities and differences, and in conventional patterns as in ads, a form of persuasive discourse, designed to convince readers that the sponsor's product is better than all the others on the market:

"Puerto Rican white rum can do anything better than gin or vodka."

"Our Puerto Rican rum has started a new trend in Bloody Marys."

"People everywhere are discovering that the rum Bloody Mary possesses a smoothness and refinement you won't find in the vodka version."

"White rum also mixes marvelously with tonic or soda. And makes an exquisite dry martini."*

The impact of descriptions often depends on the contrasts they draw between two scenes or states of mind:

Contrast — Quiet Scene and Rapid Motion

Contrast — Silence, then Sound

Contrast — Change in Emotion

Broken, dry grass and hay crackled and crunched as I proceeded down the footpath. On my left was a spacious field, where the tall hay swayed gently with the teasing winds. I shifted my gaze to the right. Clusters of strong pine trees, frail dogwoods, elms, oaks, and maples were scattered along the side. Suddenly dipping across the path came a daring blue jay. After weaving its way in and out of the red and orange tree tops, it finally perched on one that was a kaleidoscope of colors. There was short moment of complete silence, and then the blue jay began giving its sermon in a loud, high-pitched tweet. Soon an angry blackbird answered with such a vigorous squawk that the flustered blue jay quickly departed.

I shifted my gaze further down the path, spotting sweet-smelling apple trees laden heavily with fruit. I ran down the path listening to the snapping of brittle pine needles beneath my feet, and the shuffling discarded leaves. Boom! Clumsily, I tripped over an ugly brown root and landed with a jolt on the hard ground. Tenderly, I picked myself up and headed more cautiously for the first apple tree.

— Laurie Burns

"But," you may well ask, "if comparison is such an essential pattern of thought, and if it is widely used in combination with other patterns of expression, aren't there occasions when it is used as the primary pattern of a speech or essay?" The answer is, "Yes, there are, but fewer than you might expect."

Comparison is often useful as the primary pattern of discourse on occasions calling for evaluation or for new insights (particularly for a reversal of widely-held opinions), as well as in a variety of academic tasks — preparing term papers, writing critical papers, composing essay questions.

When your potential audience is facing a choice among two or more alternatives, comparison may be an appropriate pattern for thought and expression. Choice is an essential feature of our society. Our political system asks us to choose among competing candidates, our economic system asks us to choose among competing products, our social and religious systems ask us to choose one way of living from among many and to distinguish between good and evil. Audiences, therefore, often look for help in evaluating alternatives; they want to know which choice is best or which product compares most favorably with an ideal standard.

---

*Reprinted courtesy of Rums of Puerto Rico.

Stockbrokers find ready listeners for presentations like "Bonds, Mutual Funds, Common Stocks: Which is the Best Investment for You?" and "Investment Choices for the 1980s." People look to their religious leaders for advice on moral and spiritual matters: "Personal Salvation *vs.* Social Action — Where Does Our Responsibility Lie?" "Faith and Intermarriage — What Are the Choices?" Campus organizations sponsor speakers and turn out pamphlets on the choices college students face in careers, in living arrangements, and in social activities. Magazines like *Consumer Reports* and *Motor Trend* have attracted a large readership by evaluating things like ice cream ("We tested vanillas and chocolates. Many tasted quite good, but only a few lived up to the ideal"), automobiles, and self-propelled lawn mowers ("Four of these rear baggers were superior performers").

The audience for this kind of discourse does not expect a balanced, completely neutral issue analysis, nor does it want to be persuaded — urged to choose a particular alternative. Instead, the audience expects value judgments — a discussion of relative weaknesses and strengths — but it wants to be left free to make a final decision based on individual circumstances and preferences. In short, evaluation may be in some ways comparable to issue analysis and persuasion, but it is nonetheless distinct.

When your potential audience holds a point of view you wish to change substantially, even reverse, comparison can be a useful tool. Often an audience's beliefs rest on the assumption that two situations are similar (or different):

If we can put a man on the moon, we should be able to solve the nation's social problems. (Assumption: technical and social problems are similar.)

If this marketing strategy worked in Seattle, it will work in Washington, D.C. (Assumption: the two cites have similar economic and social patterns.)

The kinds of things you did to get good grades in high school won't help you in college. (Assumption: the system of rewards changes as you move from secondary school to college.)

A comparison speech or essay can help change attitudes like these by showing that the assumptions underlying them are incorrect and that the two situations are actually related in a way different from the one the audience supposed (for example, technical and social problems are dissimilar).

When some people hear of experiments that have taught apes to use sign language and message boards, they leap to the conclusion that apes can use language as humans do and may in the future be able to communicate with us. They also tend to view anyone who argues against this interpretation as a spoilsport, someone who is standing in the way of progress because of professional jealousy. In a situation like this, a critic of the research would be wrong to try to present a straightforward analysis identifying its faults because such a critic would end up sounding like an ill-tempered fault-finder, and readers or listeners would be inclined to automatically reject that analysis. Comparison, however, can provide a positive approach, showing that despite some obvious similarities with people, the supposedly-talking apes are more like trained animals than human beings. This excerpt from a magazine article takes just such an approach:

Performing Animals: Secrets of the Trade*

So-called talking animals are nothing new. They have appeared in European circuses for centuries and on American television for as long as the medium has been popular. Roy Rogers' horse, Trigger, could count; he answered with his hooves just about any question requiring a yes or no response. Except for the fact that there is no intended deception, the linguistic apes of recent fame are part of the same tradition of animal-human communication as four-legged performers and talking horses.

Thirteen years ago, Beatrice and Allen Gardner of the University of Nevada began their now famous effort to teach Washoe, a chimpanzee, American Sign Language (ASL), the gestural language used by the deaf in the United States. Other experiments to teach chimpanzees to speak had failed, the Gardners reasoned, because chimpanzees lacked the apparatus to vocalize. Within a year, they were able to report that Washoe had command of about 10 signs and was beginning to invent combinations of them, such as *gimme tickle*. Washoe was capable of language. It seemed that humans were not the only species in the universe capable of language. Other researchers, some using ASL and some using artificial languages of various forms, found evidence that appeared to support the Gardners' results. Now Herbert Terrace, through careful linguistic analysis of chimpanzee-human conversations, has concluded that we may indeed still be the only talking animals. But Terrace's approach is only half the critique. The other half is to to be found in unconscious bias, self-deception, magic, and circus performance.

Man trains animals in one of two distinct ways: *apprentissage*, or scientific training, and *dressage*, or performance training. In apprentissage, the animal's behavior is, in theory, guided not by its relation-

---

*Thomas A. Sebeok and Jean Umiker-Sebeok, from "Performing Animals: Secrets of the Trade." Reprinted from *Psychology Today* Magazine. Copyright © 1979 Ziff-Davis Publishing Company. Used by permission.

ship with a trainer, but by a fixed set of rewards and punishments consciously applied according to the classic rules of behavioral psychology. Rats are taught to run a maze and pigeons to peck at different shapes and colors by apprentissage. In dressage, the emotional interaction between man and animal is a crucial part of the training, since the animal must learn to read the verbal and nonverbal cues of its trainer. Horses taught to perform for the purpose of exhibition and porpoises taught to play basketball are trained by dressage.

The most thorough examination of dressage to date is Oskar Pfungst's study of the circus horse Clever Hans early in this century. The stallion, it was claimed, could spell, read, and solve problems in math and musical harmony. But Pfungst, a psychologist at the celebrated Berlin Psychological Institute, noticed that as the distance between Hans and his questioners increased, the animal's accuracy increased, and that if the questioners did not know the correct answer, Hans's performance suffered. Pfungst then began a series of experiments in which a number of elements of the question-and-answer procedure were systematically altered. He was able to uncover several types of visual and auditory cues that were unwittingly being given Hans by his questioners. The feats of Clever Hans amounted to nothing more, Pfungst concluded, than go and no-go responses to minimal cues provided by the people around him.

One way to distinguish apprentissage from dressage is to examine the variation in an animal's performance with different experimenters. People vary in the amount of nonverbal cuing they do, so that a dressage-trained animal will do better with some people than with others. Pfungst noted that certain questioners were more successful than others at eliciting correct responses from Hans. Hans preferred, and performed best for, people who exhibited an "air of quiet authority," "intense concentration," a "facility for motor discharge," and the power to "distribute tension economically." In other words, after giving the animal the cue to begin, the successful examiner would tense and lean forward slightly to focus intently on the horse's tapping response or on other correct movement. When the horse had completed the correct response, the questioner would relax with a barely perceptible movement that would signal Hans to stop performing. Whenever the questioner was inattentive, tired, unaware of the correct answer, or for some other reason incapable of producing the necessary muscular signal, and Hans was left to his own, somewhat limited, horse sense, he produced the wrong answer.

A similar dependence on human guidance seems to arise in training apes to use language. David Premack once attempted to test his chimpanzee Sarah with a "dumb" trainer, one who was unfamiliar with Sarah's language of word tokens. The trainer was to present Sarah with a problem on a display board and to report the token she selected by microphone to another trainer in an adjacent room.

Under these conditions, Sarah's accuracy decreased sharply and, to Premack's surprise, she reverted to an earlier form of sentence production. "Early in (her) training," writes Premack, "she had not produced sentences in their final order: she put correct words on the board in incorrect order and then made one or two changes before settling on a final order. Although she had abandoned this mode of production at least 10 months earlier, she reverted to it with the 'dumb' trainer." This is precisely the sort of behavior one might expect from an animal searching for clues from the experimenter. She would display the word tokens and then move them around, waiting for some unintentional sign from the trainer that one particular arrangement was considered acceptable.

Aware of the Clever Hans phenomenon, researchers sometimes go to great lengths to eliminate possible cuing in their experiments. Some experimenters have attempted to limit the social interaction between the animal and trainers in order to create conditions appropriate to apprentissage, but in every case that has proved to be a major impediment to learning. Sarah's trainers first worked inside her cage so that they could guide her hands, turn her head in the proper direction when her attention began to wane, and even pat her back and encourage her with words of affection. After many months of training in these intimate conditions, Sarah became sexually mature and sometimes dangerous (the project started when Sarah was already six years old). Thereafter, training had to be carried on through a small door in her cage, and Premack noted that under these conditions she rejected far more lessons than before.

(Sebeok and Umiker-Sebeok, 1979)

The authors of this piece begin with the assumption that their readers believe talking apes are something new and are examples of an unusual kind of animal behavior. They then set out to show that, on the contrary, the talking is similar in many ways to the behavior of many trained animals. To establish this similarity, they distinguish between two types of training, apprentissage, which the apes' supporters claim to use, and dressage, which is the procedure the authors believe the experimenters have unconsciously employed. Thus comparison helps organize both the essay and the argument it contains.

Academic situations often call for comparison papers. Though comparison is seldom the primary pattern of scholarly books, articles, or speeches, college teachers often assign comparison essays — for two very good reasons. First, comparison enables students to gain an extensive understanding of a subject by seeing how it is related to other phenomena and by examining all its features in detail in the course of discovering similarities and differences. Here is a typical understanding question:

Compare and contrast the development of race relations in Hong Kong and South Africa; or in Hong Kong and the United States.

(Smith and Preston, 1977)

Comparison gives students a chance to evaluate competing theories or interpretations and to choose one as a basis for their own work. Here is a typical evaluation question:

Stalin and Hitler represented two opposing ideological systems, yet some historians see their methods of rule as strikingly similar. Compare and contrast their actual methods of governing. Do you agree or disagree with these historians?

(Maimon, et al., 1981)

There are, of course, other occasions for using comparison; you may wish to use it to examine your past experience, to convey ambivalent feelings about a subject, or to highlight the contradictions you find in people's everyday behavior. Whatever the occasion, you need to make sure the topic you choose can be dealt with effectively by the comparison pattern and that you have a clear purpose for using the pattern.

Getting Materials

Finding a good topic for a comparison essay or speech can be a relatively difficult job. In the first place, the subjects you choose need to be similar enough to make comparison worthwhile. Far-fetched comparisons will fail; you are best off comparing two or more things of roughly the same kind: cares, political candidates, economic theories (capitalism and socialism), kinds of housing (apartments versus condominiums), pets (fish, birds, dogs), or friends (the quiet one, the funny one).

In the second place, however, the subjects have to be different enough so that there is a real choice between them or so that the process of comparison can reveal unique qualities in each. Apartments and condominiums, for example, are similar in most physical respects, but so different in cost and financial commitments that they offer a real choice for someone looking for a place to live.

In the third place, the subjects have to be worth comparing; you have to be able to say something about them that your audience will consider worth its time and attention. You can compare Cadillacs and Chevrolets, concluding that the Cadillacs are better automobiles, but most people will not be much interested in what you have to say because they will already assume, on the basis of reputation and cost, that Cadillacs are better cars. If you compare Chevrolets, Plymouths, and Fords, however, many people will probably be interested in your conclusions because they will consider these three kinds of cars as legitimate competitors.

Once you have chosen your subjects and jotted down their obvious similarities and differences, you should look them over again, searching for less obvious points of comparison. You may wish to make a list of the important aspects of your subjects and arrange it in this manner:

	Subject #1	*Subject #2*
Aspect #1		
Aspect #2		
Aspect #3		
Aspect #4		
Aspect #5		

Examining your subjects systematically is a form of analysis, and as with any analysis the parts or aspects you choose to divide your subjects into will depend on the overall purpose of your comparison. Most good comparisons are those that go beyond the obvious to discover new and interesting similarities and differences. Putting your thoughts on paper during analysis will help you remember the aspects you have covered and keep you aware of those still to be examined; it will also help you to see which points of comparison are strong and promising and which are weak.

The Finished Product

Point. Even if you have chosen your topic wisely and gathered interesting material, unless you have made some clear and worthwhile point, at the end of your speech or essay your audience may still remark, "So what?" To put this another way, comparison can be a complicated exercise without much meaning unless you use it to accomplish a purpose your audience finds both interesting and rewarding.

A thesis statement like "I intend to compare X and Y" usually indicates that the author has no real point to make. Thesis statements like the following, however, indicate that the author has an aim and a strategy:

> Most people believe that public and private schools offer different kinds of education; yet in such important features as course content and academic standards there are many fewer differences than most people suppose.

> The read-summarize-respond method of studying is superior in almost all respects to the other study systems commonly used by college students.

> These two friends from my childhood were very different, yet each played a part in shaping my personality.

Comparison discourse can be difficult for readers and listeners to follow because it moves from subject to subject and from comparison to contrast, usually introducing considerable detail along the way. To give your audience some guidance, therefore, you will usually need to do some things near the beginning of your speech or essay: name the subjects you will be discussing, indicate what you will have to say about them and why this should interest the audience, and indicate what pattern you plan to follow in your discussion. Here is an opening paragraph of a student essay that does all these things:

An Alternative to Money

Before the introduction of standardized currency around 1800, the most effective method of exchanging goods and services in the United States was bartering. As our nation grew, people began to rely on money (coins, paper currency) to buy what they could not grow or make themselves. Today our country has come to rely almost totally on its monetary system, though some people, especially old New Englanders, have kept the practice of bartering alive over the years. Yet many people are beginning to discover the advantages of swapping and trading over the use of money, and bartering is a growing phenomenon.

— Grace Gardiner

This introduction names the general topic, methods of exchanging goods and services, as well as the two subjects to be compared, currency and bartering. Words like *alternative* and *advantage* indicate that the essay will contrast the subjects. The thesis, stated in the last sentence of the paragraph, not only promises to show readers the advantages of barter, but also promises to let them in on the latest trend, "a growing phenomenon," implying that they will learn how to get goods and services without spending money — that is, something for nothing.

Pattern. Because comparison discourse has multiple subjects, the pattern that underlies it is complicated; in fact, comparison speeches and essays usually follow one of two basic patterns depending on whether comparisons between entire subjects or between individual aspects of the subjects are to be emphasized.

Comparison Pattern #1 (**Subject Pattern**)

Introduction (thesis, introduce subjects, pattern)
    Subject 1
        Aspect 1
        Aspect 2
        Aspect 3, 4, 5 etc.

Subject 2
  Aspect 1
  Aspect 2
  Aspect 3, 4, 5, etc.
Conclusion (summary)

Comparison Pattern #2 (**Aspect Pattern**)

Introduction (thesis, introduce subjects, pattern)
  Aspect 1
    Subject 1
    Subject 2
  Aspect 2
    Subject 1
    Subject 2
  Aspect 3, 4, 5
    Subject 1
    Subject 2
Conclusion (summary)

The two patterns can be mixed, but the results tend to be confusing. The pattern you decide on should be the one that best fits your topic and your purpose. If, for example, you wish to emphasize broad differences and similarities between your subjects, then the Subject Pattern is more appropriate. If, on the other hand, you wish to emphasize how the subjects are similar in some aspects but different in others, then the Aspect Pattern is more appropriate.

To make the pattern (organization) of your discourse plain to readers and listeners, you can use two sets of cue words:

Words Identifying Aspects of a Subject	*Words Indicating Relationships Between Subjects*
trait	in comparison
characteristic	in contrast
element	on the other side
part	likewise, moreover
segment	in the same (different) manner
unit	in addition, then
feature	yet, but, however, nonetheless
	first, second, third
	although, still

The following essay uses the Aspect Pattern and makes use of words as cues for the reader:

All Work and No Play

While I enjoy reading, many of my friends do not. One of the most unpopular subjects that they are forced to read about is history. Many textbooks contain only page after page of dull, dry material. And historical novels, while often interesting, are notoriously inaccurate. Fortunately, there is an alternative to reading about history. Simulation gaming, commonly known as wargaming, can provide an interesting supplement to this drudgery.

Although simulation gaming has been with us for centuries, only recently has it become popular. This is due to the mass market appeal of *Dungeons and Dragons*, a swords-and-sorcery game that has caught the public's eye and led to more interest in the gaming field as a whole.

Still, when you ask the average person about wargames, you receive such a response as "What, you mean like *Risk?*" *Risk*, however, is a simple boardgame. Simulation games deal with hard facts and historical realities. They allow one to assume the role of politician, military leader, or economist, and, working within the historical boundaries, actually manipulate the situation at hand.

Reading about history may be fine for memorizing name and dates, but simulation gaming can more easily make you understand why something happened. Instead of reading glib words about the brilliance of Alexander the Great, try maneuvering your skirmishers around ponderous Persian phalanxes. That is, after you've found the timber to build the galleys to carry those troops across the Mediterranean in the first place.

Although learning a new simulation game requires time, once you have become experienced this process takes no more than a couple of hours. In the same time that it would have taken you to read that chapter on the Battle of Britain in your text, you and a few friends could have recreated the entire campaign and seen just how deadly a Messerschmitt could be at night.

Most simulations require more than one person, in order to play opposing sides. (There must be conflict, for there would be very little history without it.) With more than one person playing, ideas and alternate strategies can be exchanged. What if the French knights at Agincourt had stayed in the woods away from the English longbows? History books rarely speculate about such things, but with a simulation game you can find them out for yourself.

Simulation games are not exclusively military in nature. Picture yourself as the ruler of Spain during the sixteenth century. You are trying not to start a war with another nation. You must find colonists for the New World and priests to convert the pagans. Your stolen gold must come back safely so that you can pay off the German banking houses. The peasants must not be allowed to revolt. When things start going wrong, you too may succumb to the temptation of the Armada Syndrome. And even if your empire crumbles, you will have had a lot more fun than if you had read I.M. Turgid's *History of Spain* in twenty-nine volumes.

A good simulation game costs about as much as the average textbook. And, while it takes some experience to pick a good simulation, there are fewer bad games than ther are bad texts. There are any number of publications to aid the student in choosing an accurate and appropriate simulation. Any hobby shop is likely to have information on gaming.

Simulation gaming, then, would seem to be a supplement to merely reading about history. While a simulation game may not provide as much hard information as a textbook, its many other advantages can combine to create a powerful learning aid. We students are told that we study history in order to learn from it. However, we don't learn from names and dates; we learn from experience. Simulation gaming allows us to experience history.

— Chris Stetson

Detail. Choosing the kind and quantity of detail for a comparison can be difficult. You need to include enough to convince your audience that the differences and similarities you are talking about are real ones, but not so much that the audience gets lost in exploring one of the subjects and loses sight of the comparison. A well-chosen example that accurately represents the aspect you are discussing is usually better than a host of smaller details.

Finally, evaluations can pose a special problem. If you are comparing two or more products, all you have to do is select details that clearly and fairly represent the products; but if you are comparing a product with an ideal standard, you will have to supply the details of the perfect product yourself:

> Ideally, a kitchen fire extinguisher ought to be able to put out all three major kinds of fires — grease, electric, wood and trash; it ought to be no more than fourteen to sixteen inches high so that it can fit under counters; it ought to weigh no more than four pounds so that it can be used even by a child; it ought to have a simple, one-handed operation; and it ought to be attractive enough so that people will be willing to have it in their kitchens.

SUMMARY

Analysis, enumeration, and comparison are three static conceptual patterns that aid in understanding experience and expressing that understanding. Analysis breaks problems, situations, issues, and objects into parts, examining them to see how they fit together to form a whole. Enumeration is concerned primarily with arrangement; it can help bring clarity to other patterns of expression and can be used to organize speeches and essays on occasions when more comprehensive patterns are inappropriate. Comparison is useful in evaluations, in changing attitudes, in providing new insights into a subject, and in fulfilling a variety of academic assignments.

KEY WORDS

analysis	enumeration
problem analysis	enumeration pattern
situation analysis	comparison
issue analysis	contrast
objective analysis	subject pattern
analysis pattern	aspect pattern

EXERCISES

Analysis

1. List three current social, political, or economic controversies. Reduce each one to a specific issue and state it in concrete terms. Then divide each issue by identifying the major arguments or positions on each side of the issue.

2. Here are some topics that an audience might be interested in hearing or reading about. Divide each into parts in such a way that it would make for an effective and interesting situation analysis.
   a. an interesting region or city in this country
   b. a movie, play, or television series
   c. a sport, game, or hobby
   d. life at your college or university
   e. an interesting job or occupation
   f. a field of study

3. Think of some campus or local organizations that an audience might be interested in learning about. Jot down the various features and services of one you think would make the best topic for a speech or essay.

4. Below are four thesis statements. What kind of analysis (problem, situation, issue, object) does each one suggest?
   a. During the last five years the two sides in the dispute over nuclear energy have developed detailed arguments well worth reviewing before any decision is made about the future of the industry.

   b. The question that is on the mind of most citizens of this town, then, is: Why are the roads in such terrible shape?
   c. Since most people haven't had a chance to trudge through the jungles of Mexico looking for Mayan ruins, I'd like to take you there for a while.
   d. The American auto industry is facing a real crisis brought on by competition from foreign imports.

5. Describe a potential audience for an analysis essay of each of the following kinds: a problem analysis, a situation analysis, an issue analysis, an object analysis. Write an essay addressed to one of the audiences you have identified.

6. Describe a speaking occasion for an analysis speech of each of the following kinds: a problem analysis, a situation analysis, an issue analysis, an object analysis.

7. Survey your classmates to discover what issues, problems, or situations they consider interesting. Then prepare an analysis speech or essay that takes their interests into account.

Enumeration

1. Write out brief openings for speeches or essays on these topics. Make sure each opening announces clearly to the audience that the discourse will be following an enumeration pattern.
   a. nuclear power
   b. rape or sexual harassment
   c. the economic problems this college faces
   d. career choices for college students
   e. problems in trying to study effectively for tests

2. List as many situations as you can for which enumeration might be an appropriate pattern in a speech or essay.

3. What are five enumeration systems that could be used to organize a speech or an essay?

4. For what topics or kinds of topics might an enumeration pattern be particularly appropriate?

5. Prepare a speech or essay in which you impose an enumeration pattern on the subject because its parts do not fall into any particular order of their own.

Comparison

1. Create thesis statements for possible comparison essays or speeches on each of these topics:

    a. cameras
    b. stereos
    c. automobiles
    d. friends
    e. pets
    f. future sources of energy
    g. career choices

2. Write an opening paragraph for an essay designed to evaluate some common products or services and share it with the other members of the class to get their reaction to its effectiveness.

3. List as many writing and speaking occasions as you can for which comparison would be an appropriate pattern. Choose three of them and jot down the ideas you would use in your discourse, along with some indication of the way you would arrange them.

4. If you have been assigned a comparison essay or speech in some other class, bring in the assignment to discuss with your classmates.

5. Prepare a comparison speech or essay in which you evaluate two or more processes or products.

6. Prepare a comparison speech or essay in which you try to change your audience's point of view about some campus, local, or national matter.

7. Use comparison to probe your experience, and then prepare a speech or essay in which you compare or contrast individuals or experiences that have had great impact on your life.

8. Prepare a comparison speech or essay in which you review the options available to your audience as they prepare to make a decision or undertake an action.

REFERENCES

D'Angelo, Frank. *Process and Thought in Composition*, 2nd ed. (Cambridge, Mass.: Winthrop, 1980).

Maimon, Elaine P., et al. *Writing in the Arts and Sciences* (Cambridge, Mass.: Winthrop, 1981).

Sebeok, Thomas A., and Jean Uniker-Sebeok, "Performing Animals: Secrets of the Trade," *Psychology Today* (November 1979).

Smith, Ronald W., and Frederick W. Preston. *Sociology: An Introduction* (New York: St. Martin's, 1977).

8. Static Patterns: Classification, Description, Definition, Exemplification

CLASSIFICATION

Static patterns enable us to examine our experiences in various ways. We can examine them by means of analysis, separating them into parts for closer inspection. We use enumeration to order them for easier consideration. Comparing them with similar or different experiences helps us view them more clearly. These three types of static patterns — analysis, enumeration, and comparison — were considered in Chapter Seven. This chapter will examine the other static patterns: classification, description, definition, and exemplification.

Using Classification

What kind of movies do you like? Comedies? Love stories? Horror shows? Melodramas? Westerns?

What kind of desserts do you like? Pies? Cakes? Cheeses? Ice cream sundaes? Fruits?

What kinds of activities help you relax? Sports? Reading? Dancing? Watching television? Games?

What kind of career would you like? Medicine? Business? Teaching? Publishing? Politics?

The pattern of thought that enables you to understand and answer these questions is classification. **Classification** is the process of sorting experiences (people, ideas, events, things) into groups on the basis of common characteristics or traits. It discovers relationships among the things we experience and uses these relationships to create categories.

Classification is an essential mental activity, a part of almost everything we do. We classify our friends — those we turn to for advice, for fun, for companionship, or for sympathy. We classify our clothes — for everyday, for dirty work, for formal occasions, for special dates. We classify our favorite foods:

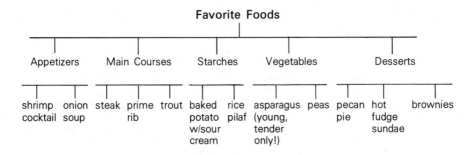

Favorite Foods

Appetizers	Main Courses	Starches	Vegetables	Desserts
shrimp cocktail onion soup	steak prime rib trout	baked potato w/sour cream rice pilaf	asparagus (young, tender only!) peas	pecan pie hot fudge sundae brownies

Classification is particularly useful when our minds are struggling with a lot of new material or information. When most people start to work on something complicated like a model airplane or a stained glass ornament, they arrange all the pieces in groups ahead of time to make them easier to find later and to get some idea of how they will fit together. If you were to sit down to work on a complicated jigsaw puzzle, for example, the first thing you would probably do would be to sort the pieces into groups like these: blue (sky pieces), green (grass pieces), solid brown (house pieces), brown with bits of green (forest pieces), pieces with one flat side (edge pieces), and so on. These groups overlap a bit, of course; a blue piece with one flat side would actually belong to two groups. (With informal classifications like this, such overlaps create no real problem; the aim is to create usable categories, not rigid ones.)

When you plan to present the results of a classification to an audience in a speech or essay, however, you need to set up the categories so that they can stand close inspection. One way to do this is to form all categories on the basis of a single, clearly identified feature. This feature, or base, or principle of division, should be used both to identify the members of a group and to separate the different groups. The distinguishing feature for a classification of land vehicles could be the number of wheels:

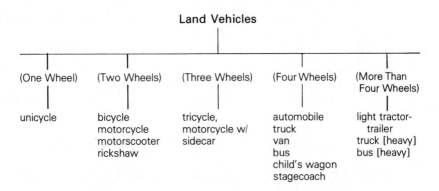

Land Vehicles

(One Wheel)	(Two Wheels)	(Three Wheels)	(Four Wheels)	(More Than Four Wheels)
unicycle	bicycle motorcycle motorscooter rickshaw	tricycle, motorcycle w/ sidecar	automobile truck van bus child's wagon stagecoach	light tractor-trailer truck [heavy] bus [heavy]

Some of these categories can be divided further into subcategories based on source of power: motor, human, or animal.

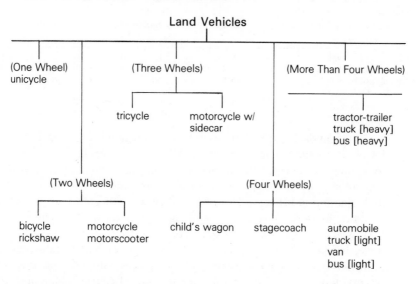

Land Vehicles

There is no overlap in the last two categories because the distinction between light and heavy trucks (and buses) is a generally recognized one.

For a thorough, formal classification, this process of dividing and subdividing may go on until all classes and subclasses have been accounted for. Biology students are familiar with such exhaustive classifications:

CLASS Mammalia. Warm-blooded vertebrates with hair and with young nourished by milk from the mammary glands of the mother.
  SUBCLASS Prototheria. Oviparous mammals with a cloaca.
    ORDER Monotremata. The duckbill (*Ornithorhynchus*) and the spiny anteater (*Echidna*).
  SUBCLASS Metatheria. Viviparous animals with skin pouch (marsupium) for the carriage of the immature young.
    ORDER Marsupialia. Kangaroos, wombats, opossums, wallabies, and the koala.
  SUBCLASS Eutheria. The placental mammals.
    ORDER Insectivora. Insect-eating mammals. Moles, hedgehogs, and shrews.
    ORDER Chiroptera. Flying mammals. Bats.
    ORDER Dermoptera. Lateral skin folds adapted for gliding. Flying lemur.
    ORDER Rodentia. Gnawing mammals. Squirrels, beavers, rats, rabbits, porcupines, mice, and guinea pigs.

ORDER Edentata. Toothless mammals (either toothless or having de-
generate teeth without enamel.) Sloths, scaly anteaters, and armadil-
los.

ORDER Carnivora. Flesh-eating mammals. Cats, tigers, lions, bears,
dogs, weasels, otters, hyenas, civets, walruses, seals, sea lions.

ORDER Primates. Highest mammals. Lemurs, monkeys, apes and
man.

— Taylor and Weber, 1961

A classification as complicated as this may be appropriate for some kinds of
scientific and technical writing, but it is too complex for most other writing
and speaking occasions. Most classification essays and speeches concentrate
on presenting their material in a limited number of categories that an audience can comprehend easily. Our minds find it much easier to understand
and remember twenty pieces of information when they are gathered into three
or four logical groups than when the pieces of information are simply presented one after the other. The strength of classification as a pattern of expression, then, is that it allows us to present complex topics in a manner that
will enable most audiences to understand them; but if the expression itself gets
too complex for a particular audience to understand, it is bound to fail.

On occasions when we have an abundance of information to convey, classification can be a very useful tool. Every day we encounter pamphlets, magazine articles, guidebooks, classified ads, catalogues, newspaper columns, and
textbooks that use classification to introduce us to new fields, to provide us
with essential information, or to make clear a complicated body of knowledge, as does this passage from a college sociology textbook:

> . . . A *crowd* may be defined as a temporary gathering of people at one
> time and place. In addition, there are different types of crowds.
>
> Sociologist Herbert Blumer discusses four types. The *casual crowd* is
> an aggregate of onlookers viewing a common event, such as shoppers
> looking in a department store window. The group has no unity or inter-
> nal organization and only a momentary existence. In contrast, the *con-
> ventionalized crowd* consists of individuals pursuing a mutual goal.
> Their behavior is considerably more established and regularized. Fans
> watching a football game and members of a congregation listening to a
> Sunday sermon are examples. Of course, the relatively few and simple
> norms and sanctions operating in these groups are quite different. A
> member of a congregation would hardly jump up from a pew, shake his
> fist, and boo the minister for a poor sermon, nor would an avid football
> fan sit placidly with her arms folded as her team was penalized by a
> "nearsighted" referee. A somewhat uncomplicated type of social organi-
> zation is guiding behavior, but instability is still present.
>
> Whereas casual and conventionalized crowds do not engage in direct
> action toward individuals and objects, the *active crowd* does. A lynch
> mob or soccer fans who square off and battle each other are examples.

In the fourth type, the *expressive crowd*, participants gather together for self-stimulation. People who shout, sing, and rejoice at a religious revival and an emotional audience that experiences a "happening" at a rock music festival such as Woodstock are examples. Blumer maintains that expressive crowds usually begin as conventionalized crowds, but as emotions become intense, the social organization guiding member behavior becomes ineffectual. Self-exaltation eventually dominates.

(Smith and Preston, 1977)

In addition, explanatory speeches frequently employ classification.

Hospital administrator speaking at orientation for new staff members

Today I would like to review for you the three different kinds of responsibilities you will have in your new position: patient care, record keeping, emergency procedures. . . .

College lecture

I want to discuss the categories into which Shakespeare's plays have been traditionally grouped — tragedies, comedies, and histories — and to ask along the way if these are really useful categories . . . .

On occasions when we want to help a potential audience deal with a situation that poses a variety of difficulties or unusual challenges, classification can be an appropriate tactic.

Report from consulting firm hired by a local government

Previous earth dams in this area collapsed, causing tragic loss of life, because the builders failed to pay sufficient attention to several kinds of problems including those posed by the harsh climate, the ruggedness of the terrain, and the lack of density in the local soil.

Presentation by up-and-coming vice president to chief executive officer and board of directors

The San Francisco market is a rich and promising one, but entering it will require rapid expansion and may expose our company to several potentially serious kinds of risks: overextension of the workforce, rapid depletion of operating capital, breakdowns in accounting safeguards, and failures in computerized inventory procedures.

Classification can also be used on occasions when we want to get an audience to take a fresh look at everyday experience — to see that human behavior falls into clear patterns, or to notice order and system in the physical world that surrounds us. Most college students, for example, would be ready to listen to a humorous classification of the teaching styles of their professors or to a serious discussion of different kinds of study systems. The following essay offers insight into the ways human beings behave:

'Tis the Season

A season, as defined by the dictionary, is "One of the four divisions of the year as determined by the earth's position with respect to the sun." Four times a year calendars and newscasters announce the change of the seasons, and people look forward to a change in the weather. There is, however, another way to tell what season it is — by the mood of the people. This method may not be common, but it is just as effective. For every season there is a different attitude, and this is evident in the actions and spirits of the people.

Winter is the time of year when cold and snow keep most people confined to warm areas. As a result of this confinement, socializing outside the home is limited, and the general mood is subdued but happy. Snowfalls, common to winter, are beautiful and serene, adding to the calmness of the season. Sometimes, however, the effect of snow may be to the contrary. Few people enjoy the chore of shoveling themselves out of the driveway! Yet even this does not seem to destroy the overall mood. Winter brings with it two very special holidays: Christmas and Hanukkah. Both of these holidays are family oriented: together with confinement due to weather they create strong family bonds. The weeks before, during, and after Christmas and Hanukkah are filled with hustle and bustle. Yet overall, spirits remain joyous and peaceful, characteristic of the winter season.

When spring arrives, the flowers begin to blossom, and so do individuals. It seems as though everyone comes out of hiding to enjoy the warm weather. The general feeling is one of friendliness and kindness; and so mingling is quite common. Easter, May Day, and April Fool's Day are holidays that exemplify the amicable disposition of this season. The bright colors of clothing and decor people choose for this season further illustrate the warmheartedness of spring.

— Kathy Canty

Getting Materials

In preparing to write a classification speech or essay, you will probably have to do two things at the same time. You will have to decide on the categories to use and you will have to collect details and examples as illustrations of the categories.

Even before you do these things, however, you will have to decide on a topic. Think about what kinds of things you know that might interest other people. What do you know about different sports, hobbies, jobs or organizations? Ask yourself questions like these:

Are there everyday things that, if classified, might reveal something about human nature? (eating habits, dating habits, choice of clothing)

Are there kinds of events and situations that irritate me (and other people as well) and that might be worth looking into through classification? (the ways police use radar; difficulties with the campus health services)

Are there sets of behavior that puzzle me but that I might understand better if I arrange them in categories? (excessive use of alcohol and drugs; cheating and plagiarism)

Here is a student essay that might have been written in response to the third kind of question ("Why do people continue smoking when they know it is dangerous?"):

Let's Smoke On It

"Warning: The Surgeon General has determined that cigarette smoking is dangerous to your health." Thousands of times a day this message is ignored by the elite group of people known as smokers. It seems ridiculous in this decade of self-improvement and self-preservation that anyone could fail to notice such a warning. And yet, the tobacco industry is booming, mass producing countless brands of cigars, cigarettes, and pipe tobacco.

But why? Why do teenagers, old men, and cancer victims still insist on polluting their bodies with smoke? There is, unfortunately, no clear-cut answer to the question because there are many different kinds of smokers and many different reasons why they smoke.

There is, for example, the peer-group smoker. This smoker has taken up the habit because of pressure from his social environment. He smokes only to be able to fit in with the crowd and to be accepted. This kind of smoking habit is frequently found among teenagers, for whom social acceptance is particularly important. The peer-group smoker is usually not an intense smoker, and he tends to get little pleasure from the act since he has been forced into it. Consequently, he may eventually decide to stop as soon as he gets a bit older and begins to feel independent of the "group."

Not unlike the peer-group smoker is the fad smoker. A fad smoker begins smoking because it is trendy, because it is chic, because it is "in." Although the fad smoker doesn't have to smoke to fit in with a group, she chooses to anyway, just to develop a certain image. Thanks to the media, many people believe that the lighting of a cigarette or cigar creates a mystique. Cigar and cigarette ads constantly promote the "macho cowboy" and "blond bombshell" look through advertising, hoping to add glamour to smoking. The fad smoker is also not a heavy smoker because she lights up only when it suits her purposes, not her pleasures.

The casual smoker is inclined to be more serious. He smokes because he wants to and enjoys it. He usually smokes when having a drink and in other social settings. This type of smoker also varies in his consumption of cigarettes. Sometimes he may have as little as two or three a day, and other times as many as a pack or two in only a few hours, depending on his social setting. Common claims from this casual smoker are, "Oh, I don't really smoke" and "I can quit anytime I want." In many cases, this latter statement is true. The casual smoker can eventually quit if he really wants to because smoking has not yet become an overriding force in his life.

This, however, is not the case for the addicted smoker. He cannot quit as readily as the casual smoker can because of one key factor: habit. When the phone rings, he quickly grabs his ashtray and cigarettes and chats. When having a cup of coffee in the morning, he simply must have a cigarette because "the coffee won't taste as good without it." And always, without fail, a good meal is followed by a good cigarette. The addicted smoker also smokes on a regular basis — a pack or two a day, never more, never less. He becomes irritated when he discovers he is down to his last butt and rushes to buy another pack. He also plays games in his mind by buying only packs instead of cartons, rationalizing that because cigarettes aren't always on hand he can't be smoking too much. He is constantly trying to cut down and tells everyone so, but never actually does, because in reality, he is addicted to smoking.

The last and most dramatic (and drastic) example is the compulsive smoker. This smoker cannot imagine life without cigarettes. They have become a part of his life and most of the day's actions include "lighting up." It has become almost a psychological torment for the smoker to think of a day without smoke. It has been found in some studies that people like this actually wake themselves every few hours at night to have a quick drag, and then drift back to sleep. Such rationalizations as "it helps me to relax," "it keeps my weight down," "it makes me feel comfortable," and "I just enjoy it" are the only explanations the compulsive smoker offers.

Even as his appearance and health become damaged, the compulsive smoker will not stop. He continues to smoke as he gradually acquires dingy, yellowing teeth; smoker's breath; discoloration of the eyes; and a "nasty little cough." More seriously, bronchitis, emphysema, and lung and throat cancer may develop, which sometimes may still not cause the smoker to quit the habit. Compulsive smokers often state, "I am going to die anyway, so why not from smoking?" And in many cases, unfortunately, that is the compulsive smoker's fate.

These five basic types of smokers pretty well describe the many kinds of "inhalers" and their reasons for doing so. In the future, when you see a person light up a butt, it may be easier for you to understand how "somebody could do that to himself."

— Margi Janucci

Once you have decided on a topic, you can set up tentative categories and begin to decide what kinds of detail you will need to illustrate the characteristics of the categories. Details should not be difficult to find; you probably have encountered many good ones in your search for a topic.

The Finished Product

Point. If you expect your readers or listeners to follow you through the many categories, subcategories, and details of a classification, you need to give them some reason to pay attention to what you have to say. Your classification must have a purpose, and you should make that purpose clear to the audience near the beginning of the discourse, in a fresh way if possible. To give audiences further guidance, many writers and speakers state the purpose again in a brief form somewhere in the discussion of each major category and, in addition, give memorable names to the categories. Naming can be fun and it can help your audience to visualize what you are talking about. These excerpts from a long essay make good use of such strategies:

Hair Apparent

. . .Hair has always been a statement for men, variously representing strength (Samson), fashionable virtue (King Charles I of England, whose wigs were long-locked and elaborate), bravado (General Custer), and genius (Einstein). Hair's considerable practical uses — for keeping the head warm and dry and unsunburned — have often mattered less than its symbolic value. To express their grim efficiency, Prussian officers favored the shorn look. In the Fifties, greasers and preppies declared their social differences tonsorially. Hippies made long hair the flag of the Woodstock nation.

Politicians and their publics are historically hair-minded. Whenever Odysseus had to make a good impression, Athena conveniently swooped down and thickened his mane, then massaged in a few drops of olive oil, the dry look apparently having held no magic on the shores of the wine-dark sea. Certain tribes in Africa ritually murder their chiefs as soon as a gray hair appears on head or in beard (Clairol take note).

As atavistic as it may seem, hair remains a crucial factor in a rise to power even as businesslike as an American presidential campaign. As television totemizes candidates, their power as icons is emphasized. Hair is the *sine qua non* of victory at the polls. Nearly axiomatic in U.S. politics is the unwritten rule-of-pate that no bald man can become president. In the 20th century, only Dwight Eisenhower has succeeded in being elected without the benefit of hair, but he was a military hero whose image had come to the public wearing army hats. Significantly, he twice ran against Adlai Stevenson, a bald civilian.

. . . The current covey of presidential candidates probably differs more from the hairline back than in their politics. But that, as my old friend (and Holy Roman Emperor) Charles the Bald used to say, is what makes hirsute races. Taking it from the top, the contenders for the White House look like this:

... RONALD REAGAN Like many products of Hollywood's studios, the Republican front-runner's hair looks slightly suspect, a kind of maroon special effect somewhat less convincing than a mid-priced toupee. Though Reagan is nearly 70, his hair has just turned 40, and the anachronism is disturbing. Before the election, voters may want to know more about the candidate's roots.

... JERRY BROWN The current California governor has the opposite problem from his predecessor. His hairline is maturing faster than his face, with unfortunate results. In the ancient way of seeing things that probably influence the election of presidents, Brown is losing strength but not gaining character. To draw attention from this problem, Brown surrounds himself with distractingly well-tressed supporters, like Jane Fonda.

... JOHN CONNALLY In Italian politics, the former Texas governor and treasury secretary might be called something like the "Silver Fox." In African politics he might be dead. In America, his sleek, grizzled locks single him out as the only gray-haired candidate (except, of course, for Harold Stassen), a distinction that may appeal to the growing percentage of voters over 60. Should Connally succeed, his hair, combined with his politics, could cause the reappearance of powdered wigs in Congress.

... EDWARD KENNEDY Like his brother Jack, Ted Kennedy has power hair. (Robert had soulful hair.) If he could make it to November on hair alone, no one could beat him. Graying just so at the temples, thick, wavy, Kennedy's formidable mane can only be the envy of all his rivals. The trouble is that Kennedy is probably not as good as his hair. Unluckily for him, voters still pay some attention to what the mouth is doing.

(Edwards, 1980)

Perhaps the best way, however, to make sure your classification is easy to follow is to make the pattern of the discourse particularly clear.

Pattern. Here is the basic pattern for classification discourse:

Classification Pattern

Introduction (including thesis)
   Category 1 (group, class)
   Category 2 (group, class)
   Category 3 (group, class)
   Category 4, 5, 6 (group, class) . . .
Conclusion (summary)

In classifications, the categories are often arranged in ascending order of importance, interest, or difficulty, and individual categories are frequently introduced by such cue words as the following:

category	division	class
sort	set	family
kind	variety	subgroup
group	species	subcategory
type	breed	subclass

Indeed, sometimes classifications seem to follow a formula of sorts. They announce a category, name it, define it, and then provide examples. These two paragraphs from a student discussion of jobs with distinctive styles of life are typical.

> The life of a stockbroker is hectic and demanding. A stockbroker sits in a crowded office surrounded by phones constantly ringing, typewriters constantly clacking, people continually talking, and stock prices moving steadily across a screen. In other words, they are part of the action and keep very busy. Successful brokers are most likely workaholics, arriving at the office around six o'clock in the morning, putting in a regular day, and, after the market closes, talking on the phone with clients. At home, brokers usually spend time catching up on paperwork. They may also give investment seminars that demand considerable preparation time and effort. A stockbroker's income can range as high as $100,000 if the market is on the upswing. This compensates for the long hours and the hectic pace. Brokers usually live in posh city apartments to be as close to their place of business as possible. If brokers are away from the market for very long, they get anxious, and vacation trips to Acapulco, Bermuda, or the Virgin Islands usually consist of client meetings in the daytime and evenings of leisure.

> College professors lead a more casual life than the physician or stockbroker does. Anxiety does not seem to dominate their activities as it does the lives of the others. Professors usually live "comfortably," on or near campus in an average but picturesque middle- to upper-class home surrounded neatly by grass, trees, attractive shrubbery, and brightly colored flowers. Campus facilities are always available to faculty members. Instructors are welcome at campus poetry readings and little theater productions. While working, professors can leave their children at the college-sponsored nursery school. Professors have responsibility for approximately ten teaching hours, along with faculty meetings, class preparation, and research for book writing. This keeps them busy during the semester. Time for rest comes between semesters and during at least two months of the summer. Professors make approximately $20,000 to $30,000 a year. Because of their salaries, professors manage their spending funds

carefully; they are not lavish in their spending but use practicality in making purchasing decisions.

— Pam Ganosel

The relationship of each of these paragraphs to the pattern of the whole essay is made plain in the opening sentences. Moreover, the paragraphs themselves have similar structural patterns: each covers the different kinds of activities — social, occupational, financial — that characterize the occupation. These two patterns, one linking the paragraphs and the other operating within the paragraphs, enable the writer to present a considerable amount of detail in a way that makes it easy to understand.

Detail. To be successful, a classification needs plentiful, vivid detail to illustrate, explain, and explore each category. Like all good examples, the illustrations you choose have to be representative of the category as a whole and also have to support the point you are trying to make. Short examples and clusters of details can be very effective, particularly if you cover the same topics for each category. Often, however, more fully developed examples of paragraph length are appropriate because they provide a thorough examination and allow you to draw on techniques like narration and description to create memorable illustrations.

The following student essay makes good use of details drawn from research in order to support its claims. Because many people might find the events described hard to believe, the author goes to considerable lengths to make them vivid and realistic. She also reminds the reader again and again that the examples are typical and that they have been verified in a number of ways.

Apparitions cover a wide range of psychic phenomenon. G. N. Tyrell, a former president of the Society for Psychical Research, dedicated his 1942 Myers Memorial Lecture to the organization of the topic of apparitions. From this lecture emerged a book, *Apparitions*, in which Tyrell classified apparitions into four categories: (a) apparitions of the living, (b) crisis apparitions, (c) postmortem apparitions, and (d) continual apparitions. These are the four major groups of phantoms generally recognized.

Although people visualize apparitions as the disembodied images of the dead, this is not always the case. A substantial portion of reported apparitions are representative of living persons. S. H. Beard was both the subject and researcher in a series of now famous experiments. Before retiring one evening, Beard attempted to project an apparition of himself to his fiancee through concentration. He fell asleep, later believing that this trial had failed. At that very instant, however, he appeared to Miss L. Verity at her bedside, clad in full evening attire. Startled, she screamed, awakening her sister, who also viewed the apparition. In order to verify his experience, Beard repeated his experiment on several occasions. He contacted Edmund Gurney, a personal friend and founding member of the Society for Psychical Research, prior to one experiment, to validate the experiment if it proved successful. Beard concentrated on Miss Verity and attempted to stroke her hair through an out-of-body experience. Miss Verity subsequently commented that the figure of S. H. Beard had appeared to her and stroked her hair, while she was fully awake.

Crisis apparitions can neither be classified as those of the living nor as those of the dead, usually appearing at the exact moment of the death (or accident) of the agent, or shortly after. The following case is typical. Flying his plane over France, World War I pilot Eldred Bowyer-Bower was shot down on March 19, 1917. That very morning his half sister, Mrs. Spearman, saw his apparition in her sitting room in India. Mrs. Spearman revealed, "I had a great feeling I must run around and did, to see Eldred; he looked so happy and had that dear mischievous look . . . and I was just putting my hands out to give him a hug and a kiss, but Eldred had gone. I called and looked for him. I never saw him again." *The Census of Hallucinations*, published in 1894, described most cases of crisis apparitions as occurring at the exact moment of death, and gradually declining with the passage of time.

Postmortem apparitions — that is, apparitions of the dead, are defined as those seen twelve hours, and often years, after the agent's death. Such occurrences have been cited as proof of life after death. The scratched-cheek case has become classic because of the peculiar evidence offered by the apparition. A young woman, identified only as F. G.'s sister, died of cholera at the age of 18, and appeared to her brother at a hotel room in St. Joseph, Missouri, nine years later. F. G. was resting and pondering the business matters that had prompted his trip when he suddenly became aware of a figure standing beside him. Glancing around, he was amazed to see the apparition of his long-deceased sister, disfigured by a long red scratch on its cheek. The apparition vanished just as quickly as it had appeared. Upon relating this experience to his parents, he nearly caused his mother to collapse at mention of the scratched cheek. After she had recovered herself, the woman admitted to having accidentally scratched the girl's cheek in an attempt to "touch up" the face of the dead girl before burial. The mother had, however, concealed the accident by carefully covering the scratch with makeup. No one but she had known of the mishap.

The figure of F. G.'s sister was sighted only once. Some apparitions, however, are seen more often, appearing, in fact, from time to time. Such figures are popularly called ghosts, and are usually identified with "haunted houses," thus falling into the category of continual apparitions or hauntings. In many instances hauntings are observed by witnesses over a long period of time and include auditory experiences (footsteps, pounding on the wall) and tactile experiences (cool breezes, feelings of being pushed, etc.) as well as visual experiences (apparitions).

In the 1970s, the Chin family of Philadelphia reported a haunting to the Psychical Research Foundation of Durham, North Carolina. W. T. Joines, associate professor of electrical engineering at Duke University, was one of the people sent to carry out an investigation. The family claimed to have seen apparitions, heard footsteps, and witnessed the movement of objects in the house. One daughter had had her bed covers pulled off. The same girl once saw an apparition and screamed, waking a sister who also saw the figure. Hauntings such as this one are often associated with poltergeists, "noisy spirits," and with the ability to move objects, start fires, attack victims, bite people (also cause bloating, lesions, and demonic possession, hurl objects, levitate people and things, and cause showers of water, rocks, and other objects, and destroy such religious items as crosses, rosaries, and Bibles). No plausible explanation has yet been offered for all forms of apparitions, and until one is accepted, I believe people will still enjoy sitting around a campfire with a good ghost story.

— Angela Fedorcuk

This essay clearly identifies each category so that despite the wealth of information it presents, the essay is very easy to read and understand. The detail is so interesting, in fact, that most readers will pay attention to it rather than to the careful way the author has organized the essay.

DESCRIPTION

Using Description

You look out over the water as the sun sets, turning the sky pink and making the lake seem like a mirror or a pool of mercury. The lake reflects the light so brilliantly that your eyes begin to hurt, so you look over towards the pine trees lining the shore, noticing for the first time the light breeze blowing against your face, carrying the rich scent of the pines mingled with the smell of the damp earth beneath the trees. . . .

You look out your apartment window at the street below, seeing groups of people walking along, the evening sun touching their faces and arms which range in color from pinkish white to the angry red of an early summer sunburn to rich olive to a dark chocolatey brown. As you raise the window, the air rushes in carrying the smell of exhaust, the fatty scent of hamburger being fried for dinner on the stove next door in 9B, and the sounds of people talking loudly, laughing and joking but in tones that threaten to spill into anger.

The sounds echo off your apartment building and those down the street, eventually mingling with the sounds of traffic coming from 53rd street two blocks away. . . .

Consider what role your mind plays in these experiences. Your eyes, ears, nose, mouth, and skin take in hundreds of sense impressions in a minute's time. Your mind combines all of these, ignoring some and emphasizing others until it puts the experience together as a scene you can contemplate, understand, react to, or even remember, if you wish. Every few seconds the incoming information changes — new sounds, new smells, new movements, new angles of light. Your mind has to react to all these new stimuli, changing the image in your brain, but not so drastically that it creates a new scene for you to react to every second or two.

Stop for a minute to think about all this.

You have probably assumed that it is your eyes that see things. You can, however, prove to yourself that although it is your eyes that gather the information, it is your mind that organizes it. Look directly at an object for ten seconds, noticing all you can about it. Now turn your head around and look at something else. Your eyes will begin to take in information immediately, but for a split second the scene will remain disorganized and blurred until your mind organizes it and you can recognize what you are looking at.

It is in this split second that the mental process called **description** takes place. In this moment your mind asks your eyes, "What are the physical features of the scene you are reporting on? How is the scene organized in space?" It asks similar questions of your other senses. The process ends when your mind recognizes the scene.

One clear sign of recognition (and understanding) is your ability to name what you are looking at. Try the head-turning experiment again. At the end of the moment of disorganization, your mind will, in effect, name what you are looking at: "Ah ha! That's a picture, a plant, a window, a wall, a tree, a person."

Recognition means being able to place the sense impressions into some familiar category, being able to say of a loud screeching noise, "That's someone slamming on brakes to avoid an accident," or of a rich, exotic scent, "That's perfume." If your mind fails to locate an exact category for impressions, it will try for an approximate category: "That loud bang sounded like an explosion"; "That dog looks like a cross between a poodle and a beagle."

At any one time our five senses record many more stimuli than our minds can deal with effectively. In response, our minds select those stimuli that contribute directly to a recognizable image, shutting out those that seem irrelevant or difficult to understand. To see how selective your mind is, close your eyes for ten or twenty seconds and note how many sounds you ignored when your eyes were open and bombarding you with visual impressions.

To sum up: The descriptive power of the mind sorts through impressions of the world as they come to us through our senses, selecting and assembling them into images that fit into categories we have developed unconsciously as the result of our experiences.

The descriptive process, however, is not limited to things we can see, hear, touch, feel, and taste. It also helps us understand things we know exist even though we cannot experience them directly. These include things like a friend's personality, and emotions like anger, fear, and joy. We know these things exist because of their effects, not because we can reach out and touch them or use surgery to isolate them in the brain or the heart. The descriptive process enables us to isolate all the effects that point to a person's character — what that person does and says, how the person acts, what others think of the person and to reach a conclusion: "He's nasty"; "She's kind and witty"; "He's a mixture of generosity, fear, and envy." We go through a similar process with emotions: "Her face is red; she's shouting; she's making broad, abrupt gestures with her hands — she's angry."

The main purpose of description as a pattern of expression is to recreate for readers or listeners a scene, emotion, or personality. The special features of description as a pattern of thought have a number of implications for it as a pattern of expression.

First, general terms are insufficient. Readers and listeners perceive the subject of a description in much the same way as we perceive a real scene, so describing something in general terms alone — "It was a beautiful autumn day"; "She looked alert and intelligent"; "I felt angry" is ineffective because it fails to provide the details (the sense stimuli) that will allow the mind to recreate the scene or experience.

Second, the details that make up a descriptive passage have to be carefully chosen so that they contribute directly to the impact the author wants to create; otherwise the minds of the readers or listeners may rearrange the details and arrive at a different impression.

Third, descriptions should use a variety of senses; otherwise they may seem thin and unrealistic.

Description is an essential part of most narratives. It provides details of the setting while aiding characterization and the portrayal of emotions. It is hard to imagine an effective narrative in speech or writing that lacks description. Any other form of discourse that involves examination of people, places, or things is likely to make use of description, and it is particularly common in analysis and classification.

The mind is much better able to process descriptive detail through written language than through spoken language. Therefore, while many speeches make use of descriptive detail, it occurs more frequently and in a more complex form in writing. In writing, moreover, description is often found on its own, presenting a particularly memorable scene or character, capturing the emotion in a scene or presenting it directly, or making a point about the world around us. Each of these uses of description is illustrated in the essays used as examples later in this discussion.

Getting Materials

You can find materials for a description in the world around you, in your memories of scenes and events, and in your imagination. Wherever you turn in your search, however, you will need to fight against two tendencies of your mind: its tendency to summarize a scene in a few words ("It was a beautiful day") and its tendency to screen out all but the most prominent sense stimuli. If you let these two operations go unchecked you will end up with descriptions that are thin in detail and that fail to take the audience there to see what you see.

As you look at a scene, reconstruct it in your memory or create it in your imagination; force yourself to pay attention to the details, letting the overall impression come later as you put it into words. If you are going to describe a scene, ask yourself if you have paid attention to all five senses; sight, smell, taste, touch (movement), and hearing. The following description covers four of the five:

The Accident

Sight and Movement (Touch)

The automobile was jerked from the long, newly-paved Texas road onto the gravelly, bumpy shoulder of the road. The car "jumped" quickly as though it were a dog whose leash had been tugged by its master. The vehicle then zigzagged wildly from one side of the road to the other; it seemed that the car was traveling in a trench that was cut by pinking shears. The lush, dark green foliage ran from the side of the road to the windshield and brushed past the sides of the car without slowing down, while rich brown mud splattered its way past in the same rude manner as the bushes. The long deep trench filled with murky water lifted, like a steel beam being hoisted by a crane, to envelop the dented and dirty car.

Sound

There was noise, too: the tires screamed out in pain at each hairpin turn of the zigzag; metal moaned with each punch from the merciless ground; and chrome squealed as it was ripped from its mount. Once the trench had the automobile firmly in its grasp, all movement and sound ceased.

Smell

A pungent odor permeated the car, creeping slowly toward it from a nearby manure-cultivated field. The stink from the field, with the smell of blood and smoke from the hissing engine, merged to create a stomach-churning stench.

Touch   My face burned because of the intense heat of the sun earlier in the day, but the left side of my face was not as fiery as the right side; liquid that was trickling down my cheek didn't feel warm because of the condition of my skin. The same warm liquid that flowed down my cheek was spewing out of my hand, forming deep rose-color splotches on my white shorts. Pain was not present, only an uncomfortable and weak feeling was in my wrist, back, temple, hand, and knee.

Sight   My dazed eyes made everything look strange inside the car: the shattered windshield distorted the scenery outside and made it look like the pieces of a jigsaw puzzle that were forced together incorrectly; the control buttons for the radio and air conditioning looked as though they had been smashed with a sledge hammer; and Barbara was crumpled in the corner, tossed there in the confusion, like an old, worn-out, unwanted ragdoll. Bright colors were not in abundance; however, the deep brown shade of the automobile, the dark blue sky, and the fogged blackness around me dominated. Suddenly, brilliant red flashes of light illuminated the destruction of the night.

— Karen Hoyle

If you are going to describe a character, pay attention to what the person looks like, says, or does, what other people say about the person, and how they react to the person's individuality. Here is a character description that does these things:

Nancy

Nancy was my favorite camper. I met her during the summer when I worked with the mentally retarded and handicapped. We were introduced as counselor and camper on a Sunday, which was the first day of our long two-week session together. She was twelve years old and stood at about three feet ten inches high. Her dirty blond hair hung just below her tiny shoulders and was usually pulled back into a pony tail. She didn't speak understandable words but I was told that she did know some. On the edge of her tiny nose hung her thick plastic glasses — which she looked better without. Her smile and laughter made my whole summer worth all the hard work and long hours. She loved physical affection and would frequently want me to carry her, which I did for the first few days until I got to know her better. She would give anyone a kiss who asked her for one. Frequently when I was resting on my bed she would come in quietly and sit on top of me and start laughing.

Her walk was different depending on her mood. When she was excited and happy, she walked briskly, almost in a run. If I scolded her for something she would walk slowly beside me holding my hand loosely. She would make little or no reaction to me if I squeezed her hand playfully. Her ordinary walk was a rocking from left to right, as if her pants were wet. This was the way she was taught to walk while she lived at Zambarano Hospital. All of the children who go to or live at that hospital walk the same way.

Some days when I would return from being out during rest period I would find Nancy sitting at the edge of her bed bouncing wildly up and down and making the strangest noises. It was at those times that it was hardest to calm her down and get her to be quiet. She only did the bouncing when I wasn't around so it was hard to stop her when she had been doing it for a while without anyone saying anything to her. I usually just brought her with me to watch TV. There she would climb up on my bed with me and quietly listen to the TV. I found this the easiest way in which to calm her down. Sometimes I was tempted to sit there and bounce with her while I watched her pony tail flop around erratically. I forced myself to get her to calm down.

Nancy could dress herself although it took her a long time because she liked being told what to do and to hurry up. She ate by herself and understood most of what I told her. She hated showers — cold ones especially. When she was happy and excited she ran around making a lot of noise. After being scolded she would become very quiet and look at me only through the corner of her eye. I only wish she had been able to talk to me.

— Cindy Houston

The Finished Product

Point. Since the purpose of description is to recreate scenes, characters, or emotions, descriptions seldom contain thesis statements of the kind found, for example, in patterns like analysis or classification. Descriptive passages contain general statements ("It was a beautiful day"), but these can occur at any point, not just near the beginning, and they serve to sum up the impressions made by the descriptive detail rather than to organize the discourse as a whole.

The point, or dominant impression, of a description must be made by all the details working together to convey the impact of a scene or character. If the details in a description of a thunderstorm, for instance, fail to adequately convey its beauty, its power, and the fear it can create, merely telling the audience that "watching the thunderstorm was an exciting but terrifying experience" will not be enough to make the description effective. It is the experience provided through the details that is the heart of a description, not the general statements.

Nonetheless, general statements play several important roles. For the communicator, they can be a way of controlling audience response, of making sure that readers and listeners respond to the description in roughly the way the communicator desires and not in some completely different manner. The statements can often serve as guides for revision, reminding the communicator of the effect the details need to achieve.

For the audience, general statements are both resting places and guides. The amount of detail in a description can sometimes be overwhelming — hard, at first, for an audience to combine into a complete image. General statements break up the density of a passage and give the audience a place to rest and an opportunity to relate the details to each other. In addition, general statements indicate to the audience how all the details are related, making it easier to form an image of the whole.

Pattern. The organization of a description is determined in part by the shape of the material being described, but this is not the only pattern a description follows. A description must have a point of view, like the lens of a camera or the eye of a beholder, and the order in which this observer sees things also helps determine the organization of the discourse. Finally, any description longer than about one hundred words (the length of an average paragraph) usually incorporates a third kind of pattern: some principle of movement or change. Movement is necessary because any description that concentrates for long on a single object or topic runs the risk of becoming either overly detailed or boring. Most long descriptions, therefore, have either some pattern of movement, as of a person walking through a forest, for instance, or some pattern of change — contrasting scenes, perhaps, or a skeletal narrative. The danger in using a narrative frame is, of course, that the emphasis on "What happened?" will end up being greater than the emphasis on the descriptive details, and the discourse will cease being a description and turn into a narrative. The technique is useful, however, as long as the narrative remains a bare skeleton, a vehicle for the description and not the primary focus of the discourse.

The order in which the parts of a description are arranged, then, depends on what is being described, on the point of view, and on the principles of movement. As a result there are many possible patterns of arrangement for descriptions, more than can possibly be listed here. Nonetheless, the patterns fall into three categories that can be discussed briefly: spatial patterns, dominant impression patterns, and fantasy patterns.

The details in a description that follows a **spatial order** may be arranged to present the subject from left to right, top to bottom, inside to outside, front to back, in a clockwise manner, counterclockwise, or in a spiral. The sequence may also reflect the order in which the details appear to an observer, to someone sitting in the woods and looking around, as for example in this selection from a student essay:

> As I sit on the soft, green moss, leaning my back against a rough tree trunk, the bright gleaming sun tries to break through the towering

trees, and the gentle wind plays with my loose hair. The silence is almost complete, although there are many things happening.

To the left of me a black ant is struggling to carry a small white object that looks too heavy for the insect. Determined to bring the catch home, the little fellow defiantly climbs over bits of tree bark, weaves around blades of wild grass, and clambers over blockading pebbles. I soon lose sight of the ant as it proudly plunges into its hole with the white object.

All about me, small red bugs are hurrying, scampering around and bumping into each other. I keep my body perfectly still as one of them tries to make its way up my arm. I flick it off my arm with my finger and watch it continue on its way.

Soon my eyes drift over to the winding brook directly in front of me. I immediately notice that the brook is higher and faster than it was during the dry summer months. About twenty water bugs are darting back and forth in the water, while a family of tadpoles swims serenely below them. As I follow the path of the brook westward, it disappears from my view behind a sharp bend. A lanky tree lazily stretches over the brook, gently shedding its first colored leaves onto the rapidly moving waters. They, too, soon drift out of sight.

Slowly my eyes drift upward to the sky, and I watch the first of many clouds approach. A chill in the wind breezes by my face, and a big black crow on an extended branch signals the sound of impending rain. Other birds take up the warning and soon the cool silence turns into a squawking circus. Below the crow, a light brown chipmunk with black and white pinstripes down the side of its body sits up on its haunches and nibbles down its remaining meal before racing away under a decaying, hollow log. My gaze lingers there for awhile, but the frightened chipmunk fails to reappear. Suddenly, I hear the distinct sound of raindrops throughout the wooded area, and the leaves of plants and trees reluctantly bend downward as the drops touch them almost pleadingly. All I hear is the gentle patter of drops on the plants and the silence of the birds.

— Mary Denton

The principle of movement in this passage is the movement of the observer's head and eyes. This movement has little significance in itself; it simply serves to shift the reader's attention from section to section of the scene being described and to prevent the accumulation of detail from becoming monotonous.

In a description designed to present a **dominant impression**, the details may be arranged in many different ways, but each segment of the description must repeat the dominant image, object, emotion, or quality that the description is designed to emphasize and develop. In the following description the central focus is indicated in the title, "Yellow"; by the end of the student essay, this everyday color takes on a significance that may help to alter permanently the audience's perception of it:

Yellow

I always notice colors and today as I drive to the beach I am more aware of them than usual. Red apples that have been dropped along the side of the road catch my eye. A large patch of blue paint spilled and blended into the grey pavement looks like an expensive abstract painting I once saw. But mostly I am noticing yellow.

All the colors are intensified by the overcast sky and the mist. They are more brilliant today because they do not have to compete with the sun. I always wonder why people don't enjoy a day without sun. The experience of seeing things is different but just as enjoyable. As I think about this I begin to notice that more and more today is becoming a yellow day.

All of a sudden this color, which I have always thought of as meek, seems to dominate the world. I always noticed that it was the first color to appear in the fall and the last one of the spring colors to leave, but today I suddenly feel it is surrounding me. Yellow — the color that divides the streets, edges the sidewalks. Yellow, on signs that direct me, warn me, stop me! I wonder why I have never noticed how much yellow there is in the world before now.

Just as I tell myself this is coincidence, a yellow light stops me. Now children in yellow raincoats cross the street between yellow lines. Suddenly the color becomes so aggressive it dominates every other. It assaults me from signs, trash cans, store fronts. A gas station is painted with such bright yellow it seems to be magnetic. I can't get my eyes off it and I nearly drive off the road while I am looking.

Yellow cars, yellow houses, fences, birdbaths, bicycles. Yellow is captivating me. Help!

I turn onto the highway to get some relief. A policeman slows me down to let a yellow maintenance truck drop a yellow line onto the road. It is brilliant and drops shining and wet like an egg yoke onto the new black tar. It hypnotizes me.

The policeman signals me on aggravatedly and I drive past wishing I could stay to watch like a motorist who passes an accident.

Just as I am starting to regain my sanity four yellow school buses, empty except for the drivers, enclose me on both sides. We seem to drive for miles like this. I am getting claustrophobic. Finally they pass me and weave dangerously in and out of the traffic, dominating the road because of their size and bright color, and startling the other motorists. They seem to have some plan in mind but no one can figure out what it is. Finally the four buses move into a single line and drive so close they seem to be connected. They keep like this at the side of the road for miles as neatly as a military formation. I wonder if being inside all that yellow has "driven" them mad!

I decide the country roads are probably more peaceful and I leave the highway. No relief. I turn on the radio and the Beatles are singing Yellow Submarine. As I round a corner I see boys in yellow football jerseys scrimmaging on a highschool field.

YELLOW: PRIMARY COLOR is shouting at me from every-where. Yellow saturates the landscape. It is woven into the grass and weeds. Wheat colored, straw colored, it is laid onto leaves, brushed through every kind of vegetation.

Willow trees drop yellow confetti like leaves onto everything, and make patterns on the wet road. The design they make is delicate, and the color is not so bold. I start to feel relieved. Yellow is still surrounding me but it is becoming less aggressive. I see little yellow flecks on the skins of fruit at the open road stands. The corn is mercifully covered over with leaves.

Now I begin to notice how much variation yellow has. It can be delicate buff or ivory sophisticated beige, ecru or amber.

I have seen all these yellows and their variations all my life. I have put yellow on hot dogs, worn it in uniforms, squeezed it from tubes. I have examined it for transparency and for its effects on other colors when I paint. Yet like so many daily experiences my knowledge of yellow was catalogued along with other practical information and dismissed. Yellow, the color of cowardice. Yellow, the color of the intellectual.

I start to become aware of a soft light, a gleam, a yellow color that is spreading over the earth. The sun has decided to make an appearance, just as the day is ending. But this is a golden yellow that softens the landscape. It is soothing and peaceful. — I can take "mellow yellow."

— David Briden

The point of view in the following student essay is that of a dreamer, and the principle of movement is a journey or quest; the content is shaped by the physical condition of the dreamer, who is suffering from indigestion.

Character descriptions usually follow a different kind of pattern, presenting a series of impressions based on what the character looks like, says, and does, and so on, or a group of loosely connected incidents that reveal personality (see "Nancy," above).

The narrative element in the essay to follow is more fully developed than in the one that precedes it, but it avoids becoming an end in itself, and its purpose is still to help shift scenes and move the reader's attention to a new set of details.

The order of **fantasy** is the order of dreams and of the imagination; descriptions of this sort are shaped by the state of mind of the observer. If the observer's mind is in the grip of illness, insanity, or a powerful emotion, the details and their arrangement will reflect this. The succeeding description follows just such a pattern. The events described in this piece are so complicated that it might be called a narrative except that the focus is not on the events themselves but on the series of grotesque and fantastic images they present.

Indigestion

It was a dark and gloomy night as I crept warily down an ominously winding path. There was neither moon nor stars to give me comfort. It was as though a selfish and powerful being wanted to hide them from my sight. Every shape, sound, and smell seemed to contribute to the sinister atmosphere of the evening.

Nothing appeared familiar. The shapes I once knew as trees looked like misshapened and deformed beings, waiting impatiently to entrap me with their twisted, pointed talons. Their outstretched, warty arms reached out to drag me even deeper into the dank forest. The howling wind bellowed, "Go back! Go back!" The rushing leaves charged at me, as if I were an intruder in their private domain, a domain that no one had dared to enter before that night. Roots sprang up to block my path and bushes clawed at my hair, like demons possessed by the forces of the damned. A detestable, musty odor descended upon me, attempting to squeeze every precious breath from my tormented body.

On I stumbled, tripping and gouging my way through that cruel and profane forest. I ached to get away. "Please let me go home," I tried to scream. No sound escaped from my throat. Suddenly a shrill and piercing screech escaped from deep within those deformed and nameless hulks. I froze with stark terror. Needles, like sharp, broken fingernails, grasped and tore at my clothes. As I struggled to free myself, I could feel my flesh being ripped from my bones. I desperately reached out for anything that would help me escape. Suddenly every morbid shape and sound magnified into a swirling, thunderous blast of noise. My tearing fingers dug into the murky, chilling soil and I pulled with all the power I had left. I was free!

Although I was still bleeding and shaking from my horrifying experience, I realized I had to go on. If I did not, I would be risking another attack. I tried to force my legs to run faster, but I seemed to be running in place. I could hear crashing sounds behind me as my pursuers drew nearer and nearer. As suddenly as everything had magnified, it became deadly silent. It was as if a soundproof barrier had been thrown around me. My blood started racing through my veins as though it would be its last lap through the narrowing and winding paths of my physically drained body. I gasped with horror! Before me crouched a disfigured, grotesque mound of flesh. It slowly began to ooze its hideous flab nearer and nearer. Blackness began to engulf me as I hazily felt my feet begin to leave the soggy ground.

Once again every sound began to magnify and consolidate into a torturous, thundering din. A force, stronger than either I or my enemy below, was pulling me up and out of the evil darkness. Through my grogginess I could dimly see a lighted face, hands and numbers. A groan escaped my lips, as I, exhausted from my night of terror, stretched up and snapped off the alarm.

— Michelle Smith

Detail. Since all descriptions consist primarily of detail, most of the preceding discussion has of necessity dealt either directly or indirectly with detail, leaving little to say here.

There is, however, one kind of detail that requires special attention: detail based on similes and metaphors. A metaphor identifies one object with another and gives to one the qualities of the other. A simile is a comparison of two similar objects using *like* or *as*.

> He is a tiger. (metaphor)
> My love is like a red, red rose. (simile)

This kind of detail is particularly important in descriptions of emotions and other things that cannot be seen or perceived directly. Descriptions of emotions often make use of such statements as "Anger is like a tiger on the loose." The following student essay uses this and other kinds of detail to describe emotions:

Feelings

Feelings can be about something that cannot be seen or heard, something deep inside you: a wish, a dream, love, hate, anger. A feeling inside your body seems harder to describe than an object in your hand. But a feeling, like an object, makes you stop and take notice. Feelings make you want to do something: to kiss a friend, tear up your room, or run away from the world. Feelings make you want to change things, pull them down or build them up. Feelings make you think you're something else — a lonely gull, an angry wind, a frightened mouse.

When something makes you angry, take notice of what happens to your body — how your lips tighten, your teeth clench, your breathing deepens, your heart beats, your face pounds. You get angry when you get a bad deal, or when your best friend gets hurt. Or because of war and pollution the whole world gets hurt. Most of all you get angry at people, at people you don't like and at people you do. You even get angry at people you don't know, both at a person who accidentally bumps into you and at dictators in distant countries.

Loneliness is a quieter feeling than anger and less sudden. It creeps in slowly like a silent mist, and it can pass by in a moment or linger for weeks. It comes along when you are alone and abandoned or when you are in the middle of a noisy crowd. If you were to paint its picture, you would choose quiet, gentle colors, such as grays, maybe, or pale lavenders and baby blues. If you were to record its music, you would use quiet, gentle notes. Imagine a barren beach, an empty field, a bleak sky, a deserted street: all are quiet places to dream and relax.

Fear can come on all at once or it can come a little bit at a time. It can come in response to the real things and people in your life or it can come from the world of make-believe. When it does come, it strikes at every part of the body — your heart, your teeth, your knees, and even the ends of your hair. It leaves you speechless or it makes you scream. It leaves you frozen or it makes you run.

For all that, people like to be frightened now and again, to shiver at the sight of a fearful figure on the movie screen. You don't need a movie camera to make a scary scene. A door can open just as silently in real life as on film, and a mouse can scurry just as easily across the floor. Shutters can bang and chimneys howl. Fear is part of everyone's being.

If you were asked to draw up a list of all the things that made you mad and another of all the things that made you happy, you might find the angry list a good deal longer. Feelings of hate and anger have a way of announcing themselves more strongly than feelings of happiness, which are quieter and may pass by unnoticed. Still, your life has its joyful moments, which can make a day seem wonderful. Getting a new car can make you happy, and showing off that new car can make you happier. Loving somebody, a guy or a girl, your mother or your father, or having a crush on someone, can make you happy; and being loved back can make you happier still. You can be happy for no reason: you suddenly feel good and you tingle all over. A single moment of happiness rather than long periods of undefined good feeling often cause the most joy — the first snow fall of the season, mist from the ocean air, a fresh breeze on a spring day. Simple things, yet each provides a second of joy and makes it, somehow, permanent.

Maybe you spend more time wishing for happy moments than actually knowing them. Suppose you could make the whole world different for one day. Everybody would seem nice to you. You could have everything you wanted out of life.

Some of your feelings may stay with you a long time, seemingly forever, and others may come and go in a flash. They may all get mixed together; you may feel happy and lonely at the same time and you may hate someone even while you love him. But your feelings are yours alone. No one feels exactly the way you feel, and this is why we are all individuals.

— Sue Wink

DEFINITION

Using Definition

A **definition** pins something down, tells what it is and what it is not.

A **formal definition** takes an idea, object, or word, names it, places it within a group or class, and distinguishes it from other members of the class, as in these examples:

Name	*Class*	*Distinction*
a go-getter	is a person	who is enterprising, hustling
to abort	is to terminate a pregnancy	prematurely
to abort	is to terminate an operation or mission	before it is completed
to gabble	is to speak	rapidly or incoherently
inflation	is a rise in price levels	that is sharp and continuing

If words and ideas all had clear and unchanging meanings, there would be little need for definition; but this is not the case. Words and ideas change their meaning over time. Take, for example, the word *housewife*. In the 1500s it meant "a woman who manages or directs the affairs of her household," just as it does today. It also meant "a light, worthless, or pert woman or girl," a "hussy." By the 1600s it had also come into use as "a local name for some kind of fish," and a hundred years later it had been extended to refer to "a pocket-case for needles, pins, thread, scissors, and so on."

Moreover, a word may have several meanings at the same time. Today *housewife* has several meanings depending on who is using it and how it is being used:

> She's bright, but her only ambition is to be a *housewife*. (used in a negative sense)
> She is a wonderful mother, wife and *housewife*. (used in a positive sense)
> Occupation: *Housewife* (used in a neutral sense on a tax form)

One reason a word can have so many meanings is that it can have both a **denotation** (a literal, dictionary meaning) and **connotations**, the extra meanings or nuances it conveys to different people. As the list above indicates, the word *housewife* today has many different connotations.

Definition is an essential process of thought and expression because it enables us to fix and limit the meaning of a word or concept, at least for as long as we need it to complete a train of thought or for a discussion with other people.

One of the most common places in which we frequently make use of definitions is near the beginning of speeches or essays; there we define terms and concepts we plan to use in the discourse so that the audience can more easily follow what we have to say. Patterns like analysis, classification, and cause and effect often use special terms to identify categories, causes, and characteristics, and it is not surprising that definition frequently appears at the beginning of speeches or essays using these patterns. Here is the beginning of a classification essay written by a student:

> What is a dream? "A dream is something to look at while you sleep" is a child's definition of a dream. It is an accurate definition because

it highlights two important features of a dream: it occurs during sleep and is a visual experience.

We can have other experiences during sleep besides dreams. While we are falling asleep or waking up, images may pass before our eyes. The falling-asleep imagery is called hypnogogic; the waking imagery is called hypnopompic. Neither of these experiences, however, can actually be called dreams.

A dream is like a play in the sense that it has a setting, props, characters, interactions among characters, and expressive behaviors. These elements can help a person classify his or her dreams and find the meaning behind them.

— Lisa DuPont

Informative discourse often uses technical terms that need to be explained to an audience. Argumentative discourse may use terms whose meanings are themselves the subject of debate, like *abortion, capitalism,* and *socialism*. They must be clearly defined before an argument gets underway.

On some occasions definition can stand by itself as the primary pattern of a discourse. Dictionary entries and discussions of language and its meaning frequently use definition as a pattern of expression, though most such discussions are relatively brief. Occasionally a speech or essay will use definition to suggest a new way of looking at a common word or concept.

The Finished Product

Point, Pattern, Detail. Formal definitions are relatively short; they can, however, be extended by a number of other methods of definition. These methods can stand on their own or can be combined to suit the communicator's purposes and the occasion.

We can define by synonyms, that is, equivalent words or phrases:

Inebriated means *drunken, intoxicated, smashed, potted, blotto.*

We can define by giving examples:

Hawthorne effect, an improvement in the performance of workers, students, etc., resulting from the attention of researchers seeking means to achieve such an improvement.

In the Oak School experiment the fact that university researchers, supported by Federal funds, were interested in the school may have led to a general improvement of morale and effort on the part of the teachers . . .

(named after the Western Electric Company's *Hawthorne* Works in Chicago, where experiments during the 1920's to improve working performance yielded this effect)

(Barnhart, et al., 1973)

We can define by indicating what the word or concept is not:

> Hoarse means rough and coarse, the sound of a voice that is not as smooth and clear as it ought to be.

We can define by tracing the history of a word or concept:

> The first *mavericks* were unbranded calves running loose on the open range in Texas. They were so named because an enterprising rancher, Sam Maverick, deliberately left his own cattle unbranded so that, at roundup time, he could claim that all unbranded strays were his. The definition of *maverick* as "an unbranded stray calf or colt" is still the primary one in most dictionaries.
>
> (Morris and Morris, 1975)

Extended definitions often follow a pattern like this:

Definition Pattern

Introduction (name of thing to be defined; may include formal definition)
  Definition Strategy 1 (synonyms, examples, etc.)
  Definition Strategy 2 (synonyms, examples, etc.)
  Definition Strategy 3, 4, 5 (synonyms, examples, etc.)
Conclusion (summary)

No matter what tactic you choose to use to make the meaning of a word or idea clear to an audience, start by making sure that you have decided what the meaning is and can state it to yourself in concise terms. If you can do this, then it will be much easier to make the meaning — that is, your point — clear to the audience. You may even wish to include a formal definition of sorts somewhere in your extended definition; doing this will assure that your audience understands precisely what your definition is.

Definitions need not always be serious; the following student essay, for instance, looks at an everyday event in fresh and interesting ways, extending our understanding of it:

Why Are You Smiling?

There are more than thirty muscles that give expression to the human face, and each time you smile, many of these muscles go into action. To be more specific, whenever you crack a smile, your *zygomaticus* and *resorious* muscles stretch your mouth up and back, while simultaneously, your *orbicularis oculi* muscles contract to narrow your eyes.

"Smile, it makes people wonder
  what you've been up to."

A person's smile can be just as expressive as verbalization. Have you ever considered how many types of smiles your lips have formed?

Why do we smile? We normally equate smiling with happiness; however, we seem to be expected to smile even when we are sad. In sports, when our team wins, we smile triumphantly; when our team is defeated, we tend to smile to show that we're good losers. When someone we don't like says something dumb, we smile. When someone we *do* like says something dumb, we smile. Upon introduction to someone, we smile.

"I'd walk a million miles
    for one of your smiles."

I'm always moved when I happen to witness two old friends meeting accidentally on the street, or wherever it may be. Both faces literally light up, and for a brief moment, the two people take on their own identity, ceasing to be just anonymous faces in the crowd. Then, when they say good-bye, and go their separate ways, their smiles gradually fade, and once more, they assume a deadpan expression.

"A smile is the whisper of a laugh."

Not that people don't smile when they're by themselves. All of us smile at times at our own private thoughts. Occasionally, when I'm alone reading a book and something the author has written amuses me, I find myself smiling. Have you ever caught someone, thinking he or she is unnoticed, looking in a mirror? We all tend to allow the corners of our mouths to curve upward when we are pleased with our appearances.

"Say, 'cheese.'"

How does one sincerely smile at an anonymous voice coming from underneath a black cloth behind a box? The idea does sound atrocious. One may smirk at the thought of an adult instructing someone to say foolish things; but this thought doesn't provoke an "ear-to-ear" grin.

We're all too familiar with the politician's classic campaign smile. Maybe one of the reasons that campaigning for political office is so exhausting is that the candidates are required to smile nonstop. (After all, without a "winning smile," how can one be expected to win?)

Sometimes it's more important to express more pleasure than you actually feel. Do you remember the green and purple striped feet-pajamas that Aunt Sophia gave you last Christmas? Yes, of course you smiled even though you have six additional, similarly obnoxious "feeties" starched and folded on the top shelf of your closet.

We tend to wear a smile on our faces as naturally as we wear shoes on our feet. Just think what the world would be like if suddenly people stopped flexing their zygomaticus and risorious muscles. And yet, despite what the song says, a smile is a whole lot more than a frown turned upside down. The only way to understand the *real* meaning of a smile is to look behind it.

— Karen Hoyle

EXEMPLIFICATION

Broad statements — generalizations — are an essential part of discourse. They represent our conclusions about experience:

Today's professional athletes make too much money.
Working in a restaurant is difficult, demanding work.
Motorcycles may be dangerous, but they are a lot more fun than cars.
Alcohol abuse can be a terrible thing.

Any worthwhile generalization is based on experience; it represents conclusions reached after observation of many particular incidents. When we hear or read a generalization, our minds naturally inquire about the particular events behind it. In short, we look for an example to support the generalization. The mental process we use for finding examples is **exemplification**. As a pattern of expression, exemplification consists of a generalization followed by one or more examples that support and illustrate it.

Exemplification Pattern

Introduction (including generalization)
    Example 1
    Example 2
    Example 3
    Example 4, 5, 6
Conclusion (Summary)

Speeches and essays that follow this pattern are often referred to as thesis-and-support. Examples are frequently introduced by cue words:

for example	typically	one particular case	cite
as an example	generally	for one thing	sample
for instance	to illustrate		

In selecting examples, make sure they are representative of the experience to which the generalization refers. Chapter Three of this text contains a detailed discussion of examples as supporting material, and Chapter Ten contains a model of an argument by example on pages 278–279.

SUMMARY

Classification, description, definition, and exemplification are static patterns of thought and expression. Classification assembles experiences into groups of categories to make plain the relationships among them. Description recreates for an audience the experience of a scene, character, or emotion. Definition helps fix and make clear the meaning of words and concepts. Exemplification provides a means of supporting and illustrating general statements about experience.

KEY WORDS

classification	definition
description	formal definition
spatial order	denotation
dominant impression	connotation
fantasy	exemplification

EXERCISES

Classification

1. What categories can you find within each of the following topics?
   a. auto accidents
   b. fraternities or sororities
   c. jobs
   d. automobiles
   e. college instructors
   f. embarrassing experiences
   g. dates
   h. styles of clothing

2. Write an opening paragraph for a classification essay or speech on some topic you think would interest your classmates. Then share it with them to get their reaction.

3. Look at the list of words below and see how many different groups (categories) you can form from it in three minutes. Be ready to state the basis or distinguishing feature of each group.

apple	shoot	parched	anchor
I	dock	battle	yellow
mosquito	sail	sun	puffy
elephant	gull	she	lizard
by	carnivore	warm-blooded	peach
four-legged	white	desert	robin
ate	they	orange	was
closet	clouds	he	snake
the	tiger	on	hung
rock	rope	to	cold-blooded
will	six-legged	herbivore	wind
banana	above	across	boat

4. Revise the following passage to make it an effective opening for a classification speech or essay. Feel free to add material.

> Last summer I worked in a gas station. I worked evenings, which is when the most interesting people seem to come in. For example, there are the "Hurry-ups" who act as if they are going to drive away while the hose is still in their cars, and sometimes do. And there are the "Cheapskates," who ask for $4.75 in gas and still expect you to clean their windows and check the oil. I would like to tell you about these and the other kinds of people that come into a gas station.

5. Describe three possible occasions for a classification speech, and prepare a speech for one of them.

6. Describe three possible audiences for a classification essay, and prepare an essay addressed to one of them.

7. Survey your classmates to find out what topics for a classification speech or essay might interest them, and prepare an essay or speech directed to them.

Description

1. Write three short descriptions of a scene, each four or five sentences long and each drawing primarily on a different sense: sight, taste, smell, touch, hearing.

2. Close your eyes and use all your senses to register the world around you. When you are finished with this step, write a description of what you felt and experienced.

3. List as many places in a speech as you can where description would be appropriate and useful.

4. Write a descriptive essay on one of these topics or a similar one.
    a. emotions
    b. a relative or friend
    c. a place you like to go to be alone
    d. a loud party
    e. a particular time of day
    f. a scene you remember from your childhood

5. Think of a person whose character you want to describe, and then jot down ideas for each of these topics:
    a. what the person says
    b. what the person does
    c. what other people say about the person
    d. what the person looks like
    e. how the person reacted in a typical situation
    Develop these materials into a description; feel free to add other material as you go along.

6. Focus your mind on a particular scene, emotion, or character. List as many similes as you can think of that describe the subject.

Fear is like . . .
Annette is like . . .
My old shoes fit me like . . .
This clearing in the dark woods feels like . . .

7. Keep a journal for a week or ten days. Each day write a brief descriptive passage based on your experience during the day or some experience you have remembered. At the end of the time, work up one of the descriptions (or a combination of them) into a finished essay.

Definition

1. Write a definition of one of these terms or a similar term, drawing as heavily on your experience or on unusual examples as you can.
   a. beauty
   b. fat
   c. anger
   d. excitement
   e. fear
   f. friend or enemy

2. List a number of speaking and writing occasions for which definition would be an appropriate pattern. Consider definition as the primary pattern for a speech or essay or as part of some other pattern. Indicate what functions the definition pattern might serve for the potential audience, and if definition is part of some other pattern, how it might be related to the primary pattern.

3. Look through a newspaper or news magazine or listen to a current events discussion on radio or television in order to see how often definitions are used and what purposes they serve. Make note of what other patterns definitions are likely to be combined with.

4. Define some controversial situation, idea, or issue in several different ways, each reflecting a different point of view on the subject.

5. Words often have different meanings to different people. Prepare a speech or essay that indicates how different people would define concepts like the following:
   a. peace
   b. strength
   c. fun
   d. love
   e. money
   f. success

Exemplification

1. Write a general statement that you would like your audience to agree with. Then list the examples you might use to support and illustrate this statement. Share with your classmates what you have done.

2. Think of a general statement that you would like to support with examples. Then ask your friends and classmates what examples they would use to support or deny the statement. When you have gathered enough good examples, turn your material into a speech or essay.

REFERENCES

Barnhart, Clarence L., Sol Steinmetz, and Robert K. Barnhart. *The Barnhart Dictionary of New English Since 1963* (Bronxville, New York: Harper & Row, 1973).

Edwards, Owen, "Hair Apparent," *Saturday Review* (April 12, 1980), pp. 80–81.

Morris, William, and Mary Morris. *Harper Dictionary of Contemporary Usage* (New York: Harper & Row, 1975), p. 388.

Smith, Ronald W., and Frederick W. Preston. *Sociology: An Introduction* (New York: St. Martin's, 1977), pp. 305–306.

Taylor, William T., and Richard J. Weber. *General Biology* (Princeton, N.J.: Van Nostrand, 1961), p. 320.

9. Conventional Patterns: Sharing Information

Social conventions are based on the way people expect one another to behave in a given situation. It is customary in this country, for example, to shake hands when introduced. If we happen to be at a cocktail party with people we barely know, we are expected to make small talk, to ask the other guests where they are from, what they do, and so on.

Some occasions for formal communication may also entail social conventions. An audience brings a set of expectations to the occasion; the experienced speaker or writer knows what these expectations are and responds to them. Businesses expect standard reporting from their employees. Journalists have standard procedures for reporting the news. In politics and government — legislatures and student governing bodies, for example — the assembled groups expect to hear issues argued in a standard pattern. When faced with such a situation, it is essential that one have a conventional way of proceeding — a **conventional pattern**. Conventional patterns are based upon questions that must be answered in the course of a discussion. Because the same questions arise over and over again, and because we have learned that responding to these questions leads us most efficiently through a discussion, we call them standard questions.

A **standard question** is one that arises frequently in the course of discussion about an idea or an issue. By using the standard questions to probe a topic and to organize discourse we can anticipate audience expectations and construct a speech or essay that will meet the needs of the occasion.

There are two types of speeches or essays for which conventional patterns are frequently appropriate: information giving and argumentation. As educated persons we will want and need to be involved in the social process of idea exchange. Some occasions will demand that we present data neutrally; others will demand that we argue for a particular cause or point of view. In both cases, however, we will need to understand how to organize the event.

All the conceptual patterns of thought and expression discussed in Chapters Six, Seven, and Eight (time patterns and static patterns) may be used on occasions calling for a conventional pattern. A process essay can help us understand how a computer works; a cause-and-effect speech may outline the effects of pollution on a local lake or stream and help us argue for change. The major difference between the conceptual and the conventional patterns lies in the way the communication is organized. Conventional patterns are merely widely accepted combinations of the basic conceptual patterns, combinations that the audience has come to expect and even demand. The standard questions listed in the next two chapters are a way of anticipating these expectations. On business and professional occasions, for example, audiences will frequently want to know specific kinds of things about a topic. A business manager might thus look for answers to these questions about a new product or process:

> Potential? Risks? Scope of Application? Commercial implications? Competition? Importance to company? More work to be done? Any problems? Required manpower, facilities, and equipment? Relative importance to other projects or products? Life of project or product line? Priorities required? Proposed schedule? Target date?

A consumer's outlook might be represented in a different set of questions:

> Practicality? Safety? Range of uses? Durability? Reasonable cost? Ease of operation? Appearance? Readily available? Repair record? Alternative processes or products? Compatibility with related equipment? Appearance?

The sharing of information is a basic activity in our culture, not only in business but in private life.

INFORMATIVE DISCOURSE

Every day we turn to informative discourse for knowledge of facts, ideas, people, and events. At work and in school we read business magazines, textbooks, technical reports, and manuals; during meetings and lectures we listen to speeches. At home we turn to newspapers, books, pamphlets, and television programs for help in preparing income tax forms, deciding on a decorating scheme, cooking an omelette, or repairing an automobile. When we want to relax or be entertained we buy *Newsweek* and *People* to read about current events, the state of the arts, fashionable people, and the latest fads. We sign up for talks on wine tasting; borrow library books describing the habits of insects, the history of whaling, and the joys of quilting; and watch television programs that offer glimpses at the lives of the wealthy or scenes of romantic tropical islands.

Imagine, if you will, a clock face with sixty minutes on it. The sixty minutes represent the entire body of information, the knowledge, that human beings have about the world. If you wanted to show all the information known before the year 1900 you would mark off only the first minute on the face of the clock. The final fifty-nine minutes would represent information generated in the past eighty years (see Figure 9-1).

Not only has the amount of information grown at an astronomical rate in the last century, but the means for spreading and sharing it have also

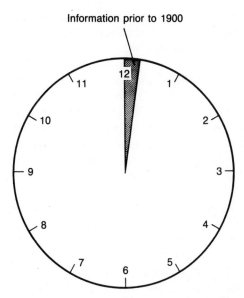

Figure 9-1 The Clock of Information

changed radically, from the telegraph and telephone of the nineteenth century to the radio, television, computer, satellite, and video device of the twentieth century. No wonder, then, that people complain about information overload and data stress.

And yet we all need information. It can provide us with practical or technical knowledge we can use immediately; it can contribute to our understanding of the world around us; and it can also satisfy our curiosity. While you most often find yourself in the role of information receiver, situations frequently occur when you are asked to give information to others — to prepare informative reports, either spoken or written.

AIMS AND FEATURES OF INFORMATIVE DISCOURSE

Informative discourse aims to increase an audience's knowledge or to introduce an audience to something new. For instance, avid coin collectors might attend a lecture on "New Markets for Trading and Selling Coins," or a general audience might read a magazine piece entitled "ESP: New Evidence for an Old Phenomenon." In both cases the discourse is designed to inform the audience in an interesting, thorough manner.

The conceptual patterns of discourse discussed in chapters Six through Eight (narration, process, cause and effect, analysis, enumerations, comparison, classification, description, definition, exemplification) can all be used to inform, of course. A classification can provide information about the different kinds of careers available to college graduates; an enumeration can present the warning signs of cancer; and a narrative can provide information about World War One. But at some point while you were reading about patterns like narration, analysis, and comparison, you probably said to yourself something to the effect that "These are useful patterns, but I often find myself in situations in which I am expected to use different, more varied organizational schemes." Further, you might have noticed that some informative speeches and essays you have encountered contain elements of all the patterns: a bit of narration, some analysis, some comparison, some description, and some classification. These observations were quite accurate: there are many situations that call for speeches and essays that combine several conceptual patterns and that answer the variety of questions posed by these patterns.

You may find, for example, that an organization to which you belong — a business, perhaps — wants information presented in response to a set of questions that reflect its particular interests: What is the potential of the new product? What are its risks? What does the competition have to offer? Moreover, for conveying information the organization may have a standard format it considers the most efficient method. A school paper or a popular magazine for which you are writing an article may have its own set of standards and may give you a set of guidelines to follow in planning and drafting your article. The patterns these occasions call for are conventional patterns — that is, they are patterns that meet the needs and expectations of particular audiences. This chapter provides a list of questions that will help you respond appropriately to the conventions of particular writing and speaking occasions and also discusses patterns suitable for a variety of information-reporting occasions.

Most of the time it is easy to distinguish between discourse intended to present information and discourse intended to argue and persuade; however, there are times when the information presented in a speech or essay seems designed not simply to add to the audience's knowledge but also to make a point and get the audience to accept it. We can expect new information to change attitudes, of course, and we would expect a speaker or writer to be enthusiastic about the information being presented, but there are some important differences between informative and argumentative discourse. In informative discourse the speaker or writer plays the role of fact-finder, observer, and reporter. In an argument the speaker or writer is an advocate, someone who attempts to persuade an audience to accept one particular point of view over another. It is this role, then, that distinguishes the informer from the persuader.

Here is an example that illustrates some of the differences between these roles. Much has been written recently about "creationism" versus "evolutionism." Briefly put, creationists argue that the world began as an act of God, as recorded in the Bible, beginning with the creation of the universe and proceeding to the creation of human beings, to whom power over the earth was given. Creationists argue for the existence of God and the supremacy of human beings over other creatures. Evolutionists argue that the universe began billions of years ago as a series of gaseous reactions that evolved over the millenia into the world as we know it today. Evolutionists neither affirm nor deny the existence of God, but argue that humans are a part of the natural order, neither above nor below other creatures, but simply co-inhabitants of the planet.

The informer and the persuader would approach this controversy in different ways. The informer's role would be to explain one or both of the positions. An informative report on the subject might begin this way:

> Recently school committees and state legislatures throughout the country have been the scene of heated arguments between supporters of the creationist explanation of existence and supporters of the evolutionist position. But this conflict is not new; it has been going on for decades and has involved such important figures as William Jennings Bryan and Clarence Darrow. The issue is a complicated one: each side has a series of arguments and evidence to support its position, and each position has strengths as well as weaknesses. This controversy is important, not simply because it has already begun to affect the way school texts are written but because it is likely to have a significant effect on the way future generations of Americans will view the world around them.

In contrast, the persuader might explain both sides but would end up taking a clear-cut position on the issue. An argumentative essay might have a thesis like this: "Creationism should be taught in the schools as an alternative to evolutionism."

At times, however, an informative speech or essay will need to contain an element of advocacy just as a piece of persuasive discourse will need to contain information. Sometimes it can be difficult to distinguish informative speaking and writing from argumentative. Look, for instance, at "Hobie Cat" below. In this piece is Paul playing the role of informer or observer? His intent was to inform the audience about Hobie Cats, but you may feel that he has crossed the line and has lost his objectivity in a gush of enthusiasm. Does his final call for us to "give it a try" affect his credibility as an informer, or is the final line acceptable, given its location in the piece and given that Paul is not arguing in favor of Hobie Cats over any other particular sailboat?

Hobie Cat

A brightly colored boat streaks through the ocean chop, leaving all contenders far behind. Everyone on the beach watches intently as the craft, with blazing speed, stands up on one edge and fights the wind for more speed. It's a "Hobie Cat," one of the most popular and fastest small sailboats on the market today.

The second part of the name, "Cat," is an abbreviation for "catamaran," a multi-hulled boat. Multi-hulled sailboats have no known origin, but were first seen by Europeans in their early travels to the Polynesian Islands of the Western Pacific. Although they were in use several hundred years ago, it was not until about eighty years ago that boats of this design appeared in the West. Around 1900, Nathaniel Herreshoff (Bristol, Rhode Island) designed and built several successful catamarans that were about thirty feet in length. With one of these designs he accepted a challenge to a race with the New York Yacht Club; he then soundly beat all comers. Yet the boat was branded a "freak" and prohibited from racing at the club again. Over the next several years many people, including Herreshoff's son and grandson, designed and perfected large multi-hulled sailboats. However, it was not until about fifteen years ago that the design was applied to smaller sailing craft by a surfboard builder in California named Hobie; and thus the Hobie Cat was born. The design has since become very popular, and many manufacturers besides Hobie build the boats.

A Hobie Cat has two parallel fiberglass pontoons separated about five feet by a lightweight aluminum frame. Strapped to the frame is a six-foot by five-foot nylon trampoline that the user sits on; also attached to the frame is the mast and most of the boat's sailing hardware. The Hobie is sloop-rigged, that is, it has a large triangular main sail and a foresail called a jib; the mast is held rigid by stainless steel stays (wires) that are attached to both pontoons. The boat is equipped with two rudders, one on each pontoon, so that when one pontoon leaves the water, as it often does in a good wind, the person steering the boat is able to maintain control.

Some of the other features that the Hobie boasts are hiking straps on the trampoline that the user straps his feet into so that he may lean over the windward side to give the boat more leverage against capsizing when it is up on one pontoon; a trapeze, which is a wire with a handle attached to the mast that the sailor holds onto when hiking; and a mast that rotates so that the main sail can be used more efficiently.

There are two models available, both fully equipped and ready for the water: the fourteen-foot model, which costs about two thousand dollars, and the sixteen-foot model, which costs about thirty-three hundred dollars. These prices are a little bit higher than those for conventional sailboats of equal size, but the prestige and added speed are well worth the extra cost.

A Hobie Cat has a long, lean, racy appearance, and it comes in red, blue, yellow, or orange. Sails for the Cat come in a variety of brilliant colors and designs. The boat is fairly lightweight and two people can easily drag it up onto the beach; special trailers are also available for about four hundred and fifty dollars. The boat may be sailed just about anywhere there is a large body of water, be it a lake, a bay, or the ocean.

Sailing is fun, relaxing, and sometimes invigorating, especially when it is done with a Hobie. The boat can be sailed by an individual or by a group of up to four people; even a beginner, with some practice, can master the Hobie. But the Cat is a highly strung machine that is prone to capsizing; it is a good idea to learn to swim before sailing and it is wise to always wear a life jacket. Once the boat has capsized it can be easily righted if one knows how; this is where instruction helps. Sailing this boat is much like sailing any other boat, but if one is a beginner and doesn't know what *sail trim, reaching, tacking,* and *running* are and what the rules of the road are, too, then the sailor is asking for trouble. It is wise to take lessons or learn the ropes from a friend before striking out on one's own.

The Hobie: fun, excitement, prestige, speed, and good looks, all at an affordable price — you ought to give it a try.

— Paul Sisson

PLANNING INFORMATIVE REPORTS

Anyone preparing an informative speech or essay has two responsibilities: to present accurate, thorough information about the subject and to provide the audience with the kind of information it wants and needs. To avoid being pulled in opposite directions by these responsibilities, writers and speakers can use a set of **standard questions** to help prepare an informative report. The standard questions reflect what most audiences will want to know about a topic and can be used as probes to help uncover worthwhile information about a subject. The standard questions also help form some of the basic conventional patterns for informative discourse, patterns that can be easily adapted to the demands of a wide variety of situations.

Analyzing a Topic

The standard questions that follow reflect most of the things an audience will want to know about a topic. The questions can be used to explore a topic, to reveal interesting aspects, and to suggest subjects for further investigation.

Significance: What is the topic and why is it useful to learn about it?

Background: What is the history of this topic? What terms need to be
   defined?
Features: What are its special characteristics, capabilities? What is its
   appearance?
Good/Bad: What is good about the topic and what is bad? How does it
   compare with others?
Procedures: How does it work? Where can it be gotten? How can it be
   done?
Applications: What is the present and future importance of the topic? How
   will it affect people? What should they do?

As you begin preparing a speech or essay using the standard questions to
probe your topic, you may discover that one or more of them lacks
application to your topic, or that some of them deal with matters unlikely
to interest your audience. On the other hand, the standard questions may
help you come up with questions of your own, questions that the particular audience you are planning to address will want to have answered.
Moreover, the standard questions, in the order they are listed above,
provide a basic pattern for informative reports. Even if your final essay or
speech does not answer all the standard questions, it is worth asking them
as you begin your work because they will help you probe a topic effectively
and will suggest ways of arranging what you have to say.

Significance. The first standard question, significance, directs attention
to any unusual, intriguing, or dramatic aspects of a topic. This material is
often necessary in informative discourse so that an audience will understand why it should be concerned about the information to be presented.
In reporting to a management class on the topic of "Listening to Subordi-
nates," for example, you might want to begin by noting a study showing
that most managers listen at only a fifteen percent efficiency rate and that
most managers, when asked, cannot say what the term listening means.
   Significant information is used in the introduction of a report to gain
audience attention. Further, it is used to get members of the audience
thinking about how they might use the information. The speaker addressing a management class might follow up a reference to the study about the
listening ability of managers by saying, "Managers who listen well are rated
highly by others, create a healthy work climate, and tend to get promoted
faster. If your goal is to be a good manager and a successful one, then you
ought to listen carefully to what I have to say today." Consider the
significance question as a way to get you and your audience off to a good
start.

Background. Informative reports usually contain a section on the history
of the topic. Such background information as important dates, places,

persons, and events gives the audience some context into which to place later information. The background question also points out the need to provide definitions for unclear or technical terms that may be used later in the report.

How much background is enough? One rule of thumb is to consider the time or space the complete presentation will take and give the background only as much attention as you give the other questions. If you can, try to find out what the audience already knows about the background. Some audiences will need only a quick sketch of the background; others will require all the time or space you can spare.

Features. The features question points out the need to gather and present information about the characteristics, capabilities, and appearance of the subject. Presenting this information might require descriptions, classification, comparisons, or analysis to help the audience visualize and understand the various features. You might, for instance, want to discuss the features of digital watches by describing external parts first, then internal, or by classifying the parts as moving and fixed. You could divide the features of a controversial issue into pros and cons, or you could present them in categories: political implications, economic implications, and social implications.

When working on the features section of an informative report, consider your audience's needs and the use you want listeners or readers to make of the information. How much description will your audience need to understand the subject? Will visual aids help? How much commentary will the audience need to accompany the visual aids? What features will your audience need to know about and which will be irrelevant?

Good/Bad. This standard question, Good/Bad, suggests a need to evelute the subject matter for the audience without becoming an advocate for a particular point of view. What are the advantages and disadvantages of a particular course of action? Is a particular product expensive or reasonably priced? What are the strengths and weaknesses of the pros and cons that make up the different stands on this issue?

Good/Bad information is often characterized by terms like efficiency, morality, durability, value, attractiveness, practicality, and safety. An informative report on a new kind of word processor or office computer, for example, might deal with such matters as overall cost, rate of repair, type of warranty, availability of service, and capacity for information storage.

Procedures. The procedures question directs attention to the way a subject operates or how it can be used. In an informative report on a Big Brother-Big Sister Program, for example, the program director might use the procedures question as a reminder to tell the audience how participants are chosen, how meetings are arranged, how the relationship can be ended, and how interested persons can get more information or sign up for the program.

Applications. The final standard question, applications, is usually answered at the end of an informative report. This question directs attention to information that shows the implications of the subject for the future. Members of the audience will want to know what effect the material presented in the speech or essay will have on them, or what implications it has for a group to which they belong or for the whole society.

The applications question also deals with information that can be used to conclude a report. Memorable quotations, repetitions of the thesis, and data that has a lasting impression all work well at the end of a report because they help the audience remember what the report had to say.

The six standard questions help in probing a topic for information. In some cases your presentation may use all the information generated by the questions; in other cases it may use only part of the material. Which information you finally use should depend on the needs of your particular audience and on the time or number of pages you have in which to present your speech or essay.

ANALYZING THE AUDIENCE

By probing a subject using the standard questions, you are taking into account the expectations and needs of the potential audience for a speech or essay. While the standard questions will alert you to the expectations of most potential audiences, they need to be refined and adapted to the particular audience you are planning to address; that is, the standard questions will tell you what all the vice presidents in the company would want to know about a subject, but you will still need to analyze the needs and interests of the particular vice president (your supervisor, perhaps) who will read or hear your report.

After probing a subject using each of the standard questions, and perhaps after preparing a draft or two of your speech or essay, you need to start thinking about the special needs of your audience. By considering these needs carefully you can avoid producing a report that is crammed with detail but is neither very interesting nor appropriate for the audience and occasion. The following example shows how information generated using the standard questions can be turned into an audience-centered report.

The report below was written by a dental hygiene student in response to this assignment: "Write an informative report about a relatively technical or complicated subject in such a way that it can be easily understood by a general audience or by an audience that already knows a little bit about the topic, but not much. Indicate at the top of the paper whether the essay is directed to a general audience or a special one." Here is the version of the essay the student first turned in:

Audience: First-year Dental Hygiene Students

Acute Necrotizing Ulcerative Gingivitis

Acute necrotizing ulcerative gingivitis, commonly called ANUG, is an inflammatory, destructive condition of the gingiva (gums). The majority of cases are seen among people between the ages of fifteen and thirty.

ANUG itself has a sudden onset, but there are many prior steps involved in the process. First there are predisposing factors: local, stress, and general health and resistance.

Local factors include preexisting gingivitis, inadequate personal oral hygiene and neglect, and smoking. Stress factors include such things as exams and important decisions as well as emotional stress. Stress factors are the reason ANUG is frequently found in college students. General health and resistance factors include dietary and nutritional inadequacies, vitamin deficiencies, recent illnesses, and fatigue . . .

— Kathy Wilson

After reading this paper, the instructor and the students in the class made comments like these:

"Kinda boring."

"Doesn't indicate what all this information means for me; doesn't tell me what use I can make of this information or why I should want to know it."

"Hard to understand. Uses a lot of big words and doesn't explain them. Doesn't include examples that I can relate to my own experience."

"Needs a better opening. Has to get the reader interested in the topic before moving into a complicated decision. The paper presents a lot of new, technical information to the reader without giving him or her a chance to absorb and understand it. Stretch out the discussion a bit — add explanations and examples."

After working on the paper and resubmitting it, the student discussed the new version and the revision process with her instructor:

Instructor: When you added detail to the original version, where and why did you add it?

Kathy: I added to the detail that was already there . . . I looked for terms that needed to be explained and described so that my readers could visualize what I was talking about.

Instructor: Did you start viewing your subject in a different way?

Kathy: Yes, from the point of view of the audience; I looked at the essay as if I were in the audience, wanting to know what the author is talking about, wondering if I will be able to understand what she is saying.

Instructor: So when you were writing, you imagined an audience in front of you? A live audience?

Kathy: Yes. About the size of the class I'm in now, all pre-Dental Hygiene, all about nineteen.

Instructor: What things did you think about them as you were writing?

Kathy: That they were just starting the program, and that they may have heard these terms before but never really knew what they meant — and that they were going to have to know about them sooner or later. So this would be a kind of introduction to the terms, and it would also give them an idea of the things they will encounter.

This paper isn't just to explain something; it is to open up their eyes — to let them know what they're getting into, to let them know that many things they will encounter in the program aren't very nice. I meant this to be a kind of introduction to the whole program.

Instructor: Were you trying to persuade them to drop out of the program?

Kathy: No, only to open their eyes.

Instructor: This paper is different from the original; how did you go about putting the first one together?

Kathy: I just wrote. I took down my books and I started writing. I didn't aim it at anyone in particular. I was just paying attention to the material. I just took my books down and started adding things, following the standard questions we were given, not aiming it towards anyone in particular, just to myself, I suppose, because I knew what I was talking about.

But when I rewrote it, I put myself in the position of someone who didn't know anything about it . . . The amount of detail depends on whom you are talking to. If it's someone who's already in Hygiene I wouldn't have to be quite so descriptive, and if it's someone who hasn't been in it yet, then I'm going to have to be more descriptive because they're not going to know what I'm talking about.

. . . I could picture them looking at each other, making faces because it sounded kind of gross — and I wanted to get that reaction.

Here is the revised paper Kathy submitted:

ANUG

Significance   People enter the Dental Hygiene program for a lot of reasons: some like to work with people; others believe it offers good career opportunities; and still others think they will enjoy the work. The work involved in Dental Hygiene is usually challenging and pleasant, but there are times when it can be downright unpleasant. This is the case with ANUG, one of the most serious and unpleasant conditions a Hygienist will be called on to face.

Background   Acute necrotizing ulcerative gingivitis, commonly called ANUG, is an inflammatory, destructive condition of the gingiva (gums). The majority of cases are seen among people between the ages of fifteen and thirty. ANUG is also known as trench mouth because it was commonly found in soldiers who had been in the trenches during World War Two.

ANUG itself has a sudden onset, but there are many steps to the disease. First there are predisposing factors including local, stress, and general health and resistance factors.

Features   Local factors include preexisting gingivitis (inflammation of the gums charaterized by redness and swelling along the margins), inadequate personal oral hygiene and neglect (such as lack of brushing or flossing), and smoking. Stress factors include things such as important decisions, emotional upset, and exams. ANUG is frequently seen in college students, especially during exam week when students may have four finals in two days. General health and resistance factors include dietary and nutritional inadequacies, vitamin deficiencies, recent illnesses, and fatigue.

Features   After the predisposing factors come the initial signs and symptoms and the characteristic clinical findings. The initial signs are pain and soreness in the mouth, especially on touch; bleeding, both spontaneous and upon probing; and a metallic taste in the mouth. There is death of the tissue cells and ulceration of the triangular gum tissue between adjacent teeth, called papillae. As a result, the tip of the triangle (papilla) becomes blunted until the tissue that is left is covered over by a grayish colored membrane. When this is wiped off, shiny, bloody gum tissue is exposed.

Good/Bad   A person who has this condition avoids brushing, of course, because of the sensitivity of the gums. And the hygienist who treats ANUG at this stage will find his or her job made particularly unpleasant by the bad breath caused by the combination of disease and neglect.

Procedures   A hygienist, therefore, clearly should try to treat ANUG as early in its progress as possible. If ANUG is left untreated, loss of the gum tissue will ultimately lead to exposure of the roots of the teeth. This can cause even greater discomfort for the patient because the roots are not covered by enamel like the crowns of the teeth, and as a result, heat, cold, touch, and certain foods can cause a lot of pain. If the disease is allowed to progress further, the result will be tooth mobility, and, eventually, tooth loss.

Applications   As unpleasant as ANUG is for the hygienist, it is even more unpleasant (to put it mildly!) for the patient. One of the best reasons anyone can have for entering the field of Dental Hygiene is to help see that as few people as possible develop conditions like ANUG, and that those who do get prompt and effective treatment. Dealing with ANUG may not be a pleasant job, but it is an important one.

— Kathy Wilson

The revised paper is much better, though by no means perfect. It does, however, cover the subject thoroughly and accurately, and it makes plain the role the information should play for the audience. Notice also how Kathy used the standard questions to organize her report.

SOURCE CREDIBILITY

The communicator's role in informative discourse is to be a resource for the audience, to present information objectively, thoroughly, and accurately. This means that your audience must regard you as a reliable source of information. Here are three pieces of advice on how to create and maintain your credibility as a source of information.

First, be an authority on the subject, and let your audience know you are an authority. If you have personal experience with the topic, plan to use it in the presentation. If you have no direct experience, do enough reading and talking about the topic so that you feel authoritative and have mastered the information you are going to present. If necessary, use direct quotes and other forms of objective support to reinforce what you have to say.

Second, because distortions of fact are frequently used as argumentative tactics, an audience is always likely to wonder if a speaker or writer is slanting or shaping information in an effort to persuade rather than to inform. If you have an opinion, state it separately from the information you present, and indicate that it is your opinion. Let your readers and listeners make up their own minds; avoid trying to shape what you have to say so that they will agree with your point of view.

Third, know enough about your topic to be able to answer questions about it, and encourage audience response or inquiries from readers. Sometimes a list of references or a handout to accompany a presentation will give readers or listeners a greater feeling of trust in the information you present.

THE FINISHED PRODUCT

Informative speeches and essays have special features in terms of point, pattern, and detail that set them apart from argumentative discourse, on one hand, and from discourse organized around conceptual patterns, on the other.

Point

In most informative discourse, the opening section (significance) serves to let the audience know the specific purpose of the discourse and to get the audience interested in the information it will present. To accomplish this the significance step must do several things: announce the topic in such a way that the audience will want to learn more about it, let the audience know how it can use the information, and give the audience some idea of the way the information will be presented. Since a single sentence usually cannot accomplish all these things, the entire opening section of many informative speeches and essays frequently takes the form of a purpose step or a thesis paragraph.

The following student essay openings illustrate a few of the wide range of strategies available to writers and speakers:

Opening 1:

You rush from your car to your house; your face is frozen, your feet are numb, and you curse the wretched snow. Imagine learning to love the harsh New England winters you are destined to face. That is the aim of *The Cold Weather Catalogue*. In five intriguing sections it reveals the "facts" and joys of winter in an effort to show people how they can come to appreciate and enjoy the season.

— Gayle Patnode

The first sentence of this opening creates a scene, and then both the topic and role of the speaker are announced in the second sentence. The purpose of the information is restated in the last sentence, and the phrase "in five intriguing sections" suggests that the "Features" section of the speech will follow an enumeration pattern.

Opening 2:

This is it! This is the year to eat better, feel better, and look better. How? This is the year to join the growing throng of people who seasonally practice the art of organic gardening. With a modest amount of exercise and an appreciable amount of sunshine and rain, your own natural creativity can result in a garden of paradise. Your organic paradise will produce a bounty of haute cuisine that will titillate your family and friends.

— Marguerite Clifford

In this opening, sentence three announces the topic, "the art of organic gardening." The value of this art for the audience is suggested in sentences two and five. While the pattern this informative report will follow is not directly stated, the clear suggestion is that it will be a demonstration (see p. 246).

Opening 3:

Today I would like to report on recent changes in government regulations that will make it possible for us to expand our production for the domestic market for the first time in ten years. Understanding these regulations is important not only for the decisions we will have to make in the next few months, it is also important for the way we view our company's relationship to other parts of the manufacturing sector and to the economy as a whole. I would like to briefly review the history of government regulations that have affected our participation in the domestic market and then move on to discuss the features, advantages, disadvantages, and implications of the recent changes in government policy.

— Bob Schultz

This opening fails to grab the attention of the listeners. You might even say that it is boring. There is no buildup to the topic. It does say how the information can be used, and it announces the plan of the discourse in the last sentence, but this last sentence seems rather far removed from the beginning of the paragraph and only loosely related to it. If you are addressing an audience that is already strongly interested in a topic, then you might use such an approach; however, a bit of imagination, as demonstrated in the other openings, is usually much better.

Pattern

Informative discourse comes in a wide variety of patterns; most of the patterns you are likely to encounter, however, are related to the standard questions. The patterns discussed here should prove useful to you on many occasions and should help you recognize other, related patterns that a particular audience may expect you to follow.

Standard Questions Pattern. The standard questions used to probe a topic may be used to organize a report. The ANUG essay on p. 239 and the Hobie Cat piece on p. 232 follow all six questions and use them as an organizing principle. The following student essay also uses the standard questions to organize what it has to say:

Outward Bound

Attention

Spend your vacation exposing yourself to physical pain, fear and the natural elements and return a new person? Well, it just might be possible with Outward Bound Inc.

Background

The Outward Bound program is designed to test endurance and give people the opportunity to discover more about themselves. It was started in Colorado in 1962 by a man named Kurt Hahn. He had developed a similar program for British seamen during World War Two and recognized the benefits it provided.

Features

Since then six additional schools have opened across the country. Their goal is to demand a great deal from the body in order to strengthen the mind. They do this by involving students in activities such as sailing, rock climbing, rappeling, canoeing, skiing, cycling and mountaineering. The staff introduces participants to basic skills, equipment, and techniques for preserving resources in an effort to prepare for the expeditions ahead. The exact content of each course differs with location and season; however, all courses contain certain basic elements. For example, in a typical three-week course the first week is spent learning to adapt to the wilderness and improving physical conditioning. Students are taught the necessary skills for success in the particular course. These include such skills as first aid, map reading, and cooking. The second week is spent utilizing these skills on an expedition with the group. The final week concentrates on the "solo." This consists of three days and nights spent in the wilderness with minimal equipment and provisions. During this time the group also plans a final expedition and completes it without an instructor's help.

Each course also contains a service performed by the group to benefit others. This may include improving the environment or including underpriviledged children in a project. The program then wraps up with a foot marathon and a discussion of impressions of Outward Bound. This includes revealing feelings recorded in journals kept during the three weeks.

Good/Bad

All programs in Outward Bound strive to teach people to work as a unit. They must cooperate and encourage one another as well as compensate for one another's strengths and weaknesses. By challenging people with physical and mental risks the staff forces them to use their own resources and perseverance. Outward Bound believes that "people learn best by doing — especially by doing that which is most immediately useful." They hope that when students leave the school they feel somewhat changed. Moreover, they hope that in stretching the body and mind to great limits, the participant is more confident and better able to cope with everyday life.

Procedures I

This standard program is open to those over sixteen years of age. There is no maximum age; however, all participants should be in good health. The tuition is $525–$650 and includes food, equipment, and instruction. Each student must provide personal items such as clothing, and provide his own transportation to and from the school. Some scholarship money is also available for those who are in need so as to vary the economic background of the group.

There are also some special courses offered at each school. These include separate programs such as those for fourteen- to sixteen-year-olds and senior citizens. They run from three to twenty-eight days and cost anywhere from $150 to $900.

Applications It should be noted that Outward Bound is not a program for everyone. The activities are rigorous and often painful and frustrating for those expecting an adult version of summer camp. Although extreme precautions are taken, some activities involve stress and
Procedures II danger. If, however, with these factors in mind, you are still interested in enrolling in an Outward Bound course, more information can be obtained by writing to the following address:

> Outward Bound Inc.
> 165 W. Putnam Ave.
> Greenwich, CT 06830

Outward Bound will send a brochure with full listings of all schools, courses, costs, and limitations. They will also enclose an application, which must be submitted for admissions to any Outward Bound course.

— Gayle Patnode

The standard pattern can be varied in a number of ways depending on the type of information and the needs of a particular audience or occasion. There are at least three types of informative reports that audiences are likely to expect in special situations: the curiosity report, the demonstration, and the practical (or technical) report. The occasions that call for these three kinds of informative discourse also require some variation on the standard questions used to prove topics.

Curiosity Pattern. Information is often presented simply to appeal to our natural curiosity. This pattern may be called the **curiosity pattern**. People like to know about local historical buildings or monuments or about the lives of famous people; they like to hear about heroic deeds and famous events. They like to know about other topics, too — about how helicopters work, how beavers build dams, and how small computers work. Of course, interest in such topics may be of a practical nature, but the broad appeal of such discourse is to curiosity.

Informative discourse designed primarily to appeal to an audience's curiosity rather than to its practicality must be rich in detail; therefore, while a curiosity speech or essay may cover some or all of the standard informative questions, their arrangement and the emphasis placed on each is quite flexible. Sometimes the approach of a curiosity piece is largely historical; in this case, the background and features of the subject may be the most important matters. Sometimes an historical article concludes with material that might be termed present-day significance. There is one element, however, that always receives special treatment in discourse that appeals to curiosity: the significance step.

The opening of an effective curiosity speech or essay creates a scene that appeals to the audience's taste for the unusual, the picturesque, the humorous, the exciting, the touching, or the romantic. The success of a curiosity piece depends heavily on the communicator's ability to hook the audience immediately. Here is a student speech designed to appeal to an audience's curiosity.

Significance   The beer you drink when you are relaxing this evening or at a party this coming weekend is not a modern invention.

Background   Beer is probably as old as agriculture. As soon as man learned to harvest the products of the soil, he learned to work them into his diet. A type of beer bread was produced in Mesopotamia some six thousand years ago. Beer was also enjoyed in Greece, Rome, and Egypt. Records on clay tablets show that among the provisions Noah took with him on his voyage was — beer. Despite its antiquity and general use, however, beer gained little commercial value until the sixteenth century. Until this time, beer production was confined mainly to monasteries. The monks produced the brew for ceremonial and festive occasions. The word *bridal* comes from the words *bride ale*; the bride would serve ale to her guests in exchange for her wedding presents.

During the exploration of America, beer was essential for long sea voyages because water stagnated quickly — as opposed to beer, which remained fresh for long periods. The dietetic properties of beer also helped ward off sea illnesses. The 1622 records of the *Mayflower* show that among the reasons for picking Plymouth Rock as a landing spot was not only that the Pilgrims were low on provisions — but out of beer. Beer brewing became popular in the colonial period. Among the colonial brewers were John Adams, William Penn, and George Washington. George Washington's recipe for beer is on file at the New York Public Library.

The years between 1840 and 1900 were the most innovative in the brewing art. The introduction of German lagered yeasts and the process called pasteurization improved the quality of the product and made the process commercially feasible. Although beer was illegal during prohibition, this never lessened the demand. In recent years the United States has outproduced all other nations by some one hundred and thirty million barrels. Although we are far ahead in production, we are behind in consumption — behind Germany, England, and other European nations.

Features   One term commonly used in beer production and in ads is lager. Hops is the flowering part of the hop plant and is used in beer production to add flavor. Pilsner is the name of a Czechoslovakian beer brewed in the sixteenth century and has now become synonymous with quality. Ale is darker, heavier, and has a higher alcoholic content than most beers. Variations of ale are stout, porter, and bock. Beer can be made from grain, corn, or rice. American brewers use a hybrid strain of barley for their product.

Procedures   There are basically eight steps in the production of beer. First, the grain is toasted and, to prevent further growth of the plant, it is then ground into a coarse mixture called malt. Second, the malt is then mixed with water and cooked at precise temperatures. This is done to convert the malt starch into sugars. The result is called mash. Third, the mix is filtered and the liquid remaining is placed in a copper kettle where it is mixed with hops and then strained to remove the hops. Fourth, the mixture is now called hopped wort; the hopped wort is cooled, aerated, and introduced to the brewer's yeast. American brewers use the top-yeast method. There are two different types of yeast. There's top yeast, in which the yeast rises to the top after fermentation is completed and is then removed. European brewers use the bottom-yeast method with a different strain of yeast, which sinks to the bottom after fermentation. Fifth, the brew is placed in fermentation vessels where the yeast enzymes convert the malt sugars into alcohol and carbon dioxide gas. During this process, the excess carbon dioxide gas is removed and stored to be used later on. This takes approximately a week, after which the yeast is removed to be used for later batches. Sixth, the brew is placed in aging tanks where it is allowed to clarify by sedimentation. This takes approximately eight weeks. Seventh, the brew is reunited with the carbon dioxide gas, then packaged in kegs, bottles, or cans. Eighth, if the beer is to be canned or bottled, it must first pass through a pasteurization process. This is done to prevent the further fermentation of the beer while it is being stored.

Applications   Beer is then shipped to bars and liquor stores across the nation where you or I, if of age, can purchase a six-pack of [pulls out a six-pack] beer.

— Jerry Thibeault

Demonstration Pattern. The **demonstration pattern** is particularly useful for introducing a new process or product; as an element in a lecture-demonstration, textbook, or manual; or to draw attention to an unusual (healthful, entertaining) sport or activity.

Demonstrations frequently use visual aids: the objects themselves or models of them; tapes, slides, movies, and records; maps, graphs, diagrams, and charts; drawings, blackboard illustrations, and handouts. If the usefulness or importance of a subject is not immediately clear to the audience, then a background section may be necessary. The same is true of the applications step: for some audiences it may not be enough to mention the uses of the product or process at the beginning; the readers or listeners may have to become directly involved.

Here is a demonstration speech delivered by a student to about a hundred classmates of the speaker, all of whom were enrolled in a speech course:

Attention   Baton twirling is an up-and-coming sport that will soon become an Olympic event. But the problem is that most people don't understand or appreciate baton twirling. Yet perhaps by the time it becomes an Olympic event, most people will understand it and its history.

Background   As you can tell [she is wearing a rhinestone-studded leotard and holding a baton], I'm going to demonstrate baton twirling. But first I'd like to explain to you how the sport started and where it originated. The art of baton twirling started many years ago in the Samoan Islands. The natives of these islands used to perform ceremonial dances using knives and spears in much the same way that a baton twirler uses a baton today. The first appearance of baton twirling in America was with the early drum majors and they used the large batons that are almost as tall as they are; they weigh about thirty pounds. But in the 1930s women started twirling, so batons had to be changed because they were just too heavy. So they became much smaller and lighter — such as this baton right here.

Today baton twirling is a very competitive field which involves both men and women. In fact, the best baton teacher — and the most well-known — is a man who lives in California. He makes a hundred dollars an hour giving baton lessons.

Features   Before you can take lessons, you have to learn about the baton itself. The baton has three main parts. The big end is called the ball; the little end is called the tip; and the middle part is called the shaft. Batons are made in different sizes according to the person who is twirling it. The way you can tell what size is right for you is by the length of your arm. You take the tip and measure it against your arm [demonstrates] and if your fingertips almost touch the end then you know it is the right size. For example, this is twenty-eight inches long. If my fingertips came right over the end like this, the baton would be too short and I would have to get a larger size.

Procedures   The proper kind of baton isn't like the ninety-nine cent batons you got at Woolworth's when you were a little kid. These batons are perfectly balanced and they cost about fifteen dollars apiece.

There are four major types of twirls. [moves to center front of the room] There are full hand moves. [demonstrates quickly] There are tosses. [demonstrates quickly] Rolls. [demonstrates quickly] And finger twirls. [demonstrates quickly]

Now I'm going to demonstrate each one for you more slowly and explain what I am doing. A full hand move is any move in which your hand is on the baton the whole time, such as a circle [demonstrates], pass [demonstrates], and reverse circle [demonstrates]. These are full hand moves because the baton is in my hand the whole time I'm twirling.

The second is tosses [demonstrates throughout the explanation], called thumb tosses because the baton rolls off your thumb. You have to practice getting used to tossing the baton and once you get used to tossing it, then you have to do different exercises — like fifty of these basic tosses a day, fifty switching from one hand to the other; fifty in the other hand. The practice limbers up your hand; you get used to doing it.

Once you can do these you may vary the routine with different catches — such as a catch under the leg, behind the back, or a backhand catch. These are the different catches you can use.

The third is rolls. In rolls your hand is not allowed to touch the baton at all. [demonstrates throughout the explanation] There are many different types of rolls — a wrist roll, an elbow roll. And all this time my hand doesn't touch the baton, the baton is just rolling across my elbow.

Now, rolls are very difficult. It took me a year and a half to learn elbow rolls like these. I'd say rolls are the hardest type of twirling.

The fourth and final type is finger twirls. There are many types of finger twirls. [demonstates throughout the explanation] Split fingers are used with just the first two fingers going back and forth. There are also four fingers — the baton goes through your four fingers. And then there's the eight finger walkover, which goes through four fingers, and then back across on the top of the hand through four more fingers. Then there's also the four finger carry. You take the baton through four fingers, flip it, and keep going through all your fingers; you keep flipping it from your finger to your fist going back through all your fingers.

Applications   Now you've all seen how easy it is. [laughter] Does anybody want to come down and learn anything?

How about Mike?

Anybody else?

Betsy?

We're going to learn a combination roll and spin.

Now put it under your neck.

Now put out your arms and the baton is going to roll down your arms. Now, once it gets to the end the first time, just lift it; when it gets down to the end lift right away. [they try — laughter] Now when it gets down here lift your left hand higher, and it will spin like that, [demonstrates] so it rolls down and spins. [they try and succeed — much laughter and applause]

Conclusion   As you can tell, baton twirling really isn't hard; it takes dedication, a lot of practice; and you have to put up with getting a lot of black and blue marks once in a while.

— Holly Morin

As she prepared this speech, Holly worried that many people in her potential audience might not be interested in the topic, so she included a background step to convince them that the topic is interesting and an applications step to show them how much fun the sport is. Not every demonstration needs to include these steps, but most will probably follow a plan of organization similar to the one Holly followed.

Practical (Technical) Report. This pattern is useful in two related but slightly different situations. It can be used to present the results of an investigation of a situation or problem, or it can be used to present a record of activities undertaken with regard to a problem or situation. The standard questions that help organize reports of this kind differ slightly from those behind the other patterns:

Significance: definition of problem or situation; indication of why action was taken, or why the subject was investigated

Background: what other investigators have said about the subject; description of the subject before the action or investigation was undertaken

Methods: method used to examine the subject; description of activities undertaken

Features: analysis of the features of the situation or problem; results of activities undertaken

Applications: what was learned from the investigation; what was learned from the activities

Most reports of this sort are relatively long and complicated. The following selections are taken from a straightforward report written by a police sergeant for a magazine distributed to police officers. The first selection describes the background, telling of the situation before the activities described in the report were undertaken. The second selection is a description of some of the activities undertaken; it is drawn from the methods section of the report.

> In October 1975, the Fox Hills Mall opened its doors for the first time in Culver City, Calif. The 130-plus store mall, with its large, expansive parking lots and three-story parking structure, set on over 60 acres of land, is one of the largest shopping malls on the west coast. To complicate matters, the mall opened its doors at the very beginning of the Christmas shopping season.
>
> The immediate effects upon the police patrol function were seen in increased calls for service to the mall and an increase in the number and type of crime reports being generated. Chainstore security personnel began almost at once to arrest both adult and juvenile shoplifters. In the beginning, responding officers were required to do

all of the crime and arrest reports, as well as handle the transportation of suspects to the station for booking procedures.

Working in conjunction with the Fox Hills Mall Security Department, the Culver City Police Department set aside and equipped a room containing report writing equipment, fingerprint facilities, and the necessary desk and telephone. This office is connected to the mall security office and is centrally located within the mall.

Members of the chainstore security departments were taught the proper methods for completing basic misdemeanor crime and arrest forms. They were also instructed to bring arrestees, when possible, to the centrally located security/police office and to complete the necessary forms there. After completing the paperwork, they were to contact the police dispatch for a patrol unit.

(Mahoney, 1981)

Detail

Details — examples, facts, descriptions, graphs, and pictures — aid understanding. Whether your purpose is to be purely practical, to aid understanding, to satisfy curiosity, or some combination of these, you want listeners or readers to take the maximum amount of information away with them. Detail helps you accomplish this goal.

Details works best as an aid to understanding when it is clear, memorable, and lively. Clarity is achieved by carefully defining terms and by using a clear pattern to move through the material. Recall for a moment the commentary by Kathy on pages 237–238. Notice that her first paper was simply a list of facts, one piled on top of the other, with few definitions, little description, and no real sense of audience. After her discussion with the instructor Kathy's revision was much clearer. She used common terms to explain technical ones; for example; Acute Necrotizing Ulcerative Gingivitis became trench mouth. She also used the standard informative pattern so that her audience could follow the development of her point that dental hygiene work can be unpleasant.

Memorableness is achieved by spacing out facts and figures, by using cue words to help the audience follow the stages of development, and by repeating key words for the audience. Look once again at Kathy's essay, both the original and the revised version. Notice how the first try is a dense, highly technical approach to the topic. The revision, however, spaces out the facts so that they are easier to digest. Kathy also provides internal previews, short paragraphs that tell us what is to follow in the features and good/bad portions of the essay, and during the discussion she repeats the key terms identified in the previous section.

Liveliness is achieved by vivid descriptions. Notice how Kathy's description of the mouth into which the hygienist must look and the condition of the patient's breath reinforces her point about this being a sometimes unpleasant task.

The point to be drawn from this second look at one student's work is that there is a difference between knowing about the various forms of supporting material (see Chapter Three) and knowing how to use them in an informative speech or essay. It is not enough to simply have the information; rather, the information must be communicated in a clear, lively, and memorable way.

SUMMARY

This chapter has introduced you to the conventional forms for conveying information and has demonstrated some of the patterns used with these forms. As they apply to information, these forms may be used to provide practical knowledge, to add to our understanding, or to satisfy our curiosity. When your aim is to be informative you will want to make sure that your speech or essay does not assume a persuasive tone and that you have sufficiently prepared your topic so that you maintain your credibility.

The standard questions, if used thoroughly, will provide you with much to say about your topic and may also serve as organizing principles. Remember that each broad issue suggests a number of questions that will aid in finding the aspect of your topic most appropriate to the audience. They will also help you during composing to probe your topic for its unusual and intriguing facets.

In addition to using the standard questions, analyzing the audience is essential to the success of a conventional pattern. A great deal depends on whether your audience is a general one or one with expertise in the topic you are addressing. If you keep the above points in mind, and shape your point, pattern, and detail accordingly, you will become effective at an important skill in our society: information-giving.

KEY WORDS

conventional pattern	curiosity pattern
standard questions	demonstration pattern

EXERCISES

1. Think of three audiences that would expect an informative report to answer specific questions (for example, executives in a large manufacturing company, college administrators, amateur photographers). Then draw up a list of the questions that each audience might pose.

2. Pick up a mass circulation magazine like *Mademoiselle* or *Gentleman's Quarterly* and look at some of the informative articles it contains. Do they answer any or all of the standard questions? Are they organized according to some variation of the patterns described in the chapter?

3. Select a topic about which you know a good deal: sailing, ice skating, cooking, repairing cars; imagine three different audiences you might present your knowledge to. Then write the opening for a speech or essay addressed to each of the audiences.

4. Here are some topics that might be suitable for an informative speech or essay addressed to a general audience:
   a. a local historical site
   b. a local custom
   c. an unusual sport (lacrosse, wall/ball)
   d. an unusual dish or cooking method
   e. a new process or product

   Choose one of these topics or one of your own, and prepare a speech or essay addressed to your classmates or a similar general audience.

5. Prepare an informative essay and bring a draft of it to class to share with your fellow students. After sharing it with them, ask them if it took into account what they already knew about the topic and what they need to know. If it did not, ask them how they think you should revise it.

6. Go through the same process as in #5 with a speech you are preparing, but instead of presenting the speech in rough form, simply tell the members of the audience in some detail what you plan to talk about; then ask them what they already know about the topic and what they need to know.

7. Is the following passage informative or argumentative in aim? If it is argumentative, how could it be made informative?

   > Unemployment is at its highest mark since the Vietnam War: 8.7 percent in December, 1980, according to a March, 1981, article in *New Society*. In a study conducted by the United States Department of Labor, it was found that this figure includes 6 percent of white males, 12.7 percent of black males, 15.6 percent of white teenagers, and a shocking 36.6 percent of black teenagers. There are two factors determining unemployment: which people become unemployed and how long they remain out of work. Christopher Byron, in an August 11, 1980 article in *Time*, stated that the two groups that suffer most from unemployment are the nation's twenty-five million blacks and twelve million Hispanics. Their rate of unemployment is double the national average and the jobs they do get are at the bottom of the

income ladder. There is a need in our society today to lower the unemployment rate, specifically among black teenagers.

REFERENCES

Mahoney, Tom, "Shopping Malls: New Problems for Law Enforcement," *FBI Law Enforcement Bulletin*, March 1981.

10. Conventional Patterns: Composing an Argument

Professor of Rhetoric: What a dull world this would be if we were all of the same mind.

Voice in the back of the room: Not if it were *my* mind.

Sometimes it seems that life would be simpler if only people would see the situation our way. There would be no quarrel over which movie to see, which driver caused the accident, or which customer is always (or never) right. There would be no need for our judicial system, the legislature, or the United Nations. But life, though more peaceful, would be much less interesting.

In fact, from the Revolutionary War through civil rights movements to the more current debates over bilingual education and abortion, the social upheavals in this country have been based on the rights of individuals not only to hold their own opinions but also to voice them — in essence, the right to argue. Argument is a natural social phenomenon. For those times when we want to voice these opinions, when our purpose is to influence others, we need to use the standard questions that govern the conventional patterns of argument. Just as with presenting information, arguing effectively requires that we anticipate the expectations of an audience. This chapter will provide you with the standard questions appropriate for moving audiences toward your point of view, while providing them with the information necessary for deciding the merits of your argument.

The ways in which we argue change as we grow older and become educated. Where once we saw everything in polarized terms — this is right, that is wrong — we eventually begin to see events in a more relative way. Certainty becomes probability in a world that is constantly changing. Rules and laws, though slow to be amended, are challenged frequently as value systems shift and as knowledge increases. The science of medicine for instance, is involved in a new course of study, bioethics. As technological advances lead to more sophisticated life-sustaining devices, physicians, nurses, and families are faced with decisions they never expected to be called upon to make. Courses in bioethics allow new medical students to consider these decisions and to argue about them. Argument, far from being an evil to avoid, is a social necessity. It is a method designed to help us reach agreement about the proper conduct of human affairs.

Because of its importance argument has been the subject of endless study from several viewpoints, the philosophical, the psychological, the political, and the sociological, to name a few. This chapter will help you with actually composing an argument, while Chapter Eleven will help you understand on what bases arguments can appeal to and work for an audience, as well as the bases on which some arguments can be refuted.

AIMS AND FEATURES OF ARGUMENT

Argument aims to provide reasons for and against an issue. Issues are topics that provoke controversy, stir emotions, and divide people into opposing groups: pro-life *vs.* pro-choice; pro-nuclear *vs.* anti-nuclear, supply-side *vs.* demand-side, and so on. In turn, these groups provide the public with slogans that promote their points of view: "Make love, not war"; "Split wood, not atoms"; and any number of others.

The goal of argument is to gain the support of others for a particular position. To do this successfully an argument must present a clearly articulated idea, support it with ample detail, and anticipate the concerns and viewpoints of a potential audience. It is important to know what an argument is and what it is not, so before going any further we need to distinguish argument from two other related methods for making choices: **coercion** and **logic**.

An argument can occur only when there is a free choice available to the disputants or to the audience. Coercive communication reduces choice so that only one option is available to the parties involved. When a thief trains a gun on a bank teller and demands money, the thief is attempting to coerce the teller into a choice: the money or a life. When supervisors order workers to either carry out a task or lose their jobs, the workers' choices are severely reduced. When stubborn children threaten to run away from home unless they are given their way, they are attempting to reduce the choices available to the parents to only one.

Coercion is not a reasonable form of communication. It is the strategy of those who have lost faith in or fail to understand the process of argument. Coercion contributes nothing to social harmony, leads to no constructive end, and creates an environment of mistrust and antagonism. The skeptic might say that coercion is the way the real world works; but the consequences of coercive communication, when seen in the light of fallen officials, shattered careers, and broken relationships, should lead even the most skeptical to search for a more effective method for bringing about change. We cannot argue about matters unless all parties involved remain open to persuasion.

In a speech or an essay, coercion takes the form of inflexibility in one's position on an issue. Coercers refuse to recognize opposing views, exaggerate the consequences of not accepting their position, and make emotional attacks on their opponents. Argument is a process of give and take, and of seeking agreement through reasoning. It is a more difficult process to learn than coercion, but the results are far longer lasting and more satisfying to all parties concerned.

Argument is natural as we concern ourselves with human affairs, a realm in which there are no exact answers. Logic, however, is a method for arriving at exact answers, at certainty. Mathematicians and physicists apply logical formulas to solve problems in the physical world. Engineers can determine the stress capacity of a particular metal by applying a strict set of criteria in their measurements. In each example, the goal is absolute knowledge, and the method is formal logic.

But human affairs are seldom entirely logical, and applying a strict logic to achieve final solutions to human problems is often futile. If an answer to a problem may be arrived at positively, the best course of action is not to argue but to find the right source for the answer. We would not argue, for instance, about the volume of a container when a scientific formula could give us an exact answer. Although we do it occasionally, it is silly to argue about who won the World Series in 1975 when a record book is available to tell us.

We need, of course, to gather as many facts as we can when arguing, and we should try to arrange our information systematically; but we should not reduce a decision about human problems to a logical formula. An engineer can tell us how to build a dam but cannot tell us if we should build it. A statistician can tell us that the average family has 2.5 children but cannot tell us how many we should have. Building a dam or having a baby are broad questions with logical, social, and moral consequences. The best way to decide complex matters like these is through open discussion of all available opinions.

If we cannot argue about matters in which there is no free choice or about matters in which there is an absolute choice, what can we argue about? We can and should argue about any topic that involves reasonable alternatives, especially when these alternatives may lead to significant change in some aspect of our personal and social lives. Should the drinking age be changed? Should gambling be legalized in our community? Are professional sports too violent? Should women be subjected to military draft? We can never be certain about such questions or countless others that confront us; therefore, we must argue.

PLANNING THE ARGUMENT

Succeeding in an argument requires careful planning. Three primary elements of the argument must be addressed before we actually begin to construct the message: the issue, the audience, and ourselves. This section will show you how to prepare for an argument by discussing issue analysis, audience motivation and source credibility.

Probing the Issue

Effective argumentation requires us to probe an issue thoroughly and accurately by considering the three main elements an audience will expect to hear about: needs, plans, and benefits. Just as with informative discourse, these elements involve responding to a standard set of questions that help us understand the issue completely and anticipate objections from our opponents or from the audience.

The **standard questions** for argument help us examine the controversy thoroughly and develop a pattern for arranging the argument. The actual argument may or may not contain a direct response to all the standard questions. As with preparing informative discourse, we may need to emphasize some questions and leave out others; however, we should use all the standard questions as probes when preparing an argument.

The six standard questions for an argument are the following:

1. Topicality: Is this a problem worth arguing about? Does the argument address the right problem?
2. Significance: Has the problem reached critical proportions?
3. Inherency: Is the solution proposed the right one for the problem? Who should solve the problem?
4. Workability: Has the solution worked anywhere else? Can the solution be demonstrated?
5. Plan-Meet-Need: Has the solution been tried some place else? Can we provide evidence that it has worked?
6. Disadvantages: What counterarguments could be raised, and how can the counterarguments be refuted?

Responding to these six questions will insure that we have probed the controversy thoroughly. Because thorough planning for an argument is so important, the standard questions are discussed below in some detail.

Topicality. Topicality includes two questions: Is this a problem worth arguing about? Does the argument address the right problem? The first question concerns the level of interest in our topic. There is no need to construct an argument about something trivial or for which there is an absolute answer. We would not argue, for instance, that a football field is wider than a soccer field, since we can find this out with a simple measurement. Similarly, we would not argue that "Each of us should attempt to find success in life," since there would be no reasonable objection to the statement. While these examples are trivial, topicality can involve more. Sometimes an argument is topical for one audience but not apparently topical for another. An argument concerning discipline in the schools may seem immediately relevant when addressed to the local school board but may not be to the residents of a senior citizens' housing complex. For this audience it would be necessary to build topicality into the argument. We would need to show the senior citizens that a lack of discipline in the schools leads to vandalism, burglary, and mistreatment of the elderly outside the classroom. The point is this: We must make an argument both interesting and appropriate to an audience before we can expect them to pay attention to it.

Topicality also involves addressing the right problem. Many of us have heard the expression, "treating the symptoms but not the disease." This familiar expression reminds us that what often appears to be a solution to a problem is only a short-term remedy. Does increasing unemployment benefits solve the problem of the unemployed? Does increasing the supply of consumer goods lead to lower prices? Will boycotting sponsors result in more wholesome television programming? Quite often the proposed solution appears to solve a problem but really addresses only a part of the problem or another problem altogether.

Significance. The significance question asks: Is the problem critical? For the most part, problems are addressed only when they become urgent. The expression *crisis management* points out how most problems are handled — only when they must be. Significance, of course, is in the eye of the beholder; a problem that we might consider urgent may not even be on the minds of those who could solve it. Thus when developing an argument we need to consider what it is that makes the problem critical.

How significant an issue is for the audience is often a matter of how significant we make it. The average person hears many arguments in the course of a day and may find no particular reason to listen to us. The significance question forces us to look at our argument from the audience's point of view and make it purposeful and critical for its members. This may require a lengthy discussion of the problem or simply a brief review. Our approach to the issue's significance will determine how much attention is given to our argument.

When probing an issue for its significance it is useful to list all the problem aspects of that issue. For example, what will build significance into your argument for a change in the litter laws? How many problems are associated with the random disposal of litter? If you focus on the fact that litter makes roadsides unsightly, this aesthetic aspect of the problem may not be significant enough to convince an audience that the litter issue is a critical one; however, if you probe the litter issue thoroughly you will discover that there are economic and legal aspects to the problem that increase its significance. Sometimes an issue becomes significant not because of one particular problem but because of the multiple problems it involves.

Arguments, then, begin with the development of the problem. Once we are certain our argument is both topical and significant, we can move to the next two standard issues: inherency and workability.

Inherency. The inherency question asks: Is this the right solution to the problem? Often, what appears to be a proper solution to a problem is not, especially when it comes to the question of who should solve the problem. We need to be certain who is responsible for solving the problem and what measures need to be taken. Is the solution to the energy crisis a federal, state, local, or individual matter, or a combination of some of these? Who has the power to legislate taxes, pass laws, prohibit building projects? By considering the inherency question we discover who should solve the problem.

Inherency also involves the degree of change that we are proposing. If we are arguing that the postal service is inefficient, is our solution to abandon the present structure altogether or simply to change it to make it more efficient? Should we do away with the primary system for electing presidents, or should we change the nature of the system so that the convention delegates are not bound to the outcome? If money is the root of all evil does that mean we should not make money, or that we should use it wisely? Probing our argument with the inherency question assures us that we have considered who is responsible for solving the problem and to what degree we have to go to solve it.

Workability. The workability question forces us to ask: Is the solution to the problem practical and/or workable? A solution that cannot work is unacceptable in an argument. Classroom teachers often hear speeches on such topics as "prostitution should be legalized" or "marijuana should be legalized." While these are clearly topical and significant issues, the speech often fails to convince its audience because the speaker has not considered how the system would operate. In the case of marijuana, who would control the industry (inherency)? and would legalization involve so many rules, regulations, bureaucratic red tape, agencies, and tax laws that it would simply not be practical (workability)? Legalizing marijuana might solve the problem of criminal enforcement, but would it solve the problem of marijuana use and abuse? We might ask, from another point of view, if the present system solves the problem of marijuana use. Does the present system work? Is enforcement possible? Does the present system address the right problem (topicality)? and does it give us a practical solution to the problem (workability)? We might do the same kind of probing for any number of issues that confront us. Unless we confront the practical nature of our solutions we will seldom be taken seriously in an argument.

Workability considerations lead to arguments that are sharpened by the realities of time, space, and politics. If an argument fails to be practical it will surely be refuted by opponents or rejected by the audience. Workability questions help us avoid pie-in-the-sky solutions to complex problems.

Plan-Meet-Need. The fifth standard question asks: Can we demonstrate that the solution we are proposing will work? Members of an audience often have a difficult time visualizing in their minds what the future will be like if the change we propose in our argument should come about. It is therefore necessary to dramatize the solution for them. This can be done in a variety of ways.

If the solution we are proposing has actually been tried in other places, we can make comparisons. If we are arguing that a women's crisis center is needed for our community we might be able to show, in the plan-meet-need phase of our argument, that such centers have worked in other communities. By doing so we would help the audience visualize what such a center might look like and accomplish in our community.

If the solution being proposed has not been tried anywhere else, we can still describe for our audience how the solution might look. In the case of the women's crisis center we might say something like the following:

> I see a place with open doors and open arms, a place of comfort and shelter where the battered and the abused, the lost and the frightened, those who need our help, can come with assurance. Such a center would make our community a more human place, a place with a heart. Crimes will be prevented before they occur, people will be saved before they are lost. . . .

Plan-meet-need questions force us to consider if our argument can eliminate all or most of the problems we have indicated in the significance portion of the argument. By showing that the solution is practical (workability), and that it can work or already has worked, (plan-meet-need), we create an argument that is difficult to refute.

Disadvantages. The final standard question asks: What objections will opponents or audience members raise to the argument? This issue deals with potential arguments by others, including refutations of our proposal and the suggestion of alternative proposals. By raising the disadvantages question, we anticipate reactions to our argument and deal with them before they are raised. Suppose, for instance, that you favor a women's crisis center, while your opponents favor stiffer penalties for cases of abuse of women. You need to anticipate this alternative in your argument and refute it before your opponents have the chance to make their case.

The disadvantages questions also asks us to consider weak points in our own argument and to deal with them before someone else does. If our solution is very expensive, or if it is risky or potentially unpopular, the disadvantages question reminds us to respond to these weak spots. By using the disadvantages question to cover possible problems not accounted for in other standard questions and to refute potential opposition, we assure ourselves that the argument will be complete.

These six standard questions allow us to probe and analyze virtually any problem and prepare a reasonable solution for it. Remember that in some arguments all of the standard questions will apply and may actually be used as an organizational scheme (see model on pp. 271–274), while in other arguments only some of the questions will be relevant. As we probe the issue with the standard questions, we need to pass our argument through each one.

Now that we have considered an analytical scheme for probing an argument, let us turn to the role of audience analysis in argumentative discourse.

ANALYZING THE AUDIENCE IN AN ARGUMENT

Arguments are constructed for audiences, since it is the audience that ultimately decides if the argument works. Lawyers tailor their arguments for the judge or jury; legislators argue for the voting assembly; advertisers target their appeals to those most likely to buy the product. Effectiveness in argument requires the arguer to turn toward the audience, to see the issue as the audience might, and to adapt the argument to the audience being addressed. Of course, all discourse is directed toward an audience (see Chapter Two). In argumentative discourse, however, we need to analyze members of the audience to discover how they might benefit by accepting our position on the argument. That is, audience, members will be more likely to accept an argument if it meets some need of theirs.

We need to think of two audiences when planning an argument: the **general audience** and the **particular audience** to whom we are speaking or writing. The general audience is an imaginary group of people. Think of this audience as all the reasonable people who might form a judgment about the argument. The concept of general audiences leads us to view an issue, develop all the possible reasons for our position, and think of all the possible counterarguments. By considering all the reasons and potential objections to our stance on the issue, we can then select various points to emphasize depending upon the demands of the situation. Thinking about the general audience forces us to reason out the whole issue and construct an argument that can be read or heard by anyone.

The second audience we need to think about is the particular audience. The particular audience is the specific group of persons who will actually read or listen to our argument. Once we have analyzed the issue and developed a total case, we need to think about those reasons that will be most important to the particular group. If you think back to the chapters on composing, you will recall a chart illustrating the special points of view of various audiences on hazardous waste dumping. Turn now to that chart on page 31. Each of these three audiences — town residents, biology professors, and owners of the dump sites — is a particular group with special needs, and your argument must speak to those needs. On the other hand it is important to draw the specific case from the total case. Although you may change the emphasis of your argument, you need to avoid making statements to one group that contradict statements made to another. We have all heard of people who say one thing to one group, something else to the next group, and so on, shaping their argument to please whoever happens to be listening. More often than not such people are found out, lose their credibility, and thus forfeit their effectiveness as advocates.

Look now at a real example of the concepts of general and particular audience analysis working together in the planning of an argument. Remember that the goal of audience analysis in argumentative discourse is more specific than the general audience analysis we do for all discourse. Here our purpose is to determine the motives operating in the group to be addressed so that the argument will be convincing.

Suppose you are working as a recruiter for the United States Army. Your task is to get persons between the ages of seventeen and twenty-one to enlist for a three-year term in the noncommissioned ranks — that is, as privates. How do you prepare for such a task?

You would begin by considering the general audience, finding all the possible reasons persons in this age group would and would not enlist in the Army. In the process of gathering this list of reasons, you obtain the Army's research study based on a public opinion survey. In the study you find the top four reasons for and against enlisting given by thousands of potential recruits in this age group who were interviewed by the survey company. The points favoring enlistment are:

1. skills training
2. travel
3. pay
4. supervision and personal growth (development of discipline)

You notice also that the four most-commonly-given reasons that persons in this age group would not join the Army are the following:

1. fear of combat
2. loss of personal freedom
3. basic training
4. peer pressure

In preparing for your role as recruiter you can assume that these are the underlying concerns of prospective recruits. You then develop a total argument for enlisting in the Army using the two lists as the basis for your detail; that is, you fill in each reason with supporting material or evidence. You have a reasonable case for enlistment based upon a composite of your general audience.

You now know what will work and not work for anyone in general, but what you still need to know is what will work for the particular individual who walks through the door of your recruiting station. Once again you look at your research polling data, and you find that when the list is broken down into college and non-college persons, different reasons are emphasized for liking and disliking the Army. College-level and college-educated persons have indicated that, above all else, they favor travel and fear loss of personal freedom. Non-college-educated persons most favor training in a skill, and most fear basic training.

On the basis of such distinctions you now know which arguments will work best for individuals who enter the station. You would not be misleading the individuals; rather, you would be making your arguments relevant to the person with whom you are speaking. You would be able to anticipate and respond to the objections most likely to arise.

On the basis of your analysis you can construct hypothetical arguments. You might make the following argument to a college-level prospect who shows an interest in joining the Army.

Proposition of Action

Jim, thanks for stopping by to talk. Getting right down to business, I'd like you to consider enlisting in the United States Army. Let me tell you, for a moment, about the opportunities available to you in the military.

Appeals to Desires

Aside from the skills training you already have, and the excellent pay, which you could probably match outside the Army because of your education, I think there is one opportunity the Army offers that you'll find hard to match elsewhere. I'm talking about travel. Jim, you are at a time in your life when travel can be exciting and educational. Once you get married, settle down, and have children, traveling can become difficult and expensive. Besides, once you get tied down to the routine of work in a situation where vacation time is limited, traveling can become all the more difficult.

The Army offers an excellent opportunity to see the world. You can, for instance, choose your first duty station in Europe, the Middle East, Asia, or somewhere in the United States. Once at your base, you'll be free to travel when off duty and during your thirty-day leave. You might, for instance, be stationed in Munich, Germany, a great jumping-off spot for skiing in the Alps, motoring down to the French Riviera, or sampling foods in a Roman garden in Italy. Your expenses to and from your base station are paid for by the military. Do you realize what a trip like that would cost at civilian rates?

Minimizes Concerns

Look, Jim, the Army is not all gravy. There is plenty of hard work, important work, to be done, and there is some regimentation; but you'll probably find that rules and regulations are pretty heavy duty in the business world too. Once you are accustomed to Army ways, you'll see that loss of personal freedom is minimal and comparable to what you'll experience in a civilian career.

Jim, I've talked long enough. Let's hear from you.

I'm ready to answer any other questions you might have.

The speech given here, of course, is hypothetical; it is a composite, however, of many that have actually been given. The value of this model may lie in the fact that many of you will hear a speech quite like it and will have to understand its motivational basis. The speech may or may not be convincing to Jim, but at least it is relevant to his concerns. The model shows how the concepts of general and particular audience work together in an argument.

Understanding the motives operating within human beings occupies much of our daily lives. The attitudes, beliefs, and values surrounding a particular topic are different for each situation and so are difficult to reduce to formulas. Some professional communicators, like advertisers, make their living by understanding the basic motives that lead people to choose one product over another. Psychologists are continually searching for the motives and values that shape human behavior. What makes an argument convincing is that it fulfills some need in the audience.

One theory of **motivation**, based on the work of psychologist Abraham Maslow, suggests five basic universal needs: physiological and social needs, and the needs for security, self-esteem, and self-actualization. We should ask ourselves these questions: Does my argument gratify the audience? Does it promise greater material wealth, security, self-esteem? Does it offer a chance to grow intellectually or spiritually? What appeal does it contain to such ideals as integrity, wisdom, popularity, equality, or personal freedom? Your goal is to relate your proposition to something for which the audience is searching.

Motivational arguments are often abused, or at least the charge is leveled that human motives are exploited; for example, some advertisers imply a promise of a more satisfying sex life to those who buy a particular car, or use a certain cosmetic, or eat special foods. Consumer advocates argue that people are then led to buy the products for reasons unrelated to their intrinsic value. As you read the following example, ask yourself with whom you agree: the author, Smith Hempstone, or the defense attorney, Jerry Paul.

Joan Little's Lawyer Told Nothing But the Truth

WASHINGTON — For a criminal trial lawyer, Jerry Paul did an absolutely shocking thing the other day. He told the whole truth and nothing but the truth.

In an interview with *New York Times* correspondent Wayne King, Mr. Paul, the North Carolina lawyer who successfully defended Joan Little, asserted that he can "win any case in this country, given enough money."

Certain it is that it took bundles of the green stuff — an estimated $325,000 — to beat Miss Little's murder rap.

And to get that sort of money, said Mr. Paul in yet another unlawyerlike burst of candor, you have to "orchestrate the press." And Mr. Paul did exactly that at Miss Little's trial in Raleigh last August.

You may recall the case: Miss Little, a 21-year-old black, was in Beaufort County jail appealing her conviction on a 7-to-10 year sentence for breaking and entering; she killed her 62-year-old white jailor, Clarence Alligood, with an ice pick, and took off for the tall timber.

After giving herself up eight days later, Miss Little claimed that she had killed Mr. Alligood in self-defense, after he had forced her to perform oral sex as he held the ice pick to her head (Mr. Alligood's body, naked below the waist, was found in her cell).

The state charged her with first-degree murder, a charge later amended to second-degree by Superior Court Judge Hamilton Hobgood.

Now not for every trial can the defense scare up $325,000. But the Little case had everything: black vs. white, female vs. male, prisoner vs. jailor, youth vs. age. Before one could say Angela Davis (who, of course, put in an appearance at the trial), Mr. Paul had civil rights groups, women's libbers, prison reform advocates, The Black Panthers, and anybody else dissatisfied with his lot falling all over each other to contribute money and assistance.

Miss Little's lawyers had no trouble in getting her trial shifted from conservative, rural Beaufort County to the more liberal state capital of Raleigh (the Watergate defendants had no such luck when they sought a change of venue).

In her pre-celebrity days, when she was but an unknown burglar, Miss Little had experienced difficulty in retaining counsel. No more:

When the time came for trial, she was represented by no fewer than seven attorneys.

On hand, in addition to Angela Davis, were celebrities such as Georgia legislator Julian Bond and radical attorney William Kunstler. More than 150 reporters showed up for her trial from nearly 50 newspapers, magazines, and broadcasting stations, including one from as far away as Sweden.

In addition to paying for her battery of high-powered lawyers, the money contributed to Miss Little's defense was vital in the jury-selection process. At a cost of more than $50,000, the defense's 28-member team of psychologists, private investigators, and mathematicians probed the attitudes of potential jurors, first in Beaufort County, later in Raleigh and surrounding Wake County.

By testing the attitudes of potential jurors on everything from their taste in magazines to their feelings about policemen's veracity, the defense was able to fashion a profile of a "friendly" juror. And through the use of the challenge right, to see to it that the jury selected — six whites, six blacks, seven of whom were women — was ideal for its purposes.

Result: After only 78 minutes of deliberation, the jury found Joan Little not guilty.

Granted that the North Carolina police work was shoddy, and that the prosecution did not exactly win for itself a place in the history of jurisprudence (it failed for instance, to make much of the fact that Mr. Alligood was stabbed 11 times, which might have thrown some shadow on the self-defense theory). And it is always possible that the jury simply found Miss Little transfigured by an aura of innocence (Mr. Paul says that he believes she was innocent, but that the question is "almost irrelevant").

In the end, one is forced to agree with Mr. Paul that such tricks as parading Miss Little in front of press photographers while she was carrying a copy of "To Kill a Mockingbird" (a gentle novel about a miscarriage of Southern justice), and his skill in obtaining a friendly jury, were crucial to her acquittal.

As for the 33-year-old Mr. Paul he's too busy speaking for $1,000 fees, planning a book on the Little trial and participating in a movie about the case to practice much law. "What I'm really like," Mr. Paul confided to *Times* man King, "is Elmer Gantry."

Gantry, you will recall, was the religious charlatan anti-hero of a Sinclair Lewis novel. Exactly.

(Hempstone, 1975)

Of course, Hempstone is arguing that Paul not only manipulated his audience by analyzing their motives, but also that he actually picked his audience through motivational analysis in such a precise way that he could not lose the case — in fact, in such a way that the actual case became a secondary matter. Paul is arguing, on the other hand, that his job is to win the argument, and that he did nothing illegal — in fact, nothing more than what he was hired to do. Hempstone's objection to this process is that the actual issue, Joan Little's guilt or innocence, could not be reasonably considered given the prior maneuvers of the defense attorney. What is your reaction?

When considering the audience for an argument, it is important to keep in mind that argument is a social mode of discourse intended to lead us to reasonable solutions to problems. You should remember that argument is your primary weapon against irrationality, and then make some decisions about your personal ethics.

The next critical subject for consideration when planning an argument is source credibility.

SOURCE CREDIBILITY IN ARGUMENTS

Source **credibility** is a term that refers to the character, intelligence, and good will attributed to the communicator by the audience. Generally, members of an audience make a preliminary judgment about the speaker or writer, one they may modify during the reading of the argument or presentation of the speech. Later, during the events that follow the speech or the reading of the essay, they may change their judgment again. The judgments made about the communicator's character, competence, and attitude during these three time periods form an image. Research indicates that this total image affects the way the argument is heard or read. We should therefore understand the bases for the image we create and decide how to improve our credibility in an argument. Look at the credibility chart shown in Table 10-1. The chart shows the three characteristics of source credibility across the three time periods of a communication event.

The term *character* refers to the communicator's personal reputation. Are we considered trustworthy? Do we inject too much of our own opinion into the argument? Do we behave according to the principles we argue for in our discourse?

The term *competence* refers to how intelligent or authoritative the communicator appears to be on the topic at hand. Do we look intelligent? Does our vocabulary suggest intelligence? Can we answer off-the-cuff questions about our topic? Can we answer questions about the other side of the issue?

Finally, good will refers to how much the communicator appears to like the audience. Are we known to have a personal antagonism toward the event or the audience? Do we appear enthusiastic about the topic or the event? Are we defensive during the question-and-answer period?

Table 10-1 Communicator Credibility

	Character	Competence	Good Will
Before	Determined by: a. group affiliation b. perceived biases c. perceived morality d. stereotype and personal reputation	Determined by: a. listing of credits and titles in introductory remarks b. such nonverbal cues as dress, posture, facial expressions, and so on c. relationship between communicator and topic	Determined by: a. relationship between audience and communicator b. audience's attitude toward topic c. perceived and manipulative intent
During	Determined by: a. relationship between image and issue b. objectivity achieved in speech or essay c. perceived congruence between attitudes actually held and attitudes exhibited	Determined by: a. errors in data presented b. associations developed between self and authorities cited c. type and validity of reasons presented d. grammar, vocabulary, style	Determined by: a. tone of voice, facial expressions, and punctuation (general presentational style) b. introduction
After	Determined by: a. shifts in social grouping b. modifications of personal reputation	Determined by: a. ability to answer questions about topic b. ability to provide sources of data	Determined by: a. interaction of audience and communicator following communication b. social behavior between time of presentation and decision made by audience and topic c. response to criticism

You or your instructor may want to add to or subtract from the entries in Table 10-1. The purpose of the chart is simply to make you more sensitive to some of the causes for your image as a communicator. You might also decide, as you look at the chart, which reasons would apply only to writers, or only to speakers. Which reasons apply to both speaking and writing? Where does the notion of clean copy fit into the chart on credibility?

Finally, how can you use or change your image? Can a person's image overwhelm the audience so that the message becomes a secondary feature? Source credibility in argument is a subject of much research and discussion; its value to us as successful advocates must not be understated.

Planning an argument carefully by considering the proof value of the message, the audience, and the message source moves us toward shaping a convincing final product. We are now ready to draft an argument.

THE FINISHED PRODUCT

An argument has five essential components: point, pattern, detail, introduction, and conclusion. The introduction and conclusion are composed using the guidelines discussed in Chapter Three. The point, pattern, and detail of an argument need special consideration here.

Point

The point of an argument is called a **proposition**. A proposition is a judgment or a conclusion that has been reached about a controversy. The proposition is the focal point of the argument, and each statement before it or after it must somehow relate to the proposition. In an argument as in informative discourse, the proposition is usually stated directly; however, the point of an argument may be implied, or be unstated, if you have a particular reason to do so. Sometimes you may want the audience itself to discover the point, as in the Kennedy-Kruschev model on pp. 304–307.

There are two basic types of propositions: propositions of fact and propositions of action.

Propositions of fact state that something is or is not the case. Look at the following propositions:

- Argentina is ruled by an authoritarian regime.
- Great athletes are born, not made.
- Gambling is a social disease.

Each of the above statements sets forth a specific premise that must be supported; there is a clear risk that the arguer must accept, and members of the audience know what they are to judge. Notice that in propositions of fact the audience is not being asked to act upon anything. The judgment to be made in propositions of fact revolves around whether the statement itself is reasonable. Propositions of fact are quite common in the normal course of events. We often hear such statements as "High protein diets are dangerous" and "College professors are too liberal." Similarly, in magazines and newspapers we read think pieces that ask us to change our attitudes toward some topic of human concern. In such cases the focus of the argument is on the accuracy and reasonableness of the statement. A proposition succeeds or fails according to the composer's ability to use terms the audience can respond to, and to support the proposition with concrete detail.

Propositions of action state that something should be done. Look at the following propositions:

- The United States government should restrict trade with Argentina until its authoritarian regime has stepped down.
- Social Security funds should be separated from funds for Medicare.
- Vote against legalized gambling in the referendum next week.
- Convicted murderers should be punished by death.

In each of the above propositions the argument revolves around an action that should be taken. Terms will need to be defined, but the argument requests a specific action, and that is its point.

Action propositions may be stated with a wide variety of topicality and significance. Notice that the statement above relating to trade with Argentina would be quite topical if made to a high-level government agency responsible for United States' trade relations, but would be only indirectly topical to a group of classmates. The propositions against legalized gambling would be relevant only to those who will actually vote or to those with some influence on voter behavior.

When drafting propositions of action it is essential to keep the readers or the audience in mind so that the proposed action will be possible for that group. If you cannot make the proposition relevant to the immediate group addressed, consider rewording the proposition so that it is a proposition of fact: for instance, if you want to argue for legalized gambling in your state to a group of classmates, you might decide that a proposition of action is not feasible, since class members are unable to enact such a law or to influence such legislation. In this instance you might decide to put your argument into a proposition of fact something like this: "The state has no right to prevent its citizens from gambling."

The specific action proposed in a proposition of action may or may not be actually stated. You might argue, for instance, that "The State legislature should establish a low interest loan fund for middle-income college students." If your argument is addressed to the state legislature, the specific action is explicit in the proposition; but if you compose this argument as a letter to the editor, you must include the specific actions you want your readers to take. Often an audience agrees wholeheartedly with an argument, but nothing results because the speaker or writer has not suggested an action the audience can take. Remember the political adage: it is not enough for me to convince you that I am the best candidate; I must also convince you to vote.

Propositions of fact and action are related. If you argue that "Toxic waste dumping is America's number one problem," it is only a short step to asking that something be done about it. The differences are real, however, and you should choose the type of proposition based upon what you believe can be accomplished on the particular occasion.

Pattern

Once you have decided upon the type of proposition and have stated it, you need to begin gathering your total argument into some organized form. The organization of an argument is designed to fulfill the expectations raised in the minds of the audience by your proposition and the situation.

The Standard Questions Pattern. An argument based upon a proposition of action has a conventional pattern of arrangement. This pattern follows the order of the standard questions. Once you have decided which standard questions you will need to comment on in the argument, you can organize the argument around them. The following argument is based on a proposition of action and is organized according to the standard questions.

A Model of a Stock Issues Argument

Introduction (gains attention)

A comedian recently quipped that his garbage was beginning to feel heavier than his groceries.

From 1958 to 1971, food consumption in America increased only 2.3 percent while packaging consumption increased 33.3 percent. This "buy the sizzle instead of the steak" attitude is the dominant factor in what many experts have called the single most pressing but least talked about problem in America: garbage. In this argument, I would like to show just how pervasive the garbage problem is in America, and what the implications of this problem are for you as consumers. Then, I would like to suggest what you can do to bring about the container deposit legislation that we desperately need.

Statement of Proposal

Significance (shows that the problem is critical)

In this year, 1979, the average American will produce approximately 1,500 pounds of garbage, as compared to 250 pounds per person in the early 1950s. This refuse totals approximately 150 million tons of garbage annually. The *Washington Post* refers to this disgrace as the "Gross national trashpile." The fastest growing segment of packaging waste in the past generation has been the beer and soft drink container. The price of "convenience" packaging is shockingly high. The Environmental Protection Agency estimates that, in 1975, Americans purchased over 65 billion throwaway containers. The 1.5 million tons of steel, 6.8 million tons of glass, and 475,000 tons of aluminum used to make these containers were tossed in dumps or along roadsides. These plastic, nonbiodegradable containers, manufactured from petroleum and natural gas distillates, may soon become the leading source of container waste, with an estimated 10 billion being produced by 1980.

Container waste affects all American citizens, whether or not they use disposable containers. Container litter-related injuries have soared into the millions, and have become the fourth most common cause of emergency room treatments for children between 0 and 4 years. Further, we are all affected aesthetically, as roadsides, parks and waterways become pocked with an estimated 4.1 billion littered containers annually. Finally, we are affected economically since we are forced to pay as much as 5¢ for a container that we use only once, forced to support costly programs designed to process all these containers, and asked to pay increasingly high taxes for litter crews which clean up the mess created by that most euphemized of criminals, the litterbug. Clearly, and finally, something must be done.

Topicality
(solution
actually
addresses
the problem)

During the past five years a number of our nation's leaders have been addressing the problem of container waste. Senator Mark Hatfield (Oregon), and Representative James Jeffords (Vermont) have proposed a solution. They have introduced legislation which calls for a 5¢ deposit on all beer and soft drink containers that are used by only one brand, and a 2¢ deposit on containers that are interchangeable; that is, which can be returned to two or more companies. In effect, the bill would mean that when consumers purchase beer or soft drinks, they would rent the container instead of buying it. Hatfield, Jeffords and a number of other legislators see the "bottle bill" as a direct response to the container waste crisis for a number of reasons.

First, by paying a deposit, consumers would be encouraged to return the container in order to get their deposit. Secondly, littering would be curtailed since the container is worth money, and, even if some containers were to be littered, they would be picked up by others and redeemed for the deposit. Thirdly, the containers could then be recycled or reused by selling them to glass or metal recycling firms, of which there are many, thus relieving the burden on landfills and incinerators.

Because the container industry makes enormous profits from its present system, a one-way movement of goods and packages (only 25 percent of all beer and soft drink containers are returnable, compared with 97 percent in 1947) they are unlikely to assume responsibility for attacking the litter problem. State and local governments cannot solve the problem. Each state with a bottle bill has a slightly different version, causing problems for both consumers and producers. For example, Vermont has established redemption centers, Oregon mandates returnable containers, and some states ban only flip-top opener tabs. Consumers will not voluntarily solve the problem, as evidenced by the yearly increase of litter.

Workability
(solution)

There is ample evidence that a federal container deposit law can work, demonstrated in a revealing study of the issue conducted by the Comptroller General of the United States. The study, "Potential Effects of a National Mandatory Deposit on Beverage Containers," is extensive and well-documented. The conclusions it reached on a national bottle bill are as follows:

- Reductions in beverage container litter, total litter, and post-consumer waste.
- Empty container handling costs would rise because of increased jobs.
- Industry's income would rise, since not all containers would be returned.
- Reduced raw materials consumption.
- Reduced energy use.
- Reduced systems costs for containers.
- Increased systems' costs for using refillable bottles.

Plan-Meet-Need (solution can eliminate problem) Seven states have passed bottle bills, and their experiences, especially the experience of Oregon, have been studied intensely. Oregon's bottle bill was passed in 1972 as a litter control measure, and has reduced container litter by 88%. There are other benefits. Most significantly, Oregonians saved energy: enough to heat 55,000 homes for one year. Employment also increased by approximately 365 jobs, with the shift back to labor-intensive returnable bottles.

In addition to the benefits mentioned, the bottle bill produced none of the negative side effects predicted by opponents. Prices for beer and soft drinks did not increase; sales did not decline. Public acceptance was high. Further, there was no significant shift in the type of container produced, with glass, steel, and aluminum retaining about their same share of the market as before the bottle bill. These facts led Governor Thomas McCall of Oregon to call his state's bottle bill, "A rip-roaring success."

Grocers, retail liquor dealers, and the packaging industry have all strongly objected to a nationwide container deposit law. Each segment has its own concerns. Retail grocers, whose profits have already been cut drastically by the impact of fast food chains and general inflation, fear a number of consequences: needing additional employees to sort and stack returned containers, using present profit-space for container storage, and creating health hazards in their stores. Retail liquor dealers share these concerns.

The container industry, on the other hand, worries about losing employees and decreasing production, and of course, the resulting loss in sales and profits. And finally, they resent the idea of federal restrictions on freedom of packaging. Brewers and soft drink manufacturers fear increased labor and transportation costs caused by a decentralization of manufacturing centers.

In Vermont, opposition to the bottle bill was fierce, especially by retailers. But the bill passed, and industry adapted. Some grocers opened redemption centers, and have turned a nice profit from them. Others have discovered that youths who pick up empties along the road and in parks redeem them, and then spend the deposit on store goodies, thus generating profits. One Vermont grocer summed up his new attitude when he said:

"At first there were problems, but they were solved within the first two or three months. It took the general public awhile to adjust to the deposit bill but their acceptance is now quite favorable since they see the positive results that have come about."

This mandate can come only from consumers who express their concern on the litter issue. I urge you to write or call your local representative and your representative in Congress. Ask your grocers why they stock only non-returnable bottles, which damage the environment and cost you more money in the long run. Get the people who can enact this legislation, and those who will be most affected by it, to think of how widespread the litter problem really is, and of its deeper implications. If not, this gross waste of raw materials and energy will eventually force container legislation of some sort upon us. But it may be too late to correct the damage. The better approach is to plan ahead.

Conceptual Patterns. Propositions of fact may be organized around one or more of the conceptual patterns. Sometimes, but not always, they combine a conceptual pattern with the standard issues. This combination of a conceptual pattern with a conventional pattern has the following advantage: it allows the arguer to present complicated factual material in a familiar thought pattern as well as to anticipate the special needs of the conventional situation. This double organizational scheme can enhance the effectiveness of an argument. In some cases, as in the first model below, an argument based on a proposition of fact uses the standard questions to make a proposition of action in response to that fact.

Time Patterns. The following student model is an argument based on cause-effect reasoning. This argument will, of course, work only if the audience accepts the causes named as being responsible for the effects stated. Tracing the causes requires both the composer and the audience to think backwards, since we never seek the causes for something until the effect occurs. In the model below, the student uses one variation of the cause-effect pattern, going from the cause (television violence) to effect one (imitating violent behavior) to effect two (desensitization to violence). Both the standard questions and the cause/effect markers are indicated in the margin. Notice that the cause/effect pattern dominates, and that the stock questions are addressed in an order different from the bottle bill model.

Introduction   Do you care what your children watch on television? Are you aware of the adverse effects violent television shows can have on young people? For over six hours per day, children sit passively in front of the television, watching programs now dominated by violence, or an "overt expression of physical force against others or self, or the compelling of action against one's will on pain of being hurt or killed." On children's weekend shows, the incidents of hurting or killing has increased from 15.6 per hour in 1976, to 25 per hour in 1977. More than fifteen years ago, 200 hours of television per week

Significance were devoted to crime scenes, where 500 killings were shown. With the dramatic increase of violence on TV, ninety percent since 1952, children by age eighteen will have viewed approximately 18,000 TV murders.

Topicality Does all this violence on television actually affect children adversely? Many psychologists, psychiatrists, therapists, social scientists,
Proposition and researchers believe that this large amount of violence does affect
of Fact children, specifically in two areas: imitation and desensitization to real-life events.

People opposing violence on television rely somewhat upon the theory that children, especially young children, imitate actions they frequently see or are exposed to. Because impressionable children view so much violence on TV, their inhibitions against behaving aggressively are reduced, and therefore, they tend to be more aggressive and imitative of violent acts they have seen on TV. This is
Support for supported by a study done by Michael Rothenburg, a child psychia-
Reason 1 trist at the University of Washington. After reviewing twenty-five years of hard data and the fifty most comprehensible studies involving 10,000 children from every possible background, Rothenburg came to the conclusion that the showing of violence tends to produce aggressive behavior among the young. Even "network apologists" concede that some children, under certain conditions, will imitate antisocial acts that they witness on the tube.

The fact that "antisocial acts" on TV are often imitated by children is supported by many studies and actual cases. One study
Support for commissioned by ABC found that out of 100 juvenile offenders,
Reason 1 twenty-two of them confessed to having copied criminal techniques from TV programs. Actual cases include the Niemi case, where nine year old Olivia Niemi, while playing near her home, was raped with a discarded beer bottle, by four children, ages fifteen and under. This incident occurred just four days after the airing of the movie "Born Innocent," in which an inmate, played by Linda Blair, was cornered by four girls, and raped with the help of a plumber's helper, in a graphic five minute scene. This movie was claimed, by Valerie Niemik, Olivia's mother, to have been the model for the rape of her daughter.

Support for In another incident, a woman was burned to death in Boston, in
Reason 1 circumstances almost identical to those shown in a film in which a group of young teenagers doused a derelict with gas, and set him on fire. This film was broadcast by a Boston TV station.

Support for
Reason 1   One last example, perhaps not as dramatic as the previous two, is
of a young child, who, after watching a TV show where one character was suffocating another character with a pillow, promptly
picked up a pillow and pressed it over the family dog's face. This
example, along with the other two, clearly illustrates that impressionable children will sometimes imitate violent acts they have
viewed on TV, and proves that violence on television can have
adverse effects on children.

The second way in which violence on television can adversely
Support for
Reason 2   affect children is through desensitization. "Too much TV too early
instills an attitude of spectatorship, a withdrawal from direct involve-
ment in real life experience. What television basically teaches children is passivity. It creates the illusion of having done something and
seen something, when in fact, you've been sitting at home," reports
Stanford University researcher, Paul Kaufman. As children watch
more and more violence-filled programs everyday, their sensitivity to
real events is dulled and their tolerance of violent behavior in others
is increased. "They tolerate violence . . . because they have been
conditioned to think of it as an everyday thing," says Ronald Drab-
man, psychology professor at the University of Mississippi. Because
sensitivity is reduced, children are able to react to real-life events less
emotionally, more as spectators. A seventeen-year-old boy illustrates
this point. After having survived a devastating tornado, he exclaimed,
"Man, it was just like something on TV."

Support for
Reason 2   The emotional detachment created by the large amounts of violence on TV is very dangerous because it allows kids to watch and
commit real crimes passively, with the absence of emotion, of guilt,
of remorse. One afternoon, a young woman was murdered in her
courtyard, with many people not coming to her aid, passively watching as if it were a television drama. An eleven year old boy voices his
opinion on the subject; "You see so much violence (on TV) that it's
meaningless. If I saw someone really get killed, it wouldn't be a big
deal. I guess I'm turning into a hard rock."

Support for
Reason 2   Results from experiments by doctors and researchers have proven
that the viewing of continual violence on TV has dulled children's
sensitivities. Dr. Victor Cline, from the University of Utah Laborato-
ries, compared emotional responses of two groups of boys, ages five
to fourteen, to a graphically violent TV program. One group of boys
had watched little or no TV in the previous two years, while the
other group had watched approximately forty-two hours of TV, per
week, for two years. After both groups had viewed an eight-minute
sequence from the movie "The Champion," their emotional responses were recorded on a physiograph, which measures heart action, perspiration, respiration, and other body responses. Of the two
groups, the boys who had watched more TV were less aroused by
what they saw; they had become "so emotionally habituated to
emotion-arousing events on TV, that their sensitivities had become
blunted."

Support for
Reasons 1
and 2

   The combination in children of desensitization and imitation, created by violence on TV, can be very dangerous. The Ronnie Zamora case, in which a fifteen year old boy in Florida shot to death his elderly neighbor, Elinor Haggart, while burglarizing her home, illustrates this point. Having seen over 50,000 TV murders, Zamora was considered, by his lawyer, to have been "suffering from and acting under the influence of prolonged, intense, involuntary, subliminal, television intoxication." Because of all the violence Zamora had witnessed on TV, he became desensitized, and developed an emotional detachment and passivity to violence in real-life situations. This, together with the fact that Zamora's crime was imitative of scripts from "Kojack" and a "Dracula" movie, led to his lawyer's comment that Zamora did not realize he was committing cold-blooded murder, but "was just acting out a television script." The effects of violence on TV, upon children, in this case resulted in the death of an innocent woman.

Inherency

   The responsibility for the problem of violence on television rests with two groups: the advertisers and the general public. Television receives all its financial support from advertisers, who, in return for placement of their ads on TV, pay the stations various amounts of money, depending upon which program their ad is broadcast with. Attempting to reach as many people as possible, advertisers pay large amounts of money for the placement of their ads on the most popular, widely watched shows, as determined by the Nielson ratings. Unfortunately, the most popular programs are the ones primarily dominated by violence. As long as people demand to see these violence-filled shows, advertisers will continue to finance them. Therefore, it is up to the public to see that violence on television is controlled, if not eliminated.

Solution 1
(appeals for
action)

   There are three main routes the public can follow in the control or elimination of violence on TV, in order to protect children from its adverse effects. First of all, letters protesting the violence in various programs could be written to the advertisers sponsoring each program, to let them know the feelings of the public. Unfortunately, this method will not accomplish much if it is not practiced by many people. On the other hand, if a lot of people do write to advertisers

Plan-Meet-
Need

complaining about specific shows, the advertisers might think twice about sponsoring those shows, because they do not want to risk losing money on unpopular programs. Also, the advertisers could put pressure upon the networks to shift the programs to different time slots, in which the viewing by children could be reduced.

Solution 2

   The second method also includes group action. There are many groups devoted to "cleaning up" television. Two more prominent

Plan-Meet-
Need

groups are Action for Children's Television, which deals with violence and commercials on and during kids' shows, and Coalition for Better Television, which opposes sex, profanity and violence on TV, and has already cost networks between ten and fifteen million dollars in lost advertising. Through these groups, tremendous pressure is

Workability   exerted upon the advertisers, as well as upon the Federal Communications Commission, which regulates TV and renews stations' li-
censes every three years. If real results in controlling or eliminating
violence on television are desired, it is important that the public
become more involved with these influential and effective groups.

Solution 3   If neither of these methods seems to be accomplishing the goal of
controlling or eliminating violence on television, it is then time for
parents to take on the responsibility for regulating what their children
can and cannot watch on TV. Carefully, parents should check and
see exactly which programs contain a lot of violence. These violent
shows should be restricted from viewing by the children, and instead
the parents should have their children watch the non-violent, educational or instructional shows, or resort to drastic action; turn the set
off, and participate in some activity with their children. "The tube
has displaced many of the normal interactional processes between
parents and children. . . . Those kinds of interactions are essential
for maximum development," comments Dr. David Pearl of the
National Institute of Mental Health. The time children spend sitting
catatonic in front of the TV, watching violent programs, has been
exacted from such "salutary pursuits as reading, outdoor play and
even simple, contemplative solitude." Parents can encourage their
children to participate in these "salutary pursuits," thereby replacing
passiveness with activeness. Through this final method, constructive

Plan-Meet-   alternatives to replace the time spent by children in watching TV are
Need   developed, and therefore, the violence on TV can no longer have
the adverse effects of desensitization and imitation on children.

                                                    — Laurie Burns

Static Patterns. *Exemplification:* In the second model of an argument
based on a conceptual pattern, in this case, an argument by example, an
accepted generalization is either supported or refuted through specific
instances. Unlike the previous model, the model below is a straight
proposition of fact, an argument that asks us to change our thinking on a
particular topic but calls for no specific action. This argument by syndicated columnist Sidney Harris shows how a widely-held generalization is
refutable by example.

Catch-22
Money Can Indeed Buy Poverty — Servant
Becomes a Master

Introduction   The late, great saloon entertainer, Joe E. Lewis, was fond of saying,
Proposition   "There's one thing money can't buy — poverty." It always raised a
of Fact   large laugh. But it doesn't happen to be true.
Example 1   Money in large amounts bought poverty for many entertainers like

Lewis — not to mention his homonym, Joe Louis, the boxer, who made millions and ended in hock to the U.S. government.

Example 2 It has bought poverty for many families who suddenly won huge sweepstakes prizes, went on binges and a year or two later found themselves more broke than before they waved the winning ticket in their hands.

Example 3 It has bought poverty for gamblers, for investors, for companies and for countries. For money, just like fire, is a splendid servant but a ruthless master: If you cannot control it, it can ruin you.

Example 4 Intellect is no protection against it. Mark Twain lost a fortune in backing bad inventions; so also, in England, did Thackeray and Sir Walter Scott. Many an artist, an actor, or inventor, has died broke after running through not one but several fortunes.

Example 5 If John Barrymore had not been so hugely successful, he would not have been able to indulge his tastes so extravagantly and would have remained a serious actor until his last days, instead of the pathetic buffoon he became.

Example 6 Norman Mailer's vast popularity and equally vast earnings as an author propelled him into multiple marriages and fatherhoods and dilatory domiciles, and a way of life that may take him until death to pay off accumulated alimonies and taxes and assorted obligations. Success goes to people's pockets as well as to their heads.

Example 7 Even those with so-called "business heads" are not immune from this emotional ailment. The chronicles of commerce are studded with cases of entrepreneurs who went wild with profits, overextended themselves and ended in bankruptcy court, or worse. Had they not risen so high so fast, they could not have fallen so far so precipitately.

Example 8 Spain is a striking example of a country in which money bought not only poverty but nearly permanent depression. It became so rich and greedy with gold raided from the New World that dissipation and degeneration soon set in, and the proud empire sank to a third-rate power. The peasants lived in greater misery after the "golden age" than before, and Spain never again regained its early eminence.

Conclusion Money is as much a myth as romantic love. Both are easier to find than to keep, easier to misuse than to handle, easier to become victimized by than master of. Too much is as bad as too little — the trouble being that we know when we have too little, but we learn we have too much only when it is too late.

(Harris, 1981)

Enumeration: Some arguments are best organized in an enumeration pattern according to emphasis. Of course, the order in which we emphasize our arguments requires that the composer first go through the process of analysis. We must analyze our reasons for a particular proposition according to their strength, putting our best reasons at the beginning and the end, and our weaker ones in the middle.

Look, for example, at the following speech on water conservation, prepared to be delivered to the Town Council. The speech has a five-minute time limit, so naturally the speaker cannot cover all the reasons why the town should pass a water conservation ordinance. The speaker has chosen four, deciding that the economic argument is the most convincing and should be stated first. Two environmental arguments follow, and the speech concludes with a conservation argument.

Statement of
Proposition

I am here to speak in favor of the proposed ordinance pertaining to water conservation.

Reason 1

As a taxpayer, I am concerned about the possibility of having to pay for construction of a new reservoir. Such an expenditure would not be necessary if the right steps were to be taken to conserve water in the first place. My research shows that if all new living units were required to install low-water use toilets and shower heads, our town could reduce water consumption by approximately 40 percent, using Environmental Protection Agency estimates.

Support for
Reason 1

Reason 2

If we could reduce water consumption by 40%, our precious fresh water sources would be conserved. Given our present aquifer output of 120,000 gallons per day, a 40% reduction in that amount would assure us of ample water supply should we be without rains for any reasonably extended period of time.

Support for
Reason 2

Reason 3

Furthermore, the water conservation ordinance would reduce completely the flow of untreated waste water into our local lake, Lake Walton. At the present time our sewage treatment plant is capable of treating our waste water, but if water consumption caused by new construction continues at its present rate Lake Walton will be accepting raw sewage by the year 1989. We cannot wait until then to solve our problem.

Support for
Reason 3

Reason 4

Water should not be wasted. There is no reason to waste it. If new living units were required to install low-water use toilets and shower heads, we would conserve precious resources with absolutely no inconvenience to anyone. After all, what differences does it make to people if their toilets flush with 2½ quarts of water or 8 gallons? The result is the same.

Support for
Reason 4

Conclusion

The point is that this will not happen voluntarily — the average person is not conscious of water as a precious natural resource, and contractors are not going to spend the time obtaining the right kinds of appliances unless they are forced to. You must act to save us from a needless expense, pollution, and shameful waste.

Of course, the argument could continue, time permitting, to present other reasons, or to address potential disadvantages other speakers might raise. The important point is that the reasons given for the proposition have been clearly enumerated and supported.

Comparison/Contrast: Comparison/contrast is perhaps the type of argument used most frequently by advertisers. Much of advertising consists in arguing the superiority of one product over another, the familiar "Brand X" approach: "Our mouthwash has been proven 30 percent more effective than the leading mouthwash;" "In actual on-the-spot tests, 53 percent of those tested preferred our cola to its leading competitor."

In the following student model, the writer argues the advantages of living at home and commuting to college as opposed to living in a dorm or in an apartment near campus. Notice that her opening introduces three aspects on which she will base her comparison: academic, economic, and social.

A Commuter's Viewpoint

"The time spent driving back and forth could be used for studying."

"With the price of gas increasing all the time, how will you afford it?"

"How will you meet new friends if you spend only a few hours a day on campus?"

Have you heard arguments against commuting such as these? If you are a high school senior considering commuting to college, my guess is that you have. At the University of Rhode Island approximately one out of five freshmen commute. The number of students commuting increases with upperclassmen. With so much emphasis placed on the tradition of living at college the commuter aspect is often overlooked. A closer look should be taken at the advantages of commuting.

The picture most people have of living at college is not quite accurate. Marcia Appolonia, a freshman resident at the University of Rhode Island, found this to be true. "I thought that living in the dorms would be nothing but fun. I soon discovered that it was not fun; simply convenient." Marcia particularly missed good, home-cooked food and the privacy of her own room. She has decided to live at home next semester.

I should mention that living at home is not the only type of commuting. Another possible alternative is commuting from an apartment or house rented out alone or with a group of friends. When speaking of "commuting" here, I am referring strictly to living at home. Commuting from a residence other than home (i.e. Mom, Dad, sisters, brothers, etc.) would be more closely related to living on campus. You would encounter the same types of distraction commuting from a residence other than home that you would encounter on campus.

Living at home offers much-needed security to the incoming college freshman. Mary Legacy, a junior commuter from Bryant College in Rhode Island, feels that many freshmen want this added security. "The transition from high school to college is difficult enough without having to adjust to a whole new way of living," she said. The college work load is much more demanding than that of high school and takes time to get used to. If you combine the additional work with the new-found freedom of on-campus living it becomes more difficult.

It is important that you do well during your freshman year. As Normand Desmaris, a freshman commuter at Rhode Island College, states, "It is the period that will make you or break you." Normand maintained a "B" average throughout his freshman year, something he feels would have been impossible had he not been living at home. "I don't think I could have done as well if I had been distracted by on-campus activities. I may live at college next year when I've gotten accustomed to the work," Normand said. Lisa Blanchette, a freshman commuter at U.R.I., has also adopted this plan. "Now that I know I can handle the work, I can start trying new things. I never could have lived in the dormitories as a freshman. It would be too much at once," she said. Lisa noted that she will probably live on campus just one year to see what it is like. Gary Levillee, a freshman residing in a fraternity at U.R.I., agrees that it is hard to set your priorities at first. "Freshmen are overwhelmed with the new freedom that is handed to them. Many of my friends living on-campus are on probation from first semester because studying was forgotten until it was too late," Gary said.

So living at home you can study more efficiently. Is that all? Not according to Mary Legacy of Bryant College. She finds it a benefit of commuting that she can make new friends in school while remaining in close touch with friends at home. "It's like having a double set of friends!" she said. But, as skeptics are bound to ask: "How do you make new friends if you spend only a few hours a day on campus?" One tip is to join as many clubs and organizations as you have the time for. This gives commuters a chance to mingle with students living on campus in other than academic areas. Colleen Christiansen, a sophomore commuter from Rhode Island College, has another idea on how commuters can meet new friends. "Most colleges have a freshman orientation session. At this time everyone is just a future student, not a resident or commuter. There is no distinction between the two groups. I became friends with six or seven girls at orientation that I still see often." Frank Romano, a freshman commuter from U.R.I., also made a few good friends through orientation. "We roomed together during the overnight orientation. Since orientation was split into different majors we chose many of the same courses. Whenever I have a problem with one of my subjects one of these guys can usually help me out," he said.

Most colleges have organizations to help commuters adapt to college life. At U.R.I. there are two such organizations, U.R.I.C.A. (University of Rhode Island Commuter Association) and C.I.R.C. (Commuter Information and Referral Center). Located in the commuter lounge, a place for commuters to relax between classes, these

Aspect 1, Academic

Aspect 2, Social

two organizations help organize carpools, offer career-planning sessions and provide information on off-campus housing available in the area. This is only a small portion of the duties performed by these groups. So, contrary to what you may have believed, commuters are not forgotten faces. Gary Mariorenzi is a freshman commuter at U.R.I., yet he also belongs to a fraternity. He mentioned that he has attended many parties at his fraternity and doesn't feel at all forgotten. Sue Thompson, a sophomore commuter at R.I.C., explains that she and her friends from school get together every Friday night. "Either we go out to a club or I'll go to a party on campus," she said.

Considering comments made by both resident and commuter students, I feel that as a freshman college student it would be advantageous to commute, at least for the first year. This would enable the student to break into college life gradually, retaining the security of home. As proven by interviews with commuting college students, it's easy to make friends on campus. By commuting you can become included in on-campus activities by making new friends, yet still have the privacy and comforts of home. Of course, one of the major advantages of commuting is the cost. A student can save close to $1,000 a year at U.R.I. by commuting.

Aspect 3,
Economic

In my opinion, college should be first an intellectual education and then secondly a social one. Many students enter college with notions of neverending parties and constant excitement. To enter college with such expectations is sure to bring disappointment. Students should give themselves a chance to adjust to the work before trying to adjust to a new lifestyle. Making the transition from high school to college doesn't have to be a disaster. By commuting during your freshman year you will be better prepared to live on campus during your next year at college, if you wish.

— Kathy Bucklin

Notice that the comparison/contrast pattern, when used for argument, does not attempt to treat a topic even-handedly as it might if the purpose were to inform. Rather, the comparison is organized all the way through, from introduction to conclusion, to favor one alternative over the other. Throughout the argument, comparison/contrast uses the standard question "Disadvantages" to refute the opposition; in fact, the aspects being compared and the disadvantages question become the major organizing principles for an argument based on comparison/contrast.

Refutation Pattern. In some cases you will find yourself in the position of responding to an argument made by someone else. On these occasions you will need to refute the other person's point of view on the issue. Although you will probe the issue with the standard questions just as you would if you were initiating the argument, the organization will follow a refutative pattern. The following student model, a speech, illustrates this pattern of argument — counterargument, counter-proposal.

Introduction   What would you do if given $25,000, tax free with no strings attached, by the U.S. government? Buy a new car? Pay bills? Invest? A Mr. Bert Nakano, from the National Coalition for Redress-Reparations, has proposed to Congress that the U.S. government give the approximately 120,000 Japanese Americans who suffered in concentration camps this very amount. Each.

Argument   He claims the $25,000 would compensate for the mental anguish caused these people by the evacuation and four years detention time during the years 1941 through 1945. But stop and think for a moment about what would happen if the U.S. government tried to compensate all victims of civil rights injustice. We, as citizens, would be forced to move out of the country, either because of unbearably high taxes or because the U.S. had to declare bankruptcy.

Counter-argument   Realistically speaking, if we compensated the Japanese we would have to compensate everyone else. On the top of the list are the Black Americans. This group of Americans suffered segregation and separation for many more years than the Japanese did. This separation of Blacks from society was as real as any fence around the Japanese detention camps. And just as some Japanese were denied citizenship, the Black men were denied the right to vote, and is not the right to vote the basis of citizenship? If a Black man's business or farm was successful, a white man would force a sale, just as the Japanese were forced to sell before the evacuation. Surely the case of the Black American is comparable, if not identical, to the case of the Japanese American. Therefore, if we accept Mr. Nakano's proposal, all the Blacks who lived through this time should be compensated. But the list does not end here.

Counter-argument   The American Indians, who are truly the first Americans, are still in relocation centers, which we call reservations. But unlike the situation in Japanese concentration camps, the reservations's Indians are not supplied with free food and health care as the Japanese centers were. What meager financial assistance is given to the Indians by the government must be spent on necessities. Robbed of his land and pride, the Indian is another example of a people suffering mental anguish caused by a civil rights injustice.

Argument   But Mr. Nakano doesn't see the cases of the Indian and Black people as comparable to the case of the Japanese. He argues that the Black and the Indian's plights were not brought on by a direct government order. I beg to differ.

Counter-argument   It was the United States Supreme Court that upheld segregation as constitutional for so many years. Can Nakano argue that a law passed by one of the three main branches of government is not a direct government action? And it was the government that bought and stole Indian territory. It was the government that founded the reservations. It was the government that supplied the cavalry to move or kill the Indian. So as Mr. Nakano points out there are differences in the cases, but government intervention is not one. If there is a difference, it is in the matter of protection afforded to the Japanese.

By relocating the Japanese in concentration camps, the Japanese were protected from panic-stricken Americans. There were no burnings of crosses on Japanese land. There were no lynchings of Japanese people. There was no fear for the Japanese to walk down a dark street alone. How could there have been? The Japanese were safe behind fences with soldiers to protect them. There were no Japanese widows because of one group's perverted sense of justice. No cavalry men mowed down women and children. The Japanese never knew the equivalent of a rancher's "Injun" hunt. These people should be thankful to have been spared the posse and the Ku Klux Klan, but instead some ask for payment. Imagine! Getting paid for being protected! In addition, some of these people have already been paid.

Counter-argument

Over $160,000,000 was expropriated by the government for the maintenance of the camps. The California legislature appropriated $200,000 for the enforcement of the Alien Land Laws. The Department of Justice paid over $38,000,000 in settlements of Japanese claims. Not all of the Japanese saw this money, but some did. By giving each victim $25,000 more we will be duplicating what has already been done.

In many cases it appears mental anguish was minimal. If the Japanese felt these camps were so bad, why then, did several camps set up Japanese committees to try to keep the camps open after the government ordered them closed? Surely these camps must have been terrible, since the occupants refused to leave? And we are to compensate these people on the grounds of mental anguish?

Counter-proposal

Presently there is no support in Congress for Mr. Nakano's idea. If the tide should turn, all we can ask is that compensation will be carried through sensibly and not by the arbitrary methods and amounts that Mr. Nakano suggests. Americans have priced almost every commodity, but mental anguish is one that escaped this pricing. Instead of compensating the Japanese for something as abstract as mental anguish, compensate them for the financial losses suffered. This would include property loss, business loss, and salary loss.

The Japanese would bring such proof as tax records, sales receipts, and salary records before the federal commission studying the World War Two internment. This commission would put the amount of past dollars into terms of today's dollar. Then whatever tax rate these people would have had at the time of detention would be levied on the amount to be paid. Before actual payment, an investigation would be made to verify that the person had not been compensated previously. The point is, if we are forced to compensate we should give compensation only where and when due.

Conclusion   For the U.S. to try to undertake financial compensation for its civil rights victims now would be a grave mistake. We are in the midst of an economic crisis as is, without adding weight to a nearly lame horse. All we can hope is that by educating and informing people about these injustices, we can prevent them from recurring.
— Kathy Flannery

You may find certain weaknesses in reasoning in this argument, and you may not agree that reasoning by comparison is justifiable as support for the proposition. The pattern, however, is coherent and it allows the audience to follow with little difficulty the chain of reasoning used, and to make a judgment as well. It should be pointed out that even though Kathy did not use the standard issues pattern, she did probe her topic with the standard issues.

Detail

To repeat a point made earlier, an argument is the giving of good reasons for or against a proposition. Argumentative detail involves both stating the reason and supporting it with data, which is called **evidence**. A clear example of the reason-support method is the speech on water conservation that appears on p. 280. In this model the speaker lists her reasons and then immediately provides evidence for each reason.

The various ways to support any idea have been discussed at length. In an argument, however, we need to be particularly concerned with the value of our detail as proof for our propositions. We need to know how to test the quality of our evidence, and to know what possible weaknesses in our evidence opponents of propositions are likely to spot. In order to do this we need to know the tests of evidence.

There are four major tests of evidence: recency, relevance, consistency, and sufficiency. Whether our support is as personal as an experience or as seemingly objective as a statistic, we should apply the four tests as a check on the quality of our argumentative detail.

The Test of Recency. The test of recency requires us to check the time during which our evidence was gathered as well as the context in which it was gathered. Time changes the value of data and its applicability to the proposition being considered. For instance, during his presidential campaign in 1980, Ronald Reagan spoke out forcefully against registration for the military draft. In January, 1982, President Reagan renewed the draft registration program. Theoretically, a speaker or writer could quote directly from President Reagan to support or to oppose draft registration. The ethical person will state the exact date of the quote, the context in which the statement was made, and the fact that a change in position has occurred, as well as the reasons for the change.

Statistical data is often used out of time and context, thus reducing its value in argument. Authoritative support is often taken out of context; that is, statements made to support one argument are used to support another. In all argumentative discourse it is important to ask: When was the data originally gathered, and how was it meant to be used?

The Test of Relevance. The test of relevance requires us to ask if the evidence presented actually goes to the heart of the argument. We want to be certain that our data really supports what we are proposing. For instance, we often see famous people advertising and endorsing products. If the proposition is that people should buy the product because a celebrity does, the celebrity's words are clearly relevant; however, if the argument is that the product is better than others of its type because of its ingredients, the opinion of the celebrity is less relevant.

The following excerpt from a student speech is helpful in showing how relevance can be used to test evidence in an argument:

> Sex education programs have been a miserable failure in the school curriculum. Last year, for example, over one and a half million unwanted pregnancies occurred in the United States, most resulting from a failure to use birth control methods. This is the result of millions of federal tax dollars being pumped into the sex education program. I think it is clearly a waste of money, money which could be used to support back-to-basics education such as reading, writing, and mathematics.
>
> — Gerri Ebsen

The question here is one of relevance. Is there a valid causal relationship between sex education programs and federally-sponsored sex education programs? Could the opposition show, for instance, that more unwanted pregnancies occurred before the program was in effect? Could the opposition show, perhaps, that the statistic itself is not applicable to what actually happens in the sex education classroom? Could this statistic be the result of other forces, such as a breakdown in family-centered sex education information? Is the generalization made at the end of the statement regarding back-to-basics courses relevant to the discussion of sex education courses and unwanted pregnancies? In reading Gerri's statement you might have raised questions in your own mind about it other than those raised here: the point is that statistics can be used to support many things, and they may not actually support what they claim to. Check the data carefully for relevance.

The Test of Consistency. The test of consistency means that all the detail is consistent with itself, or that it is not inconsistent with other data on the same subject. In the debate over container deposit legislation (see model on pp. 271–274), for instance, some opponents of the bill argue that it will lead to unemployment, while other opponents argue that it will raise the price of beverages because of the need for more employees to drive trucks and to sort, stack, and handle empties in the supermarket. Such statements are inconsistent with each other and lead to a weakness in the total argument.

Inconsistencies crop up in any number of different situations. In politics the candidate who advocates increased spending for federal programs may also vote against the appropriations to fund them. In the classroom the student speaker who urges the audience to give blood may, in the question and answer session, admit to never having given blood personally. A famous baseball player addresses a youth group on the topic of team loyalty and teamwork, and shortly thereafter signs a huge free-agent contract with the highest-bidding team. Is the preaching consistent with the practice? Are you consistent with your message? If you are, the chances of success are improved.

The Test of Sufficiency. The test of sufficiency asks whether there is enough evidence or enough variety of evidence to support the proposition. Be careful about such words as *most, always,* and *never.* When such terms are used be certain they are used accurately. We often hear an advocate say, "In a poll conducted on campus, it was found that seniors most often do such and such." How many were polled? Was the polling conducted randomly or in a way that would include sufficient variety of response? One recent guide to choosing a university, for instance, based its entire writeup of the universities surveyed on twelve questionnaires sent to adminstrators and twenty-five sent randomly to students. Is that enough data upon which to base conclusions?

Authorities or experts are often used to support a point. In fact, it is usually possible to find expert opinion on both sides of every issue. The test of sufficiency asks if there are two experts, or three experts, who say the same thing. Can the opposition find four experts to support their side of the issue? There is no clear answer to the question, "How many experts are enough?" This is a matter of judgment; however, it is common sense to find as many experts as one can for an issue.

As a way of helping you to think about the tests of evidence as they apply to particular forms of support, use Table 10-2 to check the quality of your argumentative detail.

Table 10-2 Tests of Evidence

Type of Support	Recency	Relevance	Consistency	Sufficiency
Facts	1. When were they gathered? 2. In what context were they generated?	1. Do they support the proposition or something else? 2. Are the facts firsthand or secondhand?	1. Do other facts show the opposite?	1. Are there enough facts to support the proposition? 2. Can the facts be easily verified?
Authorities	1. Were they authorities on the subject under discussion when the statement was made? 2. Are the statements taken out of the context in which they were made?	1. Are they authorities on the subject under discussion? 2. Is the statement an opinion or a researched conclusion?	1. Have the experts made contradictory statements? 2. Do the experts practice what they preach?	1. How many support the proposition? 2. How many authorities oppose the proposition?
Statistics	1. When were they collected? 2. Were they collected as support for this proposition?	1. Do they support the proposition? 2. Are they accurate? 3. Were they gathered properly?	1. Do the statistics refute other statistics? 2. Are the tests repeatable? Could the same results accrue from an independent test?	1. Was the sample large enough to warrant the generalization? 2. Are there other studies that show the same results?
Comparisons	1. Are the comparisons from the same time? 2. Are the comparisons used within the same context?	1. Does the comparison shed light on the proposition? 2. Do the terms of the comparison help the audience understand?	1. What other comparisons could be used to support opposing views?	1. Are the terms of the comparison closely enough related? 2. How far can the comparison be carried?

SUMMARY

In this chapter we have examined argument from the point of view of the composer. Argument was defined as the giving of good reasons for and against an issue, and was distinguished from both coercive and logical communication.

The composer of an argument must consider both planning and presentation. Planning for argument requires consideration of a standard set of questions for probing an issue, audience motivation, and source credibility.

Presentation of an argument requires drafting it out and including in it a point, pattern, and detail. The point of an argument is called the proposition, and it may call for a new belief or some action on the part of the audience. Pattern in an argument may follow the standard questions, or some combination of both a conceptual pattern and a standard questions model. The detail of an argument is called evidence, and it must pass four tests of evidence: recency, relevance, consistency, and sufficiency.

Having read this chapter, you should be able to write or present orally a sound, reasonable argument. The question that remains is: Will the argument work? Will the argument be convincing? An argument works because the audience senses that something is right about the whole discourse. What is right about an argument is the subject of the next chapter, in which we look at argument from the point of view of the consumer.

KEY WORDS

argument	credibility
coercion	proposition
logic	evidence
standard questions	recency
general audience	relevance
particular audience	consistency
motivation	sufficiency

EXERCISES

1. In a brainstorming session, or as an out-of-class assignment, make a list of four issues: a local, state, national, and international issue. In a sentence or two state your opinion on each issue. Then state what the other side of the issue is, offering good reasons to refute your opinion. We often find that having taken a position on an issue, we are no longer able to verbalize what the other side is thinking. It is also difficult to imagine what it would be like to be someone on the other side of an issue. What kind of person would oppose you on these

issues? Can you get a picture of that person in your mind? Use this exercise to become sensitive to the inherency of opposing sides for issues.

2. Advertisements often use the standard questions format. Either in the pictures or the text or both, you should be able to find all the standard questions represented in national ads. In order to prove this to your self, look at an ad in a magazine and see how many standard questions are represented in the ad. Label each part of the ad with one of the standard questions. Finally, ask yourself why the advertisers have done this.

3. Write a three-to-five-page argument in favor of a proposition of fact. If the assignment requires you to present the argument orally, use the directions in Chapter Four to put your speech into outline form.

4. Do the same as in the previous assignment, except this time write an argument based on a proposition of action. As you think about your action step, consider what the audience can and cannot do.

REFERENCES

Harris, Sydney J., "Money Can Indeed Buy Poverty," *Chicago Sun Times* (July 30, 1981).

Hempstone, Smith, "Joan Little's Lawyer Told Nothing But the Truth," *Washington Star News* (October 15, 1975), p. 12.

Katula, Richard, and Richard Roth, "A Stock Issues Approach to Writing Arguments," *College Composition and Communication*, 31 (May 1980), pp. 183-196.

11. Beneath the Surface: What Makes An Argument Work

In the previous chapter we considered argument from the composer's point of view. But as citizens, consumers, and decision makers we need to become as skilled at evaluating the arguments of others as we are at constructing our own. Think for a moment about the number and variety of arguments we read or hear everyday: the abbreviated slogans on bumper stickers, the incessant pitch of the advertisers, the propaganda machines of special interest groups, and the thoughtful arguments of syndicated columnists, teachers, and political leaders. Whether we are conscious of it or not, arguments constantly shape our attitudes; the more we know about them, the better off we are.

Chapter Ten divided the composition of an argument into a number of components for purposes of study. The consumer, however, experiences only the finished product — the actual argument. Our acceptance or rejection of an argument might come from a word, a piece of detail, or something outside the actual message, such as source credibility. More often than not, however, we judge an argument on some sense that we have of the whole package — its reasonableness as an entire piece of discourse.

What makes an argument reasonable? What gives an argument its persuasive power? The answer to these questions lies in the structure of the argument, the essential basis of the argument hidden beneath the surface. We call this deep structure of an argument a **scheme**.

Each of us has a common sense definition for the word *scheming*. A schemer is someone who is looking for a strategy, a way to win the argument. Scheming is often thought of in a negative way; yet all of us engage in it quite naturally, whether we are conscious of it or not. Because it is the scheme that gives the argument its reasonableness, we need to look closely at this notion of scheming.

All arguments fit into one of two universal schemes: association and dissociation. An **associative scheme** appears reasonable to an audience because the argument is based upon something the audience already views positively. Statistics are generally viewed favorably, for example, because they give the impression of certainty. Although nothing is absolute when dealing with human affairs, the effective arguer can create an appearance of certainty by skillful use of numbers. An argument based upon a **dis-**

sociative scheme appears reasonable to an audience because the topic is distinguished from something the audience views negatively or positively. One thing that people view negatively is the phony. Thus the Coca-Cola people advertise their product as the real thing, with the implication that all other colas are imitations, phonies. In fact, dissociation is the type of argument most widely used by advertisers: "Unlike any of its imitators, X does . . ." is a common advertising phrase. These two concepts, association and dissociation, are difficult at first. This section will, however, provide detailed explanations and numerous examples so that when you have finished you will have a clear understanding of association and dissociation. Moreover, you will be able to see how real arguments work in the realm of human affairs.

ASSOCIATIVE ARGUMENTS

There are three associative arguments: quasi-logical arguments, arguments based on the structure of reality, and arguments that aim at establishing the structure of reality. Consider each type of argument.

Quasi-Logical Arguments

Quasi-logical arguments establish an association with the formal reasoning patterns of logic or mathematics. The arguer sets forth the formal pattern to be used and then inserts detail into this model. To the degree that the audience recognizes a similarity or makes a positive association between the detail and the established logical pattern, the argument seems reasonable. Consider, for example, the way in which numbers were used by one professional persuader, a lawyer, in the strange case of Janet and Malcolm Collins.

Trial by Mathematics

After an elderly woman was mugged in an alley in San Pedro, Calif., a witness saw a blonde girl with a ponytail run from the alley and jump into a yellow car driven by a bearded black man. Eventually tried for the crime, Janet and Malcolm Collins were faced with the circumstantial evidence that she was white, blonde and wore a ponytail while her black husband owned a yellow car and wore a beard. The prosecution, impressed by the unusual nature and number of matching details, sought to persuade the jury by invoking a law rarely used in a courtroom — the mathematical law of statistical probability.

The jury was indeed persuaded, and ultimately convicted the Collinses (*Time*, Jan. 8, 1965). Small wonder. With the help of an expert witness from the mathematics department of a nearby college, the prosecutor explained that the probability of a set of events actually occurring is determined by multiplying together the probabilities of each of the events. Using what he considered "conservative" estimates (for example, that the chances of a car's being yellow were 1 in 10, the chances of a couple in a car being interracial 1 in 1,000), the prosecutor multiplied all the factors together and concluded that the odds were 1 in 12 million that any other couple shared the characteristics of the defendants.

Only One Couple. The logic of it all seemed overwhelming, and few disciplines pay as much homage to logic as do the law and math. But neither works right with the wrong premises. Hearing an appeal of Malcolm Collins' conviction, the California Supreme Court recently turned up some serious defects, including the fact that not even the odds were all they seemed.

To begin with, the prosecution failed to supply evidence that "any of the individual probability factors listed were even roughly accurate." Moreover, the factors were not shown to be fully independent of one another as they must be to satisfy the mathematical law; the factor of a Black man with a beard, for instance, overlaps the possibility that the bearded Black man may be part of an interracial couple. The 12 million to 1 figure, therefore, was just "wild conjecture." In addition, there was not complete agreement among the witnesses about the characteristics in question. "No mathematical equation," added the court, "can prove beyond a reasonable doubt (1) that the guilty couple *in fact* possessed the characteristics described by the witnesses, or even (2) that only *one* couple possessing those distinctive characteristics could be found in the entire Los Angeles area."

Improbable Probability. To explain why, Judge Raymond Sullivan attached a four-page appendix to his opinion that carried the necessary math far beyond the relatively simple formula of probability. Judge Sullivan was willing to assume it was unlikely that such a couple as the one described existed. But since such a couple did exist — and the Collinses demonstrably did exist — there was a perfectly acceptable mathematical formula for determining the probability that another such couple existed. Using the formula and the prosecution's figure of 12 million, the judge demonstrated to his own satisfaction and that of five concurring justices that there was a 41% chance that at least one other couple in the area might satisfy the requirements.*

---

*The proof involved is essentially the same as that behind the common parlor trick of betting that in a group of 30 people, at least two will have the same birthday; in that case, the probability is 70%.

"Undoubtedly," said Sullivan, "the jurors were unduly impressed by the mystique of the mathematical demonstration but were unable to assess its relevancy or value." Neither could the defense attorney have been expected to know of the sophisticated rebuttal available to them. Janet Collins is already out of jail, has broken parole and lit out for parts unknown. But Judge Sullivan concluded that Malcolm Collins, who is still in prison at the California Conservation Center, had been subjected to "trial by mathematics" and was entitled to a reversal of his conviction. He could be tried again, but the odds are against it.

(*Time*, April, 1968)

The Collins example demonstrates that association is a powerful persuasive device. Associating the probable, uncertain world of human affairs with the certain world of mathematics created a compelling argument for this audience to untangle. The persuasive nature of so-called scientific evidence, such as statistics claim to represent, lead to their being frequently used in advertisements and political communication. We should be alert to such uses of apparently certain data, and remember that the argument's force lies partly in the data itself but mostly in the favorable impression created by the association of the uncertainty of human affairs with the certainty of numbers.

There are many other quasi-logical arguments we hear over and over again in the normal course of our lives; for example, there are, as explained in Chapter Five, some established rules for defining a term. Etymology, defining a term by tracing its history, is one logical way to define. An argument by definition would attempt to establish its validity by adopting a formally accepted pattern, such as etymology, as its basis of proof. Look at the following example by Barbara Lawrence:

_____ Isn't A Dirty Word

Introduction | Why should any words be called obscene? Don't they all describe natural human functions? Am I trying to tell them, my students demand, that the "strong, earthy, gut-honest" — or if they are fans of Norman Mailer, the "rich, liberating, existential" language they use to describe sexual activity isn't preferable to "phoney-sounding, middle-class words like 'intercourse' and 'copulate'?" "Cop You Late!" they say with fancy inflections and gagging grimaces, "Now what is that supposed to mean?"

Well, what is it supposed to mean? And why indeed should one group of words describing human functions and human organs be acceptable in ordinary conversation, and another, describing presumably the same organs and functions, be tabooed — so much so, in fact, that some of these words still cannot appear in print in many parts of the English-speaking world?

The argument that these taboos exist only because of "sexual hangups" (middle-class, middle-age, feminist), or even that they are a result of class oppression — the contempt of the Norman conquerors for the language of their Anglo-Saxon serfs — ignores a much more likely explanation, it seems to me, and that is the sources and functions of the words themselves.

The best known of the tabooed sexual verbs, for example, comes from the German *ficken*, meaning "to strike"; combined, according to Partridge's etymological dictionary "Origins," with the Latin sexual verb *futuere*; associated in turn with the Latin *fustics*, "a staff or cudgel"; the Celtic *buc*, "a point, hence to pierce"; the Irish *bot*, "the male member"; the Latin *battuere*, "to beat"; the Gaelic *batair*, "a cudgeller"; the Early Irish *bualaim*, "I strike"; and so forth. It is one of what etymologists sometimes call "the sadistic group of words for the man's part in copulation."

The brutality of this word, then, and its equivalents, is not an illusion of the middle class or a crochet of Women's Liberation. In their origins and imagery these words carry undeniably painful, if not sadistic, implications, the object of which is almost always female. Consider, for example, what a screw actually does to the wood it penetrates; what a painful, even mutilating activity this kind of analogy suggests. "Screw" is particularly interesting in this context since the noun, according to Partridge, comes from words meaning "groove," "nut," "ditch," "breeding sow," "scrofula" and "swelling," while the verb, besides its explicit imagery, has antecedent associations to: "write on," "scratch," "scarify," and so forth; a revealing fusion of a mechanical or painful action with an obviously denigrated object.

Not all obscene words, of course, are as implicitly sadistic or denigrating to women as these, but all that I know do seem to serve a similar purpose: to reduce the human organism (especially the female organism) and human functions (especially sexual and procreative) to their least organic, most mechanical dimensions; to substitute a trivializing or deforming resemblance for the complex human reality of what is being described.

Tabooed male descriptives, when they are not openly denigrating to women, often serve to divorce a male organ or function from any significant interaction with the female. Take the word, "testes," for example, suggesting "witnesses" (from the Latin testis) to the sexual and procreative strengths of the male organ: and the obscene equivalent of this word which suggests little more than a mechanical shape. Or compare almost any of the "rich," "liberating" sexual verbs, so fashionable today among male writers, with that much-derided Latin word "copulate" ("to bind or join together") or even that Anglo-Saxon phrase (which seems to have had no trouble surviving the Norman Conquest) "make love." How arrogantly self-involved the tabooed words seem in comparison to either of the other terms, and how contemptuous of the female partner.

The more deforming the analogy, incidentally, the stronger the taboo is likely to be. The most severely censored of all the female descriptives are those suggesting (either explicitly or through antecedents) that there is no significant difference between the female channel through which we are all conceived and born, and the anal outlet common to both sexes — a distinction that pornographers have always enjoyed obscuring.

This effort to deny women their biological identity, their individuality, their humanness is such an important aspect of obscene language that one can only marvel at how seldom, in an era preoccupied with definitions of obscenity, this fact is brought to our attention. One problem, of course, is that many of the people in the best position to do this (critics, teachers, writers) are so reluctant today to admit that they are angered or shocked by obscenity. Bored maybe, unimpressed, esthetically displeased, but no matter how brutal or denigrating the material, never angered, never shocked.

And yet how eloquently angered, how piously shocked many of these same people become if denigrating language is used about any other minority group than women; if the obscenities are racial or ethnic, that is, rather than sexual. Words like "coon," "kike," "spic," "wop," after all, deform identity, deny individuality and humanness in almost exactly the same way that sexual vulgarisms and obscenity do.

Conclusion   No one that I know, least of all my students, would fail to question the values of a society whose literature and entertainment rested heavily on racial or ethnic pejoratives. Are the values of a society whose literature and entertainment rest as heavily as ours on sexual pejoratives any less questionable?

(Lawrence, 1973)

You may or may not agree with Lawrence's argument. You should recognize, however, that what makes it convincing is its association with a formal logical pattern. Even if you are saying to yourself "Yes, but words don't mean today what they once meant," what you are really doing is going beneath the surface of her argument to look for its basic logical pattern: definition by etymology. Unless you can refute this method by another type of reasoning, Lawrence's argument is convincing.

A third type of quasi-logical argument is the argument by stereotype, a commonly-used form of quasi-logical argument by association. Arguments by stereotype frequently begin with the phrase, "I treat all people the same way." There is logic in this phrase, because it creates a positive association we have with the notion of equality. The bureaucrat thus argues that his book of regulations governing welfare eligibility applies to all individuals equally. The police officer argues that "A thief is a thief" regardless of the conditions surrounding the commission of the crime. Whenever someone says, "I don't discriminate by race, creed, sex, religion, size, or age," that person is attempting to win the argument by a favorable association through stereotyping.

So far, you have seen three examples of associative argument based on quasi-logical relations. There are other examples, of course, but the point has been made. Quasi-logical arguments work in situations in which it is important to associate your proposition favorably with some formally accepted pattern of thinking. If you have particularly emotional or sensitive topics (as Lawrence did, for example) you may want to underplay the emotional component of the issue by associating your topic with its logical elements. The next section deals with arguments based on the structure of reality.

Arguments Based on the Structure of Reality

In an argument based on the **structure of reality**, arguers use accepted beliefs, values, and attitudes and then attempt to provide a link between these and the judgment they want to promote. Every culture sees relationships among events. In composite form, such beliefs, values, and attitudes form the basic structure of a culture's reality.

Arguments based on the structure of reality do not presume to show reality the way it is; they begin instead with a widely held notion, whether true or not, and proceed to argue from this accepted premise. Arguments by consequence are one common form of structure-of-reality arguments. Superstitions, for instance, are based upon a connection that is seen between an act and its consequences: "Don't step on the sideline," "Don't whistle on a fishing vessel," "Make the sign of the cross before batting," "Cross your fingers for good luck." These expressions and dozens like them may appear completely irrational; even those who practice superstitions may see their own behavior as irrational; but remember that arguments based on the structure of reality do not presume to present the truth; they attempt only to make a positive association between some accepted truth and the proposition being argued. If the arguer is able to gain adherence for the consequences predicted, the argument is successful.

In the following argument notice how the consequences of not following a generally accepted belief, a logical belief, become the basis for providing the proposition:

What the Hedgehog Knows

Introduction   Among the fragments left us by the Greek poet Archilochus there is a line, dark in meaning, that says:

The fox knows many things; the hedgehog knows one big thing.

Ecologists, in my opinion, are hedgehogs. The one big thing they say is this: *We can never do merely one thing.*

This simple sentence imperfectly mirrors the one big thing ecologists *know* — the idea of a system. So large an idea is best defined ostensively, i.e., by pointing to examples.

Here is a completely serious example. Everyone has heard of the Aswan Dam in Egypt. Actually, a succession of dams has been constructed on the Nile at Aswan during the twentieth century, of which the "High Aswan," built with Russian help, is only the latest. The builders meant to do only one thing — dam the water — and that for two purposes: to generate electricity and to provide a regular flow of water for irrigation of the lower Nile basin. Ecology tells us that we cannot do merely one thing; neither can we do merely two things. What have been the consequences of the Aswan dams?

First, the plain has been deprived of the annual fertilization by flooding that served it so well for five thousand years. Where else in the world can you point to farmland that is as fertile after five millennnia of cultivation as it was in the beginning? (Much of the farmland in the southeastern United States was ruined in half a generation.) Now the Egyptians will have to add artificial fertilizer to the former floodplains of the Nile — which will cost money.

Second, controlled irrigation without periodic flushing salinates the soil, bit by bit. There are methods for correcting this, but they too cost money. This problem has not yet been faced by Egypt.

Third, the sardine catch in the eastern Mediterranean has diminished from 18,000 tons a year to 400 tons, a 97 percent loss, because the sea is now deprived of floodborne nutrients. No one has reimbursed the fishermen (who are mostly not Egyptians) for their losses.

Fourth, the rich delta of the Nile is being eroded away by storms on the Mediterranean. In the past, a nearly "steady state" existed between the deposition of silt by the river and the erosion of it by the sea, with a slight positive balance in favor of deposition, which gradually extended the farmlands of Egypt. With deposition brought to a virtual halt, the balance is now negative and Egypt is losing land.

Fifth, schistosomiasis (a fearsomely debilitating disease) has greatly increased in the Nile valley. The disease organism depends on snails, which depend on a steady supply of water, which constant irrigation furnishes but annual flooding does not. Of course, medical control of the disease is possible — but that too costs money.

Is this all? By no means. The first (and perhaps only a temporary) effect of the Aswan Dam has been to bring into being a larger population of Egyptians, of whom a greater proportion than before are chronically ill. What will be the political effects of this demographic fact? This is a most difficult question — but would anyone doubt that there will be many political consequences, for a long time to come, of trying to do "just one thing," such as building dams on the Nile? The effects of any sizable intervention in an "ecosystem" are like ripples spreading out on a pond from a dropped pebble; they go on and on.

Ironically, in the end, the whole wretched game will return to the starting point. All dam-ponds are transient: in the scale of historical time they are soon filled by siltation behind the dam, and then they are useless. Theoretically, a dam-pond could be dredged clean, but engineers, inclined though they are to assume they can do anything, never suggest this. Evidently the cost is, in the strict sense, prohibitive.

Conclusion
So in a short time — perhaps a century, certainly nothing like the fifty centuries during which Nile agriculture prospered before the dams were built at Aswan — in a short time the dams themselves will be useless and then the silt-laden waters of the Nile will once again enrich the river bottom.

Will history start over again then? Certainly not. Too much will have happened to Egypt in the meantime, most of it bad; and perhaps much to the rest of the world, as the Egyptian people struggle desperately to free themselves from the net in which their well-wishers have unwittingly ensnared them. Things will never again be the same. History does not repeat.

(Hardin, 1972)

Hardin's scheme is an argument by consequences. He asserts that the consequences of constructing a dam on principles contrary to the way the world works are disastrous. The argument is effective to the degree that the audience associates the consequences of which Hardin speaks with the violation of the axiom, "We can never do merely one thing." How might you refute such an argument?

One way to refute an argument based on an axiom is to point out to the audience that axioms are often contradictory: for example, the advice is often offered to those in love that "Absence makes the heart grow fonder." Conversely, the lovesick are also warned, "Out of sight, out of mind." Which axiom is closer to reality? The answer to this is that while axioms may be popular sayings, none mirrors reality accurately all the time. It is on this basis that you can refute an argument that uses an axiom as a proposition.

A second type of argument based on the structure of reality is the well known argument by waste. This argument invokes the commonly held notion that once one has begun a project, worked and sacrificed for it, one should see the project through to a conclusion. To do otherwise would be to waste what has already been expended. This is the argument exhausted marathon runners use one mile before the finish line to convince themselves to give it their all. It is the argument parents use to keep their children practicing the piano or the baton so that the lessons will not go to waste. Students who may be deciding to drop out of school after one year are often exhorted to continue so as not to waste the first year. Such examples may seem trivial, but the argument by waste can have significant consequences, as we see in the following example, also about a dam.

Tellico Dam: Politics At Its Worst

In our cautious system of government, change is usually incremental and mistakes can be corrected. But every once in a while we sense that a government decision has done permanent damage: to the country, to faith in the system. The realization is painful. We find it hard to read about the event; we want to turn the page.

An article by Peter Matthiessen, the naturalist, has just had that effect on me. It told a story so painful that I wanted to escape, but I stayed and learned. The piece appeared in the current issue of *The New York Review of Books*. It concerns the decision, maneuvered by Sen. Howard H. Baker, Jr., to complete the Tellico Dam in Tennessee and destroy the Little Tennessee Valley.

It is only one dam, in a place unknown to most Americans — a parochial question, one might think. But it is not. The Tellico Dam is an extreme example of a widespread phenomenon in this country: the destruction of the land and the people who have worked it. What makes the Tellico extreme is the way the thing was done. Logic, law and economics were overwhelmingly against it, but the facts availed nothing against the guile of cynical politicians.

The valley drowned by this dam had 16,000 acres of the richest riverbottom farmland in the United States. Running through it was the last free-flowing stretch of the Little Tennessee. What had once been 2,500 miles of wild river — the Tennessee and its tributaries — had already been dammed by the Tennessee Valley Authority.

The clean swift water of that last unspoiled stretch was the best brown trout stream in the East. It also was the habitat of the snail darter, the tiny fish that for a time forced a halt in construction of the Tellico Dam because it would violate the Endangered Species Act. The snail darter at first attracted a kind of amused national sympathy — a fish fighting the interests — but Baker and his cohorts turned the argument around.

Logical
Belief

Proponents of the dam argued that a "useless minnow" should not be allowed to stand in the way of progress — to "waste" a $120-million project that would produce energy vital to the area. The shoreline of the lake to be created by the dam would attract industry, providing jobs for an economically depressed region. Anyway, the snail darter could be moved elsewhere.

Those were the arguments. Every one of them was a fake, as Matthiessen devastatingly showed. The compelling power of his account can't be reproduced in a brief newspaper column. But these are some of his points:

Refutation

According to the TVA itself, the annual cost of maintaining the dam will be greater than its income. The "benefits" from the new lake will be nearly $1 million a year less than the income from the lost farmland.

The dam was not in fact "a $120-million project" as most of us would understand those words. Construction of the dam and embankments cost $22 million. The rest went for roads and land around the proposed lake. Farmers' land was taken even when only a small portion of the acreage would be flooded; they were evicted to make room for speculators in lakeside lots.

There will be no electrical generator in the Tellico Dam. A diversion canal carrying water from there through another dam may produce 23 megawatts — out of a current TVA regional capacity of 27,000 megawatts.

Industry does not need new lakeside sites for jobs in the area. There are 24 existing major dams and lakes within 60 miles of the Tellico Dam, and most of them have long undeveloped stretches of shoreline. The TVA found that the dam would cost the area more jobs than it would create.

Three attempts have been made to transplant snail darters to other streams. In two places the fish died; in the third they are threatened.

Baker, speaking for the local developers and labor unions and politicians, helped push through a bill amending the Endangered Species Act. It set up a review committee to consider exemptions from the Act for worthwhile projects. But the new committee studied the Tellico Dam and decided unanimously that it was not worthwhile.

Foiled by the new rules he had helped to draft, Baker simply eliminated the rules. A House Republican colleague from Tennessee, in violation of House procedure, sneaked on to an appropriation bill an undebated amendment that exempted the Tellico project from all laws of any kind. Baker made the necessary deals to get it through the Senate. And President Carter, evidently afraid of retaliation from the Senate's Republican leader, did not have the courage to do what he knew was right: veto the bill.

In the Republican forum in Iowa the other day Baker said: "Politics is an important secular mechanism in this country. It's not just a game. It's not beneath us, it's how we decide our future."

The sentiments are admirable. But Howard Baker's behavior in the affair of the Tellico Dam shows why millions of Americans have come to despair of politics.

(Lewis, 1980)

In this example by Anthony Lewis we see how an argument by waste can be refuted. Refuting Baker's argument required Matthiessen to attack Baker's predicted consequences with another set of consequences. Even though Matthiessen was able to do this, Baker maneuvered the project through, seemingly with a little coercion. If you were to think back to the

Hardin example now, could you refute his argument by attacking the consequences the way Matthiessen attacked Baker's?

One final type of argument based on the structure of reality is the argument by causality. A model for this type of argument was provided by Laurie Burns' essay on the effects of television violence on children, pp. 274–278. What we actually do in a causality argument is to reconstruct past events, hoping that the flow of these events will lead indisputably to the effect. Notice that the Laurie Burns model refrains from blaming television programming alone as the cause of children's imitating violent behavior; it also blames parents who fail to monitor what their children see. Because the cause/effect scheme appears reasonable, the only way to refute such an argument is to attack the data itself.

In reviewing the principle of arguments based on the structure of reality, remember that they use a widely accepted premise and work best when the audience has a positive association with a widely accepted premise, perhaps an axiom like "Money can't buy happiness," or with some cultural ideal, such as patriotism or equality. When you sense that your audience's moral values or basic beliefs have been violated, you may want to use an argument based on the structure of reality. The next section turns to the third type of argument by association, the argument that attempts to organize reality for us.

Arguments that Attempt to Organize Reality

Each of us has a picture of the world around us. As the section on reality-based arguments stressed, we see an argument as real to the degree that it squares with, is consistent with, our view of the world. An argument can also work, however, by creating for us some new reality. In fact, there are whole books based upon this kind of argument — George Orwell's *1984*, for example, and Sir Thomas More's *Utopia*. The novel *1984* attempted to provide a vision of what the future could be like if a government controlled its people to the utmost, and if technology controlled humanity instead of the other way around. Orwell's purpose was to picture an unpleasant reality that we should take steps to avoid. Sir Thomas More's *Utopia*, on the other hand, attempted to present an ideal reality that we should strive for. To the degree that the new reality seems a reasonable possibility, we will work toward it if the vision is favorable and against it if the arguer has painted a bleak picture.

A commonly used type of argument based on the construction of reality is the argument by example. Through such arguments an accepted generalization is either supported or refuted by means of specific instances. The argument by Sidney Harris in Chapter Ten (pp. 278–279) showed how a widely held generalization, that money cannot buy poverty, may be refuted through argument by example. Harris's argument works to the degree that his examples organize reality for us in a new and acceptable way. If we agree that the examples are sufficient in number and accurate as given, we will associate them positively with the way things really are, in this case, that money can buy poverty, as opposed to what we had previously believed.

A second type of argument that attempts to organize reality for us is the argument by model. In a quite trivial way, we might exemplify this by thinking of a new car model or a new fashion design that attempts to show us the newest look in cars or clothing. Models tell us how we are to see a process, product, or person, and to the degree that we link the model with something we like, the argument works.

Look at the model for the communication process offered in Chapter One, on p. 7. Your acceptance of that model is based upon how thoroughly and accurately it depicts for you the abstract process of communication. Molecular models, logical models used by philosophers, and model homes all attempt to construct for us a picture of something we cannot see clearly for ourselves.

A third type of argument that attempts to structure reality is the argument by analogy. The basic premise of an analogy looks like this: as A is to B, so C is to D. In the argument by analogy, the arguer tries to compare an abstract idea with one that is more concrete, one that can be visualized by an audience. To the degree that the audience associates the abstract concept with the concrete idea, the argument works. The successful analogy allows the audience to see the abstract idea in a new form.

Argument by analogy has been used persuasively in the most serious of circumstances. In the following example we see how an understanding of the power of analogy turned the tide of a critical argument:

President Kennedy and the Russian Fable

On October 6, 1961, President John F. Kennedy met at the White House with Andrei Gromyko, Soviet Foreign Minister. The President spoke to Mr. Gromyko about a major issue threatening the future of the United Nations.

The men met against the background of a crisis in the U.N. that had been precipitated several months earlier by the death, in a plane crash, of Dag Hammarskjöld, U.N. Secretary General. Attempts to select a successor to Hammarskjöld were at first complicated and then blocked by the objections of the Soviet Union. Premier Nikita Khrushchev doubted that any of the various men whose names had been advanced for the job would be able to overcome their partiality to the West. He said he thought it impossible, in fact, to find any individual who was impartial enough to satisfy both the Soviet Union and the United States, to say nothing of the uncommitted nations.

Khrushchev's proposed solution was a triumvirate — three men who would share the responsibilities of the office of the Secretary General. The Soviet proposal became popularly known as the "troika," the Russian word for a sled or wagon pulled by three horses.

Week after week, the Soviet Union pressed its opposition to the choice of a single successor to Dag Hammarskjöld, who obviously had been too much of a statesman-leader and not enough of a caretaker-administrator for Mr. Khrushchev's taste. Unwilling to risk another Hammarskjöld, Mr. Khrushchev gave the clear impression that the U.S.S.R. would withdraw from the U.N. if its troika proposal were defeated.

President Kennedy was equally determined to keep the most important job in the United Nations from being fragmented. Appearing before the U.N. General Assembly on September 25, 1961, the President said that, "however difficult it may be to fill Mr. Hammarskjöld's place, it can better be filled by one man rather than by three." He pointed out that the three horses of a troika did not have three drivers, all going in different directions. "They had only one — and so must the United Nations executive. To install a triumvirate, or any panel or rotating authority, in the United Nations' administrative offices would replace order with anarchy, action with paralysis, confidence with confusion. . . . Whatever advantages such a plan may hold out . . . we reject it. For we prefer world law, in the age of self-determination, to world war, in the age of mass extermination."

The battle echoed in the corridors of the U.N. There appeared to be no visible prospect of breaking the deadlock. The life of the United Nations, always difficult, now seemed terribly precarious. President Kennedy was determined not to cripple the U.N. by concurring with the Soviet proposal. Neither did he wish to force the issue in a way that would result in the withdrawal of the Soviet Union from the U.N.

At the height of the controversy, the President was told by Timothy Reardon, his administrative assistant, of an interesting visit Reardon had just had with Walter Besterman, a legislative staff assistant to the House Judiciary Committee. The President recalled having met Besterman during his own service in Congress. Besterman had come to the White House with ammunition for the President's fight over the troika. It was a little book, printed in Russian, of fables written by Ivan Andreevich Krylov, the Russian counterpart of Aesop. Besterman had recalled the fables from his youth in Poland. One of the fables had been translated. Its title was "The Swan, the Pike, and the Crab." It told of a combined effort by the three animals to pull the same wagon. The swan tried to pull it into the sky. The fish tried to drag it into the sea; and the crab tried to yank it backward. Result: no forward motion.

The President thanked Reardon. He reached for the phone and

called the Government Printing Office. He said he had a little
illustrated book in Russian he wished to have reproduced in several
copies on fine parchment in a handsome format. It was to serve a
special purpose, a very special purpose, and the President wanted to
be sure that not even the original edition was more attractive.

The next thing the President did was to invite Foreign Minister
Gromyko to the White House.

Two days later, the Government Printing Office delivered to the
White House several superb reproductions of Krylov's *Fables*.

Mr. Kennedy was in a pleasant, relaxed mood when Mr. Gromyko
was ushered into the oval office. He told the Foreign Minister he
hoped the United States and the Soviet Union could find some way
out of the impasse over the selection of a successor to Dag Hammarskjöld. Gromyko said he welcomed the opportunity to explore the
matter, but he hoped the President would understand that the Soviet
Union would have little confidence in the United Nations unless the
top post were impartially administered, something it was unreasonable to expect a single individual to do. The ability of the United
States to swing enough votes in the U.N. to elect a single candidate
could not be minimized by the Soviet Union.

The President reached over to a side table and picked up the
crisply printed booklet of Krylov's fables.

"I happen to have a delightful little book here," the President said.
"It's in Russian. It's by Ivan Andreevich Krylov. You're familiar with
it, I'm sure. I enjoyed it enormously."

The President handed the booklet to Mr. Gromyko, who seemed
puzzled. Then the President called the Foreign Minister's attention
to the illustrated fable about the swan, the pike, and the crab. While
his guest read the original, the President reread the translation:

Proposition of fact	When partners with each other don't agree Each project must a failure be, And out of it no profit come, but sheer vexation.
Analogy	A Swan, a Pike, and Crab once took their station In harness, and would drag a loaded cart; But, when the moment came for them to start, They sweat, they strain, and yet the cart stands still; what's lacking? The load must, as it seemed, have been light; The Swan, though, to the clouds takes flight, The Pike into the water pulls, the Crab keeps backing.
Conclusion	Now which of them was right, which wrong, concerns us not; The cart is still upon the selfsame spot.

It didn't take Mr. Gromyko very long to get the point.

"Mr. President," he said, "you are thinking of making this public?"

"Not at all," said the President. "I was just eager to give you this specially printed American edition as a gift which I hope you might share with Mr. Khrushchev."

There was a second's silence. Gromyko's ordinarily stern face dissolved into a broad smile and then into generous laughter, which the President fully shared.

Mr. Gromyko said he would be happy to deliver the President's message to the Premier and got up to leave. The President shook his hand, then presented him with an extra copy for himself, on the chance he might send the first one to Mr. Khrushchev.

Several days later, the President received a reply. The Soviet Union would withdraw its opposition to the election of a single successor to Dag Hammarskjöld.

On October 12, 1961, a messenger from the White House delivered a small package to Walter Besterman's desk in the House Office Building. It was a copy of Krylov's *Fables*. On the frontispiece, in the President's hand, appeared the following:

> For Walter Besterman — This won
> the argument! — With thanks and
> best wishes — John F. Kennedy.

So far, there is no account of what happened on the Soviet side, after Mr. Kruschev received the message from Mr. Gromyko. The newly published book *Kruschev Remembers* has no light to throw on the incident. One thing, however, seems clear. Whether or not Krylov's fable was directly responsible for the change in the Soviet position, as President Kennedy believed, the United Nations might not be alive today if the issue had gone unresolved.

Of equal importance, too, is the fact that the withdrawal of the troika scheme cleared the way for the election of U Thant, who, during the past ten years, has demonstrated qualities not just of impartiality but of initiative and courage, and who has attempted from the start to elevate the concept of the United Nations so that it might some day meet mankind's greatest need, a planned planet.

(Cousins, 1971)

In this incident Kennedy's argument was effective because it created for Kruschev a mental picture of what the United Nations would be like under a Troika form of government. Kruschev's transference of the concept of three animals pulling a cart to the concept of governance of the United Nations made the argument compelling.

Of course, in reality, pulling a cart and governing an organization are unrelated, but by use of the analogical scheme an association was made, and the meaning of one phenomenon (cart-pulling) became the meaning for the other (governance of the United Nations).

Effective analogical schemes are difficult to invent. Some research suggests that skill in using analogy, or for that matter any type of metaphorical structure, develops only with maturity in writing and speaking. While you may not find the analogy to be a scheme you actually use in your own discourse, it is a scheme you will want to understand as an analyzer of argument.

In reviewing arguments that attempt to organize reality, remember that such schemes are convincing to the degree that the audience accepts the new vision as reasonable. Confusing models, stereotypical or extreme examples, and trite or exaggerated analogies will be unconvincing. The example, the analogy, the model must excite and convert the audience. Arguments that attempt to organize reality are best suited to situations for which we have no sense of reality and to topics with which the audience has little or no previous association: for example, what will a nuclear war be like in the year 2000? What will be the advantages and disadvantages of solar-powered cars? Because the audience may have no factual knowledge of the subject, arguments that attempt to organize reality must therefore be easily visualized and well remembered.

DISSOCIATIVE ARGUMENTS

The second universal scheme is dissociation. Remember that a dissociative argument was defined as one that separates the idea under consideration from something the audience views negatively or positively, depending on the point we want to make. This might seem like a difficult concept, but it is a common argumentative scheme — one we hear or use all the time. Think, for example, of how often you have heard something like the following: "I love all kinds of music [positive association], but that stuff [dissociation], that's not music."

Of course, emotional statements like the one just given usually do not lead to real argument; however, the same kind of reasoning occurs in serious argumentative discourse. In the past decade much has been said and written, for example, about the delayed stress many Vietnam veterans are suffering. This delayed stress is caused by the experience in Vietnam, of course, but also by the way Vietnam veterans have been treated since their return. The national antagonism toward the war, the outcome of the war, and the handling of the war by government officials has caused many Vietnam veterans to feel great anxiety about the role they played. For most Americans the Vietnam veteran is part of the same reality as the Vietnam War and, as such, has suffered by association.

In an issue of *Time* magazine devoted to the plight of the Vietnam veteran, correspondent Anne Constable argued that it is time to take a new look at the Vietnam veteran. She did so by invoking an argument by dissociation, as she wrote: ". . . antiwar politics had prevented me and my generation from separating the war from the warrior. I hope we can finally welcome them home." Similarly, former antiwar activist and now journalist Doug Kamholz is quoted as saying, "I have been feeling guilty about blaming the war on the warriors. I never yelled 'baby killer' but I didn't oppose it either. It was a moral and political mistake for the antiwar movement not to see the difference. I hope it's not too late." In both of these statements dissociation is at work. The argument is based on the ability of the writers to separate (dissociate) the Vietnam veteran from the war in Vietnam. To the degree that they are successful, the argument becomes convincing.

Dissociative arguments are a common scheme in advertisements. We often see the words *new* or *improved* used to describe a product. The goal of such statements is to invoke a positive reaction to the product by dissociating it from previous versions of the product, or from other products of its type. Dissociative arguments are also used by parents who warn their children to "Be your own person. Don't just go along with the crowd." It is the main argument parents have against the peer pressure they fear may influence their son or daughter in the wrong direction.

Dissociative schemes often underlie arguments that attempt to define a term in a new way or to define it more precisely. Definition is a form of quasi-logical argument, as has been noted earlier in this chapter; however, definition is also a means by which to dissociate terms from their customary usage to their so-called real meaning. This type of argument appears when someone feels that the original meaning of a term has been corrupted by popular usage. In the following essay, we can see this type of argument at work:

Discrimination is a Virtue*

When I was a child, my grandmother used to tell me a story about a king who had three daughters and decided to test their love. He asked each of them, "How much do you love me?" The first replied that she loved him as much as all the diamonds and pearls in the world. The second said that she loved him more than life itself. The third replied, "I love you as much as fresh meat loves salt."

This answer enraged the king; he was convinced that his youngest daughter was making fun of him. So he banished her from his realm and left all of his property to her elder sisters.

As the story unfolded it became clear, even to a 6-year old, that the king had made a terrible mistake. The two older girls were hypocrites, and as soon as they had profited from their father's generosity, they began to treat him very badly. A wiser man would have realized that the youngest daughter was the truest. Without attempting to flatter, she had said, in effect, "We go together naturally; we are a perfect team."

King Lear: Years later, when I came to read Shakespeare, I realized that my grandmother's story was loosely based upon the story of King Lear, who put his daughters to a similar test, and did not know how to judge the results. Attempting to save the king from the consequences of his foolishness, a loyal friend pleads, "Come, sir, arise, away! I'll teach you differences." Unfortunately, the lesson comes too late. Because Lear could not tell the difference between true love and false, he loses his kingdom and eventually his life.

We have a word in English which means "the ability to tell differences." That word is *discrimination*. But within the last twenty years, this word has been so frequently misused that an entire generation has grown up believing that "discrimination" means "racism." People are always proclaiming that "discrimination" is something that should be done away with. Should that ever happen, it would prove to be our undoing.

Discrimination means discernment; it means the ability to perceive the truth, to use good judgment and to profit accordingly. *The Oxford English Dictionary* traces this understanding of the word back to 1648 and demonstrates that for the next 300 years, "discrimination" was a virtue, not a vice. Thus, when a character in a nineteenth-century novel makes a happy marriage, Dickens has another character remark, "It does credit to your discrimination that you should have found such a very excellent young woman."

Of course, the "ability to tell differences" assumes that differences exist, and this is unsettling for a culture obsessed with the notion of equality. The contemporary belief that discrimination is a vice stems from the compound "discriminate against." What we need to remember, however, is that some things deserve to be judged harshly; we should not leave our kingdoms to the selfish and the wicked.

Discrimination is wrong only when someone or something is discriminated against because of prejudice. But to use the word in this sense, as so many people do, is to destroy its true meaning. If you discriminate against something because of general preconceptions rather than particular insights, then you are not discriminating — bias has clouded the clarity of vision which discrimination demands.

One of the great ironies of American life is that we manage to discriminate in the practical decisions of daily life, but usually fail to discriminate when we make public policies. Most people are very discriminating when it comes to buying a car, for example, because they realize that cars have differences. Similarly, an increasing number of people have learned to discriminate in what they eat. Some foods are better than others — and indiscriminate eating can undermine one's health.

Yet in public affairs, good judgment is depressingly rare. In many areas which involve the common good, we see a failure to tell differences.

Consider, for example, some of the thinking behind modern education. On the one hand, there is a refreshing realization that there are differences among children, and some children — be they gifted or handicapped — require special education. On the other hand, we are politically unable to accept the consequences of this perception. The trend these days is to group together students of radically different ability. We call this process "mainstreaming," and it strikes me as a characteristically American response to the discovery of differences: we try to pretend that differences do not matter.

Policy: Similarly, we try to pretend that there is little difference between the sane and the insane. A fashionable line of argument has it that "everybody is a little mad" and that few mental patients deserve long-term hospitalization. As a consequence of such reasoning, thousands of seriously ill men and women have been evicted from their hospital beds and returned to what is euphemistically called "the community" — which often means a roach-infested room in a welfare hotel.

Or to choose a final example from a different area: could any unbiased observer believe that our foreign policy is marked by discrimination? How was it possible for the Iranian revolution to surprise us as it did, if it were not for a failure of perception? And for that matter, how was it possible for our President to feel betrayed by the Soviet invasion of Afghanistan, if he were not guilty of an inability to discriminate? Like Lear, he put his faith in hypocrites and was then astonished to discover that there are those among us who do not always tell the truth.

So as we look around us, we should recognize that "discrimination" is a virtue which we desperately need. We must try to avoid making unfair and arbitrary distinctions, but we must not go to the other extreme and pretend that there are no distinctions to be made. The ability to make intelligent judgments is essential both for the success of one's personal life, and for the functioning of society as a whole. Let us be open-minded by all means, but not so open-minded that our brains fall out.

(Miller, 1980)

Miller's argument is based upon dissociation of the term *discrimination* from the narrow negative connotation that popular usage has given it. Similar arguments might be made for such terms as *chauvinism, stereotyping,* or *ambitious,* essentially useful terms for which popular usage has created a negative image. Do you accept Miller's argument? If not, why? If so, is it because you accept his dissociation?

A dissociative argument, then, can be useful when you want to reverse the way an audience thinks on a topic about which they already have a definite attitude, be that attitude positive or negative. The dissociative argument separates the particular topic from the general category by describing the characteristics and functions that set it apart. In short, when your message is essentially "But this isn't the same thing," you will want to use a dissociative argument.

SUMMARY

What makes an argument convincing — what makes it work — has been a subject of interest since the ancient Greeks first conceived of a civilization based on the principle of democracy. Each argument we encounter has value, of course, only in the situation in which it is given, but if we look beneath the surface of any argument we can find one of two universal schemes operating: association or dissociation. These two universal schemes give to an argument its essential reasonableness.

Associative arguments appear reasonable to an audience because the argument is based upon something the audience views positively. There are three types of associative arguments: quasi-logical arguments, arguments based on the structure of reality, and arguments that attempt to organize reality. In each of these three schemes the arguer bases the proposition on a favorable association the audience makes as it considers the whole argument.

Dissociative arguments appear reasonable to an audience because the topic under consideration is distinguished from something the audience views negatively or positively. Common dissociative themes are appearance *vs.* reality, letter of the law *vs.* spirit of the law, fact *vs.* opinion, and democracy *vs.* communism. Dissociative arguments also take the form of definitional essays, in which the term is given a new meaning by dissociating it from terms it was formerly identified with.

As citizens in a democratic society we are constantly asked to make judgments about the world of human affairs. In order to do so, we need to be aware of the underlying forces that make an argument compelling. This chapter has described and modeled these underlying principles of argument.

KEY WORDS

scheme   quasi-logical arguments
associative scheme   structure of reality
dissociative scheme

EXERCISES

1. Professional advocates write essays in newspapers, magazines, and journals. We hear professional arguers on television, too. As consumers of argument it is important that we know the structure of the argument as

it is presented. In order to sharpen your awareness of this structure, bring into class an argumentative essay by a syndicated columnist, or an essay from a magazine like *Time*, and read it to a small group, or to the whole class. Indicate which type of argument you think is operating, associative or dissociative, and then give your reasons for your choice. Do you think the argument works? On what bases would you refute the argument? What scheme would you choose for refuting the argument?

2. Try writing a dissociative argument. You might focus on such common dissociative pairs as appearance *vs.* reality, spirit of the law *vs.* letter of the law, or fact *vs.* opinion. One of the easier dissociative arguments to write is the argument by definition, in which you take a term that has a familiar meaning and associations for the audience and try to redefine the term, making it mean something completely new. You might take the word *fun*, for example, and try to show its common meaning, and then redefine the term as you see it.

REFERENCES

Cousins, Norman, "President Kennedy and the Russian Fable," *Saturday Review* (January 9, 1971).

Hardin, Garrett, "What the Hedgehog Knows," in Garrett Hardin, *Exploring New Ethics for Survival* (Baltimore: Penguin, 1972).

Lawrence, Barbara, "_____ Isn't a Dirty Word," *The New York Times*, October 27, 1973, p. 29.

Lewis, Anthony, "Tellico Dam: Politics at its Worst," *Providence Journal*, January 18, 1980, p. A–10.

Miller, Robert Keith, "Discrimination is a Virtue," *Newsweek* (July 21, 1980), p. 15.

"Trial by Mathematics," *Time*, April 1968.

12. The Paragraph: Details that Make a Point

What are paragraphs?

Paragraphs are sentences separated from those that come before them by means of an indentation.

Why use paragraphs?

Paragraphs can do a number of things: call attention to an idea or expression; help avoid confusion, as in the case of dialogue, where a new paragraph signals a new speaker; or provide visual breaks in overly long stretches of prose. Most important of all, paragraphs mark the major sections in the pattern underlying an essay.

How long should paragraphs be?

Paragraphs for special purposes — to provide emphasis, to mark dialogue — may vary greatly in length, from a few sentences to many. Paragraphs that represent sections of an essay are relatively long, often containing six to eight sentences, because they need to contain all the ideas, examples, and experiences that are appropriate for the particular part of the essay. And because paragraphs of this sort play such important roles in an essay — highlighting the structure, developing ideas and details — this chapter concentrates on them, discussing how they can be made to fit into the pattern of the whole essay, examining how the sentences they contain can be made to fit together, or cohere, and reviewing some standard formulas for writing paragraphs.

OVERALL STRUCTURE: FITTING PARAGRAPHS INTO ESSAYS

Most people have had an essay returned to them with this comment: problems with organization. Often the problem lies with the paragraphs, and it may have two sources. First, each paragraph in the essay may be well-organized and well-developed, but they may be poorly placed in relationship to each other and to the essay as a whole. Second, individual paragraphs may be scrambled: instead of presenting information that contributes to the central point of the paragraph and to the essay as a whole, each sentence may contain a new idea. Each of these topics needs to be examined separately.

Paragraphs Within the Essay

Sometimes the paragraphs in an essay you have written may make sense when each is taken alone, but when put together fail to create a unified essay. This problem generally has an easy solution: when you revise the essay, simply rearrange the paragraphs. In the course of rearranging you may come across some other problems; you may find a point that has not been sufficiently developed, or a short two-sentence paragraph that should be combined with another, longer paragraph. In the following student essay each paragraph makes a point, but as a whole the essay would profit from some reorganization:

Suburban Life is Great

1   Younger people have a hard time deciding where they plan to settle down and live. Some couples prefer the city while others prefer the suburbs. There are many good arguments for choosing a life-style in the suburbs over one in the city.

2   Living in the city enables a person to be closer to his job, to have much more access to public transportation, and to encounter more people.

3   But many people do not like to be close to their jobs because a job is one part of life and their families are another part. People like to get away from their business problems and enjoy life without worrying about their jobs. When people are close to their jobs, it seems as though they are called at any hour of the day when something goes wrong.

4   When living in the city, people have much more access to public transportation than do the people in the suburbs. But with more buses and taxis, there is more air and noise pollution. When there are heavy counts of air pollution, older people have a hard time breathing. Noise pollution has become a major problem in cities. Almost anywhere in a city at any time of the day, there is noise.

5   Living in the city enables one to encounter more people, but the reason for this is overpopulation. Today more and more cities are becoming overpopulated and some cities are short of housing. Under these conditions, garbage piles up, the city becomes dirty, and there is widespread disease. Throughout history, diseases in cities have killed many people.

6   There are many more advantages to living in the suburbs which outweigh the advantages of city living.

7   In the suburbs, the air is much cleaner to breathe. It seems that there is less sickness in the suburbs than in the city, mainly because of clean air.

8   A person has fewer neighbors in the suburbs, and therefore more privacy. Privacy is essential. Everyone enjoys being with friends without having other people see what is going on.

9   In the suburbs, people have more land. More land enables people to have a garden, a pool, or any other form of recreation they would like. Having worked all day, people like to get outside and enjoy life. A pool seems to be the most enjoyed family recreation today. But in

order to have a pool or a garden, a person must have the land to build one.

10   In the suburbs, the life-style moves at a slower pace. In the city, there is too much hustle and bustle, but in the suburbs people seem to be more relaxed and rested. When people are more rested, they usually are more polite and friendly.

11   In the suburbs, there seems to be less of everything than in the city. There are fewer robberies and less vandalism in the suburbs. With fewer cars and fewer people, there is less air and noise pollution.

12   People seem to work as one unit in a suburban town because they get to know their neighbors and a mutual respect forms between people.

13   There are many more positive reasons for living in the suburbs than living in the city. The suburbanites live in more of a relaxed atmosphere and seem to be healthier and happier.

— Greg Hancock

A number of things could be changed in this essay. In the first place, Greg was right to list in paragraph 2 the three advantages of living in the city that he intended to deal with; but there was no need for him to make this list a separate paragraph. It should instead have been attached to the end of paragraph 1 like this: "There are many more good arguments for choosing a lifestyle in the suburbs rather than in the city, although some say living in the city enables people to be closer to their jobs, to have much more access to public transportation, and to encounter more people."

To set up a more effective contrast between pollution levels, paragraph 7 should follow paragraph 4. Paragraph 8, which deals with people, would be better after paragraph 5, which has a similar subject. Paragraph 12 also deals with people and should come next; as a one-sentence paragraph tossed in near the end of the essay, it loses its force as an argument. With these changes the essay gains unity and a sharper contrast: air/air, neighbors/neighbors.

Paragraph 6 is repetitive and unnecessary; it can be dropped. Paragraphs 9, 10, and 11 are additional arguments for living in the suburbs that provide no contrast with the city; but since Greg believes that suburban life is better, it is natural that he drop the point-by-point comparison with the city and end with support for the suburbs. Rearranged, his paper would read this way:

Suburban Life is Great

Younger people have a hard time deciding where they plan to settle down and live. Some couples prefer the city while others prefer the suburbs. There are many good arguments for choosing a life-style in the suburbs over one in the city, although some say living in the city enables people to be closer to their jobs, to have much more access to public transportation, and to encounter more people.

But many people do not like to be close to their jobs because a job is one part of life and their families are another part. People like to get away from their business problems and enjoy life without worrying about their jobs. When people are close to their jobs, it seems as though they are called at any hour of the day when something goes wrong.

When living in the city, people have much more access to public transportation than do the people in the suburbs. But with more buses and taxis, there is more air and noise pollution. When there are heavy counts of air pollution, older people have a hard time breathing. Noise pollution has become a major problem in cities. Almost anywhere in a city at any time of the day, there is noise.

In the suburbs, the air is much cleaner to breathe. It seems that there is less sickness in the suburbs than in the city, mainly because of clean air.

Living in the city enables one to encounter more people, but the reason for this is overpopulation. Today more and more cities are becoming overpopulated and some cities are short of housing. Under these conditions, garbage piles up, the city becomes dirty, and there is widespread disease. Throughout history, diseases in cities have killed many people.

A person has fewer neighbors in the suburbs, and therefore more privacy. Privacy is essential. Everyone enjoys being with friends without having other people see what is going on. People seem to work as one unit in a suburb because they get to know their neighbors and a mutual respect forms between people.

In the suburbs, a person has more land. More land enables people to have a garden, a pool, or any other form of recreation they would like. Having worked all day, people like to get outside and enjoy life. A pool seems to be the most enjoyed family recreation today. But in order to have a pool or a garden, a person must have the land to build one.

In the suburbs, the life-style moves at a slower pace. In the city, there is too much hustle and bustle, but in the suburbs people seem to be more relaxed and rested. When people are rested, they usually are more polite and friendly.

In the suburbs, there seems to be less of everything than in the city. There are fewer robberies and less vandalism in the suburbs. With fewer cars and fewer people, there is less air and noise pollution.

All in all, there are many more positive reasons for living in the suburbs than living in the city.

Although there are other aspects of this essay that still need improvement, the overall organization is much tighter after a few relatively simple changes. Had Greg thought a bit more about the whole purpose of his paper — what all his information was leading to — he would have had fewer organizational problems.

Sentences Within the Paragraph

Sometimes the information in a paragraph you have written may fail to lead up to a central idea or a key sentence (topic sentence). If this is the case, your readers will have trouble figuring out what you are trying to say and how your essay is organized. The following example, an opening paragraph from a student essay titled "The Nursing Career," illustrates this kind of problem:

> Nursing is one profession that will never go out of style. There will always be the need for nurses all around the world, simply because people will never stop becoming ill. Computers may be taking over many jobs, but taking care of a sick patient requires the work of a skilled professional. But because nurses are underpaid, hospitals and nursing homes are understaffed. This is a major problem because there are fewer nurses for the greater number of patients; therefore, many patients get less personal care. For instance, a patient who is in the intensive care unit requires a nurse twenty-four hours a day. There must be enough nurses to care for the other less sick patients. However, I have read articles in nursing journals which state that the problem of underpaid nurses is being remedied.
>
> — Betty Healy

What exactly is the point of this paragraph? Betty began the essay with a central idea: there will always be a need for nurses; but by the end of the paragraph the reader has been led in so many other directions that the initial focus is lost. The paragraph presents too many important ideas and too much information: nurses are underpaid, hospitals are understaffed, patients may not receive the personal care they deserve. In addition, the final sentence states that nursing journals indicate that the problem of underpayment is being remedied, as though this were the point of the paragraph rather than the idea about the need for nurses that opened it. There are four, possibly five, topics in this paragraph, and the reader has reason to be confused.

Betty's purpose in the whole essay, as she explained it to her instructor, was to persuade more people to go into nursing. What happened? In an effort to show the tremendous demand for nurses, Betty wanted to explain that hospitals and nursing homes are understaffed. Inadvertently, however, she set up another topic: "But because nurses are underpaid, hospitals and nursing homes are understaffed." In an essay intended to persuade readers to enter the nursing profession, the material related to pay and understaffing are out of place in the first paragraph. They are not persuasive; moreover, they switch the topic from the need for nurses to problems in the nursing career. In the interest of being fair to her audience, Betty could have introduced the related questions of salary and understaffing later in the essay along with her reassuring evidence from the nursing journals, but in the first paragraph it is distracting.

Betty's difficulties with this paragraph did not stop with the introduction of the material about understaffing, because this led her to introduce another problem facing the nursing profession: the impersonal care of patients. Though she was still trying to say indirectly that nurses are in demand, Betty ended up creating a list of problems the nursing profession is facing. As a result, this paragraph fails to make nursing seem like an attractive career. This is unfortunate, because opening paragraphs are crucial to an essay's success. Having made a statement, Betty felt compelled to explain it again and again until she lost sight of the central purpose of the paper, the intent to persuade people to go into nursing. Instead of keeping this focus in mind, she let the writing control her.

When she sat down to revise the paragraph, Betty concentrated on leading the reader to understand the true point of her paper:

> Nursing is one profession that can never be taken over by computers. People all over the world need nurses. Although some potential nurses are discouraged from entering the profession because they feel it involves too much work for too little pay, the medical field as a whole is working to remedy this problem. Most of nursing's rewards are not financial anyway; the greatest joy is knowing you have given lonely or depressed people the feeling that someone cares about them.

In this version of the paragraph, Betty directs the reader's attention to her purpose, persuading people to enter nursing. Everything in this paragraph was included somewhere in the original essay; in revising, Betty pulled the material together, keeping in mind what she wanted her readers to know by the end of the first paragraph. Betty realized she had to make clear that despite the hardships involved, she was urging people to get into the profession. Her newly shaped paragraph fulfills that end.

Both kinds of problems — too many topics within a paragraph and incorrect placement of paragraphs within the discourse — originate from the same source: a vagueness about the overall shape of the essay or speech, an inability to see the ending. Of course, as Chapter Two of this text illustrates, even professional writers begin their writing without complete knowledge of where it will go and what direction it will take. They do, however, have a purposeful statement guiding them through the discourse. Once you have achieved direction, an end-shape, your paragraphs will begin fitting easily into the whole essay or speech.

KINDS OF COHERENCE: LEADING THE AUDIENCE

Good paragraphs cannot be written without a sense of the finished product, the whole essay or speech; and individual paragraphs must have a focus, must move the audience from one point to another. In addition, the paragraphs within a discourse should stand in a clear relationship to each other, and the ideas within a paragraph should be clearly related. The word *coherence* refers to relationships among paragraphs and ideas. A paragraph in which the ideas are clearly related is a coherent one.

There are several kinds of words that when placed appropriately help create coherence in a stretch of discourse. Audiences look and listen for these words; without them, coherence over a sustained piece of discourse becomes weak, and the audience is uncertain about what one idea has to do with the next. The following passage illustrates what it is like to read or listen to a paragraph lacking many of the words that help create coherence:

> The nation's swelling step-population includes some 12 million step-parents and 6.5 million step-children under 18. People like to think that such blended families live in rewedded bliss. The bliss can be short-lived. The impact of remarriage on a family, regardless of how high the expectations, is almost as great as the crisis of divorce. There are no guidelines for acceptable step-family behavior. One expert attributes the higher rate of divorce in second marriages — 40% as against 33% on first marriages — to the strain of trying to work it all out.

Pause for a moment. Try to remember what you have just read. Can you put it in some kind of mental order? You may find it difficult. Now try it with italicized words added:

> The nation's swelling step-population *now* includes some 12 million step-parents and 6.5 million step-children under 18. *And though* people like to think that such blended families live in rewedded bliss, the bliss can be short-lived. The impact of remarriage on a family, regardless of how high the expectations, *is second only* to the crisis of divorce. *Because* there are no guidelines for acceptable step-family behavior, *at least one* expert attributes the higher rate of divorce in second marriages — 40% as against 33% in first marriages — to the strain of trying to work it all out.
>
> (*Newsweek*, February 11, 1980)*

The underlined passages in the preceding paragraph create coherence through two kinds of words: transition words like *and* or *but* and words that indicate time or space relationships like *now, a while ago, in the future, usually, lately, below, above,* and *in a few years.* There are only a few of these words in the sample paragraph — not every sentence needs

---

*Copyright 1980 by Newsweek, Inc. All Rights Reserved. Reprinted by permission.

them. But notice how the **readability** of the piece is increased. A readable piece of discourse is one that can be summarized with little difficulty after a single reading or hearing because relationships among ideas are clearly marked. Discourse with a high readability level is easy for readers to take in because it is prepared with them in mind. In expository prose, we usually want to strive to make our material as easy to take as possible without sacrificing the element of style. **Transitional coherence** and **time/space coherence** can help.

The words that add coherence and readability to prose by clarifying relationships among sentences fall into six categories (Winterowd, 1975). The name of each category indicates the kind of relationship signalled by the words it contains.

1. Coordination. This relationship is most commonly expressed by *and* (synonyms: *in addition, also, again, too, furthermore*).

   > Children sense a deep loss and feel they are suddenly vulnerable to forces beyond their control.
   >
   > (*Newsweek*, February 11, 1980)

   Sometimes the pair "not only . . . but also" expresses the emphatic coordination of ideas.

   > In that single move, her oldest child lost *not only* his father and his home, *but also* his school and his friends.
   >
   > (*Newsweek*, February 11, 1980)

   Coordination is probably the most frequently used method of combining ideas, especially when the ideas are of equal nature. Often, though, we as writers want to imply that ideas are unequal, that there is choice involved, or that one decision precludes another. Here are some of the ways we make these implications:

2. Contrast. Often expressed by *but* (synonyms: *yet, however, nevertheless, on the other hand, although*).

   > The merchandise was expensive, *yet* people continued to buy.
   >
   > *But* no matter what deficiencies are presented to the child, the parent must present the other parent's assets *as well*.
   >
   > (*Newsweek*, February 11, 1980)

3. Cause and effect. Usually expressed by *for* or *because*.

   > But they are different — *for* divorce, though no longer a stigma, is nonetheless a wrenching series of crises that sets these children apart.
   >
   > (*Newsweek*, February 11, 1980)

4. Choice/Alternatives. Expressed by *or*, sometimes the *either . . . or* pair.

   > Were "the strongest changes binding the prisoners . . . their own universal submission and total surrender to their situation as slaves," as Solzhenitsyn rages in *Gulag*? *Or* does Soviet rule survive because

it is "inhumanly strong, in a way as yet unknown to the West," as the same work also explains?

(Feifer, 1980)

5. Conclusion. Expressed by *so, therefore, thus, for this reason.*

The fans know that the policemen won't risk their personal safety, *so* the crowds continue to smoke pot, throw firecrackers, and toss beer bottles.

Eventually, if these measures are taken, rock concerts will become safer and more interesting, *thus* encouraging more fans to see their favorite groups perform.

6. Sequence. Expressed by such transitions as *first, second, third, earlier, later, in the middle, after, then, while, during.* Sequence words can also be time/space markers.

Later these positions are usually occupied by one person *for long periods of time.*

Occasionally, transitions are implied, and, as Chapter Thirteen shows, punctuation may be used in place of a transition word, or the words may be moved around in sentences to create various effects. In any case, this list is by no means an exhaustive one. In your daily reading, look for words that signal a transition; you may find additional categories of these transitional words.

Look at the following paragraphs of a student essay to get a sense of how the transition words and time/space markers, all italicized, work in paragraphs:

While daydreaming about my summer vacation, I realized that wintertime is my favorite season. *Even though* winter can be cold and bleak, I know this signals my favorite holiday, Christmas, especially the days before it, which bring feelings of happy anticipation.

Throughout my eighteen years, I have accumulated a set of seasonal clues that remind me of Christmas time. *One December morning* I will awake to find myself curled under three heavy blankets. *Outside,* a crisp breeze will be whistling through the pine trees, *and* a thin layer of frost will be glistening on my bedroom window. *While* snuggled beneath my covers, I will eventually notice that something is different about this particular morning. *Outside,* the usual sounds have become muffled. The cars' tires won't be scraping against the rough concrete streets. *Instead,* the neighborhood sounds will have become hushed by a soft cushion. As I shuffle down the stairs in my fluffy pink slippers, I will smell the rich aroma of hot chocolate simmering on the kitchen stove. *Immediately* I'll head to the picture window. *Overnight* a blanket of snow will have covered the ground. The snowflakes on the trees will be sparkling in the sun, *and* the peacefulness of this first snowfall will be my *first* seasonal clue of the approaching holiday.

— Maria Esposito

Maria's paper (these are only the first two paragraphs) received a high rating from her fellow students in their evaluation group. Their main comment was that they could follow along, feeling as though they were actually in the scene Maria had created. Though some of this feeling is caused by the specific images Maria creates, much of it is due to her effective placement of the transition words and the time/space adverbials.

Still another type of coherence is **lexical coherence**, sometimes called an equivalence chain because closely synonymous words are equivalent to each other. This kind of coherence emerges in a paragraph through repetition of a word, a pronoun that refers to the word, or a synonym of the topic word in the paragraph. Here is an example:

> But are *separate components* really for you? *They* do give you a chance to mix and match brands, performance levels, and features just as home *stereo components* do. However, *they're* not as easily stacked, and the mounting racks available are each made to hold one manufacturer's components; *other brands* will be of different sizes. And too, spreading the controls among *several components* makes the system harder to operate while driving. On the other hand, there's nothing quite as luxe-looking as a *full set of separates*. So you may want *them* for your van or motor home where space is less of a problem and *the equipment* is less visible to potential thieves. And, of course, *they'd* look just dandy set into the bar of your Rolls Royce.
>
> (*Stereo Review*, 1980)

Proper use of lexical coherence focuses the audience's attention on the subject or topic of the paragraph and prevents the need to reread a passage to find its main idea, or to ask speakers to state their main ideas again. Skillful composers keep their referent words clear; nothing is more annoying to an audience than an ambiguous *it* or *they*. Sorting out ambiguity requires time and decreases the readability of a passage, as well as the level of understanding in a speech.

Most paragraphs, however, require supporting ideas as well as the main one, and the supporting ideas need to be introduced in a way that avoids confusing the audience. In the paragraph above on car stereo components, for example, the author explains why separate components may not be feasible: "However, *they're* not as easily stacked, and the mounting racks available are each made to hold one manufacturer's components; *other brands* will be of different sizes." The author wisely avoids saying "*they* will be of different sizes." Why? Because the subject of the sentence is a referent word, *they*, and between that subject and the end of the sentences are two other possible subjects: *mounting racks* and *components*. Even though, as an intelligent audience, we would have figured out that *they* in "they will be of different sizes" refers to *mounting racks,* and not to *components,* the author saves us the trouble. He uses the alternate phrase *other brands.*

Here are two rules that can help you avoid confusing your audience:

1. Avoid counting on a referent word to get an audience through a whole paragraph. Usually two uses of the referent in a row are acceptable; more than that can create difficulty. Find synonyms for your topic word, or if necessary repeat the word itself rather than leaving members of the audience to find their way out of a labyrinth of *its* and *theys.*

2. If a sentence contains more than one noun, be careful about where referent words are placed. Sometimes it is better not to use the referent word at all. As a general rule, a referent should always refer to the noun immediately preceding it. Following this rule will give the paragraph coherence and prevent unnecessary difficulties for your audience.

TECHNIQUES OF EXPOSITION

The first two sections of this chapter have investigated paragraphs primarily from the point of view of their impact on an audience. This section examines paragraphs from a composer's perspective, discussing ways to construct paragraphs well, techniques that should help you avoid in your writing many of the problems covered earlier in the chapter. Effective composers are aware of all their options and use them with discrimination, leaving the mark of their individual styles on what they write. There should be as much satisfaction in the writing of good prose as there is in the reading or hearing of it. Though this chapter is primarily about writing and reading, hearing is appropriate here, too, because many of the techniques to be studied in this section can be applied to formal speaking as well as to writing.

Using Patterns

Good writing is far from formulaic; however, it helps to know a few rules before we bend or break them to suit our own needs or the needs of an audience. There are also times when fast paragraph organization is essential — particularly, any time you are asked to write on the spot: in-class essays, job or graduate school applications, or complaint forms to businesses. Remembering **paragraph patterns** can help.

For these times, and for any time you sense a lack of organization in your composing, practice with the following patterns will help you to get over writer's block. They will assure you of writing a coherent paragraph; if you learn to use them fluently, you will acquire intuitions about which kind of paragraph is most effective in meshing with your overall essay or speech pattern, whether it be narration, cause and effect, definition, or process. *Acquire intuitions* is the correct phrase here because although there are some guidelines, there are no set rules for using the different kinds of paragraphs. You must manipulate the patterns yourself, know how they work as well as why and when they do. Think of your prose in a visual sense: sometimes just a small movement of the kaleidoscope shifts the focus to where you want it.

Topic-Restriction-Illustration

Many beginning composers have been taught to narrow a topic and state it in the first sentence of a paragraph in the form of a topic sentence. The following paragraph illustrates a more useful and more subtle pattern, one that is common in skilled expository prose: topic, restriction, followed by illustrations (examples).

Topic (broad topic)	In Medieval manuscripts, God is sometimes depicted as an architect, the artist who constructed the world. From at least late Renaissance times, when Vassari wrote that Michelangelo's life and works seemed divine rather than earthly, there have been hints that the metaphor could be reversed, the artist himself seen as godlike.
Restriction (narrow topic)	The 20th century, when God went into hiding, was on the lookout for the superhuman, and found it easily in Pablo Picasso.
Illustration (of thesis)	As early as 1902, a year after his first show, a critic wrote of this artist, "One might call him a young god who wanted to remake the world."
Illustration	Mythical equations kept cropping up in the succeeding years. In 1910, Picasso is called "The doubly distilled ultimate."
Illustration	In 1912, there is "something demonic in his quest."
Illustration	In 1919, his studio is "more hallucinatory than the laboratory of Faust."
Illustration	And in 1966, Roland Penrose described Picasso as "a man who deals with angels and demons alike, a man who has no need to talk of God, for is he not himself some sort of god, albeit human to the core?"

(Goldberg, 1980)

This paragraph, taken from "The Arts" section of *Saturday Review* magazine, opens by introducing a topic likely to interest its readers: changing views of the artist over the last 800 years. But this topic is, of course, too large to be dealt with adequately in a paragraph, so the paragraph goes on to limit, or restrict, its treatment of the topic to the present century and to the century's most famous artist, Picasso. The illustrations that follow support the point of view expressed in the restriction.

Though this paragraph follows a formula, the writing seems not mechanical at all because the author is a skillful writer. Look at the paragraph again: it moves from the Medieval period to the Renaissance to the twentieth century to different parts of the century. Each period is given one sentence, and each sentence moves the reader to another level: from God to artist to superhuman to Picasso and, finally, to the different stages of critical reaction to Picasso. The author supports the claim made about Picasso in the restriction by introducing the opinions of authorities from the art world, and this prepares the reader for an essay that examines various aspects of Picasso's career.

Notice also how this paragraph prepares the reader for the patterns that the essay to follow will use. It establishes a contrast between Picasso and the artists of preceding centuries, and it splits Picasso's career into stages, preparing the reader for the analytical pattern that will be important in the essay.

Broad Topic-Explanation-Restriction-Example

The basic topic-restriction-illustration pattern can be adapted in a variety of ways. The paragraphs below show how it can be expanded to cover two paragraphs and how it can be used to introduce patterns to be followed by the rest of an essay or speech:

Broad Topic
Explanation

Restriction
(narrow topic)

Illustration
(extended
example)

I've said before that I think the women's movement was probably long overdue. We're trying to redress grievances that men like me didn't even know existed. So I'm not averse to the mainstream of the new feminism. But (I can hear the rustle of millions of hackles rising ominously at that simple *but*) I think we're headed for trouble because of a couple of semantic problems.

The first problem has to do with the different meanings of *equal*. If, when we say that men and women are equal, we mean that they are equal as sides of the same coin are equal, or as partners are equal, or as components of the whole are equal, the statement makes sense. But *equal* can also mean "exactly the same, alike, identical"; and unfortunately, this latter meaning seems to have been accepted by large numbers of feminists as the meaning of sexual equality.

(Middleton, 1980)

There are several important points to notice in these paragraphs. The writer begins with the **broad topic** of the women's movement, then moves quickly into the more restricted range he intends to address: "a few semantic problems," which is the **narrow topic**. The article being introduced filled only a single page in the magazine, so the author could not afford to waste space. Swift movement is achieved in part by use of a device discussed earlier, transition words in adjacent sentences: "So I'm not . . . . But I think . . . ." By using these transitions, the author narrows his topic and clarifies the purpose of the essay, which is to persuade. This is a good first paragraph because it makes clear to the reader the final shape of the paper.

The second paragraph uses two patterns widely employed to organize entire essays. The first, enumeration, follows naturally from the final sentence of the first paragraph. The second, definition, helps serve the final purpose of the essay: persuasion. By defining immediately, the writer shows that even though he has used the colloquial phrase "a couple of . . . problems," he has no intention of being vague about his issues. The whole paragraph serves as an extended example of one of the "semantic problems" the essay will probe.

Example-Example-Example-Topic

The structure of this paragraph pattern is quite obvious, but it is nevertheless effective, especially in opening paragraphs.

Example   On November 14, 1979, the U. S. Government froze all Iranian assets in American banks.

Example   On November 21, a banking syndicate led by Chase Manhattan declared Iran in default on a $500 million loan and moved to seize Iranian deposits; Iran was a week late with an interest payment.

Example   Still later in the month, the Morgan Guaranty Trust Company took steps to attach Iran's interest in two companies — Krupp and the engineering firm of Deutche Babcock.

Topic   It looked, in short, like a bad month for the wicked Ayatollah and his red-handed fanatics. Then the Europeans started hollering.

(Davis, 1980)

You will find this type of paragraph especially helpful when using classification and comparison/contrast, because you can give three very different examples or three similar ones, depending on the point you want to make. Using dates the way the author has done here is a good arouser of audience interest. It is an effective way to begin because it creates an element of suspense; in fact, many modern films *(Three Days of the Condor, All the President's Men, The Shining)* flash dates on the screen in a cinematic use of this same technique.

Occasionally, you may want to modify the three-example technique to organize and pile up information in an analysis. Here is another example from the Picasso article quoted earlier:

Topic   He was at the forefront of several major revolutions in art: With

Example   Braque he coauthored the beginnings of Cubism and the introduc-

Example   tion of collage into the realm of high art; alone, in his 1912 construc-

Example   tions, he allowed sculpture to renounce volume in favor of planes; and in the late Twenties, with Julio Gonzalez, he established welded, direct-metal sculpture as an important modern form.

Thesis His accomplishments lived up to his gifts, a rarity in human experience, and if they did not do so at every point in his long career, that says little beyond admitting he was not a god after all.

Here the author identifies several stages in Picasso's career as examples to support her opening statement in the paragraph. These examples also lead to a thesis statement central to the essay's analysis of Picasso.

Problem-Solution

Sometimes this pattern also fits into the topic-restriction-illustration format, and is useful for persuasion. Look at this opening paragraph on toxic waste:

Problem It began with Love Canal, an out-of-control chemical dump in upstate New York that wakened the nation to the dangers of hazardous waste. Now, nearly two years later, toxic waste is fast becoming the nation's biggest environmental problem — far more pervasive and far less controlled than nuclear waste, and consequently a far
Explanation greater threat to health. Chemicals once thought benign have been shown to cause cancer, birth defects and a variety of lesser ailments. Long-buried dump sites dot the landscapes in most states, and some of them are slowly poisoning underground water supplies. Industry produces 62.8 million tons of hazardous waste each year — 500 pounds for each American — and only 10 percent of it is disposed of properly. Public alarm is growing, and after years of neglect, Federal regulators are just beginning to crack down. "Who knew what polychlorinated biphenyls were in 1976?" says Gwen Molinar, whose neighbors in tiny Wilsonville, Ill., united to shut down a chemical dump.
Solution "If industry knows how to produce these chemicals, it should learn how to dispose of them."

(*Newsweek*, May 19, 1980)*

Bang! The solution may not be as simple as Gwen Molinar suggests, but it elicits that sense of identification, a feeling of wanting to respond "that's right!" that leads the reader into the essay. Even if readers disagree with the statement, chances are they will be pulled into reading the article to see if the magazine intelligently covers the plight of industry in this area or deals with the issue one-sidedly. By placing a simple but sharply worded suggestion at the end of the paragraph, the article thumps the audience on the head.

There is another pattern here. Notice that topic-restriction (together in the second sentence) is followed by three illustrations. The paragraph patterns, like the larger thought patterns discussed earlier, seldom appear in isolation. The effective composer uses them to achieve variety and to create a setting for the main idea. For purposes of discussion, however,

---

*Copyright 1980 by Newsweek, Inc. All Rights Reserved. Reprinted by permission.

these patterns have been treated more or less as pure forms. Knowledge and practice, however, will enable you to arrange the forms as you like.

Here is one more problem-solution paragraph, one that appears in the middle of an essay entitled "The Superwoman Squeeze." As a middle paragraph, it is a more clear-cut problem-solution example. Because of its flexibility for use in presenting both sides of issues, problem-solution is found frequently in analysis as well as in persuasion.

Problem As domestic duties shift increasingly from housework to child care, new kinds of helpers are needed.

Solution 1 The National Committee on Household Employment is promoting special training and certification — along with better pay and professional treatment — for home child-care workers.

Solution 2 Because such workers are in short supply, however, increasing numbers of families turn to illegal aliens for live-in day care. "Illegal workers do work no one else wants to do, and that allows society to continue unchanged," says Marion Houston of the U. S. Labor Department.

                  (*Newsweek*, May 26, 1980)*

The final paragraph pattern that needs to be examined is question-answer. This needs little explanation except to say that it can be used in two ways. The first is as a direct question with a brief reply — sometimes a nice way to lighten a heavy section of prose or to involve a live audience.

Question How bad can a man be whose idea of a fun evening is to go home, put on his 'jamas and watch "Little House on the Prairie?"

Answer I have been asking myself that question about Ronald Reagan for some time, and I now have an answer in the form of another question.

Question (topic) The other question is: Can Ronald Reagan control his own right wing?

                     (Kraft, 1980)

In this piece the slightly whimsical question that opens the paragraph leads into the serious question that is really the writer's topic. Had he begun with the second question instead of the first, he would not have aroused as much curiosity about his topic. Now he has the readers hooked.

The second way to use this pattern is to pose an indirect question, with the answer representing a summary of information or opinion. This can be an effective conclusion in an explanation. Look at the last paragraph of the *Newsweek* essay on toxic waste:

Question Given the high cost of cleaning up and the legitimate scientific quandary about the extent of the hazard to public health, the overriding question about toxic pollution is just how much safety — and how much risk — the nation can afford.

Answer   Though some environmentalists worry about an irreversible increase in the cancer rate, the consensus view is more cautious. EPA's
regulations, says Beck, aim at a prudent reduction of the chemical
hazard — not the total elimination of risk. "The society that reaps
the benefit from chemicals must recognize that it has to accept some
risks," Beck says. With scientific knowledge so scanty, the trade-offs
will be tough to calculate — and the EPA has only begun the job.

(*Newsweek*, May 19, 1980)

All of the paragraph patterns just discussed can be integrated with the
larger essay and speech patterns discussed in preceding chapters. Perhaps
the best way to understand these relationships is to look at Table 12-1. To
begin with, assume that your discourse, an argument or an informative
essay, perhaps, involves the use of any or all of the time/space patterns
listed across the top of the chart. Notice that these time/space patterns are
grouped according to the ways they most frequently support or interact
with each other. The chart indicates four basic groups of the patterns with
subscript numerals for clarity; other groupings are, of course, possible,
depending upon your aim. Now read across the top of the chart and then
down to discover which paragraph patterns may be useful in helping you
develop the particular time/space patterns you plan to use.

Once again, these categories are by no means exhaustive. The chart

Table 12-1 Using Paragraphs as Patterns

Paragraph Patterns	Time/Space Patterns			
	1 Narration 1a Description	2 Description 2a Definition 2b Comparison/ Contrast	3 Process 3a Analysis 3b Comparison/ Contrast	4 Analysis 4a Cause/Effect 4b Classification 4c Exemplification
Broad Topic Explanation Restriction (Narrow Topic) Example		2, 2A	3, 3A	4
Topic Restriction Illustration	1A	2, 2A	3, 3A	4
Example Example Example Topic	BOTH	ALL	3B	4B, 4C
Problem Solution Solution			3, 3A	4, 4A
Question Answer	1A	2, 2A	3, 3A	4, 4A

merely suggests the way the patterns interact in the work of many good composers. In your own writing you will undoubtedly discover arrangements that work successfully for you. All writers do. That is how style develops.

CREATING EMPHASIS

Coherence is a feature essential to all successful paragraphs. **Emphasis,** on the other hand, is a technique used to highlight those paragraphs that composers find most crucial to their point. Composers create emphasis by paying particular attention to the placement and arrangement of sentences within paragraphs and of words within sentences. Because emphasis is easily listened to, as well as readable, it leaves an impression. In fact, the reason the first two examples below have been chosen from advertising is that many ads are written to be heard on the radio and television as well as to be read in magazines. To be effective in all these media, the words must be carefully chosen and carefully placed. Look at the wording of the following advertisement:

> In the craft of creating Waterford Glass, little has changed in centuries. Each piece is still an individual masterwork, from the blowing of the molten shape to the cutting by hand of the finished crystal. In the creation of such beauty, there has not been yet devised a finer machine than man. So some pieces may not always be available.
> But would you rather we rushed?*

Everything in the ad points to what the manufacturers consider its biggest selling point: its perfection, a quality maintained by humans and not machines. To emphasize this quality the advertisers have turned what competitors would consider a liability into an asset.

As a way of indicating their fairness to the customer, they warn that "some pieces may not always be available"; but what a build-up first! The ad opens with a time marker that sounds like historical precedent: "little has changed in centuries." This is followed by exemplification, using parallel structure — "from the blowing . . . to the cutting . . ." Parallel structure is a good way to build emphasis in paragraphs. The next sentence ends with another emphatic phrase: ". . . there has not been yet devised a finer machine than man." The reader is carried away — again perfection is implied. The next sentence, naming the product's one drawback, is introduced by *so*, setting up the final contrast, the appeal to logic implied by "But would you rather we rushed?" The drawback is made to seem

---

*From *Ireland of the Welcomes,* May-June 1980, p. 31.

minor, one that no reasonable person could object to. A shorter version of the ad, reduced to its premises, might look like this:

> We create perfection.
> Therefore, what you order isn't always in stock.
> Of course, perfection takes time.

The two transition words, *so* and *but*, are essential to the punch of this ad. Remember that a good way to create emphasis is to give your subject a powerful build-up, using examples and placing your most important words (especially adjectives) at the end of the sentence. Then end with a question introduced by a contrastive *but*. It works well. Consider how you would write an ad for crystal from a competitor's standpoint, one that emphasizes quick replacement of damaged pieces because of the company's rapid production of stock items.

Look at another ad, this one for an automobile. Whatever else can be said about auto ad and liquor ad creators, most of them understand language and how to use it.

> What do you think it is? Need some help? Then consider the following: the car you're looking at has a CIS fuel-injected engine that can take you from 0 to 50 in 8.5 seconds. And power-assisted disc drum brakes that can take you from 50 to 0 in less than three. It has 4-wheel independent suspension to keep you from going like this on bad roads. And front-wheel drive to give you responsive handling even in bad weather. In back, there's a trunk so large it can hold six suitcases. All standing up. And inside, there's room enough for a family of four. Got it yet? Well maybe it would help to know that for all its impressive performance on the road, this car still turns in a pretty spectacular performance at the gas pump. It gets an EPA estimated 25 mpg; 40 estimated highway. (Use "estimated mpg" for comparisons. Your mileage may vary with weather, speed and trip length. Actual highway mileage will probably be less.)
>
> You *still* don't know? Then we should probably mention one last thing. This car doesn't look like what it is, and most people have a hard time guessing. So why don't we just tell you. We call it the Jetta. Of course *Autoweek* had a different name for it.
>
> They called it, "Another winner from Volkswagen." *

This paragraph, which is of course accompanied by an impressive picture of the car itself, uses techniques different from the last one. By now all of them should be familiar to you. This simply demonstrates one way of putting them all together to create emphasis. It begins with a question, for questions, whether at the beginning or end, are always an excellent device for creating emphasis and making your words memorable. Much of the emphasis in this paragraph, however, stems from the simple

---

*Courtesy of Volkswagen of America.

use of coordination. In the beginning of the ad, every other sentence (the examples) begins with *and*. Then comes a question, then parallel structure: "for all its impressive performance . . . this car still . . ." Statement in the form of additional support is next, and then the obvious conclusion, introduced by *so*, a natural climax built up to by the list of *ands*. The paragraph's structure looks something like this:

Question
Topic (car)
Examples (using *and* as transition — coordination)
Question
Question
Conclusion (using *then* as transition word)
Emphatic structure placed at end of sentence: ". . . one last thing"
Conclusion (using *so* as a transition)
Answer (to all three questions)

Of course, the ending is spectacular in its casual understatement. **Understatement** is a device many composers neglect.

One other thing about emphasis; save your best argument till last, and then don't overdo it. If it is a good argument, there is one simple rule: Say it well, but say it only once.

This final example, with numbers added, is from a student paper that argues forcefully that baseball players deserve high salaries. While not the concluding paragraph, this is Joanne's last and strongest argument. How does she emphasize her main point — that baseball players have limited careers?

1. The major reason professional baseball players deserve high salaries is that their careers are limited.
2. The average professional plays for only twelve seasons.
3. Many are forced to retire sooner becasue of injuries or personal problems.
4. In 1973, a rookie pitcher named Bart McDonnell pitched only five games for the Chicago Cubs before he tore cartilage in his right elbow.
5. This ended his pitching career.
6. But for most (the average) players the career ends in the twelfth season, when they can no longer compete physically with the younger players.
7. Although there are exceptions, such as Carl Yastrzemski of Boston and Pete Rose of Philadelphia, who are entering their seventeenth and fifteenth season respectively, most players complain that their legs are gone around the age of thirty.
8. Others notice that they can no longer "hit a good fastball."
9. After his ninth season, Cleon Jones of the New York Mets complained that he could not time the curve ball any more.

10. Once the average professional's playing career has ended, he is not prepared for another career.
11. Only one-fifth of all Major Leaguers are college graduates, who are more likely to be prepared for an alternative career.
12. A lucky few of the other professionals acquire jobs as sportscasters after their playing careers end.
13. But these jobs are available only to the best players with the most expertise.
14. Also, these positions are usually occupied for long periods of time by one person such as Ralph Kiner, who has been broadcasting for the Mets for the last twenty-three years.
15. Another minority (about ten percent) of the players will become Major League coaches and managers.

— Joanne Barrick

Everything that should be present in good paragraphs is present here. The ending of a sentence is usually its most emphatic part, the part we tend to remember, and Joanne's sentence 2 ends with *only twelve seasons,* so that early on, the shortness of a baseball career in comparison with most other careers is demonstrated. Joanne then gives what she acknowledges to be a rare example, one that nevertheless supports her point and leads to her contrastive phrase, "But for most . . .," in sentence 6. Good writers know the value of supplying examples immediately after stating the thesis, rather than simply restating the thesis in a number of different ways.

If you look carefully at the paragraph, you will notice that Joanne achieves most of her emphasis through transitional coherence, along with time markers. Nearly every sentence begins with one or the other: *although, after, once, only, but . . . also.* Information relating to career brevity is placed at the end of the sentence, the naturally emphatic position: "Their legs are gone *around the age of 33*"; "*he could not time the curve ball anymore*"; ". . . he is not prepared for *another career*," and so on. Using this very specific information and placing it well, Joanne uses emphasis to create a strong case. Can you find anything else that helps the paragraph work?

One kind of emphasis is not discussed here, but you may have noticed it in the advertisements: variety of sentence length. This will be discussed fully in the chapter on sentences.

COMPOSING SCENE SETTERS

This section requires less explanation than the previous two because the examples speak for themselves. Perhaps the best thing for you to do is to read for and listen to techniques that are particularly effective, then in your daily writing and speaking practice the techniques you have discovered.

Scene setters work for nearly every type of writing and formal speech: narration, exposition, and persuasion. They capture your perceptions, your style, and your audience. Sometimes they make that difference, so hard to define, between a *B* and an *A*. There is really no trick to them. Like catching the perfect wave or hitting a clear high *C*, they simply require a great deal of practice and a love for the art.

The two paragraphs below open an informative article on the Dublin Zoo. Of course, description is frequently a necessary element in any type of composition. Look at this particularly effective example of it:

> The Bactrian camel looked at me happily. It was a cold winter's morning and I was its only visitor. I had never seen anything so ridiculous, all lumps and bumps and a coat that was *like a bad perm and an old rug*. It was delighted with my attention. I think it thought I was fancying it. It got all coy and coquettish and rubbed its neck in what it hoped was a sly and come-hither way.
>
> I decided not to be a tease, it wasn't fair to encourage it, so I went off and looked with mute adoration at a sulphur crested cockatoo. It ignored me. I whistled and cooed and was just as silly as the Bactrian camel had been with me, but it was useless. *The Zoo is Just Like Life* I thought to myself philosophically and left the aviary in a sulk.
>
> (Binchy, 1980)

Much of the effect here is created by use of **figurative language**. The overall effect is to endow the animals with the human capacity of flirtation, with all its whims and wiles. The analogy in the last sentence expresses this cleverly. It makes the reader smile. In a smaller way, the author uses figurative language in the form of a simile (underlined in sentence three). The author could have begun the article this way: "The Dublin Zoo is located in the heart of Ireland and entertains 600,000 visitors a year," but then she would not have made her readers care. As it is, her opening is hard to resist.

A good essay or speech needs a good start. It is a simple rule but one that deserves serious reflection. Many students enjoy writing or speaking about sports. Sports writing above all must move; it must evoke action. The paragraph below is from a student speech detailing the whys and wherefores of the Boston Celtics' 1980 comeback:

> When Larry Bird shoots, he flicks his wrist, causing the ball to rotate with a beautiful arc. The result more often than not is two points, sometimes three if it's beyond 23 feet. The moment the ball passes the rim it tingles the twines with a swish that is pleasant to the ear. Other times, the shot kisses or banks off the glass backboard like a feather and again the ball goes through the iron.
>
> — John Grossaminides

John did not arrive at this opening the first time around. His first try went like this:

> The Boston Celtics have made a remarkable comeback this year. They have made a 180-degree turnaround from last year. A large part of their success comes from their acquisition of Larry Bird. But there are other factors, too.

Not a bad opening, but not an exciting one, either. In fact, the problem with this paragraph is that because of its last sentence, John felt compelled to list and discuss every single factor in the Celtics' comeback when what he really wanted to do was focus on Larry Bird. The result was a disorganized speech. It was suggested to John that he begin by putting his audience right into the game, centering on Larry Bird. It worked. He reshaped the speech, and he made his audience care. Look also at how he ended the speech:

> The fans go wild, with thoughts of another Championship flag hanging from the rafters at Boston Garden. All because of this young man from Indiana. Larry Bird has been the catalyst in changing the team's mediocrity to superiority and dominance. He made each player blend his talent into a cohesive, close-knit team, a sort of family, with everyone rooting for the other. This is why this team could do the same thing the old Celtics did in the 50s and 60s — win 12 World championships in 13 years. A dynasty reborn.

Notice that a sentence fragment is often an effective stop. It's abrupt — and unforgettable. After all the struggle of composing, most of us like what we have said to be remembered.

Consider how *Newsweek* wrote about one of the most spectacular geologic events of the century, the eruption of Mount St. Helens:

> For geologists, it was the chance of a lifetime: to study the earth from the inside out. For photographers, it augured a season of spectacular sunsets; 1981 should be a vintage year for wall calendars. For everyone outside its deadly penumbra of ash, Mount St. Helens' eighteen hours of rage may pass unnoticed — or it may cause noticeable disruptions in the world's climate. Scientists say they aren't sure — and a lot will depend on what the unpredictable volcano does in the next few weeks.
>
> (*Newsweek*, June 2, 1980)

Sometimes a good method of approaching a really *big* subject is to describe its implications for several groups of people, as the author did above. Notice the buildup: "for geologists . . . for photographers . . . for everyone else . . ." — parallel structure again. Composing from the particular to the general can encompass several viewpoints at once — and involve your readers and listeners as well, since they are likely to fit into one of the categories you name.

As some point in college courses or later on the job, you will want to tell someone how to do something. Sometimes this is done perfunctorily; a simple explanation will do. At other times you may want to lead into it more gracefully by supplying a rationale for doing whatever it is or by providing an anecdote explaining what piqued your interest in the subject. Here are two paragraphs from *Bon Appétit* magazine, the prelude to a recipe:

> It is our custom on the Feast of St. Valentine to blow the budget on a less than economical dinner for two. By the middle of February we figure we deserve it. As it happens, we have no birthdays or other excuses for extravagance in the late winter and, inevitably, the optimistic plans we made for a vacation somewhere closer to the equator have evaporated in a hail of deadlines or been sacrificed to some pressing — but boring — cause like buying a new furnace.
>
> One of the nice things about cooking just for two is that it's possible to splurge occasionally at the market without going into debt. While it's true that the price of the cut of beef called for in this month's main course is reminiscent of those quoted on the Zurich Gold Exchange, two fillets cut from the small end of the loin cost less than, say, tournedos for a family of eight. The same can be said of the tiny shrimp which, judging from the rates we've seen in the fish markets lately, must be practicing some form of population control. This recipe for two, however, requires only a few of them.
>
> (Morgan, 1980)

The authors empathize with their readers — they know people are on tight budgets, and February can be a dull month; they have found a way to make both plights a little brighter and are willing to share it. (By the way, the recipe is excellent: shrimp in cucumber nests with dill dressing.)

The paragraphs used as examples in this chapter have been designed to give pleasure to the audience as well as to communicate ideas and information. Perhaps they will inspire you to compose paragraphs that are enjoyable to read; but remember, practice is essential.

SUMMARY

There are three general goals to strive for when composing paragraphs: directing paragraphs toward the aim of an essay or speech, writing with coherence, and writing with style. To achieve these goals, revision is often necessary. The discourse will not shape itself on the page the first time around.

Remember the possible problems. To begin with, information in the paragraph should lead to only one topic, or thesis, depending on the position of the paragraph in the essay or speech. Thesis statements usually occur early in an essay or speech and may be restated at the end. Topic sentences, on the other hand, are present in all good paragraphs.

Next, paragraphs should be arranged to fit the larger time/space pattern of the discourse. Compare or contrast like elements in adjacent paragraphs — in other words, keep apples with apples, and not with oranges or pears. Effect should follow cause, and so on.

Always look for three kinds of coherence. Transitional coherence is achieved by using words like *and, but, although, again, so, thus,* and *therefore*. Other words, adverbials like *during, later, occasionally, next, first,* and *in the middle,* provide time/space coherence. Finally, to facilitate lexical coherence, keep pronoun referents clear.

Polish paragraphs by arranging them in patterns, by creating emphasis, and by writing scene setters where appropriate. Remember to check the table on page 330, as well as to manipulate the patterns to suit your own needs. Create emphasis by shifting transition words, by using parallel structure, and by placing the most important information, the punch line, at the end of a sentence or paragraph. Read and listen widely, study creative scene setters, and practice them in your own composing.

KEY WORDS

transitional coherence	narrow topic
time/space coherence	emphasis
lexical coherence	understatement
readability	figurative language
paragraph patterns	scene setter
broad topic	

EXERCISES

1. Look through old essays for any with organizational problems. Can you revise or rearrange your paragraphs to give the essay more unity? Are your paragraphs coherent? Would a scene setter help the essay?

2. Read the following paragraph, an opening paragraph from a student essay. Which techniques discussed in this chapter has Linda used? Is it an effective paragraph? Can you change anything to make it better?

   My body radiated heat, my skin felt like leather, my chest blossomed with blisters, and my eyes were swollen shut. No, I had not contracted a rare disease. Unfortunately, however, I had recklessly broiled myself in the Miami beach sun. While my lobster-red skin sizzled in the hotel's cool bathtub water, I tried to recall where I had gone wrong. Since my primary goal had been to impress my high school friends with a golden tan, I had forgotten that there is a proper art to bronzing one's body. A complex strategy is involved in acquiring, enhancing, and preserving an ideal suntan. I had neglected to consider the hazardous aftereffects of careless sunbathing; in addition, I had also disregarded the precautionary steps that must be followed before, during, and after the frustrating struggle to obtain a perfect tan.

— Linda Meltzer

3. Identify the coherence levels in the following two paragraphs from a student's persuasive essay. Should some coherence markers be shifted to achieve emphasis? Where are they used most effectively?

One of the students' main grievances concerned the school's high cost, yet they ignorantly contributed to an increased charge by wasting enormous amounts of food. In five minutes, the students threw enough garbage to have filled every air molecule with food that could have fed thousands of starving children. This waste was both selfish and stupid. Eventually, it was the students who felt the financial burden of their pointless food fight. Every year, the meal book expense increased, reflecting the previous semester's Halloween disaster. In addition, the charge may have risen when dining hall structures were damaged or students were hurt by flying glass and silverware. It seems so senseless to have wasted such large amounts of food, especially when the students inevitably paid for their impulsive foolishness.

Furthermore, food fights simultaneously triggered hostility throughout campus. As the local newspaper tore the school's reputation to shreds, hostile feelings flared across the University. Initially, the administration blamed the dining services. Consequently, the dining service punished the students with bag lunches and security guards at every tension-filled meal. Unnecessary anger raged as innocent bystanders were struck with flying glass and silverware. Food fights left a painful reminder long after Halloween week.

— Linda Meltzer

4. Looking back at the examples in the chapter, practice the five paragraph patterns. First, bring in several examples of each pattern from magazine or newspaper articles. Discuss them in class. Did the patterns mesh with the larger time/space framework of the essay? Did you find any opening paragraphs with weak patterns, patterns that left you vague about the topic of the paragraph? Revise any paragraphs the class decided were ineffective. Then practice writing original paragraphs in each of the five patterns.

5. Using the same topic for all, write a paragraph to fit at least three of the patterns. Which pattern seems most appropriate to your topic? Why?

6. Using your favorite hobby as a topic, write one or two lead-in paragraphs for a how-to essay or speech. You might want to tell your

classmates why they might enjoy the hobby, or how you yourself became involved with it.

7. Collect six examples of scene setters from magazines or newspapers. Bring them into class and read them aloud. Discuss which you like best, and why. Then try practicing your own scene setters for the following topics:

a local disaster (fire, transportation strike, flood, snowstorm)
a childhood memory
the computer revolution
alternative energy
review of a movie (book, play, television show)
a recent sports event
the student union
your favorite red-tape complaint (postal service, school financial aid, computer errors on bills)
a local museum

REFERENCES

Becker, A.L., "A Tagmemic Approach to Paragraph Analysis," *The Sentence and the Paragraph* (Champaign, Illinois: National Council of Teachers of English, 1966).

Binchy, Maeve, "Close Encounters of the Bactrian Kind," *Ireland of the Welcomes* (May-June, 1980), p. 18.

"Car Stereo," *Stereo Review* (June, 1980), p. 62.

"Children of Divorce," *Newsweek* (February 11, 1980), pp. 59, 63, 66.

"Coping with Toxic Waste," *Newsweek* (May 19, 1980), pp. 34–35.

Davis, L.J., "Banker's Casino," *Harper's* (February, 1980), p. 43.

Feifer, George, "The Dark Side of Solzhenitsyn," *Harper's* (May, 1980), p. 58.

"Gauging the Fallout," *Newsweek* (June 2, 1980), p. 27.

Goldberg, Vicki, "Monument to Tempestuousness," *Saturday Review* (May, 1980), pp. 48–49.

Kraft, Joseph, "Ronald Reagan and the Right Wing," *The Providence Journal* (June 18, 1980), p. 33.

Middleton, Thomas H., "Light Refractions," *Saturday Review* (May, 1980).

Morgan, Jink and Jefferson, "Cooking for Two," *Bon Appétit* (February, 1980), p. 30.

"[The] Superwoman Squeeze," *Newsweek* (May 26, 1980), p. 78.

Volkswagen Advertisement, *Harper's* (June, 1980), p. 12.

Waterford Crystal Advertisement, *Ireland of the Welcomes* (May-June, 1980), p. 31.

Winterowd, W. Ross, "The Grammar of Coherence," in W. Ross Winterowd, ed., *Contemporary Rhetoric* (New York: Harcourt Brace Jovanovich, 1975), pp. 225-232.

13. Sentence Varieties: Style as Choice

Sophistication of style is one of those things like love or happiness: writers and speakers who try too hard to achieve it lose it. Yet there are many successful ways of improving style. Nearly all of them begin at the sentence level, and all of them require practice.

Think of the suggestions and the exercises provided in this chapter as finger drills at the piano, or as scrimmages before the big game. The idea behind all these activities is the same: to practice the basics so precisely that variations on them begin to come naturally, so that to the observer they appear to be without effort or strain. We shudder with the pianist who misses several notes in the trill or glissando, or with the football player who muscles his way to the goalline only to drop the ball. As an audience to writers and speakers we shudder at words that torture and twist themselves into sentences instead of flowing smoothly, calling little attention to themselves because of their careful arrangement. It is an old cliché but a true one that a professional makes the difficult appear graceful and effortless.

There is a distinction here between grammar and style. If you are having difficulty with grammar, you should ask your instructor for help and refer to the handbook required in your course. The concern of this chapter, however, is with making your sentences clear and, beyond that, graceful. The preceding chapter on paragraphs introduced the concepts of readability and ease of listening, which refer to how well an audience can understand a text or process the information given in a speech. For stylistic reasons, we do not compose every sentence in the manner easiest for an audience to process. If we did, our discourse would be boring, and that in itself lessens understanding. In fact, the main purpose of this chapter is to increase your awareness of the variety of sentences, particularly in the composition of written discourse. There are some factors, however, that lessen a work's readability without contributing to its style; on the contrary, they detract from both style and ease of understanding because they force the reader to re-read a sentence two or three times in order to process its meaning.

These factors are a result of many things, from simple failure to edit carefully to an unawareness of how to match the ending of a sentence with its beginning. This first section of the chapter will demonstrate some ways in which writers cause their readers confusion, and then suggest methods for eliminating this confusion.

AGENCY: WHO DID WHAT TO WHOM

Agency can be most clearly defined by the above heading; that is, agency concerns the question "Who did what to whom?" Because English is primarily a subject-verb-object language, the agent of the sentence, the doer, is frequently in the subject position. There are times, however, when writers want the agent in something other than subject position, or choose not to name the agent at all. If these choices are made purposefully the sentence will still make sense. When there is unintentional vagueness about who is performing the action, however, a sentence can leave readers with the feeling they have missed something. This feeling will cause them to read the sentence over, looking for the missing agent. They may read the sentence two or three times and then give up. The meaning has been lost.

Checking sentences to make sure that verbs are accompanied by someone or something doing the action solves many common writing problems. The examples provided in the next sections illustrate the various difficulties caused by a misplaced agent. Remember, grammar is not necessarily the point here; clarity is. Here is an opening sentence from a student essay on nuclear energy:

> The famed movie *China Syndrome* created much concern over nuclear energy. The major concern is of the decreasing amount of supplies, in reference to energy.

The author created a trap for herself in the second sentence by not identifying whose major concern she was writing about. The concern of the movie? Or of the viewers? She chose an abstract subject for her sentence rather than a concrete one (*concern* instead of *movie* or *viewers*), then followed it with a weak verb. After she wrote "decreasing amount of supplies," she feared she had not identified the supplies, and so added the wordy phrase *in reference to energy*. To clarify her thought, she might have left *concern* as the subject, but given it a stronger verb, like this:

> The major concern revolved around the decreasing amount of energy supplies.

Now the subject of the sentence is doing something. There are times when the verb *to be* is the only one that will serve; however, when coupled with an abstract noun like *concern* it frequently produces a vague sentence.

Another way to handle the sentence would be to clarify whose concern it was. The sentence might be worded like this:

> The major concern of its viewers was the decreasing amount of energy supplies.

Here, using *concern* with the verb *to be* creates little confusion because we have the identifying phrase *of its viewers*.

Here is a short section from the same essay. Keep in mind that when dealing with a technically complex issue like nuclear energy, it is especially important that ideas be clear.

1. There is no reason for imposing danger upon surrounding communities.
2. Examples of imposing danger upon communities with unsafe leakage in containments, as transportative compartments are sent to various sites.

Look at sentence two. Again, there is no doer at the beginning of the sentence; instead, there is a *noun phrase*: "Examples of imposing danger upon communities." This is called a noun phrase because the noun *examples* is followed by an explanatory prepositional phrase beginning with *of*. Had she ended the sentence after *communities* with a verb (Examples of imposing danger upon a community *abound*; or Examples of imposing danger upon a community *are numerous*), her sentence would have been readable; but she decided to include an example within her sentence: "with unsafe leakage in containments, as transportative compartments are sent to various sites." Unfortunately, she began her sentence with a structure, the noun phrase, that did not lend itself to her ending. Her prose plunged ahead, losing control of the sentence and creating a structure we will deal with later, the misplaced modifier. It sounds from the sentence as though *communities* rather than *compartments* have "unsafe leakage in containments."

Begin the sentence with an *agent*, a *doer*, and see how it gains clarity.

Nuclear plants send transportative compartments to various sites, sometimes endangering communities because of unsafe leakage in containments.

The key to making the sentence readable is to track down the verb, *are sent*, ask "Who sends?" and make the answer the subject of the sentence. The rest falls into place.

Sometimes writers create mazes in the course of trying to integrate unfamiliar material from a magazine article into a sentence of their own writing. It is usually better either to quote directly or to put the material all into your own words, even though you will, of course, footnote those ideas that are not your own. This ensures that you understand what you have read, and prevents you from tacking on a phrase that destroys the meaning of your sentence.

Gerunds: -ing Subjects

Here is another sentence with a different kind of problem. Again, awareness of agency would have rescued the author.

Undercoating a car will not be forced into buying a new car every few years.

The meaning is disrupted — we want to read the sentence over to see if we have skipped a word. There are several ways to rewrite this:

> The person who undercoats his car will not be forced into buying a new car every few years.

> If you undercoat your car, you will not be forced into buying a new one every few years.

> Undercoating a car prevents buying a new one every few years.

The word *undercoating* is a **gerund**, a verb used as a noun. We use gerunds all the time in both speech and writing: "Swimming is my favorite sport"; "Cooking relaxes me." Sometimes writers or speakers pile them up, forgetting that they are, after all, actions that must be performed by someone or something; they themselves cannot perform. Here is another example:

> Driving a car on the lift, using the four security bars, and placing them on the frame are the car's balance.

The three gerunds *driving, using,* and *placing* are not the car's balance; they are not the agents; but that is what the sentence implies. The same agent who drives, uses, and places must be responsible for the balance of the car. The author apparently decided in mid-sentence that the security bars are the car's balance, and overlooked the fact that he had already created three actions with no doer. Since he is writing a how-to essay, it would have been appropriate to address the reader directly, like this:

> After driving the car on the lift, you must balance it. Use the four security bars and place them on the frame.

In this version, the driver (you) is the subject. If the author wished to keep his gerunds, he could say:

> After driving the car on the lift, using the four security bars and placing them on the frame will balance the car.

Using and *placing* can balance the car; they cannot be the balance.

One last example of gerunds in trouble:

> Editing, cutting and being able to alter the finished product are only a few examples of the technical superiority that a movie has over a play.

The problem is similar to the last one — the gerunds have no agent. The movie does not edit and cut; nevertheless, that is the only agent the sentence supplies. So who does? The film director. Rewritten, the sentence reads:

> Because a film director can edit, cut, and alter the finished product, a movie is technically superior to a play.

Once again, it is possible to keep the gerund structure and still make sense:

> Editing, cutting, and altering the finished product are the prerogatives of a film director, but not of a play director.

This discussion does not imply "Don't use gerunds," but it does caution against using them carelessly. Remember that they are verbs, and do not allow them to perform actions that only animate subjects are capable of.

Dangling Modifiers

The concept of agency is especially useful in dealing with a sneaky little construction that finds its way into the prose of even the most polished writers and speakers. It can create uncontrollable laughter or simply a lot of red marks in the margin of the paper, depending on the degree of change in meaning. Finding the agent will help you to track it down. It is called the **dangling participle**, the verbal without a subject. Here are some examples from student papers: (Participial phrases are underlined.)

> <u>Feeling helpless,</u> my face turned a fiery red.
> <u>Checking for leaks,</u> the car drove smoothly off.
> <u>Having on lots of warm clothes,</u> the cold didn't bother us.
> <u>Worrying about my sister-in-law,</u> school became unbearable.

Look at the examples above. Who felt helpless? Who checked for leaks? Who wore the clothes? The problem with participles arises when a writer forgets to follow the participial phrase with its proper agent and instead introduces a new agent-verb construction. Why does this go unnoticed by a writer or speaker? It is because frequently, though not always, the writer or speaker is, in fact, the doer of the participial action. In every case above, the authors themselves performed the action of the -*ing* word, and in every case the authors forgot about audience. Since they were writing about incidents that had happened to them, the authors's minds were focused inward, on themselves as doers of the action. This is understandable, but the inward focus caused confusion for readers.

Composing, as we described it in the second chapter, is an egocentric activity. Once the prose is on the page, however, we must step back from ourselves to scrutinize meaning as others may interpret it. The microscope is for writing; the telescope is for revising.

Before revising the above examples, look at a second kind of participial error, one in which the author is not the agent of the action expressed. This is perhaps a less noticeable error; the sentences just fail to sound right, and the reader or hearer may have difficulty identifying the source of the trouble:

> Whether it be *asking questions, sticking up for your rights,* or *becoming more educated on the subject,* it's up to the consumer to do it.

Passing by the white flag, it was now or never for the three-time champion.

In these sentences, the agent of the *-ing* action is named in the main clause; in the previous examples, the agent was not named at all, making the error more obvious. Fortunately, there is a single rule applying to sentences that open with participial phrases: the agent performing the action expressed in the participial phrase must immediately follow that phrase. Following are some possible sentence revisions, with agents italicized, that apply this rule:

Feeling helpless, my face turned a fiery red.
Revision: Feeling helpless, *I* turned fiery red.
Checking for leaks, the car drove smoothly off.
Revision: After checking for leaks, *we* drove the car smoothly off.

Notice that to revise these sentences, the missing agent (the narrator of the event) was supplied, but the verb already present in the main clause was used. The following two sentences require a different kind of change:

Passing by the white flag, it was now or never for the three-time champion.
Revision: Passing by the white flag, *the three-time champion* knew it was now or never.
Whether it be asking questions, sticking up for your rights, or becoming more educated on the subject, it's up to the consumer to do it.
Revision: Whether it be asking questions, sticking up for your rights, or becoming more educated on the subject, consumers must accept responsibility.

This time in revision, an agent named in the main clause was used, but a new verb was supplied to make the sentence work. You can avoid dangling participles if you remember that like the verbs they are derived from, participles must have an agent, someone or something who performs the *-ing* action.

A third kind of participial error occurs when it is impossible to revise the sentence in either of the two ways demonstrated above; that is, when the main clause of the sentence contains neither the appropriate verb nor the appropriate agent as in the following sentence:

Having on lots of warm clothes, the cold didn't bother us.

To maintain the opening participial phrase in this sentence, we would have to supply both agent and verb in the main clause:

Revision: Having on lots of warm clothes, we were not cold.

When both subject and verb must be applied, however, it is sometimes more graceful to reword the sentence, changing the participial phrase into a clause to supply the needed information:

Since we had on warm clothes, the cold didn't bother us.

Here is another headless modifier:

Worrying about my sister-in-law, school became unbearable.
Revision: Worrying about my sister-in-law, I found school unbearable.
More gracefully: When I was worrying about my sister-in-law, school became unbearable.

Changing from a phrase to a clause eliminates the problem of agency, since clauses contain or imply agents and verbs within their structure.

When both are grammatically possible, choosing between a phrase and a clause is a stylistic option. The briefer structure of the phrase connotes continuous action; on the other hand, adverbial clauses can indicate necessary time elements, creating the time/space coherence studied in the chapter on paragraphs. The final word is this: agency is all-important in sentences opening with participial phrases. Look for it when you revise.

Misuse of Passive Voice

Passive voice means that the agent, the performer of the action, is not in the subject slot of the sentence.

Active: The boy hit the ball.
Passive: The ball was hit by the boy.

There are times when a writer wishes to switch the focus of a sentence to achieve emphasis, to shift responsibility, or to create suspense, and so prefers to place the subject as the last word in the sentence. Here are some brief illustrations of the passive voice.

(Emphasis) The commencement address at Clifton University this year was delivered by none other than Robert Redford.

Small children might use the passive voice to avoid responsibility: "It got broken"; or "It got dirty." Sometimes this avoidance of responsibility is used in a more sinister way:

Bombs were dropped today on a tiny village in a little-known part of the world.

Whatever the viewpoint on the morality of that last sentence, it illustrates our main point in this brief section: the passive voice should be used for a reason, either stylistic or semantic, and it should not be overused. Research has shown that sentences in the passive voice are more difficult for readers to process; this extra difficulty should be created purposefully rather than at random, and it should clarify emphasis or focus rather than obscure it.

Sometimes writers encounter difficulty when creating a descriptive scene in which there is no active observer. Rather than using first person, they write as though all actions are observed or performed by some invisible being, and unintentionally detract from the scene they are creating. Here are two examples:

> The sun sits in a sparsely woven nest of white clouds against a blue sky. A slight but steady breeze whispers through the trees. The sound of birds is heard. In the distance, a small grayish cloud is seen.
>
> — Mary Denton

> Placing oneself in the waters of Narragansett Bay manages to keep the pressure down and temperatures cool; however, the constant routine of summer has got to be broken. Then a ticket for a Motels concert in Providence in a week is purchased indiscreetly, almost unnoticed entirely.
>
> Then about mid-week, word makes its way down from Boston that the Motels have sold out two shows in advance. Interest is heightened, so now when the Motels' latest record is played, the radio volume is turned up.
>
> — Jeff Riccio

Both Mary (who described the suddenness of a spring shower) and Jeff wrote good essays with lively details; but students in their evaluation group commented that several sentences "sounded awkward," or were "hard to follow." Jeff's last sentence, containing three passives, received a lot of criticism on this point. Jeff solved his problem by rewriting the essay in the first person, making himself the performer of the actions. His last sentence then read:

> My interest was heightened, so now when I heard the Motels' latest record on the radio, I turned up the volume.

Mary, on the other hand, decided to keep her observer anonymous, but provided her agent with actions so that her last two sentences changed from:

> The sound of birds is heard. In the distance, a small grayish cloud is seen.

to

> Birds chirped throughout the woods, while off in the distance, a small grayish cloud appeared, scudding across the horizon.

In this way she removes the questions in the reader's minds: "Who saw?" "Who heard?"

Passive voice requires that writers think carefully about where they place the agent of a sentence as well as about the reasons for that placement. It is a stylistic option to be chosen consciously and where appropriate.

THE RELATIVE CLAUSE: PROPOSITIONS

The **relative clause** is a useful structure for embedding information within a sentence. It sometimes functions as a referent, directing our attention toward a particular person, place, or thing:

1. The person *who rents the house is responsible* for all damage done to the house.
2. The only other noise in the bus terminal was a sleepy voice, *which announced that my time of escape had arrived.*
3. The causes *that led to his downfall* were numerous.

To fully understand the relative clause (as well as all other sentence structures), how it is used, how it may be misused, and why it is occasionally preferable to replace a relative clause with another structure, it is important to know something about the nature of sentences. Every sentence is either one proposition or a combination of propositions. A proposition is a main word or phrase around which other words and phrases organize themselves into meanings. A relative clause, then, is one sentence (proposition) embedded within another. In looking back at sentence 1 above, we find that we can separate its propositions as follows:

A. The person rents the house.
B. The person is responsible for damage done to the house.

The main word of each proposition, the word around which the meaning revolves, is *person*. This is why when the propositions are combined, the word *who* (a relative clause marker) directly follows the word *person*. Sentence 3 is similar. Here are its propositions:

A. The causes led to his downfall.
B. The causes were numerous.

Here the main word of both propositions is *causes*, followed by the relative clause marker *that*.

As readers or listeners, we have little trouble processing the relative clauses in sentences 1 and 3. Because of our intuitions about the language, our native competence, there is no need to consciously separate the embedded propositions and examine them individually.

Restrictive and Nonrestrictive Clauses

Sometimes a relative clause is potentially ambiguous. There are two possible meanings for the combined propositions. Because of this ambiguity, it is important to look at the difference in meaning between **restrictive** and

nonrestrictive clauses and to know the device used for clarifying possible ambiguity.

> 4. Professors who always lecture overtime are inconsiderate. (Restrictive)

If we look back at Sentence 1 of this section, we could paraphrase it to read:

> The person rents the house, and is responsible for all damage done to it.

However, we could not paraphrase Sentence 4 the same way.

> Professors always lecture overtime, and are inconsiderate.

The relationship between the propositions is different here; it is not one of equality. The relative clause *who always lecture overtime* is restrictive; it limits the class noun *professors* so that a paraphrase might read: "Those professors are inconsiderate who always lecture overtime."

If, though, a writer did wish to imply that all professors lectured overtime, and that therefore all professors weere inconsiderate, the writer must compose the sentence like this:

> 5. Professors, who always lecture overtime, are inconsiderate.

Then the clause *who always lecture overtime* is said to be nonrestrictive because it includes and modifies the class of all professors. The commas make the propositions equal rather than separate, so that the sentence "Professors always lecture overtime and they are inconsiderate" is now a fair paraphrase of the meaning.

Look at one more example:

> 6. Professional athletes *who are obviously more concerned with self-glory than teamwork* anger their fans.

If we said that sentence to a friend without pausing between the words, the friend would more than likely agree with us, because it uses a restrictive clause, limiting the guilty athletes to a sub-class of all athletes; but if we paused slightly in the places where the commas are below, we would more than likely end up in an argument:

> 7. Professional athletes, who are obviously concerned with self-glory more than teamwork, anger their fans.

The commas, then, are the written equivalent of an oral pause. If we say the sentence aloud with pauses, we imply that all athletes are guilty of a primary concern with self-glory, we imply no restrictions. Because of the drastic change in meaning between restrictive and nonrestrictive clauses, it is important that writers know the convention, the comma placement, responsible for indicating their desired meaning accurately. It is equally important that speakers be aware of their placement of pauses in sentences containing clauses that are ambiguous.

Relatives in Trouble: The Which-Trap

The relative clause is one kind of **modifier**. Modifiers provide various options for expanding on the two pivotal words in every sentence, subject and verb. In a later section of the chapter we will examine these options and the various rhetorical effects they create under the heading "free modifiers."

The point here is that the relative clause, while it is a very useful modifier, is also one that is overused and sometimes misused. Composition research indicates that college-level writers whose style is judged mature and pleasing to read have developed a variety of structures other than the relative to express their ideas within a sentence. In short, although they continue to use relative clauses where appropriate, they avoid depending on them as their sole device for embedding propositions. Over-use of relative clauses results in dull prose because every sentence begins to sound alike. Worse, readability suffers when writers pile up two or three lengthy relatives in one sentence, neglecting to consider that important element, agency. Here is a passage of prose too heavily dependent on the relative clause structure:

> (1) They figured that they had less time to do the same amount of work which is not necessarily true. (2) There are many parts of many courses that could simply be shortened which would solve the time problem. (3) There are some professors that I feel who think that their courses are the only ones that students are taking. (4) This semester had too many tests and assignments. (5) The professors must realize that even though material may be shortened, tests cannot be compressed that much.
>
> — Greg Taylor

What is the effect of this paragraph on you as a reader? What happens in sentence *three*? Look at the number of propositions embedded in this sentence:

1. There are some professors.
2. I feel.
3. Some professors think.
4. Their courses are the only ones.
5. Students are taking these courses.

Five propositions are not too many in one sentence — certainly, a reader can process that number with relative ease; but marking every relative clause structure is unnecessary and makes the sentence appear more complex than it is. One way to simplify the sentence is to delete the relative clause markers:

> I feel that some professors think their courses are the only ones students are taking.

Now, even though the relative clause structure is still the main embedding device, the reader need not confront a jumble of *thats*.

AVOIDING THE WHICH-TRAP: USING SHORTER STRUCTURES TO ADD DETAILS

Modifiers that Repeat

You have probably always thought of the subject and verb as the primary elements of the sentence. To the extent that we cannot have a grammatically correct sentence without the subject and verb (except for the imperative), this notion is correct; yet readers gain very little information from these two elements. For the reader, the modifier, or **comment** as it is sometimes called, is the essential part of the sentence, the part that supplies details about the **topic** of the sentence.

The president was shot today,	causing shockwaves in capitals throughout the world.
Topic: Word or words around which the sentence revolves.	Comment: Supplies details about the topic.

The kind of modifier about to be demonstrated picks up on the topic of the sentence, repeats it, and elaborates upon it. It is called a **resuming modifier** because it resumes the line of thought begun in the topic. Read the following sentence:

> His work exhibits the awareness of writing that he stressed in his first text.

Now see how the topic of the sentence may be emphasized more directly by switching from the relative clause structure to the more emphatic resuming modifier:

> His work exhibits an *awareness* of the consequences of writing, *an awareness* he stressed in his first text.

Consider another example, one that will illustrate the kind of detail the comment can allow the writer to pile up:

> We can all remember *moments* like that,
> *moments* when the October colors,
>> the chilled picnic wine, and
>> the company of a special person all merge
>>> into a perfection seldom recaptured.

Resuming modifiers need not always begin with nouns; sometimes adjectives may be the most important part of your topic:

> The Mona Lisa's smile has been called both
> *enigmatic and coy,*
> *enigmatic* because the source of her amusement
>> is out of range of the viewer and will forever
>>> remain her secret, and
> *coy* because it is only a half-smile, as though
>> she is withholding her pleasure at will.

Sometimes you will want to elaborate on the verb:

> After the accident that left him a quadraplegic, Kevin's
> only wish was to *survive,*
> *to survive* the physical torment of daily therapy
>> needed before he could perform the simplest tasks, and
> *to survive* the mental trauma imposed by the pitying stares of
>> strangers.

Resuming modifiers, then, allow the writer to emphasize the topic or key word of the sentence, whether that word be a noun, adjective, or verb. At the same time, they allow the reader to take a breath after the first phrase in the sentence and then follow the writer's main idea through the rest of the sentence.

Modifiers that Summarize

The **summary modifier** is similar to the resuming modifier in its placement and purpose. Instead of repeating the topic, however, it uses a synonym for the topic word, which is called an appositive. Once again, it is a device that allows the reader to pause and then focus on the topic of the sentence.

> In Milic's terms, then, we must somehow stimulate
> *stylistic* options,
> *those decisions* he claims are made unconsciously
>> and usually below the sentence level.

Notice how the above use of the modifier allows the writer to comment on the topic in a way that the relative clause does not:

In Milic's terms, then, we must somehow stimulate
stylistic options that are made unconsciously and
usually below the sentence level.

Here is another example:

Some residents have proposed *to close the beach
to non-residents* in order to preserve an area for themselves —
an issue that has stirred up much controversy among the towns-
people

Free Modifiers

In addition to the structures described above, there are others called **free
modifiers**, which also comment on the topic of the sentence. They are
called free modifiers because they may be easily shifted around in the
sentence. These structures also allow a writer to continue a sentence
without the clutter of *which's* and *that's*, but they are slightly different
from the other two. They function most effectively in final position in a
sentence, where they follow the verb but comment on the subject or topic.
Perhaps the most frequently used free modifier is that which begins with
the *-ing* form of the verb. Look at the difference in the flow of the
following two sentences:

It is argued that processes are initiated within the individual (such as
free association and transference) and that these act on the mental
apparatus which can imply a dualism which Freud did not practice.

It is argued that processes are initiated within the individual (such as
free association and transference),
acting on the mental apparatus, and therefore
implying a dualism Freud did not practice.

Using the *-ing* verb forms increases the readability of the sentence above,
reducing the number of relative clauses from four to one. Here is one
example of how much information can be clearly presented in free modifier form.

The diesel engine has a number of advantages, which include
operating continuously for long time periods with
minimum breakdown danger,
burning more air that sparks ignition engines, and
creating less of a fire hazard than the gasoline engine,
since diesel fuel is less combustible than gasoline.

Packed into relative clauses, the above information would be difficult to
digest, but *-ing* verb forms allow the reader to move through the three
advantages of diesel fuel with ease. Free modifiers can also begin with the
-ed or *-en* form of the verb:

In this way, solar heat is maximized,
> *focused* by the mirror on a small receiver that
>> follows the motion of the sun,
> effectively *trapped* by the longer wavelength.

The adjective phrase is a less frequently used free modifier, but is positioned in the same way as the verb phrases.

Madden writes an interesting lead,
> *effective* in part because of her well-placed alliteration.

As you practice the techniques illustrated in this section, remember these points:

1. Resuming modifiers comment by repeating a topic word and elaborating on it.
2. Summary modifiers summarize a topic word by using a synonymous word or phrase and adding further comment.
3. Unlike resuming and summary modifiers, which occur singly, free modifiers usually occur in clusters. Use them when you wish to provide your reader with detailed comment on the topic of your sentence but want to avoid a bulky pile-up of relative clauses.

CREATING COHESION: USING BOUNDARY SENTENCES TO COMBINE OLD AND NEW INFORMATION

Chapter Twelve pointed out that a paragraph in which the ideas are clearly related is a coherent paragraph. It discussed the importance of transition words for expressing such relationships as cause/effect, contrast, and conclusion, as well as the importance of words like *now*, *outside*, and *during*, which create necessary time/space coherence.

No matter how much coherence your essay achieves as a whole, however, it will lack cohesion unless the connections among thought units are clearly marked for the reader.

Boundary Sentences

Marking the connections among thought units is the function of **boundary sentences**. A boundary sentence defines a new area of thought and marks it off from the preceding material, even though it may contain some reference to information already presented.

Not every paragraph represents a new thought unit, so not every paragraph requires a boundary sentence; but it is important to recognize where boundaries occur in the mind of the reader and to help your readers relate the new information you are presenting in a paragraph to information you have previously provided in the essay — old information. Successfully relating new information to old information gives an essay **cohesion**.

Another factor that lends cohesion to an essay is repetition of the pattern words, the vocabulary associated with analysis, process, comparison/contrast, and so on. The pattern chapters contain lists of these words; now would be a good time to review the vocabulary of a particular pattern so that what is illustrated will make sense to you.

The function of boundary sentences and the importance of cohesive devices are illustrated in the following sentences from a student paper written to inform readers about alcoholism in women. Cue words are italicized.

> The *reasons* women drink are distinct from the *reasons* men drink. (1) Dr. Gomberg, who has done extensive research on women and alcohol, has determined that alcoholism *is not the same in women as it is in men*. (2) He feels that *"... physiologically and socially female alcoholism has a different set of causes and effects*. (3) Marriage, children and the inevitable frustrations and stresses lead the vulnerable woman towards problem drinking." (4) Her problem is compounded by the fact that as a woman, she must hide her drinking habit. (5) *While men can* socially drown their sorrows in whiskey, *women are* allowed such a privilege *only* in private.(6)
>
> A *double standard* exists concerning appropriate behavior for *men and women* in terms of alcohol consumption *in public*. (7)
>
> Alcohol consumption for women *is related to both psychological and biological pressures*. (8)
>
> The saddest part of all is the fact that alcohol abuse *on the part of a woman has more serious consequences than it does for a man*. (9)
>
> — Debbie Gleavey

The first six sentences quoted above belong to a single paragraph. Notice that the first sentences provide *cue words*, which set up two patterns for the reader: cause/effect and contrast. The cue words are *reasons* (cause/effect) and *distinct from* (contrast). Sentence 6 of this paragraph reinforces the contrast pattern by providing information about both men and women through the use of an introductory dependent clause.

Sentence 7 includes the words *double standard* and *men and women* to cue the reader that the basic pattern of contrast is continuing even though a new topic, alcohol consumption in public, is being introduced. Sentence 8, even though it is several paragraphs removed from the first sentence quoted, reminds the reader of the cause/effect pattern by moving into the topic of psychological and biological pressures underlying alcohol consumption. These pressures are explored for several paragraphs until the writer wants once more to focus the reader's attention on the contrast pattern. Sentence 9 introduces new information *(more serious conse-*

quences), but relies on the established pattern of contrast *(on the part of a woman . . . than it does for a man)* to fit this information into the essay's overall framework.

There are no rules for writing boundary sentences, since their content depends, of course, on the topic you are writing about. The sample sentences we have just studied are subtle in their cues to the reader, depending upon repetition of topic words and reinforcement of the two organizing patterns of the essay, contrast and cause/effect.

Linking Discourse

Sometimes boundary sentences include more obvious references to material either already covered in the essay or about to be introduced. They refer to this material through the use of **linking discourse**, discourse about discourse. Linking discourse includes phrases like "as I have previously noted," "the *next problem* to be dealt with," "*another issue* concerns. . . ." Phrases like these are direct cues to readers that although what they are about to read is linked to the previous material, they will be encountering new information. Here are some sample sentences from a student essay that discusses the benefits industries will receive by locating in Rhode Island.

This sentence is followed by a pie diagram and a paragraph detailing chronological comparisons of industry in Rhode Island.

The following model depicts the makeup of Rhode Island manufacturing. (1)

Reference to information already presented, but indicating a new topic.

But now we should look at the stories behind the figures. (2)

Reader knows advantages are about to be enumerated.

What brings about this influx of *new manufacturing*? Let's look at some of the advantages to locating your company in Rhode Island. (4)

New information, but repetition of topic word.

There are tax incentives that help to lure new manufacturing to Rhode Island. (5)

Reference to topic in beginning of sentence; proper placement of new information at end of sentence. This sentence is followed by a paragraph on one facet of the new topic.

Obviously, in the location of any new manufacturing facilities, *there must exist available and suitable real estate*. (6)

Refers to real estate; lets the reader know this paragraph is still on the same topic as the previous one.	The Department of Economic Development maintains a full-time staff, which keeps a constant inventory of *sites and available buildings*. (7)
Linking discourse allows reader to remember the general introduction; reader is now about to get information focusing specifically on high technology.	*As mentioned a little earlier in this report*, the State of Rhode Island is interested in attracting *high technology industry*. (8)

— Chris Linderson

Although you will probably find yourself unconsciously writing boundary sentences as cues to yourself during your drafting stages, be sure they are present in your final draft in a form that is cued to the reader. Add them to your revision checklist so that you may consciously provide the necessary cues. In the next section we will examine the effects created by the various ways in which you place information within a sentence. You may want to make some of your boundary sentences special by practicing these placement techniques.

Can you pick out the boundary sentences in the following student essay? What do they do for the reader?

While walking down the street proudly wearing my new pants, I heard an awful noise. No, it wasn't a whistle. I had caught my pants on the heel of my shoe and ripped them! I was totally upset; after all, I had spent half of my paycheck on them. After cursing fashion designers for making pants suitable for people six feet tall and apparently forgetting shorter people like me, I decided to head back to work. Hoping that no one would notice my less than beautiful pants, I decided to do something about the problem.

How easy everything would have been if I had known how to hem a pair of pants properly. In order to save yourself from the frustration and embarrassment I experienced, you should learn too! You'll need a pair of pants that are too long for you, scissors, thread, straight pins, and a sewing needle.

The first step is to wash and dry the pants if they are new; therefore, shrinkage will occur before you make a permanent hem. After your pants are completely dry, take down the original hem by removing the stitches. Then press the lower legs of the pants with a hot flat iron. Once this is done you are ready to begin adjusting the pants to the correct length.

Now you should try the pants on while wearing the shoes you plan to wear with the pants. Mark the desired length by placing two straight pins through the material, one in the front and one in the back. This is much easier done by a second person but can be accomplished by one. Now take the pants off and cut the excess material on each leg, leaving approximately two inches below the straight pins.

You are now ready to enter the next stage, creating the hem. First you should turn the pants inside out. Then turn the cut edge up approximately a half inch and pin. Measure at several points to be sure you have pinned correctly. Now press the pinned portion with a hot iron and remove the pins.

Next, turn the pressed portion upward to the pin mark you created earlier. Pin both pant legs at this length, placing a pin every one and a half inches. Be sure not to put the two sides together during this process. Once all the pins are in place turn the pants right side out and try them on again. Wearing the shoes you will wear with the pants, check the length in a mirror. If the length is appropriate you will move onto the next stage. If it is not, you must re-pin the hem as described above.

Now that your pants are pinned at the length you want, you are ready to sew. Cut about two feet of thread off your spool and place one end through the eye of the needle. Pull the thread through until the two ends meet. Now tie a double knot at the end of the thread. Starting at the seam of the pant leg, put your needle through a few stitches of cloth of the upper portion of the pant leg and through the bottom of the portion you have pinned into place. Pull your needle and thread through until the knot is at the edge. If your knot isn't large enough, the thread will slip through. Therefore, you must make your knot larger and begin again.

Repeat this stitching process placing your needle approximately one-sixteenth of an inch away from your last stitch. Continue until your thread becomes too short thus creating difficulty in placing the needle in the desired position. At this point you must cut the thread close to the eye of the needle. Tuck this piece of thread into the pinned portion and prepare your needle with new thread, knotted at the end. Begin sewing again, restitching approximately three to four stitches to insure permanency of the stitches at the end of your thread.

Go through the above process until you meet with the starting point. Before cutting the thread from the needle restitch back and forth about four times to insure permanency. Cut the thread close to the point where it protrudes from the material. Remove your pins and press the hem with a hot flat iron. Do the same for the other leg and you are finished.

Although the hemming process seems complicated and time consuming, the results are worthwhile. You now own a pair of pants that are the right length for you. You will never have to worry about tripping on them again!

— Gail Gariepy

CREATING SPECIAL EFFECTS: EMPHASIS AND PARALLELISM

Emphasis: Beginnings and Endings

> *Emphasis* . . . is largely a matter of controlling the way a sentence ends. When we maneuver into that stressed position our most important information, the natural emphasis we hear in our mind's ear underscores the rhetorical emphasis of a significant idea. Even that natural stress, though, can seem weak and anticlimactic if we let a sentence end on lightweight words.
>
> (Williams, 1980)

Joseph Williams, from whose book the above quote is taken, has spent a great deal of time studying the features of a rich, emphatic prose style. Learning to manipulate these various linguistic features will add style and grace to your writing. The previous chapter examined the way emphasis builds in a paragraph. Since a paragraph is, after all, an organized unit of sentences, many of the same principles apply on the sentence level. As you begin to use modifiers more frequently and fluently in your writing, your sentence length will become more varied and your range of options will widen. Some of your sentences, in fact, will be like mini-paragraphs. For these sentences the techniques of **emphasis** will be particularly important.

The ending of a sentence is where the emphasis naturally falls. For this reason, boundary sentences should contain old information in the introductory phrase or clause and should place new information, including the new topic word, at the end of the sentence. For example, one student wrote a boundary sentence like this:

> In making ear-piercing a macho and communal event, Christopher is not alone.

The next section of her paper discussed the various cultures in which ear piercing was indeed a *communal event*, a rite of passage for men. The emphasis was not, as her sentence implies, on Christopher. To use a reference to Christopher as a transitional device was appropriate; however, the order of the sentence should be reversed to read:

> Christopher is not alone in making ear piercing a macho and communal event.

Here the emphasis falls on *event*, which leads into the section nicely. Here, from the same essay, is another boundary sentence that places the old information early in the sentence and introduces the new key word *public* toward the end.

It may also be that besides choosing a more macho method for reasons having to do with rites of passages, some men are embarrassed to come to a place as public as the mall.

In addition to placing your new information at the end of the sentence, there are ways to present it with a certain amount of elegance and flair. Some words are *lightweights*. One particularly strong structure for ending a sentence (or a clause within a sentence) is the **nominalization**, the noun derived from a verb or an adjective. Another is the prepositional phrase beginning with *of*. These structures may be used separately or in combination; either way, their use allows a sentence a solid ending.

Lewis H. Lapham, editor of *Harper's*, has a most dignified style. Compare the effect of the following two sentences:

> The landscape has been encumbered with a mediocre public architecture, and American painting illustrates aesthetic theory.

Lapham's version:

> The landscape has been encumbered with a public architecture *of unsurpassed mediocrity*
> and American painting addresses itself to the *illustration of aesthetic theory*.

Lapham's version has a ring to it; the first version is ordinary. The above sentence and those following in this section are from an article of his (Lapham, 1981).

Another Lapham sentence illustrates the emphasis these particular structures can lend to a sentence.

> He risked this *observation* [end of clause]
>   in what he thought was secular company in the merchant city of
>   *New York* [end of clause]
>   but his remark produced the *shock of blasphemy* [noun phrase]
>   in the midst *of a synod of bishops*. [noun phrase]

And another:

> Listening to them talk, I noticed that
>   the *discussion of cultural subsidies*
> tends to confuse artistic and political patronage
> and that by and large the speakers neglect to make
> a number *of useful distinctions*.

The sentence might be written with the nominalizations in the forms from which they are derived, like this:

> Listening to them talk, I noticed that *discussing* cultural subsidies tends to confuse artistic patronage and that by and large the speakers neglect to make a number of things *distinct*.

Although using the verb *discussing* and the adjective *distinct* shortens the sentence by a few words, their use makes the sentence less graceful. This is in part because using the verb and adjective forms rather than the two noun forms detracts from the **parallelism** of the sentence.

Parallelism

When the emphatic structures named above are combined with a device called parallelism, style can become powerful. Parallelism simply means that when a sentence has several parts to it, these parts must all be of the same grammatical form. The following sentence does not sound quite right. Why not?

> They bear a responsibility to the taxpayers or the stockholders,/ maintaining racial harmony,/ pleasing the chairman's wife,/ tax laws,/ and the way their city or state functions.

If you take the first part of this sentence, "They bear a responsibility to . . .," and place it with any single one of the last four comments (separated by slashes), the sentence will make grammatical sense. For example,

> They bear a responsibility to maintaining racial harmony.

> They bear a responsibility to the way their city or state functions.

But since the writer chooses to include a series of comments in the same sentence, these comments must all be in parallel form, or the sentence reads disjointedly. Here is Lapham's original version:

> They bear a responsibility to the taxpayers or the stockholders,
>   to the appearance of racial harmony,
>   to the preferences of the chairman's wife,
>   to the vagaries of the tax laws, and
>   to the pretensions of the city or state
>   in which they do their principal business.

Each of the four modifiers now has the same form, a prepositional phrase beginning with *to* followed by an emphatic ending, and another prepositional phrase beginning with *of*.

> Here is another sentence illustrating effective use of parallel structure:
> The events of the twentieth century have referred the question
>   *to the politicians,*
>   who have access to the final weapons
>   and [coordinator]
>   *to the scientists,*
>   who perhaps will discover the secret of immortality.

In the sentence above, the parallel structures are linked by the simple device of coordination, which, when not overused, can make the parallelism even more powerful.

Parallelism is essential when shaping a series of modifiers, but you can vary the degree of parallelism you use in the series according to the effect you wish to create. You might write:

> In the summer, I like to fish on rainy days,
>   to swim when it's sunny, and
>   to spend my evenings with a good book.

This is a perfectly acceptable sentence, but when you begin to develop your style consciously you may choose to create a more lyrical pattern:

> In the summer, I like
>   to fish when the day is dull and rainy,
>   to swim when the sun is bright and hot,
>   and,
>   when evening comes cool and hazy,
>   to settle down comfortably with a good book.

Notice that the last item in this series reverses the order of the parallelism, putting the when clause before the infinitive (*to*) phrase. Because the paired adjectives, *dull and rainy, bright and hot, cool and hazy* create an additional level of parallelism in the sentence, lending it even more rhythm, the writer chose to alter the pattern of the final element just enough to avoid monotony.

This style is not the only one you should strive for. In fact, there are times when the first version of the above sentence, written in a lighter, chattier style, would be more appropriate. However, you must use parallelism when your sentence consists of a topic followed by a series of comments or modifiers. You may choose to use parallelism, along with coordination, when you wish to connect two elements — especially relative clauses — with a special emphasis.

The Lewis Lapham sentence was one example of such a sentence. Here is another:

> I don't know which is more deceptive:
>   the lover who pledges fidelity and forsakes it
>   at the earliest opportunity
>   or
>   the one who claims "freedom is healthy" but
>   means "don't let me catch you."

Parallelism is a pleasure for the reader, true, but for the writer who masters it and uses it well it is also a source of pride.

SPEAKING WITH STYLE: SENTENCES TO BE HEARD

The characteristics of well-formed sentences that have been discussed apply to sentences in general, whether they are to be spoken aloud or read silently, but there are some special considerations you will want to keep in mind when writing sentences to be heard. These considerations grow out of the now-familiar differences between the live audience who will hear your speech and the silent reader who is alone with your prose.

Readers have the opportunity to go over a confusing sentence or a sentence packed with information. For this reason, sentences like those we illustrated in the section on free modifiers — topics with several comments attached — represent an acceptable and even desirable style when they are to be read. Generally though, it is a style that is difficult to process aurally, particularly when the comments contain highly technical information. On the other hand, the shorter resuming and summary modifiers are helpful to hearers. They allow for an audience's need for **redundancy**, repetition of new information in a sentence. Listeners require a good deal more repetition of key words than do readers if they are to follow your topic and your ideas all the way through your speech.

Hearers also need shorter sentences, and sentences marked with heavily rhythmic patterns. Parallel structure, in fact, is an especially important speaking device. If you refer to the section on parallelism in Chapter Three, for example, you will find several sentences from student speeches that made effective use of parallelism to incorporate important details.

The speeches of Martin Luther King, John F. Kennedy, Jesse Jackson, and Edward Kennedy exhibit a number of rhetorical devices, elegant phrases long remembered because of the particular **balance** and emphasis with which they were consciously constructed. Look at the following sentences from John F. Kennedy's inaugural address:

> Let the word go forth from this time and place, to friend and foe alike, that the torch has been passed to a new generation of Americans, born in this century, tempered by war, disciplined by a hard and bitter peace, proud of our ancient heritage, and unwilling to witness or permit the slow undoing of those human rights to which this nation has always been committed today at home and around the world. (1)
>
> Let every nation know, whether it wishes us well or ill, that we shall pay any price, bear any burden, meet any hardship, support any friend, oppose any foe to assure the survival and the success of liberty. (2)
>
> If a free society cannot help the many who are poor, it cannot save the few who are rich. (3)
>
> Let us never negotiate out of fear, but let us never fear to negotiate. (4)

> All this will not be finished in the first one hundred days. Nor will it be finished in the first one thousand days, nor in the life of this Administration, nor even perhaps in our lifetime on this planet. But let us begin. (5)
>
> And so, my fellow Americans, ask not what your country can do for you; ask what you can do for your country. (6)
>
> (Kennedy, 1961)

Sentence 1, although it is quite lengthy, contains no material that is difficult to comprehend. Kennedy could therefore successfully use a series of *-ed* verb forms, then end the sentence with a coordinated parallel structure, the "to which . . . and . . . to which . . ." construction.

Sentence 2 relies for its effect on the buildup of short phrases in the present tense, so that they stir the audience to action. Try saying this sentence aloud, practicing pauses and emphasis. Rhythmic sentences can lose their power if they are not delivered well. Of course, Kennedy's delivery style, along with his resonant Boston accent, settled his phrases firmly in the minds of his hearers.

Sentences 3 and 4, like the famous sixth sentence, employ a balanced structure, putting together two phrases equal in length and form and then shifting the meaning cleverly in the second phrase. Quote 5 begins with a short first sentence. The long middle sentences uses repetition of time elements, each progressively longer (one thousand days . . . life of this Administration . . . lifetime of this planet). What creates the greatest effect, however, is the last simple, short sentence, beginning with a coordinator of contrast: "*But* let us begin." Variety of sentence length is an important factor in a speech. It helps in avoiding the natural monotony created by a single voice speaking for a long time, no matter how gifted that voice or how exciting its message.

Parallelism also marks this quote from Martin Luther King's Nobel Prize acceptance speech:

> I accept this award with an abiding faith in America and an audacious faith in the future of mankind. I refuse to accept the idea that the "isness" of man's present nature makes him morally incapable of reaching up for the "oughtness" that forever confronts him.
>
> (King, 1964)

The phrase "abiding faith . . . audacious faith" illustrates alliteration, another effective device in speaking because it allows for the repetition of language sounds, particularly initial sounds of words. The more rhythmic repetition you can build into your speech the easier you will make it for your hearers to remember what you have said. Notice we said rhythmic repetition. Random repetition will lose your hearers rather than winning them to your side.

Sentences like the ones we have just quoted from Kennedy and King are not likely, barring sudden inspiration, to surface in rough draft. They require skill in the manipulation of language as well as an appreciation of its subtleties. They require a final draft that pays attention to how well you say it as well as to what you say. To some extent, they also require ego-involvement, a desire to be remembered.

If you learn to write rhythmic sentences, your speech will be worth the effort.

SUMMARY

There are common sentence errors that can distract and lose your reader; many of them occur because the writer has forgotten to include an agent in the sentence. Check for this error whenever an essay is returned to you marked *dangling modifiers* or *misplaced modifiers*. Much of the stylistic work you do at the sentence level should take place consciously in your final draft. It is here that you should replace an overabundance of relative clauses with tighter, shorter structures, here that you should strive for special emphasis, and here that you should created rhythm through the use of devices like parallelism and balance. Developing your writing style is a lifelong pursuit requiring a sensitivity and dedication to language. The techniques we have suggested in this chapter will work, but they will work only with practice.

KEY WORDS

agency	topic
gerunds	free modifier
dangling participle	boundary sentence
passive voice	cohesion
relative clause	linking discourse
propositions	emphasis
restrictive, nonrestrictive clause	nominalization
modifier	parallelism
comment	redundancy
resuming modifier	balance
summary modifier	

EXERCISES

1. Rewrite the following sentences, supplying an appropriate agent:

   Checking the discrepancy in the data detected an error.
   Patterns of skipping class in the Spring are less inclined to study.
   Making sure you have all the ingredients for the first step when you
      begin working with stained glass.

2. Rewrite the following sentences, undangling the modifiers:

   Lounging around the room, the telephone rang.
   After raining all week, the dam burst and flooded the valley.
   Jumping from the plane, the parachutes opened.
   Listening to the radio, my favorite song came on.
   Having eaten his dinner, we saw the lion smile.

3. Add either resuming or summary modifiers to the following topics:

   The only television programs I really like are situation comedies, . . .
   Hockey, soccer, and baseball are exciting spectator sports, . . .
   Camping is one of the best of all recreations, . . .
   Registration is a fatiguing and humiliating experience, . . .
   Attending musical events of all kinds is my favorite leisure activity, . . .

4. Use free modifier clusters to comment on the topics below:

   It was an absolutely perfect summer day, . . .
   The constant beat of that music distracts me, . . .
   He had many faults but I loved him anyway, . . .
   The constant infighting of that particular department has disrupted the
      company, . . .

5. Listen to a public speech. Take a notebook with you and write down
   any sentences or phrases that seem especially rhythmic or memorable.
   Then try to analyze them in the terms we have discussed in this
   chapter. Try writing some imitations of your own, practicing parallelism and balance and building rhythm.

REFERENCES

Kennedy, John F., Inaugural Address, January 20, 1961.

King, Martin Luther, Nobel Prize acceptance speech, December 11, 1964.

Lapham, Lewis H., "The Counterfeit Muse," *Harper's* (September 1981), pp.
8–12.

Williams, Joseph, *Style 10 Lessons in Clarity and Grace* (Glenview, Ill.: Scott,
Foresman, 1980), p. 85.

14. Developing Critical Skills

> *No thinker shall suffer for his thoughts* is equivalent to the rule: Nothing important shall ever happen.
>
> (Hocking, 1937)

The point that philosopher Hocking is trying to make in this aphorism is well worth thinking about. We communicate in order to share our ideas with others; part of that sharing involves appraisal and criticism of what we have said. As we exchange views our ideas take on sharpness and sophistication. Developing skills in critical appraisal of discourse is thus essential to the ends of human communication.

Unfortunately, giving and taking **criticism** is often a painful process (although the word *criticism* means finding both faults and merits). Giving and taking criticism well is a fine art. While many of us are reluctant to criticize or be criticized, it is equally disturbing to have our ideas met with stony silence or a half-stifled yawn. The ideal path is narrow: we must be open both to the giving and the taking of criticism. On the other hand, we should not allow ourselves to be tyrannized by criticism.

This chapter will provide some practical tips on the critical appraisal of communication. The discussion is limited to the criticism of written essays and formal speeches, although when you read the chapter you may want to extend it to other aspects of communication.

ORAL COMMUNICATION

Asking and Answering Questions

Most planned communications will be followed by a question-and-answer session. You should know in advance if there is going to be one, and you should also know how long it will be. The Q-A period is no less important than any other part of the speech event; indeed, this is often the time when the speaker and audience can interact with each other naturally, when judgments are made about the speaker's credibility, and when loose ends may be tied up with regard to the topic. It is a realistic time to practice critical listening, thinking on one's feet, and managing an audience. It thus deserves special attention and involves two questions for discussion: How do we ask good questions? How do we answer questions effectively?

As a preliminary consideration, we should discuss whether to take questions during the speech or ask the audience to hold them until the speech is completed. Both ways can work. Quite often, however, taking questions during the speech can be troublesome. Questions might require clarification and repeating; they might be unrelated to the topic — or simply terrible questions. Further, one question can lead to another, and before long the sense of flow in the event is gone. It is generally wiser, except when you must do otherwise, to ask that questions be held until the end of the speech.

Asking Questions. If you are listening carefully, you will become aware of three distinct aspects of the speech, the by-now-familiar point-pattern-detail components stressed throughout this book. Just as *point, pattern,* and *detail* are key words for you in planning your communication, so are they critical variables as you listen and prepare to exchange views with the speaker.

1. *The Point.* Remember that the point is the thesis of the presentation, whether actually stated or not. If you are sure that the speaker has not made a point, that ought to be your first question:

- Senator Hall, I listened to your remarks on the proposed solid waste management plant, and I am still not sure if you are for it or against it. What is your position?
- Governor Grant, you said in your speech that you loathe garbage and waste, and that you are looking very favorably at the proposed solid waste management plant bond referendum; but are you for or against the present plans for the plant? What is your exact position?

Do not allow speakers to wiggle out of commitments or to avoid being purposeful. Even straightforward descriptions and definitions have a point:

- Carl, you described the plight of the Cambodians quite vividly. I was moved. But why? What led you to do so? (What was your point?)
- Fran, you say that obscenity is defined by community standards and situations. I may or may not agree. If you could repeat or make your point for taking this position, it would help.

Because purposeful communication is so important, make your first question somehow related to the point. If the point is clear, you should move on to thinking about questions based on pattern.

2. *The Pattern.* If a speaker's point ought to raise expectations for you, the pattern ought to fulfill those expectations. If it does not, a second level of questioning arises. Look at how this works.

If the speaker announces, for example, that a pro-con analysis of an issue is going to be given, you should note, either mentally or on your note sheet, that announced purpose. Listen carefully for the pros and cons. Are they given balanced treatment? Do biases emerge? Are the same issues treated pro as well as con? If you have doubts, ask a question about pattern:

- Jim, you promised us a fair look at the volunteer Army problem, but I don't see much in your speech against it. I'd like to know why so much is said about its having failed before I am ready to decide on this issue. What else do you know?

Every pattern raises similar expectations. Comparisons ought to be clearly equivalent, examples ought to be typical and real (whenever possible), narratives should move through events in such a way that one event prepares for the next. Arguments should lead to specific recommendations. If they do not, ask a question:

- Sue, you've convinced me that coupons are a cleverly-disguised ripoff of consumers, but what can any of us do about it?

In the conventional patterns we have presented in this book, each standard question becomes a potential topic for clarification. Did the speaker demonstrate enough needs so that a change is in order? Did the solution seem practical? Critical listeners get involved in pattern recognition and want their expectations fulfilled. If these expectations are not fulfilled, good listeners raise questions. If they are fulfilled, a third level of questioning remains: questions about detail.

3. *The Detail.* The subject of detail raises many questions for critical listeners; a few are suggested. Use this discussion as a guide to your own inventiveness.

Much of this book so far has tried to reinforce the notion that people ought to support assertions. Critical listeners insist, therefore, that assertions be followed by support. Those that are not become the crux of questions later on:

- You said, Dr. Kowalski, that nutrition is taught in American medical schools, but you failed to give us any examples of this. Which medical schools emphasize such training, and which do not? Are you generalizing, or do you really mean that some nutrition is taught in some medical schools?

- Mr. Chairman, we have seen no evidence from past years that Senior Week is actually well enough attended to warrant a mandatory fee for it during registration. Are any such figures available?

More specific questions arise out of considerations of source (first- or secondhand), accuracy and interpretation of detail, currency of data, and appropriateness of the support for the assertion made; for example, on accuracy and interpretation:

- Mrs. Arnott, as one argument against increasing federal subsidies for public television, you said that the PBS presentation of *Macbeth* received poor Nielsen ratings; but are ratings a measure of quality, or just quantity? Do poor ratings mean poor television?

On timeliness of data:

- Miss Simon, how can you define pornography on the basis of a Supreme Court decision of 1936? Weren't the standards, and thus the definition, changed by the Supreme Court decision of 1972?

On secondhand data:

- Ms. Bardelli, is it really fair to use statistics from our school paper to support your argument for required writing courses at the university? I would have preferred that you had read for yourself the report that the newspaper article was based on. Are you sure the student reporter got the information right?

Is there such a thing as being picky? Yes. There are those who accept nothing, and who feel enormous pleasure at hearing themselves ask questions. Naturally, you will want to avoid such behavior. On the other hand, it is essential to effective communication (the meeting of meaning, as we have described it earlier) that ideas be clarified through dialogue. As critical listeners we should feel no hesitancy to ask for simple clarifications or complex explanations: whatever serves to increase understanding is valuable.

Answering Questions.   In the previous discussion, although we suggested that *all* questions have some value, we concentrated on asking *good* questions. Unfortunately, from the speaker's point of view, questions come in all shades of quality, some very good and some very bad. It thus requires some thinking on your part to know how to handle the Q-A session.

Most important, effective speakers must avoid defensiveness in the Q-A session. As a speaker you will sometimes find that the ulterior purpose of the question is to see how well you handle yourself. If you respond to a nasty question in a nasty way, you have revealed something about yourself, and you will also have lost an opportunity to win an adherent. The Q-A session is your chance to manage the audience, to gain credibility, and to talk spontaneously about your topic. You therefore should look upon all questions as creative opportunities, and you should avoid **defensiveness** whenever possible. Here are some strategies to help you do this.

Be responsive. Try to answer, or at least react, to all questions, and in a positive way. **Responsiveness** can help your image as a speaker. Even a nondescript, accusatory question can be turned to your advantage:

> Q. Hey, how the hell can you say that a tuition increase is fair? Whose side are you on, anyway?

> A. If you have a better solution to the school's economic problems, I'm willing to listen. This increase hurts me as much as it does you. I didn't say, by the way, that I *liked* the tuition increase, only that, after examining the alternatives, I find it to be the most viable one right now.

In the example given above, the speaker has made two positive moves: first, the speaker has shown willingness to listen to other alternatives, and second, the speaker has clarified his or her exact position on the issue. Chances are that by turning the question back to the questioner, but still being responsive, the speaker will find that the questioner will neither be able to offer a better solution nor be able to accuse the speaker of dodging the question.

Consider the whole audience. Consider all questions to be general questions—that is, ones the entire audience would be interested in. Even though they come from one individual, answers should be given to the entire group. By following this procedure the speaker avoids getting locked into a dialogue, a situation that can lead to a general drifting away by other members of the audience.

Repeat the question, and rephrase if necessary. Quite often a question will be asked too softly. Make sure the whole audience knows what question you are answering by repeating it loudly enough. Similarly, if the question needs rephrasing or clarification, do so:

> Q. You said a lot of things in your speech that I disagreed with, especially that stuff about uniforms. Where'd you get that stuff?

> A. I guess you're referring to my comment that all of us wear uniforms whether they are called that or not. If so, I got that idea from a book I read called *With Words Unspoken*, by Rosenfeld and Civikly. You might want to read the book for yourself, and then agree or disagree with me. Let me ask you, what do you mean by the term *uniform*? It may be that we are having a problem of terms.

Keep answers brief. Whenever possible, keep your answers concise and to the point. Most audiences are bored by long-winded answers, so **brevity** is desirable. Although they are sometimes necessary, it is good advice, in general, to delay the irrelevant or the technical, time-consuming questions. Tell the questioner that a good answer would take too long in order to be adequate, and that you will see him or her afterwards. It is quite irritating to have a question ready to ask and not get a chance to ask it because the first question takes up all the time allotted. The more questions the speaker can get to, the better.

Accept the question. All too often, as speakers we feel that a question is a personal attack on us. We also find that, having made a statement, it is difficult to back away from it, even when it is found in the Q-A session to be flawed. It is a sign of maturity to overcome this type of ego-involvement. Assume that questions are addressed to the content of your speech rather than at you as a person. Disagreements can be healthy, and a sharp exchange of differences over ideas is somewhat equivalent to a tough game of one-on-one basketball or a chess match: once it is over you shake hands and get on to other things. If someone in the audience makes a reasonable comment about your presentation, listen to the comment carefully and accept it as a good point. You will find that by doing so you may gain more than by fighting back aimlessly.

Learn to say, "I don't know." If you do not know the answer to a question, say so. As speakers we often feel that we must have all the answers and that anything less diminishes our stature. Of course, it is the ideal to answer in a thorough way all questions asked, but it can also be quite helpful for us to admit when we do not know an answer. Most important, we avoid making a poor answer, one that will probably reduce our credibility, and second, we display maturity—the maturity to say, "I don't know." Finally, by admitting we do not have the answer to certain questions, we create an opportunity to involve the questioners or the audience in finding an answer, and we also create the opportunity to talk with the questioners at a later date by saying that we will find out the answer and get back to them.

Refrain from responding to loaded questions. We are expected to respond only to legitimate questions about our topic. Questions that are intentionally irrelevant or that attack us personally should be labeled as such and dismissed. On occasion, it is necessary to say, "I am willing to try to answer any questions you have about this issue, but I am unwilling to be a target of abuse, and I have no intention of speaking with you any further." You will not have to use this strategy often, we can predict, but if the situation arises, be firm.

Comments That Are Not Questions

Quite often you will find that the response you want to make, or that you receive from an audience member, is not actually a question but a statement of some sort. Here are two typical examples:

- I liked your speech. It reminded me of a situation I was in, except that I pushed the panic button and couldn't do anything. I'll have to remember what you said if I ever see someone choking again.

- You have got to be kidding! If we have no more brains than to ban hazardous waste dumping without coming up with an alternative we might as well forget about half of the things we're wearing and eating today because they all create hazardous waste.

You will note from the examples, both of which are real, that one is a positive comment and one negative. Of course, comments come in all shades in between, but as a speaker you will almost always know if they are favorable or unfavorable. What do you do?

In the case of positive comments, be positive right back. Acknowledge the positive nature of the remark and *reinforce* the critic. **Reinforcement** gives you an opportunity to develop your point. In the first example, the speaker responded approximately like this:

- Thanks for the comment about the speech. If you'd like, I'll get you a description of the Heimlich Maneuver for saving a choking victim. If anyone else would like a copy, just ask.

Of course, every comment is different, but if you will remember to acknowledge and reinforce, you will generally score points with the audience.

In the case of negative comments, respond by being **positive**. Argue, defend yourself, disagree, but be positive. You will, more than likely, catch your critic off guard, and maybe even convert the person. In the second example, the speaker rebutted something like this:

- You're right! You're right! We do need goods that produce hazardous waste, and that means we have to find an alternative to indiscriminate dumping. But wouldn't a ban give the industries involved an incentive for solving the problem? Without the ban, will they really be motivated to expend the money and time? My feeling is that without the ban, you and I, the public, will be forced to solve industry's problem, and that's neither fair nor effective. So, look, I understand what you mean, but my view of things is that we pay either way: we either suffer the loss of goods, or we die slowly by chemical poisoning. If you have a better solution, let's hear it.

That was not a bad response, though perhaps not as good as the one you might invent. The speaker did, however, try to identify with the critic by recognizing his point and showing how the two of them were really in the same boat: thus the speaker was positive. She also stated her disagreement frankly and explained why she disagreed. In short, she made the best she could out of the situation.

This chapter can provide only a few examples and bits of advice for what is a complex, continually creative situation. You will want to remember that each situation is a challenge and requires you to be constantly innovative. The key is to listen carefully to people and to avoid defensiveness and overly emotional responses. Avoid statements that label a person's comment as good or bad. Be positive, be in control; that is all that can be expected, and it is, quite often, all that you will need in order to succeed in critical appraisal.

WRITTEN COMMUNICATION

Reading and Responding to Essays

This book has emphasized that your essays are written to be read; while you may choose occasionally to submit your work for publication in the school or local paper, your most frequent audience will be your colleagues in the classroom. Peer evaluation is important to all writers. Even the most polished composers attend writer's workshops, conferences, and retreats in an effort to learn more about their work. Honest evaluation by others is essential in helping you form your own communication style and in the development of that most difficult pair of skills, giving and taking criticism.

Your instructors will provide the most suitable method of access to your classmate's essays. They may ask you to type your essays on ditto masters, which they will then have duplicated, or you may be asked to provide your own copies for a small number of people. Your class might even decide to read essays aloud and criticize them orally. Whichever method you use, the important point about this part of the process of communication remains the same: you can learn a great deal from a reading-and-responding session—critics can reflect what you cannot see from your own side of the pen and paper.

Evaluating Writing in the Classroom. Just as with the critical appraisal of a speech, approaching an essay from the point-pattern-detail paradigm assures that you will be looking at the major elements of the paper. Unless your instructor specifically requests that you edit each others' papers for spelling and punctuation, commenting on these is not essential. If you are asked to write comments on the papers and find many spelling and punctuation problems, you may want to suggest that a student proofread more carefully; but in oral discussion of the papers it is best to stick to the three larger topics of point, pattern, and detail.

1. *The Point.* You will often have only a short time to read and discuss each essay. The first time you are asked to comment on someone's essay, the temptation will often be to say "It was good," or "I liked it." There is nothing wrong with such a spontaneous reaction to what you have read;

however, you will need to be more substantive and specific, and so you will have to support your **evaluation** with concrete comments.

So what do you say? Your first comment should be directed to the point of the essay and should generally be in the form of a question to the author. Be sure that you have read and understood what the author intended, that the author has in fact "communicated," as we defined the word in the first chapter, and that a sense of **identification** has been achieved. You might say, for example, "Jane, the point of your essay was really that when students cram for exams instead of keeping up with nightly reading, they are cheating themselves, right?" If Jane agrees, fine; proceed to a discussion of pattern—how effectively was the essay structured? She may respond, however, with something like this: "No, I was trying to emphasize that professors give too much work, and cramming is the only way students can survive." Then it is necessary to assess how the distortion in meaning occurred. This is where group discussion can prove fruitful to the writer. If several students misinterpret the point the author intended, then clearly the fault lies with the writing, and not with the reading.

A good place to start in looking for the problem is the first paragraphs. Let us assume that Jane's first paragraph ended with the following sentence:

> However, no permanent long-lasting knowledge is gained; the student is mentally dull while taking the tests and tired or run-down for the remaining week; nervousness (anxiety) increases as the exam day approaches; and finally, after the exam, the student has succeeded in passing himself off as someone he really isn't.

With this ending sentence readers would naturally be led to believe that Jane believes cramming is harmful to the student, not that she is defending it as a way of survival. As critical evaluators of Jane's work, you must point this out to her, suggesting that she rewrite her lead paragraph to emphasize the inconsideration of professors in assigning too much work.

Because you have questioned her point, Jane will probably realize her mistake, a common one. She was carried away with writing about the unpleasant experience of cramming and forgot to direct her first paragraph toward the end of the essay, toward her point. Now that she knows what confusion she has created for you, her readers, she will probably not make that mistake again. By questioning her about the point of her essay, you have helped her on her way to clearer writing.

There will be times when you may read an essay that has no apparent point. Be tactful, but do not overlook this flaw. It is a major one, and it will cost dearly in professional or other real-life writing. You are doing your fellow students a favor when you discuss this shortcoming with them, especially when there is an opportunity to revise the essay.

Essays that recount trips are especially prone to rambling on without any clear focus. You might say something like this: "George, you mentioned all the things that went wrong on your camping trip. Some of them were funny, but you didn't really say whether you learned from them, or if you had a good time anyway, or whether these catastrophes were due to poor planning. I had a hard time following your point."

If George responds with something like, "Oh, yeah, well we definitely had a good time. I'd go again but this time I'd make sure I . . .," then suggest to George how he can clarify this point early in the essay and shape the incidents around lack of foresight. Learning how to respond to others' mistakes with tactful but concrete suggestions helps both of you, since it keeps you alert for similar problems when revising your own essays.

2. *Pattern*. Once you and the author have agreed on the point of the essay, the next topic of criticism is pattern. How well did the essay succeed in carrying its point throughout? Is the essay shaped around one or more discernible patterns, as they are explained in this book? Would another pattern have resulted in a more informative essay? Suppose, for example, that the essay is a narrative, a story about a childhood friendship that ended in hard feelings. Perhaps the author classified the events that led to the break-up in order of importance, or chronologically. A better method might have been an analysis of personalities, using comparison/contrast to show the kinds of differences that proved responsible for the ending of the friendship. Perhaps the essay needed more description, a setting to take the reader back to childhood.

Examine the smaller patterns, too: are the paragraphs well-arranged? Do they move the essay forward? Do they support the thesis? Sometimes authors, even professional ones, cannot resist including a comment that is irrelevant to their topic but is a favorite anecdote or a clever turn of phrase. Comments such as this distract the reader from the main point because they do not fit. As Chapter One emphasizes, digressions of the by-the-way sort are much more acceptable in casual conversation than in formal discourse. If you must tell the author to cut, do so: you may learn how to trim fat from your own writing as well.

On the next level, are the paragraphs readable as units within themselves? Can you recognize some of the patterns we have suggested, or effective rearrangements of them? If there are undeveloped paragraphs, point them out and explain to the author what kind of support they need. If, for example, the author writes: "We all know rock concerts are unsafe. We should do something about this," and then plunges into the essay, you should mention that the claim is not supported sufficiently by the words *We all know*. The author might begin with the Three Examples-Topic paradigm, demonstrating that rock concerts are unsafe before suggesting ways of improving their safety.

Whenever you point out a flaw to an author, try immediately to suggest a way of improving it. If you sense something is wrong but cannot come up with a suggestion, be honest and say something like this: "Art, I can't really say what's wrong here, but something is missing for me; I can't quite follow your argument. Is there some other way you can say it?" Invite other members of the group to help you out in offering a concrete suggestion. If the argument or the statement turns out to be clear to everyone else, read the selection again. Maybe it was you who missed the point.

On the other hand, nothing needs to be wrong with the essay for you to view it critically. If the essay succeeds, analyze it for the reasons. Discover originality in the statement of point, creativity in meshing patterns together, or techniques like humor, flashback, or analogy that are used especially well. Comments based on any of the above relate to the notion of detail.

3. *Detail.* This is the subject in which you, as critic, can help the weaker writer derive the most from those who have a flair for the art. Compliment writers who have created scene setters where appropriate, who have used emphasis, figurative language, understatement, or any other device well. If an essay leaves you with something to ponder, raises a question you had not thought about, and is well written besides, say so. Even good writers need encouragement, and you will be helping others to learn about style—to learn what it is that makes some essays a delight to read.

Use of detail can improve most essays. For example, you might say to a classmate: "I understood what you were getting at, and I like the way your information was organized; but I think if you provided some statistics about sports-related injuries, used more active verbs, and maybe put the reader right into the scene, you would sharpen the effect of the essay."

Perhaps a student has written a fairly clear essay about a scientific process—it makes a point and is well organized; but you are a drama major and science does not come easily to you. You could comment this way: "I followed what you were saying pretty well, but I'd like to understand it better. Is there some everyday activity you could compare this with? I think an analogy or an example would help me to relate the process you're describing to something I know more about."

Finally, look carefully at sentences and words. Are the sentences readable? Are they rhythmic? Would using some special sentence patterns improve the flow of the essay? Are there too many short, choppy sentences, or too many long, tangled ones? Check for overuse of *which* and *that*. Suggest shorter, less wordy sentences where appropriate. Reduce two- or three-word verbs like *make an attempt* to *try* and *reached a decision* to *decided*. If passive voice is used, is it necessary or does it dull the essay? Are there many auxiliary verbs—too many *ises* and *wases*? Be scrupulous here, but be precise. Good use of details strengthens an essay; poor use, or no use at all, weakens even the best-made point.

Accepting Criticism

This section has discussed ways of giving good criticism; now, a few words about how to receive it. A good deal of what needs to be mentioned here has been stated for oral communication, but some key points bear repeating. Writers realize that none of us like criticism, yet all of us need it. Criticism is somewhat like paying taxes; we just have to make the best of it. No taxes, no benefits. No criticism, no improvement. So it goes.

When people comment on your essay, they are saying that they think enough of you and your writing to risk communication. It is much easier, generally, though much less productive, to say nothing. Those students who comment are doing so out of a sincere desire to help. Listen to your critics; learn from them. You may feel you have to clarify something you wrote, but do not feel compelled to justify every flaw brought to your attention. By doing so, you may be closing your mind and blocking your potential development as a writer. Accept advice graciously; write down suggestions and try them in your revision or your next essay. Your classmates will be as pleased with your improvement as they are with their own.

Group evaluation is an enjoyable and valuable part of your course; but you are the group, and you must work to keep it that way.

SUMMARY

This chapter has dealt with the critical appraisal of ideas. The give and take of questions and answers and the critical appraisal of colleagues' essays can be the most rewarding part of communication. Applying what has been said here can help to make this a period of pleasure and self-growth.

KEY WORDS

criticism	reinforcement
defensiveness	positive
responsiveness	evaluation
brevity	identification

·EXERCISES

1. Read the following comments and questions. Assume they have been asked about your speech or essay. How would you respond?
    a. You sound like a do-good liberal to me. You don't really think we can afford to give food stamps to students, do you? If you do, you must not be a taxpayer.
    b. Litter is caused by slobs. I would say that you are asking that all of us pay, by having a container deposit system, for the ten percent who live like slobs.
    c. I agree with the three reasons you cited for the failure of the cooperative record store, but I think a fourth would have to be added: unfair competition from the bookstores.
    d. Do you have any proof that a proficiency test will be culturally unbiased? I agree that it would provide a measure for all students, but would it be an equal measure?
    e. You know, I really enjoyed your characterizations of fraternity men, but I do want to add that some of them don't fit into the *macho, animal,* or *elitist* categories you set up. I know many fraternity guys who are as pleasant, smart, and open-minded as anyone on the campus.
    f. Could you give me that definition of *euthanasia* again? I must have missed part of it, or else I disagree.
    g. Would you recommend European travel for all of us? Was your experience typical?
    h. O.K., you say Blacks are discriminated against on campus, and you say it's too subtle to actually document, but I think that's a copout. Give me one concrete example.
    i. Your statistics on the divorce rate — where did you get them, and have things changed?
    j. I really liked your speech.

2. The next time you hear a speech, see if you can write down, or at least think of, a point, a pattern, and a detail question. Get up the courage to ask it. What did you feel? How did the speaker handle the response?

3. Read one of your essays aloud, in class or to a friend. Ask the listener(s) to give you two comments: one positive and one negative. React to both. Analyze your feelings about the comments and the quality of your response.

REFERENCES

Hocking, William Ernest, *The Lasting Elements of Individualism* (New Haven, Conn.: Yale University Press, 1937), p. 77.

Appendix: Finding and Documenting Materials

While most successful speeches and essays begin with personal experience, it is frequently necessary for a communicator to go beyond personal experience to gather materials: to books, to magazines, or to interviews. Here are some suggestions for finding materials in outside sources and for making clear to your audience where you found the materials.

WRITTEN MATERIALS

Much of the information and ideas you will want to use in speeches and essays can be found in written sources: books, magazine articles, newspapers, pamphlets, and government publications. The library is the place to go for these, but to locate a source in a library can sometimes be difficult. There are, however, bibliographies and indexes that can help you locate printed materials.

One good place to start is with Eugene P. Sheehy's *Guide to Reference Books*. This guide will suggest reference works that will provide information to get your search going. Encyclopedias like *The New Encyclopedia Britannica*, *The McGraw-Hill Encyclopedia of Science and Technology*, and *International Encyclopedia of the Social Sciences* as well as almanacs like the *World Almanac and Book of Facts* or the *Statistical Abstract of the United States* are reference works that will give you basic information as well as a general outline of a subject.

The information in general reference works will seldom be extensive enough or up-to-date enough to satisfy your needs as a speaker or writer. At this point, then, you can turn to the card catalog of your library, looking under subject headings for books on your topic, or under author and title headings if, in your search through general reference texts, you have come across the name of a particular author or work. Magazine articles and articles in scholarly journals are also good sources of information. You can locate these by using indexes like the *Readers' Guide to Periodical Literature*, the *Humanities Index*, the *Business Periodicals Index*, the *Social Sciences Index*, *The Education Index*, and *The New York Times Index*. Your librarian will help you locate these and other useful indexes.

As you locate material, take notes on it and write down information about your source so that you can pass this information on to your audience. If the information you gather is widely known, then you need not let your audience know about your specific source. If you are quoting words or figures exactly, however, or if you are paraphrasing material or using material that is more or less unique to a particular book or article, then you need to let your readers or listeners know your source. Do this in a speech by telling your audience the author and title of your source, or by writing the appropriate information on a blackboard or on a sheet to be distributed. In an essay you can make use of footnotes and a bibliography to convey to the reader the necessary information about your sources. If you are presenting the information in written form, use standard footnote and bibliography form. Your instructor may require you to use a particular form, or you can consult handbooks like *The Little, Brown Handbook*, the *MLA Handbook* (published by the Modern Language Association), or the *Publication Manual of the American Psychological Association*.

INTERVIEWS

Sometimes you can get more complete and more up-to-date information by talking to an authority in a particular field than by going to printed sources. Scholars, politicians, business people, administrators, and even your fellow students will usually be willing to tell you what they know or how they feel about a subject; if you have a tape recorder or can take notes quickly and accurately, you can use what they have to tell you in your speech or essay. Remember to ask the subject's permission before you tape, and remember to tell the subject exactly what use of the material you plan to make. Obey any restrictions the subject puts on the use of the material.

Interviews are like books and magazines in that they need to be documented as sources of information. Your instructor or the standard handbooks will let you know the appropriate footnote and bibliography form for them.

(Continued Credits and Acknowledgments)

Walter Clemons, from "Fathers and Sons." Copyright 1981, by Newsweek, Inc. All rights reserved. Reprinted by permission.

Norman Cousins, "President Kennedy and the Russian Fable," *Saturday Review*, 9 January 1971. Reprinted by permission of the author.

Owen Edwards, "Hair Apparent," *Saturday Review*, 12 April 1980. Copyright © 1980 by *Saturday Review*. All rights reserved. Reprinted by permission.

Howard Gardner, from *The Shattered Mind*. Copyright © 1974 by Howard Gardner. Reprinted by permission of Alfred A. Knopf, Inc.

Joshua Gilder, from "Creators on Creating: Tom Wolfe," *Saturday Review* (April 1981). Copyright © 1981 by *Saturday Review*. All rights reserved. Reprinted by permission.

Vicki Goldberg, from "Monument to Tempestuousness," *Saturday Review* (May 1980). Copyright © 1980 by *Saturday Review*. All rights reserved. Reprinted by permission.

David Halberstam, from *The Powers That Be*. Copyright © 1975, 1976, 1977, 1979 by David Halberstam. Reprinted by permission of Alfred A. Knopf, Inc.

Scot Haller, from "Creators on Creating: Eudora Welty," *Saturday Review* (June 1981). Copyright © 1981 by *Saturday Review*. All rights reserved. Reprinted by permission.

Scot Haller, from "The World's Five Best Selling Authors," *Saturday Review* (March 1981). Copyright © 1981 by *Saturday Review*. All rights reserved. Reprinted by permission.

Garrett Hardin, from *Exploring New Ethics of Survival: The Voyage of the Spaceship Beagle*. Copyright © 1968, 1972 by Garrett Hardin. Reprinted by permission of Viking Penguin Inc.

Sydney J. Harris, "Money Can Indeed Buy Poverty . . ." from *Strictly Personal* by Sydney J. Harris. © 1981 Field Enterprises, Inc. Courtesy of Field Newspaper Syndicate.

Smith Hempstone, "Joan Little's Lawyer Told Nothing But the Truth," *The Washington Star*, 1975. Reprinted by permission of the author.

William Ernest Hocking, from *The Lasting Elements of Individualism* (New Haven: Yale University Press, 1937), p. 77. Reprinted with permission.

Walter Isaacson, from "The Duel Over Gun Control." Copyright 1981 Time Inc. All rights reserved. Reprinted by permission from *Time*.

Richard Katula and Richard Koth, "A Stock Issues Approach to the Teaching of Argument," (Bottle Bill Argument Model), *College Composition and Communication* (May 1980). Reprinted by permission of the National Council of Teachers of English.

Barbara Lawrence, "——— Isn't a Dirty Word." © 1973 by The New York Times Company. Reprinted by permission.

Anthony Lewis, "Tellico Dam: Politics at Its Worst." © 1980 by The New York Times Company. Reprinted by permission.

Thomas Middleton, from "Light Refractions," *Saturday Review* (May 1980). Copyright © 1980 by *Saturday Review*. All rights reserved. Reprinted by permission.

Index

Accepting criticism, 379
Action-based conclusions, 62–63
Agency defined, 342
    in sentences, 342–349
Analysis
    cue words in, 167
    detail in, 170–171
    getting materials for, 157–164
    of issues, 152
    object, 152
    pattern in, 166–170
    point in, 164–166
    as probe, 24
    of problems, 151
    of situations, 151
    uses of, 150–157
Analyzing a topic in informative
    discourse, 233–236
Analyzing the audience for argument,
    261–262
Analyzing the audience for
    informative discourse, 236–240
Analyzing the communication
    situation, 31
Anxiety
    speech, 95–98
    writing, 99–103
Apprehension
    communication, 94
    state, 95
    trait, 95
Argument
    aims and features of, 255–256
    analyzing audience in, 261–262
    associative scheme in, 292–293
    conceptual patterns in, 274
    credibility in, 267–268
    defined, 254–255
    detail in, 286–290
    dissociative scheme in, 292–293
    motivation in, 264–267

    pattern in, 271–286
    planning, 256–261
    point in, 269–270
    probing the issue in, 257–261
    proposition in, 269–270
    refutation pattern in, 283–286
    scheme in, 292–293
    standard questions for, 257
    standard questions pattern in,
        271–274
    static patterns in, 278–283
    test of consistency in, 288
    test of recency in, 286–287
    test of relevance in, 287
    test of sufficiency in, 288
    time patterns in, 274–278
Argumentation as probe, 26
Arguments
    associative, 293–308
    that attempt to organize reality,
        303–308
    based on structure of reality,
        298–303
    dissociative, 308–312
    quasi-logical, 293–298
Asking and answering questions,
    368–369
Associative arguments, 293–308
Associative scheme, in argument,
    292–293
Audience
    analysis of, 29–31
    general, 261–264
    particular, 261–264
Audience
    in communication, 7
    in composing, 29–32

Background, in informative discourse,
    234–235
Balance in speech, 364–366

Belief-based conclusions, 62–63
Boundary sentences, 355–357
Brainstorming, use in composing,
    19–20

Casual speech, 1
Cause, defined, 132
Cause and effect
    cue words in, 137
    detail in, 140
    getting materials, 135
    pattern in, 139–140
    point in, 136–139
    as probe, 24
    uses of, 131–135
Classification
    cue words in, 202
    defined, 192–195
    detail in, 203–205
    getting materials for, 197–199
    pattern in, 201–203
    point in, 200–201
    as probe, 26
    uses of, 192–197
Classroom, evaluating writing in the,
    375–379
Clauses, restrictive and nonrestrictive,
    349–351
Coercion and logic, 255–256
Coherence
    defined, 320
    lexical, 323–324
    in paragraphs, 320–324
    time/space, 321–323
    transitional, 321–323
Cohesion, 355–358
Colloquial speech, 8
Comments vs. questions, 373–375
Communication
    audience in, 7
    defined, 3
    feedback in, 7
    formal, 2
    informal, 2
    messages in, 6
    oral, critical appraisal of, 365–375
    process of, 4–5

purpose in, 5
shared experience in, 6–7
symbols in, 6
written, critical appraisal of,
    375–379
Communication apprehension,
    defined, 94
Communication situation, analyzing
    the, 31
Communicator's role, 26–28
Comparison
    cue words in, 186
    defined, 177
    detail in, 188
    getting materials for, 183–184
    pattern in, 185–188
    point in, 184–185
    as probe, 26
    uses of, 177–183
Composing
    advice from experts on, 32–34
    audience in, 29–32
    through brainstorming, 19–20
    through conversation, 19–20
    constraints and guidelines for,
        28–29
    focus in, 38
    form and organization in, 38–39
    getting started, 34–35
    with a journal, 17–18
    rereading and rewriting in, 36–37
    role of key phrases in, 37
    with a tape recorder, 17
Composing process, elements of, 16
Conceptual patterns
    defined, 47
    in argument, 274
Conclusions
    action-based, 62–63
    belief-based, 62–63
    in the finished product, 59–63
    parallelism in, 60
    quotable quotes in, 59
    reiteration in, 61–62
Connotation, 218
Constraints and guidelines for
    composing, 28–29

Contrast, defined, 177
Conventional patterns, defined, 47,
    227–228
Conventional probes, 26
Conventions
    of form, 43
    of formal speaking, 7–10
    of formal writing, 10–11
Conversation, use in composing,
    19–20
Conversational speech, 1
Coping mechanisms, 102–103
Coping with speech anxiety, 97–98
Coping with writing anxiety, 102–103
Credibility, 43
    in argument, 267–268
    in informative discourse, 240
    through use of personal experience,
    48
Critical appraisal, 368
    of oral communication, 365–375
    of written communication, 375–379
Criticism, accepting, 379
Cue words, 45–47
    in analysis, 167
    in cause and effect, 137
    in classification, 202
    in comparison, 186
    in enumeration, 175–177
    in narration, 114–115
    in process, 126
Curiosity pattern, in informative
    discourse, 244–246

Dangling modifiers and sentence
    problems, 345–347
Dangling participle, defined, 345
Definition, defined, 217–218
    point, pattern, detail in, 219–221
    as probe, 26
    uses of, 217–219
Demonstration pattern, in
    informative discourse, 246–249
Denotation, 218
Description, defined, 205–206
    detail in, 216–217
    dominant impression in, 212–214

fantasy in, 214–215
getting materials, 208–210
pattern in, 211–215
point in, 210–211
as probe, 26
spatial order in, 211–212
uses of, 205–208
Detail
    in analysis, 170–171
    in argument, 286–290
    in cause and effect, 140
    in classification, 203–205
    in comparison, 54–56, 188
    in description, 216–217
    examples, 49–50
    factual examples, 49–50
    factual support, 50–51
    figurative comparisons, 55–56
    in the finished product, 47–48
    firsthand facts vs. secondhand
        facts, 50–51
    hypothetical examples, 49–50
    in informative discourse, 250–251
    literal comparisons, 54–55
    personal experience, 48–49
    in process, 128–130
    quantitative support, 51–53
    quoting from authorities, 51
Dialogue, 7
Disadvantages in argument, 260–261
Discourse
    defined, 16
    linking, 357–359
    planned, 1
Discovering a topic, 20–21
Dissociative arguments, 308–312
Dissociative scheme, in argument,
    292–293
Doing aids
    preparation of, 88
    presentation of, 89
Dominant impression in description,
    212–214

Editing, 64
Effect, defined, 132
Effective style of presentation, 43

Elements of the composing process,
  16
Emphasis
  in paragraphs, 331–334
  in presentation, 83–84
  in sentences, 360–362
Enumeration
  cue words in, 175–177
  point, pattern, and detail in,
    175–177
  as probe, 26
  uses of, 171–174
Episodes, 113
Essay
  paragraphs within, 314–318
  reading and responding to,
    375–379
Evaluating writing in the classroom,
  375–379
Exemplification, 222
  as probe, 26
Experience
  personal, 21
  probing, 21–23
  shared, in communication, 6–7
  vicarious, 21
Extemporaneous speech, 73, 78

Facial expression in presentation, 79
Falling action, 115
Fantasy, in description, 214–215
Features, in informative discourse,
  235
Feedback in communication, 7
Figurative language, in scene setters,
  335
Filler speech, 10
Final form
  editing, 64
  in discourse, 63–67
  scripting the essay, 63–65
  unscripting the speech, 65–67
First-person narrative, 117–118
Flowchart, in process discourse, 129
Fluency, in presentation, 83
Focus in composing, 38

Form and organization, in
  composing, 38–39
Form, conventions of, 43
Formal communication, 2
Formal speaking, conventions of,
  7–10
Formal writing
  conventions of, 10–11
  semantic conventions in, 11
  syntactic conventions in, 11
Free modifiers, 354–355
Free writing, 18

General audience, 261–264
Gerund
  defined, 344
  sentence problems, 343–345
Gestures in presentation, 78
Getting materials
  in classification, 197–199
  in comparison, 183–184
  in description, 208–210
Gettysburg Address, 8–9
Good/bad, in informative discourse,
  235

Humor, in introductions, 57–58

Informal communication, 2
Information
  as probe, 26
  levels, 29–30
Informative discourse, aims and
  features of, 229–233
Informative aids
  preparation of, 83
  presentation of, 86
Informative discourse
  aims and features of, 229–233
  analyzing a topic for, 233–236
  applications in, 236
  curiosity pattern in, 244–246
  defined, 228
  demonstration pattern in, 246–249
  detail in, 250–251
  pattern in, 242–251

point in, 241–242
practical report in, 249–250
standard questions for, 233–234
standard questions pattern in,
    242–244
Informative reports, planning,
    233–236
Inherency, in argument, 259
Introductions
    humor in, 57–58
    in the finished product, 56–57
    quotations in, 58
    rhetorical questions in, 57
    startling statements in, 58
Issue analysis, 152

Journal writing, 18
Journal, use of, in composing, 17–18

Key phrases in composing, 37

Lexical coherence, 323–324
Linking discourse, 357–359

Manuscript speech, 73
Memorized speech, 72
Message preparation, types of, 72–78
Message sender, 6
Messages in communication, 6
Modifiers
    free, 354–355
    resuming, 352–353
    summary, 353–354
Motivation, in argument, 264–267
Movement in presentation, 79

Narration
    detail in, 115–117
    getting materials for, 110–111
    pattern in, 113–115
    point in, 111–112
    as probe, 24
    style of, 117–118
    uses of, 107–109
Narrator or speaker, 117–118
Notecard system, 75

Object analysis, 152

Paragraph emphasis, 331–334
Paragraph patterns, 324–331
Paragraphs
    coherence in, 320–324
    defined, 314
    within the essay, 314–318
    problem-solution, 328–330
    scene setters, 334–337
    sentences within, 318–320
    topic-restriction-illustration,
        325–326
    understatement in, 333
Parallelism
    in conclusions, 60
    in sentences, 362–363
Particular audience, 261–264
Passive voice
    defined, 347
    misuse of, 347–349
Pattern
    in analysis, 166–170
    in argument, 271–286
    in cause and effect, 139–140
    in classification, 201–203
    in comparison, 185–188
    in description, 211–215
    in the finished product, 45
    in informative discourse, 242–251
    in process, 123–128
Patterns, paragraph, 321–331
Pause, in presentation, 83–84
Personal experience, 21
Physical attributes of presentational
        style, 78–80
Plan-meet-need, in argument, 260
Planned discourse, 1
Planning informative reports,
    233–236
Planning the argument, 256–261
Point
    in analysis, 164–166
    in argument, 269–270
    in cause and effect, 136–139
    in classification, 200–201

Point (*cont.*)
   in comparison, 184–185
   in description, 210–211
   in the finished product, 43–44
   in informative discourse, 241–242
   in process, 124–125
Point, pattern, and detail
   in definition, 219–221
   in enumeration, 175–177
Posture in presentation, 78–79
Practical report, in informative
   discourse, 249–250
Preparing a questionnaire, 163–164
Presentation
   dress and appearance in, 80,
     83–84
   effective style of, 43
   emphasis in, 83–84
   facial expression in, 79
   gestures in, 78
   movement in, 79
   pause in, 83–84
   posture in, 78–79
   rate in, 83–84
Presentational style
   physical attributes of, 78–80
   vocal attributes of, 80–84
Primary cause, 135
Probes
   analysis, 24
   argumentation, 26
   cause and effect, 24
   classification, 26
   comparison, 26
   conventional, 26
   defined, 25
   definition, 26
   description, 26
   enumeration, 26
   exemplification, 26
   information, 26
   narration, 24
   process, 24
   static, 24–26
   thought patterns as, 23–26
   time, 24
Probing experience, 21–23

Probing the issue, in argument,
   257–261
Problem analysis, 151
Problem-solution paragraphs,
   328–330
Procedures in informative discourse,
   235–236
Process
   defined, 118–119
   detail in, 128–130
   getting materials for, 121–124
   pattern in, 123–128
   point in, 124–125
   as probe, 24
   style in, 130–131
   uses of, 119–121
Process of communication, 4–5
Pronunciation, in presentation, 80,
   82
Proposition
   of action, 269–270
   in argument, 269–270
   of fact, 269
Purpose in communication, 5
Purpose statement, role in
   composing, 34–35

Quasi-logical arguments, 293–298
Questionnaire, preparing a, 163–164
Questions, asking and answering,
   369
Quotable quotes in conclusions, 59
Quotations in introductions, 58

Rate, in presentation, 83–84
Readability, defined, 321
Reading and responding to essays,
   375–379
Redundancy in speech, 364–366
Refutation pattern, in argument,
   283–286
Reiteration, in conclusions, 61–62
Relative clause, defined, 349
Repair sequences, 10
Responding to experience, 16–17
Restrictive and nonrestrictive clauses,
   349–351

Resuming modifiers, 352–353
Rhetorical questions in introductions,
    57
Rising action, 115

Scene setters, 334–337
    figurative language in, 335
Scheme, in argument, 292–293
Scripting the essay, 63–65
Second person, 130–131
Secondary or contributing causes,
    135
Semantic conventions in formal
    writing, 11
Sentence emphasis, 360–362
Sentence problems
    dangling modifiers and, 345–347
    gerunds and, 343–345
Sentence style
    within the paragraph, 318–320
    in speech, 364–366
Sentences
    agency in, 342–349
    boundary, 355–357
    parallelism in, 362–363
    special effects, 360–363
Setting, 109
Shared experience in
    communication, 6–7
Showing aids
    preparation of, 86
    presentation of, 87
Significance
    in argument, 258–259
    in informative discourse, 234
Situation analysis, 151
Spatial order in description, 211–212
Special effects in sentences, 360–363
Speech anxiety, 95–98
    audience anxieties in, 97
    message anxieties in, 96
    self-anxieties in, 95–96
    situational anxieties in, 97
    understanding, 95–97
Speech anxiety peak, 97
Speech anxiety syndrome, 96

Speech
    balance in, 364–366
    casual, 1
    colloquial, 8
    conversational, 1
    extemporaneous, 73, 78
    filler, 10
    from manuscript, 73
    memorized, 72
    redundancy in, 364–366
    sentence style in, 364–366
Spontaneity in presentation, 70
Standard questions, 227
    for argument, 257–261
    for informative discourse, 233–234
    in information, 234–236
Standard questions pattern
    in argument, 271–274
    in informative discourse, 242–244
Startling statements, in introductions,
    58
State apprehension, 95
Static patterns
    in argument, 278–283
    defined, 148–149
    and time patterns compared,
        149–150
Static probes, 24–26
Structure of reality, arguments based
    on, 298–303
Subpoints in the finished product,
    44
Summary modifiers, 353–354
Symbols in communication, 6
Syntactic conventions in formal
    writing, 11

Tape recorder, use of, in composing,
    17
Test of consistency, in argument,
    288
Test of recency, in argument,
    286–287
Test of relevance, in argument, 287
Test of sufficiency, in argument, 288
Thesis in the finished product,
    43–44

Thesis statement, role in composing, 35
Third-person narrative, 118
Thought patterns as probes, 23–26
Time patterns
in argument, 274–278
defined, 106–107
Time probes, 24
Time/space coherence, 321–323
Topic, discovering a, 20–21
Topic-restriction-illustration
paragraphs, 325–326
Topicality, in argument, 257–258
Trait apprehension, 95
Transitional coherence, 321–323
Types of message preparation, 72–78

Understatement, in paragraphs, 333
Unscripting the speech, 65–67

Vicarious experience, 21

Visual aids
defined, 84–85
in written communication, 89–91
preparation and presentation of, 84–89
Vocal attributes of presentational style, 80–84

Which, misuse of, 351–352
Which-trap, 351–352
Workability, in argument, 259–260
Writer's block, 99
Writing anxiety, 99–103
audience anxieties in, 101–102
coping with, 102–103
message anxieties in, 101
self-anxieties in, 99–101
situational anxieties in, 102
Written communication, visual aids in, 88–91